Malaysia's
Original People

To Richard,
   With best wishes,
      Kirk

Malaysia's Original People

Past, Present and Future of the Orang Asli

Edited by

Kirk Endicott

NUS PRESS
SINGAPORE

© 2016 Kirk Endicott

Published by:

NUS Press
National University of Singapore
AS3-01-02, 3 Arts Link
Singapore 117569
Fax: (65) 6774-0652
E-mail: nusbooks@nus.edu.sg
Website: http://nuspress.nus.edu.sg

ISBN 978-9971-69-861-4 (Paper)

National Library Board, Singapore Cataloguing-in-Publication Data

   Malaysia's original people: past, present and future of the Orang Asli. – Singapore: NUS Press, [2016]
      pages cm
      ISBN: 978-9971-69-861-4 (paperback)

   1. Indigenous peoples – Malaysia – History. 2. Indigenous peoples – Malaysia – Social conditions. 3. Indigenous peoples – Malaysia – Economic conditions. 4. Indigenous peoples – Malaysia – Social life and customs. 5. Indigenous peoples – Land tenure – Malaysia. 6. Ethnology – Malaysia. I. Endicott, Kirk M., editor.

   GN635.M4
   305.89928 -- dc23   OCN912221234

The editor and authors have resolved all copyright issues related to material in this publication. Unless otherwise stated, images are from the authors' personal collection.

Cover: Batek woman with leaf headdress at Sungai Sat, Pahang, 2014. Photograph by Vivek Venkataraman.

Typeset by: International Typesetters Pte Ltd
Printed by: Mainland Press Pte Ltd

Dedicated to
Robert K. Dentan and Geoffrey Benjamin

CONTENTS

LIST OF ILLUSTRATIONS

Figures

Tables

PREFACE AND ACKNOWLEDGEMENTS

The Orang Asli ("original people") of the Malay Peninsula have fascinated scholars since the 19th century, but they are still little known by the general public, even in Malaysia. Although research on Orang Asli groups and topics has flourished since the 1960s, there have been only three books on the Orang Asli as a whole, the most recent published in 1976 (Carey 1976), and the world of the Orang Asli has changed rapidly since then. My fellow researchers and I believe that it is now time for a book providing a broad overview of the past, present and future of these remarkable people, with special emphasis on the changes that have taken place in Orang Asli lives since the beginning of the 21st century. The book includes chapters on a wide range of groups and topics, including Orang Asli origins and history, their cultural similarities and differences, and their responses to the challenges facing them in the modern world. The chapters also highlight the importance of Orang Asli studies for the anthropological understanding of small-scale indigenous societies in general. The chapters are written by a distinguished group of Malaysian (including Orang Asli) and international scholars with expertise in anthropology, archaeology, history, biology, linguistics, education, therapy, geography and law.

We have dedicated this book to Robert K. Dentan and Geoffrey Benjamin, whose work with the Semai and Temiar respectively laid the foundation for the modern anthropological understanding of the Orang Asli and who have inspired, encouraged and helped succeeding generations of researchers.

I thank all the contributors to this volume and also Karen Endicott, Geoffrey Benjamin, Colin Nicholas, Paul Kratoska, Lena Qua,

Lee Li Kheng, Lye Tuck-Po, Vivek Venkataraman and Tom Kraft for their valuable advice and help in their areas of special expertise. I also thank Dartmouth College for its administrative and financial assistance.

REFERENCE

Carey, I.
    1976   Orang Asli: The Aboriginal Tribes of Peninsular Malaysia. Kuala Lumpur: Oxford University Press.

Introduction

Kirk Endicott

THE ORANG ASLI

The Orang Asli are, with minor exceptions, descendants of the earliest human inhabitants of the Malay Peninsula. The term "Orang Asli", which means "original people" in Malay, was adopted by the Malaysian government in the 1960s to replace the English term "Aborigines" and the Malay term "Sakai", which have derogatory connotations. The Orang Asli consist of at least 19 culturally and linguistically distinct subgroups. Until about 1960, most Orang Asli lived in small camps and villages in interior forests and isolated rural areas and were seldom seen by other Malaysian citizens. Orang Asli communities were self-governing and mostly self-sufficient, living by varying combinations of hunting, gathering, fishing, swidden (shifting) horticulture and trading forest products. Recently, however, economic development of interior regions has replaced the rain forests with rubber and oil palm plantations, and government programmes aimed at bringing the Orang Asli into the "mainstream" of society have forced most Orang Asli to move into "regroupment" villages, where they are expected to support themselves by tending rubber trees or oil palms and growing fruit for sale.

Groups

For official administrative purposes the Malaysian government distinguishes 18 culturally distinct Orang Asli groups in three categories: Negritos, Senoi and Aboriginal Malays (*Melayu Asli*) (see Table 0.1 and Map 0.1). Orang Asli ethnic groups range in size from a few hundred (Kensiu, Kintaq, Mendriq, Lanoh and Orang Kanak) to more than 49,000 (Semai). Their total population of 178,000 in 2010 comprised only about 0.76 per cent of the Peninsular Malaysian population of 23.5 million, which was—and is—dominated by Malays, Chinese and Indians.

Table 0.1 Orang Asli groups

Group Name	Pre-1950 Economy	Location (State)	2010 Population	Aslian Language Branch	Official Category
Kintaq	Foraging, trading	Perak	234	Northern	Negrito (Semang)
Kensiu	Foraging, trading	Kedah	280	Northern	Negrito (Semang)
Jahai	Foraging, trading	Perak, Kelantan	2,326	Northern	Negrito (Semang)
Mendriq	Swiddening, foraging	Kelantan	253	Northern	Negrito (Semang)
Batek	Foraging, trading	Kelantan, Pahang	1,359	Northern	Negrito (Semang)
Lanoh	Foraging, trading, swiddening	Perak	390	Central	Negrito (Semang)
Chewong	Foraging, swiddening	Pahang	818	Northern	Senoi
Temiar	Swiddening, trading	Perak, Kelantan	30,118	Central	Senoi

Table 0.1 (*cont'd*)

Group Name	Pre-1950 Economy	Location (State)	2010 Population	Aslian Language Branch	Official Category
Semai	Swiddening, trading	Perak, Pahang, Selangor	49,697	Central	Senoi
Jah Hut	Swiddening, trading	Pahang	4,191	Central	Senoi
Semaq Beri	Swiddening, foraging	Terengganu, Pahang	3,413	Southern	Senoi
Btsisi' (Mah Meri)	Swiddening, fishing, foraging	Selangor	2,120	Southern	Senoi
Temoq	Swiddening, trading, foraging	Pahang	Included in Semelai population	Southern	Aboriginal Malay
Semelai	Swiddening, trading	Pahang, N. Sembilan	9,228	Southern	Aboriginal Malay
Jakun (Orang Hulu)	Horticulture, trading	Pahang, Johor	31,577	(Malay)	Aboriginal Malay
Temuan	Horticulture, trading	Pahang, Selangor, N. Sembilan, Malacca	19,343	(Malay)	Aboriginal Malay
Orang Kanak	Horticulture, trading	Johor	238	(Malay)	Aboriginal Malay
Orang Seletar	Fishing, foraging	Johor	1,042	(Malay)	Aboriginal Malay
Orang Kuala	Fishing, wage labour	Johor	3,761	(Malay)	Aboriginal Malay

Population source: 2010 Population and Housing Census (unpublished data). This includes the Temoq as a separate group, although the Department of Orang Asli Development now regards them as part of the Semelai group.

Map 0.1 Ethnic group divisions of the Malay Peninsula
(approximate distribution)

The areas shown on Map 0.1 are the maximal areas in which each
group lived in the early 20th century. Today some Orang Asli live in
urban areas mixed with members of other ethnic groups.

The divisions and names of Orang Asli groups are somewhat
arbitrary and artificial (see Lye 2001: 207–22 for a discussion of all

the group names that have been used in the literature). Before coming under the administrative purview of a government department (now called the Department of Orang Asli Development, Jabatan Kemajuan Orang Asli or JAKOA), most Orang Asli identified only with their local groups. If they called themselves anything, it was usually their term for people of a particular river valley. They did not concern themselves with larger categories of similar peoples, much less with the constructed category, Orang Asli, which encompasses all the indigenous minorities of the peninsula. For example, the lowland-dwelling west Semai in Perak told Dentan that the upland-dwelling east Semai in Pahang were not Semai at all, claiming that they were Temiar, while the east Semai called the west Semai Malays (2011: 92). The people grouped under the category Batek include at least three distinct language groups—Batek De', Batek Tanum and Batek Nong—who just happen to use the term Batek for humans of their type. One small group, the Temoq, officially ceased to exist as a separate group in the 1980s when the predecessor department to the JAKOA folded them into the larger Semelai group for administrative purposes (Laird, this volume).

The names of the different groups have wildly varied origins. Most terms were originally applied to the people by outsiders. For example, the name Semaq Beri was given to one group by a British colonial administrator, Howard Biles, who asked group members for their term for "forest people". The name Chewong is a corruption of the name of a pre-World War II Malay employee of the Game Department, Siwang bin Ahmat, which was misunderstood by the British game warden as the name of the group (Howell 1984: 10–4).

The tripartite division of Orang Asli groups into Negritos (Spanish for "little blacks"), Senoi and Aboriginal Malays developed from early 20th century European racial concepts, with the Negritos (short, dark-skinned, curly-haired people) being seen as the most primitive race, the Senoi (taller, lighter-skinned, wavy-haired people) being more advanced and the Aboriginal Malays (tall, light-skinned, straight-haired people) being seen as almost the equals of the Muslim Malays (Manickam, Fix, this volume). The idea that races, in Malaysia and in general, are discrete and can be ranked from inferior to superior has now been discredited and discarded in scientific discourse, though it lingers on in popular beliefs in many cultures. Recent studies show that the features said to differentiate the Orang Asli races in fact vary in continua across the groups, and the groups are not genetically distinct (see chapters in P. Endicott 2013). Most cultural anthropologists now prefer the term Semang, from an Aslian term for "human being", to the racial term Negrito.

The general correlation of Semang with hunting and gathering, Senoi with swidden horticulture, and Aboriginal Malays with farming and trade is not clear-cut either. For example, many Semaq Beri are settled farmers and are classified as Senoi by the JAKOA, but others are hunter-gatherers, while the Mendriq, classified as Negritos (Semang), are swidden farmers.

Languages

Although the southernmost Orang Asli groups (Jakun, Temuan, Orang Kanaq, Orang Seletar and Orang Kuala) now speak dialects of Malay, an Austronesian language that is the official national language, most Orang Asli groups speak languages in the Mon-Khmer subgroup of the Austroasiatic language family, which is centred in mainland Southeast Asia but also includes the Munda languages of South Asia. Nowadays most Aslian speakers also speak colloquial or standard Malay. The Orang Asli language divisions—Northern Aslian, Central Aslian, Southern Aslian, Jah Hut and Malay—do not neatly correlate with the three official categories of Orang Asli (Negrito [Semang], Senoi and Aboriginal Malay), although most Semang have Northern Aslian languages, and most Senoi have Central Aslian languages.

Economies

Until about 1950 most Orang Asli groups had subsistence economies supplemented by trade or sale of forest products. Some groups (Kensiu, Kintaq, Jahai, Batek and some Semaq Beri) specialized in mobile hunting and gathering (foraging). Others (Temiar, Semai, Mendriq, Lanoh, Semelai, Temoq, Betise', Jah Hut and Chewong) practised swidden ("shifting" or "slash-and-burn") cultivation supplemented by hunting and gathering. Some southerly groups (Temuan, Jakun and

Orang Kanak [Kanaq]) practised wet and dry rice farming, market gardening, and trading of forest products. The tiny Orang Kanak group are descendants of people who were brought "from Sekanak Island in Riau [Indonesia] by a member of the Johor royal family in the nineteenth century" (Benjamin 2002: 46). Two tiny groups living on the Johor coast (Orang Seletar and Orang Kuala [Duano]) were coastal foragers and fishermen. The Orang Kuala are an offshoot of a larger group living in Jambi in Sumatra. Since about 1980 most groups have been disrupted by logging, development projects (for example, oil palm plantations) and government-sponsored regroupment schemes, and they now live predominantly by producing commodities for the market (for example, rubber and fruit) and wage labour.

Social Organization and Practices

Most Orang Asli communities are united by kinship and ties to specific land areas. They trace kinship ties cognatically, through both mothers and fathers. Conjugal families, consisting of a married couple and their children, form the core units in most communities. Among the mobile foragers, such as the Jahai and Batek De', families come together in temporary camps but then split apart and form new camp groups, depending on changing opportunities and preferences. Some farming groups, such as the Temiar, organize themselves around extended families and shallow cognatic descent groups, tracing their descent from a common ancestor through a combination of male and female links. Orang Asli generally regard the land in their traditional territories as free to all members of the local group, although in some groups families have exclusive rights to the crops in the fields that they clear and plant. But the land itself reverts back to the residential group as a whole once the fields are left to become forest again.

Rules governing marriage, sexual access and post-marital residence vary from people to people. Benjamin distinguishes three basic patterns, which he calls "societal traditions": Semang, Senoi and Malayic (Aboriginal Malay and Malay) (1985, 2013, 2014b; Fix, this volume), although a few groups—the Batek, Chewong, Jah Hut and Semaq Beri—have mixed traditions. The Semang tradition is associated with the mobile hunting and gathering economy. People are forbidden to marry any consanguineal (blood) relative or affinal (connected by marriage) relative or to have sex with anyone but the spouse. They must also avoid physical contact with opposite-sex in-laws. These rules require people to find their spouses among distant groups, thus creating a wide-ranging network of social ties. The Senoi tradition is associated with swidden horticulture, in which new fields are opened every year but the villages move only after all the suitable land in one area has been used and left to regenerate. In these groups marriage is forbidden with consanguineal kin but is preferred with affinal kin, and extramarital sex is allowed between brothers-in-law and sisters-in-law. The result is that kin ties are concentrated within specific river valleys. The Malayic tradition is associated with sedentary villages supported by agriculture and trade of forest products with the outside world. Malays and Aboriginal Malays prefer to marry within the village or local area, even with first cousins. Benjamin argues that these kinship practices reinforce people's commitment to their particular economic systems and also lessen any temptation they might have to adopt the way of life of followers of the other traditions. He believes that these differences in practices and worldviews became "locked in" perhaps 1,000–1,500 years ago to help maintain the complementary ways of life of foragers, swiddeners and farmer-traders, who otherwise might converge on a single pattern and thus come into conflict (2011: 177, 2014b).

The Semang and Senoi ethnic groups are politically and socially egalitarian, but some of the southern groups—Semelai, Temuan and Jakun—had hereditary leaders (*batin*) and other ranked political positions. The mobile hunting and gathering peoples, including some Semaq Beri, strongly emphasize personal autonomy, and social relations are egalitarian between males and females (see, for example, Endicott and Endicott 2008). Charismatic individuals may have some influence over others, but no real authority. Senoi too emphasize the autonomy of individuals. They respect elders and may even call some of them headmen, but those leaders have no power. Collective decisions are made by consensus after open discussions by entire communities (Benjamin 1968; Dentan 1968: 65–8; Robarchek 1990).

One remarkable feature of Orang Asli societies is that they prohibit all interpersonal violence, both within their own groups and with outsiders (see, for example, Dentan 1968, 2008; Robarchek 1989;

Endicott 2013; Endicott and Endicott 2014; Hickson and Jennings, this volume; but cf. Leary 1995 for a contrary view). This may in part be a result of their having been victims of Malay slave raiders in the 18th and 19th centuries (see below). Their survival strategy was to flee from contacts with most outsiders and to teach their children to abstain from all forms of violence.

Religions

Studies of Orang Asli beliefs and rituals have revealed elaborate religious systems that make sense of the world and give meaning to people's lives. They also provide moral codes that specify how people should behave (see, for example, Schebesta 1928; Evans 1937; Endicott 1979a, 1979b; Karim 1981; Howell 1984; Roseman 1991; Lye 2004; Benjamin 2014a).

Most Orang Asli think of the cosmos as consisting of a celestial upper-world, sometimes pictured as an island or several solid layers; an earthly middle-world consisting of a disc of solid matter surrounded by sea; and an under-world containing a vast underground sea. Creation myths typically describe culture heroes, such as turtles or water-birds, creating the middle-world by bringing bits of earth to the surface from underneath the primordial sea. The separation of the earth from the underground sea is fragile and can be undermined by humans breaking certain prohibitions (see below).

These worlds are inhabited by various categories of superhuman beings—including spirits, ghosts and deities—some of which are helpful to humans (for example, spirit guides of shamans) and some harmful (for example, agents of disease). The superhuman beings are invisible to humans except during dreams and states of trance. Some superhumans are individualized, named and associated with particular natural phenomena, such as thunderstorms, floods and the production of fruit. For example, most Orang Asli believe in a thunder god, who punishes people for breaking certain prohibitions by sending a violent thunderstorm over the offender's camp or settlement, and an under-world deity, often pictured as a giant snake who causes an upwelling flood from the underground sea to dissolve the earth beneath the offender's settlement, a localized reversal of the world's creation. The offender must make a small offering of blood from his or her leg or burn some hair to persuade the deities to stop the storm.

Orang Asli explain most misfortunes—including accidents, diseases, floods, thunderstorms and attacks by wild animals—as punishments by superhuman beings for people violating prohibitions against behaviours that threaten the natural order (for example, cooking different species of animals over a single fire) or the social order (for example, sexual relations between close relatives) or that show disrespect for the superhuman beings (for example, making loud noises that sound like thunder) or for other people (for example, saying the personal name of an elder). They see their way of life as following a plan laid down by the superhuman beings.

Orang Asli rituals are intended to maintain harmonious relations between themselves and the superhuman beings that control their fortunes. The more elaborate rituals are directed by shamans, many of whom have spirit guides, sometimes conceptualized as the shamans' spouses. Most shamans practise "soul-travel" shamanism, in which the shaman, while in trance, sends his or her soul to other parts of the cosmos to retrieve the missing soul of a sick person or to ask superhuman beings for help, knowledge or magical substances (Gianno, Laird, this volume). Many people know spells that are thought to cure diseases or ensure success at some activity, usually through the help of superhuman beings. The foraging peoples perform communal rituals such as singing and dancing sessions to ask the superhuman beings for abundant crops of wild fruit. Farming groups make offerings and recite spells to ask the earth spirits for permission to plant their crops.

THIS BOOK

Part One: Studying Orang Asli

Despite their small numbers and relative obscurity, Orang Asli have long attracted the interest of European explorers, travellers, traders, museum collectors, missionaries and colonial administrators, and this has led to a large body of literature (Baer 2012). In her comprehensive annotated bibliography on the Orang Asli (2001), Lye Tuck-Po has recorded 1,715 publications and other documents relating to Orang

Asli produced between 1824 and 2001. (This invaluable work contains annotated entries for most of the 1,715 works as well as indices by topics, author's names, ethnic and language groups and place names. Most of the modern publications on Aslian linguistics appeared after the 2001 publication of Lye's bibliography, but they are discussed in Benjamin 2012 and on his *Academia* website.) The quality of the information in the pre-1900 works is highly variable, much of it based on brief encounters with Orang Asli and some even on hearsay reports from Malays. W.W. Skeat and C.O. Blagden provide a useful, though dated, summary of the outside world's knowledge of the Orang Asli at the end of the 19th century in their monumental two-volume book *Pagan Races of the Malay Peninsula* (1906).

During the first 60 years of the 20th century, a number of professionally trained scholars and gifted amateurs, especially colonial administrators, recorded their observations of various Orang Asli groups, mostly based on short-term contacts. For example, the valuable publications of I.H.N. Evans, the long-time curator of the Taiping Museum in Perak, were based on short visits to numerous groups (see, for example, 1937). However, two notable scholars carried out more extended fieldwork with Orang Asli. First was Father Paul Schebesta, a Jesuit scholar from Vienna, who spent a year living with Semang groups, especially the Jahai, in 1924–25 (see, for example, 1928, 1952–57). Also H.D. Noone, the field ethnographer of the Taiping Museum in the late 1930s, carried out extended research with the Temiar and even married a Temiar woman. His "Report on the Settlements and Welfare of the Ple-Temiar Senoi of the Perak-Kelantan Watershed" (1936) was the first general ethnography of a single Orang Asli people. His appendix on the "Proposed Aboriginal Policy" became the basis for the colonial government's Aboriginal Peoples Ordinance (1954, amended in 1967 and 1974) (Malaysian Government 1994).

The modern era of anthropological fieldwork began with Dentan's research on the Semai and Benjamin's studies of the Temiar in the 1960s (Holaday, this volume). They used sociocultural anthropology's now-standard method of ethnographic research—living for extended periods with the people, learning their languages and participating in their everyday lives. This enabled them to produce rich descriptions of these peoples and their cultures and to explain some of the beliefs and practices that make Orang Asli cultures so remarkable.

Dentan and Benjamin's research was followed by a proliferation of studies of various Orang Asli groups by trained anthropologists from Malaysia, Singapore, Thailand, Britain, the United States, Canada, Australia, Japan, France, Norway, Denmark, Sweden, Greece, Germany, Poland and Finland. This research has focused on such topics as language, religion, social organization and practices, biology and demography, economy and environmental adaptation, prehistory, history, art, music, social change and problems. (See Lye 2011 for a comprehensive review of research and publications on Orang Asli up to 2011.)

Until recently most of the anthropological research with Orang Asli was done by foreign scholars. Malaysian granting agencies and universities—except for Universiti Kebangsaan Malaysia, Universiti Sains Malaysia, Universiti Malaya and possibly Universiti Putera and Universiti Pendidikan Sultan Idris—have not encouraged faculty research on Orang Asli, and the Department of Orang Asli Development no longer has trained anthropologists on its staff. Nevertheless, Malaysian scholars —including Wazir Jahan Karim, Juli Edo, Alberto Gomes, Kamal Solhaimi Fadzil, Mohd Razha Rashid, Rusaslina Idrus, Yogeswaran Subramaniam, Shanthi Thambiah, Anthony Williams-Hunt and Zanisah Man (this volume) as well as Hood Salleh, Lye Tuck-Po, Colin Nicholas, Hasan Mat Nor, Lim Chang Ing, Alice Nah and Ramle Abdullah continue to make important contributions to Orang Asli studies. Only a few of those scholars (Juli Edo, Zanisah Man and Anthony Williams-Hunt) are Orang Asli, however. The number of Orang Asli obtaining advanced degrees in social sciences is still very low, and those who do receive them often have career goals outside academia. But we expect that as more Orang Asli succeed in higher education, more will use their skills to document the histories and cultures of their people as well as to help them adjust to their rapidly changing world.

In this volume, Holaday discusses the intellectual and political climate in which Dentan and Benjamin carried out their research in the early and mid-1960s. Howell writes about her long-term research with the Chewong during a period of rapid change in their circumstances. Manickam examines the racial classification of Orang Asli that was developed by European scholars and discusses how studies of Orang

Asli blood types and genes reinforced the conventional racial divisions current in the 1950s.

Part Two: Orang Asli Origins and History

Prehistory

The climate and geography of Southeast Asia at the time the first modern humans arrived were very different from today. During the late Pleistocene epoch, which ended about 10,000 years ago, a series of ice ages locked up a large amount of the world's water in vast ice sheets that covered the northern areas of Eurasia and North America, causing the sea level to drop 100 metres or more below present levels. The seabed beneath the shallow seas now found on both sides of the Malay Peninsula was then dry land. The Asian mainland extended east to Borneo, Java and Bali, north to Palawan in the Philippines, and west to Sumatra, forming a broad continental shelf now known as Sundaland (Vons 2000; Baer 2013, this volume). The Thai-Malay Peninsula formed a range of mountains and hills above the plains. The climate was cooler than now, and the vegetation consisted of a mosaic of open woodlands and savannah, interspersed with swamp and heath forests and with gallery forests along the rivers in the lowlands.

Recent studies of the mitochondrial DNA (mtDNA) of Orang Asli show that some of their ancestors were among the first modern humans to arrive in Southeast Asia during the late Pleistocene exodus from Africa, while other ancestors apparently arrived from other parts of Asia at later times (Hill et al. 2006; Bulbeck 2011; Oppenheimer 2011; Fix, Bulbeck, this volume). "These studies have identified mtDNA lineages that branched from the ancestral African root very early, perhaps 44 to 63 thousand years ago" (Fix, this volume). "The descendants of these *H. sapiens* colonists are well represented in the female gene pool of all Orang Asli groups, especially the Semang" (Bulbeck 2011: 236, see also 230). Other mtDNA haplogroups found among Orang Asli date from the terminal Pleistocene and early Holocene (recent) epoch, suggesting the arrival of migrants from more northerly areas of Southeast Asia who mixed with the previous occupants of the Thai-Malay Peninsula (Bulbeck 2011: 230; Oppenheimer 2011; Fix, this volume) (see below). This does not mean that modern Orang Asli physically resemble those ancient settlers, as there has been gene flow into the Orang Asli population and local evolution over the last 10,000 years. For example, skeletal evidence shows that modern-day Orang Asli are about 10 per cent shorter than the early Holocene inhabitants of the peninsula (Bulbeck 2011: 216–24).

The earliest dated occupation of the Thai-Malay Peninsula by modern humans was about 75,000 years ago at Kota Tampan in northern Malaya (Zuraina 1990; Bulbeck 2011: 213). Kota Tampan was an open-air site on an ancient lakeshore. Other early archaeological sites were in rock shelters in limestone outcroppings. The tool kit at Kota Tampan and later Pleistocene sites featured large river cobbles knapped on one or both sides and numerous flake tools. The people apparently were mobile broad-spectrum hunter-gatherers. Animal bones found at Lang Rongrien, a cave near the west coast of southern Thailand, dating from 43,000 years ago, include bones of large game, such as deer and elephants, and smaller animals, including tortoises (Anderson 1980, 2005; Mudar and Anderson 2007; Baer, this volume). Another site in southern Thailand, Moh Khiew, dating from about 25,000 years ago, contained bones of wild water buffalo, wild pig, tapir, sun bear, primates, otters and squirrels (Pookajorn 1996; Baer, this volume). Plant remains are seldom preserved, but plant residues on stone tools at Niah cave in Sarawak show that aroids (for example, taro), yam and sago-palm pith were part of the diet possibly as early as 40,000 years ago (Barton 2005).

After the last glacial maximum (LGM) about 20,000 years ago, the world's climate gradually warmed, stabilizing about 6,000 years ago. The great ice sheets melted by the beginning of the Holocene epoch, about 10,000 years ago, and the sea level rose, flooding the low-lying plains of Sundaland and creating the separate islands, such as Borneo, found on maps today (Baer, this volume). The climate of the Thai-Malay Peninsula became hot and humid, and seasonal monsoon rains developed. The vegetation in the interior gradually changed to swamp forest and tropical rain forest, and broad mangrove forests developed along the coasts.

The human inhabitants of the peninsula adapted to the changing environment. In the early Holocene they continued to hunt and gather the game and plants in the interior forest and expanded their utilization of marine and seashore resources, as shown by large middens of seashells at various points along the west coast. They also continued to produce stone tools made predominantly of river cobbles flaked on one side to produce sharp edges. They participated in a tool complex or industry called the "Hoabinhian", which was found across Southeast Asia from modern-day Vietnam to north-eastern Sumatra (see, for example, White 2011). The characteristic Hoabinhian tools are elongated unifacial cobble tools, termed "sumatraliths", but flakes, hammerstones and bifacials are also found in the Hoabinhian tool assemblage. There is good reason to believe that the stone tools were used to make a wide range of other tools, especially of wood and bamboo, as well as to chop down trees (see, for example, Higham 2013: 24; White 2011: 27–32; Baer, this volume).

Early Holocene foragers probably harvested the full range of plant and animal foods utilized by Semang hunter-gatherers in historical times. These include wild yams and other tubers, fruits, nuts, fern shoots, palm cabbage, *petai* beans, bamboo shoots, sago palm starch, honey and insect larvae (Dentan 1989). Protein would have come from game, turtles, fish, shellfish, and eggs from birds and turtles (Baer 2013). "The Gua Cha rockshelter in interior Kelantan, dating from 10,000 to 3,000 years ago, contained bones of monkeys, gibbons, pigs, deer, sun bear, cattle, squirrel, fruit bats, rats and even rhinoceros" (Adi Taha 1985, 1991, 2007; Baer, this volume).

During the middle Holocene period, 7,000 to 3,000 years ago, the ancestral Orang Asli populations and cultures underwent major changes in their biological makeup, material culture, economic practices and languages, stimulated in part by immigrants into the peninsula from more northerly parts of mainland Southeast Asia who became absorbed into the existing population (Fix, Bulbeck, this volume). Genetic studies show the arrival of mitochondrial DNA lineages that originated in modern-day Thailand, Cambodia and Vietnam (Oppenheimer 2011). These are most marked in the Senoi groups in the northern and central areas of the peninsula, suggesting that immigrant women as well as men married into the existing populations.

During this period the material artefacts characteristic of "Neolithic" ("new stone") technology—including ground and polished stone tools and pottery—begin to appear in archaeological sites in the peninsula

(Bellwood 1997; Bulbeck 2011, 2014, this volume). Presumably the knowledge and skills needed to make such objects were brought by the immigrants, although some products, such as ornaments deposited in graves, may have arrived by trade. Neolithic technology did not replace chipped and flaked stone tools. The Hoabinhian material culture "continued long after the incorporation of Neolithic material elements, before giving way to metal tools" (Bulbeck 2014: 114).

Swidden ("shifting" or "slash-and-burn") horticulture also arose in the peninsula between 7,000 and 3,000 years ago (Bulbeck 2014, this volume), although there is some evidence of forest burning and other environmental management techniques as early as 10,000 years ago (Maloney 1998; Baer 2013). Probably some of the crops grown, such as rice, were brought by the immigrants, but others, such as betel nut palms, were indigenous to the area. Stone choppers could have been used to cut down or ring-bark and kill trees to open up fields. Swidden farming is associated with semi-sedentary residence and larger and more enduring social groups than hunting and gathering. But mobile hunting and gathering continued alongside swidden farming right into the 20th century. Benjamin argues that the Semang foragers and Senoi horticulturalists in the northern area deliberately "locked in" their complementary ways of life around 1,000–1,500 years ago and traded forest produce for agricultural products (2011, 2014b; cf. Lye 2013).

The immigrants also brought the proto-Aslian language, an offshoot of the Austroasiatic language family that is centred in mainland Southeast Asia, to the Malay Peninsula (Burenhult, Kruspe and Dunn 2011; Benjamin 2012; Dunn, Kruspe and Burenhult 2013; Bulbeck, Burenhult and Kruspe, this volume). This language was adopted in stages by early Orang Asli populations, first in the centre of the peninsula and then spreading south and north. After spreading to various groups, the proto language diverged into the different Aslian languages and dialects found today. We have no direct evidence about the languages spoken by the earlier inhabitants of the peninsula or the reasons why they gave up their original languages for Aslian ones. Possibly proto-Aslian became a lingua franca used in trade and other interactions between the earlier populations and the later arrivals, and then it gradually replaced the earlier languages. Something similar seems to have happened in the Philippines, where the Negritos, the original inhabitants of the islands, adopted Austronesian languages from immigrants who spread into insular Southeast Asia by sea from a homeland in Taiwan (Blust 2013; Reid 2013).

Some Austronesian speakers (but not yet Malayic speakers) began to arrive in the Thai-Malay Peninsula, probably from Borneo and Sumatra, in the first millennium BC. They settled mainly on the coast because the interior was already populated by ancestral Orang Asli (Andaya 2002: 27, 35; Benjamin 2002; Bulbeck, this volume). Some of the early Austronesian-speaking immigrants were probably among the ancestors of the Aboriginal Malays now living in the southern Malay Peninsula.

Early History

After about 500 BC small coastal settlements sprang up, especially at river mouths on the west coast of the Malay Peninsula and on both sides of the Isthmus of Kra in present-day southern Thailand. The settlements became centres of trade, first with other communities up and down the coast and later with traders from as far away as China, India, the Middle East and the Mediterranean. Some of these grew into major trading ports with permanent populations of foreign traders (Nik Hassan Shuhaimi 1991; Andaya and Andaya 2001; Bulbeck 2004). Orang Asli became suppliers of forest products—such as aromatic woods, resins, rhinoceros horns and elephant tusks—and gold and tin ore, the last being especially sought after by Indian traders for making bronze. In return the Orang Asli received such goods as cloth, iron tools, beads and foods, such as rice. "In this role as collectors of primary forest produce, and as labourers and guides in the transhipment of goods across their lands, the Orang Asli became indispensable to the coastal trading kingdoms" (Andaya 2002: 31, 2008: 218–22).

The Malay culture as it is known today—including the Malay language, social hierarchy and Indian-influenced political systems—developed in eastern Sumatra between the 7th and 14th centuries AD, when the kingdoms of Srivijaya and Melayu "dominated both sides of the Strait of Melaka and the interior of Sumatra" (Andaya 2002: 28). In the late 14th century Malay-speaking nobles from Sumatra established trading settlements, including Melaka, at river mouths around the coast (Andaya 2002: 28). In the early 15th century the third ruler of Melaka adopted Islam, probably under the influence of Muslim Indian cloth merchants (Andaya and Andaya 2001: 55–6). Gradually Malay language and culture spread, due to the assimilation of Orang Asli and immigration of Malays and other Austronesian language speakers from present-day Indonesia. At first Minangkabau immigrants, who were matrilineal, took wives from the Orang Asli living inland from Melaka in order to establish claims to the land. As the Malay population increased, the political and economic importance of Orang Asli declined, and "the Orang Asli lifestyle, their way of dress, and even their physical bodies became objects of ridicule by the Melayu [Malays]" (Andaya 2002: 38). The Orang Asli population dwindled down to the minority that rejected assimilation.

As Malay immigrants slowly spread up rivers into the interior of the peninsula, most Orang Asli retreated into the foothills and mountains. By the 18th and 19th centuries Orang Asli had become targets of slave raiders (Dodge 1981; Endicott 1983; Dentan et al. 1997: 55–9; Dentan 2008). The slave raiders were mostly Malays from outside the peninsula (for example, Rawa, Mandailing and Minangkabau Malays from Sumatra) or from coastal and downriver settlements, who had no interest in maintaining an enduring cooperation with the Orang Asli (Dentan et al. 1997: 55–6; Endicott 1983: 227, 233). Slave raiders targeted Orang Asli because they were non-Muslim, so capturing them did not violate the Islamic prohibition on enslaving other Muslims (Gullick 1958: 104; Endicott 1983: 217–8). Debt-slaves and captured slaves (Malay *abdi*) formed the main labour force in towns and in the households of chiefs and sultans (Gullick 1958: 97–8; Endicott 1983: 216–7; Reid 1983: 29). Other captured slaves were sold in slave markets to traders who transported them to places such as Java, where labour was in demand (Reid 1983: 27–33). The raiding was violent. Usually well-armed parties would attack a village or camp at night, killing the adult men and women and capturing the children (Endicott 1983: 221–2; Dentan et al. 1997: 56–7; Dentan 2008). Sometimes Malays tempted or coerced Orang Asli into kidnapping other Orang Asli for them in order to "preserve their own women-folk from captivity" (Clifford 1897:178; see also Maxwell 1880: 47; Noone 1936: 54–5; Benjamin 1966: 8; Robarchek 1979: 565; Endicott 1983: 223). Slave raiding was stopped by the British colonial government in the late 19th and early 20th centuries.

Recent History

Between about 1920, when slave raiding ceased, and the Japanese invasion in 1941, the Orang Asli remained outside developed areas, and the authorities treated them with benign neglect (Carey 1976: 288–90). During the Japanese occupation (1941–45), most Orang Asli hid in the forest, while the Japanese exploited Malay farmers for food and labour (Dentan et al. 1997: 60–1; Endicott 1997: 39). Orang Asli and Malays shared the forest with the Malayan People's Anti-Japanese Army of the Malayan Communist Party, consisting mostly of Chinese residents, which provided the main internal source of resistance to the Japanese occupation (Dentan et al. 1997: 60–1; Kratoska 1997). After the war ended in 1945, the Malayan Communist Party tried unsuccessfully to gain influence in the post-war government (Dentan et al. 1997: 61). In 1948 members of the Party "returned to the jungle to launch an armed insurrection" (Kratoska 1997: 315). The British colonial government declared this an "Emergency", which lasted from 1948 to 1960 (Dentan et al. 1997: 61–6). During the Emergency "Communist terrorists" (CTs) controlled Orang Asli by persuasion mixed with the threat of violence (Dentan 1968: 3, 80–1; 1995; Jones 1968; Carey 1976: 290–5, 305–20; Leary 1995; Dentan et al. 1997: 61–6). By 1953 most Orang Asli in the central highlands were under effective Communist control (Jones 1968: 297; Carey 1976: 305, 311).

The British security forces treated the Orang Asli as suspected CT collaborators. They tried removing Orang Asli to concentration camps outside the forest, with disastrous results; many Orang Asli died, and others fled back to their home areas (Polunin 1953; Carey 1976: 307–8). Later the British established "jungle forts" in Orang Asli areas and attempted to win the cooperation of Orang Asli by providing them with medical aid and trade goods, with slightly more success (Carey 1976: 312–4; Dentan et al. 1997: 63–4). In 1954 the colonial government expanded the nascent Department of Aborigines, which carried on the campaign to win over the Orang Asli (Jones 1968: 299–300; Carey 1976: 312–4), and it enacted the "Aboriginal Peoples Act, 1954", which gave the federal government total control over all Orang Asli, down to what media people could bring into their settlements. The Orang Asli feared offending either the CTs or the government forces. More remote upstream Semai pretended to support the CTs, less remote downstream Semai pretended to support the government forces, and those in between just played dumb (Dentan 1968: 80–1).

In 1960 the newly independent Federation of Malaya government declared the Emergency ended, but for security reasons interior forest areas, where many Orang Asli continued to follow their traditional ways of life, remained off limits to development and outsider settlement until the late 1970s. The government retained the Department of Aborigines, renamed the Department of Orang Asli Affairs (Jabatan Hal Ehwal Orang Asli or JHEOA), as the agency responsible for administering the Orang Asli and for providing them with medical care, education and economic development. The Aboriginal Peoples Act remained in force, giving the JHEOA extensive control over the Orang Asli.

Over the next two decades, the government's goals regarding the Orang Asli slowly changed. In 1961 the government published a "Statement of Policy Regarding the Administration of the Aborigine Peoples of the Federation of Malaya", stating that the government's goal was the "ultimate integration [of Orang Asli] with the Malay section of the community" and that it should be "natural integration as opposed to artificial assimilation" (Ministry of the Interior 1961: 3, 5). The Statement added that "special measures should be adopted for the protection of the institutions, customs, mode of life, persons, property and labour of the aborigine people" (Ministry of the Interior 1961: 5), which suggested that the Orang Asli should enter into a close relationship with the Malays but remain culturally distinct from them (Mohd Tap 1990: 112–9). However, some officials in the government, which was—and still is—dominated by Malays, resented the idea that a category of Malaysians existed that was arguably more indigenous than the Malays. The Malaysian Federal Constitution provided many special privileges to Malays (and natives of Sarawak and Sabah), such as preferential access to higher education and government jobs, based on the rationale that Malays, unlike Chinese and Indians, are indigenous to Malaysia (Malaysian Government 1982 Article 153). Therefore, they argued that the government should assimilate the Orang Asli into the

Malay ethnic group, thus causing them to cease to exist as a separate category of citizens. The Malaysian Federal Constitution defines a Malay as "a person who professes the religion of Islam, habitually speaks the Malay language [and] conforms to Malay custom" (Malaysian Government 1982 Article 160). Since many Orang Asli already could speak Malay, and Malay customs were highly variable, the major task was to get the Orang Asli to adopt Islam. By the late 1970s, despite guarantees of religious freedom in the Constitution and the Aboriginal Peoples Act, the JHEOA was working with the Ministry of Religious Affairs and various religious organizations to induce the Orang Asli to adopt Islam and become Malays (JHEOA 1983; Mohd Tap 1990: 228; Dentan et al. 1997: 79–83; Nicholas 2000: 98–102; Endicott and Dentan 2004: 29–30; Nobuta 2009; Benjamin 2014a). The agencies' efforts included building community halls containing Muslim prayer halls (*surau*) in Orang Asli villages, posting "community development officers" trained by the Department of Religious Affairs in Orang Asli communities, and instituting numerous "positive discrimination" measures favouring converts to Islam, such as paying their school fees, restricting university scholarships to converts, and requiring Orang Asli public servants to convert to get promotion (Nicholas 2000: 98–102; Nobuta 2009: 253–7). The JHEOA published a new policy statement in 1983 describing its goal as "the Islamization of the whole Orang Asli community and the integration/assimilation of the Orang Asli with the Malays" (JHEOA 1983: 2).

The JAKOA (which succeeded the JHEOA in 2011) continues the efforts to assimilate the Orang Asli into the Malay ethnic group. JAKOA no longer builds prayer halls or posts community development officers, but the Islamization programme is still active, and government officials threaten to arrest, under the Internal Security Act, anyone who interferes with it (Nobuta 2009: 276). It is unclear how successful the Islamization programme has been. Many Orang Asli have nominally accepted Islam but have made no effort to change their beliefs or behaviour.

Until 2012 the JAKOA also ran a medical service, which was based at the Gombak Hospital just outside Kuala Lumpur (Nicholas 2000: 128–30; Endicott and Dentan 2004: 36; Bedford 2008, 2009, 2013). This service was established during the Emergency with the goal of providing medical care to remote, isolated Orang Asli communities.

It employed a network of simple medical posts in villages, attended by trained Orang Asli medical orderlies and visited periodically by doctors from Gombak. Orang Asli closer to towns could also use ordinary government clinics for free. The medical service was somewhat successful, although the Orang Asli standard of health lags well behind that of the general population (Baer 1999, 2010; Nicholas 2000: 27–30; Endicott and Dentan 2004: 36; Bedford 2013: 193–4). The Gombak Hospital "is under-resourced in terms of funding, facilities, and staff, and the standard of health care offered often falls below that practiced in mainstream government hospitals" (Bedford 2013: 194). In 2012— after complaints from Orang Asli, adverse reports in the media and pressure from nongovernmental organizations, including the Malaysian Bar Council—the Ministry of Health took over Orang Asli health care.

The Department of Aborigines education service also began during the Emergency and was continued after independence (Carey 1976: 300–1). Students were expected to start their studies in special primary schools in Orang Asli villages and then switch to ordinary government secondary schools, where they would be housed in hostels. The teachers were poorly educated Department of Aborigines employees in grade 1–3 schools and Ministry of Education teachers in the higher grades. Unfortunately, a large proportion of Orang Asli children dropped out after only one or two years of schooling. Government officials blamed the Orang Asli parents and children, but numerous cultural problems, including Orang Asli's lack of facility in the Malay language and their aversion to corporal punishment, and practical problems, such as school fees, as well as the poor quality of the teachers exacerbated the problem. Orang Asli children in government schools also suffered from abuse by other students and teachers (see, for example, Lim 1984; Tan 1992: 9; Nicholas 2006; Thambiah, Zanisah Man and Ruslina Idrus, this volume). In 1995 the government turned over the responsibility for Orang Asli education to the Ministry of Education (Nicholas 2000: 24–7, 127–8; Endicott and Dentan 2004: 36–9). Since then rates of Orang Asli school enrolment at all levels have improved, but still lag well behind national averages (Nicholas 2006).

The main responsibility of the JAKOA today is economic development of the Orang Asli. The goal is to "modernize" their economies, by which is meant getting them to replace their subsistence activities with activities directed toward market exchange, selling commodities or labour, and buying food and other necessities (Mohd Tap 1990: 239; Nicholas 2000: 46–52, 96–8; Endicott and Dentan 2004: 40–4). At first this was based on *in situ* improvements. Officials encouraged residents of existing Orang Asli settlements to grow cash crops, including rubber trees, oil palms, coconut trees and fruit trees. The department provided tools, seedlings, herbicides and fertilizers. Newly settled foraging groups were also given rations to tide them over until the trees began to produce income.

In the late 1970s the federal government lifted the security restrictions on most of the interior of the peninsula. State governments then sold lucrative logging concessions to logging companies and allocated the cleared land to companies and government organizations for conversion into rubber and oil palm plantations. No accommodation was made for the Orang Asli living in those areas (see below). The JHEOA then instituted a more radical form of development based on resettling Orang Asli in artificial villages, usually located in selectively logged parts of their traditional territories. These "regroupment schemes" (*Rancangan Pengumpulan Semula* or RPS) have become the standard method for "modernizing" Orang Asli economies. In theory, each RPS contains an administrative centre, school, clinic, shop and multipurpose hall. It also has electricity and piped water and access roads to the outside world. Each family gets up to ten acres of land for oil palm, rubber and fruit trees and two acres for a house and subsistence crops (Jimin et al. 1983: 96). As before, the department provides the equipment, seedlings and fertilizer, and the residents provide the labour.

The regroupment schemes have not succeeded in lifting residents out of poverty (Nicholas 2000: 30–2; Endicott and Dentan 2004: 43–4; Nicholas, Jenita Engi and Teh 2010: 45):

> Statistics provided in the Government's 10th Malaysia Plan (2011–2015) … reveal that 50 percent of the 29,990 Orang Asli households in existence live below the poverty line. Of these, about 5,700 households (19 percent) are considered to be hardcore poor. In contrast, the national poverty rate is a commendable 3.8 percent, with only 0.7 percent being hardcore poor. (Nicholas, Jenita Engi and Teh 2010: 45)

There are several reasons for the failure of these schemes. Sometimes the promised facilities do not materialize, due to inadequate funding and poor planning and execution. No alternative means of earning a living are provided during the time the cash crops are maturing. The land is often of poor quality, and the amounts of land and resources provided are inadequate to support the residents. Also, dependence on selling commodities such as rubber exposes producers to market fluctuations and exploitation by middlemen. The result is that residents of the regroupment schemes often become dependent upon government agencies for financial support.

The biggest problem facing the Orang Asli today is their lack of land rights. According to Nicholas, "The dismal record of securing Orang Asli land tenure—coupled with increased intrusion into, and appropriation of, Orang Asli traditional lands by a variety of interests representing individuals, corporations and the state itself—remains the single element that is of grave concern to the Orang Asli today" (2000: 38; see also Dentan et al. 1997: 73–6 and Subramaniam 2013). Under Malaysian land law, based on the British colonial "Torrens" system of land title, the individual states own all land that is not held by title deeds. During the colonial period states designated some of the areas where Orang Asli lived as "Orang Asli reserves" or "Orang Asli areas", where Orang Asli had exclusive rights to live and use the resources. However, state and federal governments do not recognize any Orang Asli ownership rights to the land on which they and their ancestors have lived for centuries. According to statute law, though not common law, the Orang Asli are squatters on state land, and state governments can reclaim the land in aboriginal reserves without payment or the consent of the residents. The amount of land actually gazetted (officially proclaimed) as Orang Asli reserves was never more than a small portion of the traditional land claimed and utilized (Nicholas 2000: 31–2; Nicholas, Jenita Engi and Teh 2010: 49–53). The JAKOA claims that it, being a federal government agency, has no way to obtain land for the Orang Asli. However, Article 83 of the Constitution gives the federal government ample power to acquire land from the states for purposes it considers important, which should include promoting the welfare of the Orang Asli (Subramaniam 2013 and this volume). When Orang

Asli have gone to court to claim compensation for loss of land under principles of common law and international indigenous rights, they have been opposed by all concerned government agencies, including the JAKOA, and all branches of the government except for the judiciary (Dentan et al. 1997: 76–9; Nicholas 2000: 110; Nicholas, Jenita Engi and Teh 2010: 99; Subramaniam 2013 and this volume). As Benjamin says of tribal societies in the Malay world in general, "All too often ... the requirement that the tribespeople settle down permanently ... has not been met with a parallel guarantee of land rights. The authorities who urge them not to move around are usually the same authorities who move them away when more prominent citizens desire the land they occupy" (2002: 47).

In recent decades Orang Asli—especially those who are educated and have experience outside their villages—have become aware of the common interests and problems they share with members of other Orang Asli ethnic groups (Heikkilä and Williams-Hunt, this volume). One reflection of this broader Orang Asli identity is the development of the Association of Orang Asli of Peninsular Malaysia (Persatuan Orang Asli Semenanjung Malaysia or POASM). It began as a small group of Orang Asli employees of the JHEOA, but had expanded to about 10,000 members by 2011 (Dentan et al. 1997: 153–4; Nicholas 2000: 152–6, 179n10; Khoo 2011). POASM is no longer very active, but recently the Jaringan Kampung Orang Asli Semenanjung Malaysia, an informal Orang Asli network advocating indigenous rights, has been trying to represent the interests of Orang Asli to the government and the general public.

Part Three: Aslian Languages

As mentioned above, most Orang Asli groups speak Aslian languages, a subdivision of the Austroasiatic language family. The study of Aslian languages goes back to the beginning of the 20th century with the work of W. Schmidt (1901) and C.O. Blagden (Skeat and Blagden 1906, Vol. 2: 507–775), but research by professionally trained linguists languished until the 1960s, and it has expanded dramatically in recent years. (See Benjamin 2012 for a comprehensive summary and discussion of Aslian linguistic studies and references to the literature.)

The Aslian languages have been found to contain a number of linguistically interesting features, such as extensive vocabularies for smells. In their chapter, Burenhult and Kruspe discuss the elaboration of terms for eating and drinking in the Aslian languages and show how those terms relate to their classifications of plants and animals and their modes of subsistence.

Part Four: Orang Asli Religions

As discussed above, traditional Orang Asli religions attribute most illnesses to attacks by invisible superhuman beings, sometimes as punishment for the victim breaking a prohibition. People treat many illnesses by means of herbal medicine and magical spells, but the most serious and lingering diseases require the help of shamans, religious experts thought to have the power to send their souls to the land of the superhuman beings, while in trance, to meet with them to obtain powerful medicine or spells or to retrieve the souls of victims of soul loss. The chapters by Gianno and Laird describe in vivid detail the distant reaches of the cosmos where gods, spirits and ghosts dwell as well as the methods shamans, in their spiritual forms, use to accomplish their perilous tasks. These elaborate curing rituals reinforce the Semelai and Temoq understanding of the cosmos and the connections between its human and non-human inhabitants.

With increasing exposure to outsiders, Orang Asli have been confronted by competing religious worldviews. In their chapter, Juli Edo and Kamal Solhaimi give a vivid account of the religious competition for the souls of the Western Semai of Perak, where almost half of the population subscribed to a world religion in 2011. Juli and Kamal's research reveals that Semai individuals adopt or reject religions for personal and social reasons, including concerns that adopting a world religion would undermine their Semai identity. This detailed history also shows how colonial and Malaysian government policies affected people at the grassroots level.

Part Five: Significance of Orang Asli Cultures

Orang Asli developed their ways of life over many centuries in response to the practical problems and opportunities they faced in their particular natural and social environments. However, some of their practices, which they take for granted, seem remarkable to Western scholars. Among other things, Orang Asli societies show how social life can be coordinated without a hierarchical political system (see chapters in Gibson and Sillander 2011), how cooperation and personal autonomy can both be maximized (Endicott 2011), and how societies can maintain gender equality (Endicott and Endicott 2008).

Hickson and Jennings (Chapter 11) and Gomes (Chapter 12) take the further step of suggesting that Western societies can benefit by adopting certain Orang Asli practices. One of the most striking characteristics of Orang Asli social life is the near absence of physical violence. Andy Hickson and his mother, Sue Jennings, who spent over a year living with the Temiar, describe how they have applied what they learned from the Temiar about peaceful conflict resolution to their professional practices as an educational consultant and a drama therapist respectively. Hickson works to counteract bullying in schools by having students act out dramas based on Temiar ways of interacting, and Jennings applies aspects of Temiar ritual practices to her group therapy sessions.

Another interesting feature of Orang Asli cultures is their merging of religious beliefs and economic practices. According to Gomes, Western religions represent nature as something to be exploited and dominated by humans, unlike traditional Semai religion, which regards plants, animals and the earth itself as animated by superhuman beings that must be treated with respect and restraint. Gomes argues that Semai attitudes toward nature are worthy of emulation if humans are to utilize nature in an ecologically sound and sustainable manner.

Part Six: Challenges, Changes and Resistance

Since about 1980, widespread logging and replacement of forests with plantations has seriously disrupted the lives of most Orang Asli. Without forests the former hunter-gatherers have no wild foods and game, and without adequate land the former horticulturalists can no longer support themselves on their crops. The chapters in this section document some of the problems they face, some of the changes they have made in response, and some of the ways they resist the destruction of their ways of life.

Karim and Razha (Chapter 13) and Nowak (Chapter 14) deal in part
with the Ma' Betise' or Hma' Btsisi' (also called Mah Meri), a Central
Aslian-speaking people living on Carey Island and adjacent parts of
the mainland in coastal Selangor. Before the spread of plantations,
some Ma' Betise' lived in and around the coastal mangrove forests—
supporting themselves by fishing, foraging and swiddening—while
those living on the mainland concentrated more on swidden horticulture.
These chapters show how their cultures and social organization changed
in response to their loss of land and resources and how some people are
making a successful transition to life in the market economy. However,
they are afraid to live in urban areas, and their attachment to their rural
villages is still strong.

The news is not so promising for the former foragers—the Kintak
Bong in northern Perak (Karim and Razha, this volume), the Jahai
in northwestern Kelantan (Riboli, this volume), the Batek Tanum in
northwest Pahang (Tacey, this volume), and the Lanoh of northern Perak
(Dallos, this volume)—who are now living in regroupment villages
surrounded by secondary forest and plantations and villages populated
by non-Orang Asli. The Kintak Bong have adopted subsistence farming
and continue to sell minor forest products, but they are so poor that
even food-sharing has broken down. The health of the Jahai at Rual
has seriously deteriorated due to pollution and communicable diseases,
which they attribute to evil spirits, ghosts and the black magic of
outsiders.

The Batek Tanum and the Lanoh, also former hunter-gatherers, face
similar problems of land loss, environmental degradation and pressures
from outsiders, but they have fought back in ingenious ways. The Batek
Tanum—who now learn about world events from TV, radio, videos and
newspapers—are attempting to form alliances with powerful outsiders,
including nongovernmental organizations and foreign governments, by
means of shamanic visits to other countries and letters to potential
supporters. The Lanoh keep Malays at arm's length by employing a
tactic—which probably goes back hundreds of years—of maintaining a
monopoly on the supply of minor forest products to established trading
partners. This removes the need for the trading partners to seek the
products themselves, and it protects the autonomy of the Lanoh by
keeping the Malays out of the forest.

Recently some Orang Asli have been successful in establishing their customary land rights in court. With the support of volunteer lawyers, they have demanded compensation, under principles of common law and international indigenous rights, for land seized by government agencies and private enterprises (Subramaniam 2013 and this volume). Although the legislative and executive branches of the government strongly oppose Orang Asli land claims, due to the government's desire to exploit the land and resources, the judicial branch has maintained its impartiality, at least in these cases. But Orang Asli have had to fight each case from scratch, with the government refusing to accept previous decisions as precedents, apparently with the aim of bankrupting the Orang Asli plaintiffs. Nevertheless, this avenue appears to be the most promising route to compensation for land seizures.

Part Seven: The Future

The goal of most Orang Asli is to become prosperous Malaysian citizens while also maintaining their distinctive identities and cultures. In spite of their numerous handicaps, some Orang Asli have succeeded in obtaining higher education, which has enabled them to obtain employment in the professions and skilled jobs. Shanthi Thambiah, Zanisah Man and Rusaslina Idrus (Chapter 19) describe some of the challenges facing Orang Asli women in the Malaysian educational system, including the need to be competitive, which is contrary to traditional Orang Asli sociality. Many educated Orang Asli are now computer literate and use the Internet to gather information, network with other indigenous people in Malaysia and abroad, and provide information about Orang Asli perspectives to each other and to the wider public through blogs (Heikkilä and Williams-Hunt, this volume). Some blogs educate Orang Asli and promote discourse on matters of mutual concern, such as the United Nations Declaration of Rights of the Indigenous Peoples (UNDRIP), which the Malaysian government has endorsed but has not implemented in its dealings with the Orang Asli (Nicholas, Jenita Engi and Teh 2010; Subramaniam 2012).

REFERENCES

Adi Taha
    1985   The Re-Excavation of the Rockshelter of Gua Cha, Ulu Kelantan, West Malaysia. Federation Museums Journal (New Series) 30: i–134.
    1991   Gua Cha and the Archaeology of the Orang Asli. Bulletin of the Indo-Pacific Prehistory Association 11: 363–72.
    2007   Archaeology of Ulu Kelantan. Kuala Lumpur: Ministry of Culture, Arts and Heritage Malaysia, Department of Museums Malaysia.

Andaya, L.Y.
    2002   Orang Asli and the Melayu in the History of the Malay Peninsula. Journal of the Malaysian Branch of the Royal Asiatic Society 75(1): 23–48.
    2008   Leaves of the Same Tree: Trade and Ethnicity in the Straits of Melaka. Honolulu: University of Hawai'i Press.

Andaya, B.W. and L.Y. Andaya
    2001   A History of Malaysia. Second edition. Houndmills, UK: Palgrave.

Anderson, D.
    1980   Lang Rongrien Rockshelter. Philadelphia: University of Pennsylvania Museum.
    2005   The Use of Caves in Peninsular Thailand. Asian Perspectives 44(1): 137–53.

Baer, A.
    1999   Health, Disease and Survival: A Biomedical and Genetic Analysis of the Orang Asli of Peninsular Malaysia. Subang Jaya, Malaysia: Center for Orang Asli Concerns.
    2010   Orang Asli (Indigenous Malaysian) Biomedical Bibliography. http://hdl.handle.net/1957/15784, accessed 15 April 2014.
    2012   Contacts and Contrasts: The British vs. the Orang Asli in Colonial Malaysia. http://hdl.handle.net/1957/29700, accessed 15 April 2014.
    2013   Human History and the Orang Asli in Southeast Asia. Unpublished draft paper.

Barton, H.
    2005   The Case for Rainforest Foragers: The Starch Record at Niah Cave, Sarawak. Asian Perspectives 44(1): 56–72.

Bedford, K.J.A.

2008 Gombak and Its Patients: Provision of Healthcare to the Orang Asli (Indigenous Minority) of Peninsular Malaysia. Unpublished D.Phil. thesis. University of Oxford.

2009 Gombak Hospital, The Orang Asli Hospital. Indonesia and the Malay World 37(107): 23–44.

2013 Perceptions of Leprosy in the Orang Asli (Indigenous Minority) of Peninsular Malaysia. *In* When Culture Impacts Health: Global Lessons for Effective Health Research. C. Banwell, S. Ulijaszek and J. Dixon, eds. Pp. 193–203. London: Academic Press.

Bellwood, P.

1997 Prehistory of the Indo-Malaysian Archipelago. Revised edition. Honolulu: University of Hawai'i Press.

Benjamin, G.

1966 Temiar Social Groupings. Federation Museums Journal (New Series) 11: 1–25.

1968 Headmanship and Leadership in Temiar Society. Federation Museums Journal (New Series) 13: 1–43.

1985 In the Long Term: Three Themes in Malayan Cultural Ecology. *In* Cultural Values and Human Ecology in Southeast Asia. K.L. Hutterer, A.T. Rambo and G. Lovelace, eds. Pp. 219–78. Ann Arbor, MI: Center for South and Southeast Asian Studies, University of Michigan.

2002 On Being Tribal in the Malay World. *In* Tribal Communities in the Malay World: Historical, Cultural and Social Perspectives. G. Benjamin and C. Chou, eds. Pp. 7–76. Singapore: Institute of Southeast Asian Studies.

2011 Egalitarianism and Ranking in the Malay World. *In* Anarchic Solidarity: Autonomy, Equality, and Fellowship in Southeast Asia. T. Gibson and K. Sillander, eds. New Haven, CT: Yale University Southeast Asia Studies.

2012 The Aslian Languages of Malaysia and Thailand: An Assessment. *In* Language Documentation and Description, Volume 11. P.K. Austin and S. McGill, eds. Pp. 136–230. London: Endangered Languages Project, School of Oriental and African Studies.

2013 Why Have the Peninsular "Negritos" Remained Distinct? Human Biology 85(1–3): 445–83.

2014a Temiar Religion: 1964–2012: Enchantment, Disenchantment and Reinchantment in Malaysia's Uplands. Singapore: NUS Press.

2014b Between Isthmus and Islands: Studies in Malay-World Ethnohistory. Singapore: Institute of Southeast Asian Studies.

Blust, R.

2013 Terror from the Sky: Unconventional Linguistic Clues to the Negrito Past. Human Biology 85(1–3): 401–16.

Bulbeck, D.

2004 Indigenous Traditions and Exogenous Influences in the Early History of Peninsular Malaysia. *In* Southeast Asia: Origins to Civilization. I. Glover and P. Bellwood, eds. Pp. 314–36. Abingdon, UK: RoutledgeCurzon.

2011 Biological and Cultural Evolution in the Populations and Culture History of Homo sapiens in Malaya. *In* Dynamics of Human Diversity: The Case of Mainland Southeast Asia. N.J. Enfield, ed. Pp. 207–55. Canberra: Pacific Linguistics.

2014 The Chronometric Holocene Archaeological Record of the Southern Thai-Malay Peninsula. International Journal of Asia Pacific Studies 10(1): 111–62.

Burenhult, N., N. Kruspe and M. Dunn

2011 Language History and Culture Groups among Austroasiatic-Speaking Foragers of the Malay Peninsula. *In* Dynamics of Human Diversity: The Case of Mainland Southeast Asia. N.J. Enfield, ed. Pp. 257–75. Canberra: Pacific Linguistics.

Carey, I.

1976 Orang Asli: The Aboriginal Tribes of Peninsular Malaysia. Kuala Lumpur: Oxford University Press.

Clifford, H.

1897 In Court and Kampong. London: Richards Press.

Dentan, R.K.

1968 The Semai: A Nonviolent People of Malaya. New York: Holt, Rinehart and Winston.

1989 Potential Food Sources for Foragers in the Malaysian Rainforest. Bijdragen Tot de Taal-, Land- en Volkenkunde 147: 420–44.

1995 Bad Day at Bukit Pekan. American Anthropologist 97(2): 225–31.

2008 Overwhelming Terror: Love, Fear, Peace, and Violence among Semai of Malaysia. Lanham, MD: Rowman and Littlefield Publishers.

2011   Childhood, Familiarity and Social Life among East Semai. *In* Anarchic Solidarity: Autonomy, Equality, and Fellowship in Southeast Asia. T. Gibson and K. Sillander, eds. Pp. 88–118. New Haven: Yale Southeast Asia Studies Program.

Dentan, R.K., K. Endicott, A.G. Gomes and M.B. Hooker
1997   Malaysia and the "Original People": A Case Study of the Impact of Development on Indigenous Peoples. Upper Saddle River, NJ: Allyn and Bacon.

Dodge, N.N.
1981   The Malay-Aborigine Nexus Under Malay Rule. Bijdragen Tot de Taal-, Land- en Volkenkunde 137(1): 1–16.

Dunn, M., N. Kruspe and N. Burenhult
2013   Time and Place in the Prehistory of the Aslian Languages. Human Biology 85(1–3): 383–400.

Endicott, K.M.
1979a   Batek Negrito Religion: The World-View and Rituals of a Hunting and Gathering People of Peninsular Malaysia. Oxford: Clarendon Press.
1979b   The Batek Negrito Thunder God: The Personification of a Natural Force. *In* The Imagination of Reality: Essays in Southeast Asian Coherence Systems. A.L. Becker and A. Yengoyan, eds. Pp. 29–42. Norwood, NJ: Ablex.
1983   The Effects of Slave Raiding on the Aborigines of the Malay Peninsula. *In* Slavery, Bondage and Dependency in Southeast Asia. A. Reid, ed. Pp. 216–45. St Lucia, Queensland: University of Queensland Press.
1997   Batek History, Interethnic Relations, and Subgroup Dynamics. *In* Indigenous Peoples and the State: Politics, Land, and Ethnicity in the Malayan Peninsula and Borneo. R.L. Winzeler, ed. Pp. 30–50. New Haven, CT: Yale Southeast Asia Studies.
2011   Cooperative Autonomy: Social Solidarity among the Batek of Malaysia. *In* Anarchic Solidarity: Autonomy, Equality, and Fellowship in Southeast Asia. T. Gibson and K. Sillander, eds. Pp. 62–87. New Haven, CT: Yale University Southeast Asia Studies.
2013   Peaceful Foragers: The Significance of the Batek and Moriori for the Question of Innate Human Violence. *In* War, Peace, and Human Nature: The Convergence of Evolutionary and Cultural Views. D.P. Fry, ed. Pp. 241–61. New York: Oxford University Press.

Endicott, K.M. and R.K. Dentan
    2004 Into the Mainstream or Into the Backwater? Malaysian
          Assimilation of Orang Asli. *In* Civilizing the Margins: Southeast
          Asian Government Policies for the Development of Minorities.
          C.R. Duncan, ed. Ithaca, NY and London: Cornell University
          Press.

Endicott, K.L. and K.M. Endicott
    2014 Batek Childrearing and Morality. *In* Ancestral Landscapes in
          Human Evolution: Culture, Childrearing and Social Wellbeing.
          D. Narvaez, A. Fuentes and P. Gray, eds. Pp. 108–25. New York:
          Oxford University Press.

Endicott, K.M. and K.L. Endicott
    2008 The Headman Was a Woman: The Gender Egalitarian Batek of
          Malaysia. Long Grove, IL: Waveland Press.

Endicott, P., ed.
    2013 Special Issue on Revisiting the "Negrito" Hypothesis. Human
          Biology 85: 1–3.

Evans, I.H.N.
    1937 The Negritos of Malaya. Cambridge: Cambridge University
          Press.

Gibson, T. and K. Sillander
    2011 Anarchic Solidarity: Autonomy, Equality, and Fellowship in
          Southeast Asia. New Haven, CT: Yale University Southeast Asia
          Studies.

Gullick, J.M.
    1958 Indigenous Political Systems of Western Malaya. London: Athlone
          Press.

Higham, C.
    2013 Hunter-Gatherers in Southeast Asia: From Prehistory to the
          Present. Human Biology 85: 21–44.

Hill, C., P. Soares, M. Mormina, V. Macaulay, W. Meehan, J. Blackburn,
D. Clarke, J.M. Raja, P. Ismail, D. Bulbeck, S. Oppenheimer and M. Richards
    2006 Phylogeography and Ethnogenesis of Aboriginal Southeast Asian.
          Molecular Biology and Evolution 23: 2480–91.

Hill, C., P. Soares, M. Mormina, V. Macaulay, D. Clarke, P.B. Blumbach,
M. Vizuete-Forster, P. Forster, D. Bulbeck, S. Oppenheimer and M. Richards
    2007 A Mitochondrial Stratigraphy for Island Southeast Asia. American
          Journal of Human Genetics 80: 29–43.

Howell, S.
1984 Society and Cosmos: Chewong of Peninsular Malaysia. Singapore and New York: Oxford University Press.

JHEOA
1983 Strategi Perkembangan Ugama Islam di Kalangan Masyarakat Orang Asli. Kuala Lumpur: Jabatan Hal Ehwal Orang Asli.

Jimin B. Idris, Mohd Tap Salleh, Jailani M. Dom, Abd. Halim Haji Jawi and Md. Razim Shafie
1983 Planning and Administration of Development Programmes for Tribal Peoples (The Malaysian Setting). Kuala Lumpur: Jabatan Hal Ehwal Orang Asli.

Jones, A.
1968 The Orang Asli: An Outline of Their Progress in Modern Malaya. Journal of Southeast Asian History 9: 286–305.

Karim, W-J.B.
1981 Ma' Betisék Concepts of Living Things. LSE Monographs on Social Anthropology No. 54. London: Athlone Press.

Khoo, S.
2011 Emergency Fund for Orang Asli. The Star (Malaysia), 5 September.

Kratoska, P.H.
1997 The Japanese Occupation of Malaya: A Social and Economic History. Honolulu: University of Hawai'i Press.

Leary, J.
1995 Violence and the Dream People: The Orang Asli in the Malayan Emergency, 1948–1960. Athens, OH: Center for International Studies, Ohio University.

Lim Hock Chye
1984 On the Way to a Better Future. Malay Mail, 28 July.

Lye Tuck-Po
2004 Changing Pathways: Forest Degradation and the Batek of Pahang, Malaysia. Lanham, MD: Lexington Books.
2011 A History of Orang Asli Studies: Landmarks and Generations. Kajian Malaysia 29 (Suppl. 1): 23–52.
2013 Making Friends in the Rainforest: "Negrito" Adaptation to Risk and Uncertainty. Human Biology 85(1–3): 417–44.

Lye Tuck-Po, ed.
2001 The Orang Asli of Peninsular Malaysia: A Comprehensive and Annotated Bibliography. Kyoto, Japan: Center for Southeast Asian Studies, Kyoto University.

Malaysian Government
  1982 Malaysia Federal Constitution. Kuala Lumpur: Office of the Commissioner of Law.
  1994 Akta Orang Asli 1954 / Aboriginal Peoples Act 1954 (with all amendments up to June 1994). Kuala Lumpur: Malaysian Government.

Maloney, B.
  1998 A 22,000 Year Old Record of Past Environmental Change from Trang, South Thailand. Bulletin of the Asia-Pacific Prehistory Association 17: 54–5.

Maxwell, W.E.
  1880 The Aboriginal Tribes of Perak. Journal of the Straits Branch of the Royal Asiatic Society 4: 46–50.

Ministry of the Interior
  1961 Statement of Policy Regarding the Administration of the Aborigine People of the Federation of Malaya. Kuala Lumpur: Ministry of the Interior.

Mohd Tap bin Salleh
  1990 An Examination of Development Planning among the Rural Orang Asli of West Malaysia. Unpublished PhD dissertation, University of Bath.

Mudar, K. and D. Anderson
  2007 New Evidence for Southeast Asian Foraging Economies: Faunal Remains for the Early Levels of Lang Rongrien. Asian Perspectives 46(2): 298–334.

Nicholas, C.
  2000 The Orang Asli and the Contest for Resources: Indigenous Politics, Development and Identity in Peninsular Malaysia. Copenhagen: International Work Group for Indigenous Affairs and Subang Jaya, Malaysia: Center for Orang Asli Concerns.
  2006 The State of Orang Asli Education and its Root Problems. Section of consultancy report entitled "Orang Asli: Rights, Problems, Solutions" prepared for the Human Rights Commission of Malaysia (SUHAKAM).

Nicholas, C., Jenita Engi and Teh Yen Ping
  2010 The Orang Asli and the UNDRIP: From Rhetoric to Recognition. Subang Jaya, Malaysia: Center for Orang Asli Concerns.

Nik Hassan Shuhaimi bin Nik Abd. Rahman
  1991 Recent Research at Kuala Selinsing, Perak. Bulletin of the Indo-Pacific Prehistory Association 11: 141–52.

Nobuta, T.

2009 Living on the Periphery: Development and Islamization among the Orang Asli in Malaysia. Subang Jaya, Malaysia: Center for Orang Asli Concerns.

Noone, H.D.

1936 Report on the Settlements and Welfare of the Ple-Temiar Senoi of the Perak-Kelantan Watershed. Journal of the Federated Malay States Museums 19(1): 1–85.

Oppenheimer, S.

2011 MtDNA Variation and Southward Holocene Human Dispersals within Mainland Southeast Asia. *In* Dynamics of Human Diversity: The Case of Mainland Southeast Asia. N.J. Enfield, ed. Pp. 81–108. Canberra: Pacific Linguistics.

2012 A Single Southern Exit of Modern Humans from Africa: Before or After Toba? Quaternary International 258: 88–99.

Polunin, I.

1953 The Medical Natural History of Malayan Aborigines. Medical Journal of Malaya 8: 55–174.

Pookajorn, S.

1996 Human Activities and Environmental Changes During the Late Pleistocene to Middle Holocene in Southern Thailand and Southeast Asia. *In* Humans at the End of the Ice Age. L.G. Strauss et al., eds. Pp. 201–13. New York: Plenum.

Reid, A.

1983 Introduction: Slavery and Bondage in Southeast Asian History. *In* Slavery, Bondage and Dependency in Southeast Asia. A. Reid, ed. St Lucia, Queensland: University of Queensland Press.

Reid, L.A.

2013 Who Are the Philippine Negritos? Evidence from Language. Human Biology 85(1–3): 329–58.

Robarchek, C.

1979 Learning to Fear: A Case Study of Emotional Conditioning. American Ethnologist 6(3): 555–67.

1989 Hobbesian and Rousseauan Images of Man: Autonomy and Individualism in a Peaceful Society. *In* Societies at Peace. S. Howell and R. Willis, eds. Pp. 31–44. London: Routledge.

1990 Motivations and Material Causes: On the Explanations of Conflict and War. *In* The Anthropology of War. J. Haas, ed. Cambridge: Cambridge University Press.

Roseman, M.
1991   Healing Sounds from the Malaysian Rainforest: Temiar Music and Medicine. Berkeley, CA: University of California Press.

Schebesta, P.
1928   Among the Forest Dwarfs of Malaya. London: Hutchinson.
1952–   Die Negrito Asiens. 2 volumes. Vienna-Mödling: St Gabriel-
57   Verlag.

Schmidt, W.
1901   Die Sprachen der Sakei und Semang auf Malacca und ihr Verhältnis zu den Mon-Khmēr-Sprachen. Bijdragen Tot de Taal-, Land- en Volkenkunde 52: 399–583.

Skeat, W.W. and C.O. Blagden
1906   Pagan Races of the Malay Peninsula. 2 volumes. London: MacMillan.

Subramaniam, Y.
2012   Orang Asli Land Rights by UNDRIP Standards in Peninsular Malaysia: An Evaluation and Possible Reform. Unpublished PhD dissertation, University of New South Wales, Sydney.
2013   Affirmative Action and the Legal Recognition of Customary Land Rights in Peninsular Malaysia: The Orang Asli Experience. Australian Indigenous Law Review 17(1): 103–22.

Tan, M.
1992   Orang Asli School Notes. Pernloi Gah 4: 8–9.

Vons, H.
2000   Maps of Pleistocene Sea Levels in Southeast Asia. Journal of Biogeography 27: 1153–64.

White, J.C.
2011   Cultural Diversity in Mainland Southeast Asia: A View from Prehistory. *In* Dynamics of Human Diversity: The Case of Mainland Southeast Asia. N.J. Enfield, ed. Pp. 9–46. Canberra: Pacific Linguistics.

Zuraina Majid
1990   The Tampanian Problem Resolved: Archaeological Evidence of a Late Pleistocene Lithic Workshop. Modern Quaternary Research in Southeast Asia 11: 71–96.

Part One

STUDYING ORANG ASLI

chapter 1

Notes on Politics and Philosophy in Orang Asli Studies

Duncan Holaday

Let me begin with a brief explanation of the title. By politics, I am referring to the political realities of studying Orang Asli, from the micro-politics of village life to the sweep of Southeast Asian history including such events as wars and the shift from colonies to nation states. I do not refer specifically to Malaysian electoral politics, but this subject would be relevant. By philosophy, I am referring to the assumptions about human nature and society that guide the work of those conducting and using the studies. The initial question to be addressed is how the former, the political realities, affected the assumptions of scholars and others doing the work. I use the term "Notes" in my title because this subject involves some rather grand notions on which I offer only a few short notes.

To get a handle on the subject, I will take a relatively long view of Orang Asli studies going back a half-century to the early to mid-1960s to trace developments from the time when Robert Dentan and Geoffrey Benjamin entered the scene, until about 1980. The exact dates are not important. But, it seems to me that this period represents a turning point in Southeast Asian history and studies focused on this part of the world. It also appears that the Orang Asli people have come to occupy a pivotal position, geographically and historically, for the study of a problem that is now central to Asian Studies and to social studies in general, that being the relation of nation states and world civilizations to the health and survival of non-majority ethnic groups existing within and crossing their boundaries.

In 1965, somewhere between 200,000 and 500,000 people were killed in the upheaval in Indonesia, 500,000 American troops were sent to Vietnam, and Singapore was separated from Malaysia. There were various immediate causes and circumstances for these events. In Indonesia, for example, there was reaction to Sukarno's agrarian reform and shift to the left; in Vietnam, the Cold War and strategies inspired by the domino theory; and in Malaysia the expansion of Malay dominance in the absence of British rule. All these events, though, were embedded in a larger pattern, a long arc of change having to do with the withdrawal of European colonial powers from Southeast Asia.

This was the situation into which Robert Dentan and Geoffrey Benjamin carried their anthropological wares, their theories and projects: a war brewing to the north, a coup to the south, and tension in between.

Ironically, the mid-1960s was a relatively quiet time for the Orang Asli, a sort of golden age when they were not exactly ignored, but were given a wide berth to live their lives so long as they cooperated with British and Malaysian forces attempting to maintain control over the jungle. For the visitor from the West, there was, in my experience, a real sense of peace in the jungle once one journeyed beyond the end of the last paved road and out of range of the still rather primitive electronic world. One could not ignore the presence of the Malaysian government among the Orang Asli—Department of Orang Asli Affairs (Jabatan Hal Ehwal Orang Asli or JHEOA) posts near the estuaries of inhabited river valleys, the hospital for Orang Asli at Gombak and its scattered medical posts, and the Army. But the anchors of Orang Asli economy and social life—hunting, gathering and swidden agriculture in highland sanctuaries—were still in place. Arriving in an Orang Asli village was like entering another world.

So, what were the projects and conceptual frameworks that Dentan and Benjamin carried upstream in those early days? How did the situation change over the next decade and a half? How did their theories hold up and their projects fare? These are the main questions

I will address. I should mention that Dentan and Benjamin were not the only ones working with Orang Asli in the sixties; there were Iskandar Carey, Ivan Polunin, Dee Baer and Gérard Diffloth, to mention a few. But, I will focus here on Dentan and Benjamin for their consistently excellent and widely influential research, publication, and teaching in the field. I will close with a brief discussion of their impact on my own, small contribution to Orang Asli studies.

Dentan's project was initially to examine food taboos. His research had to do with finding out what leads people who have access to a range of food sources to choose some and exclude others from their diets (Dentan 1965). The Dentans, Robert and his then-wife Ruth, were aware of the political situation in Indonesia when they went to the field in 1962. In fact, Indonesia was to be the site of their fieldwork until tensions with the US got in the way. But, this larger political context was not part of their plan of study. It was by a chance meeting with Rodney Needham, a prominent scholar at Oxford University who had studied the nomadic Penan people of Borneo, that they changed their direction toward the more receptive hinterland of Peninsular Malaysia. There, they put on Semai clothing, learned to speak Semai, ate Semai food, and to the extent they were able, lived as highland Senoi (Dentan 2002: 109).

Dentan's first book, *The Semai*, published in 1968, is written in the tradition of early to mid-20th century ethnography; like Evans-Pritchard's *The Nuer* (1940), it is a textbook example of what an ethnography should look like before the "re-thinkings" of the 1970s and later (Hymes 1972). It covers a range of topics from environment, economy, and kinship, to cultural categories that define the unique qualities of the people under study. His real passion, though, which shines through the prose, is his love of the natural world (Dentan 1967a, 1967b; Dentan and Ong 1995). His description of the forest and its animals, the spitting cobra and 35-foot long python, are evocative. "One spider," he writes, "which has a leg spread like a soup plate, eats birds and mice." And, the *agas-agas* flies, he tells us, "swarm so densely... writing or typing is almost impossible" (Dentan 1968: 26). Note the word "almost" here because writing is clearly another of his passions. In terms of his observations on human nature, none is more vivid and enduring than his photograph entitled "East Semai Man Felling a Tree" which, I believe, can be compared with Lewis Hine's 1930s images of workers perched on the steel structures of the Empire State Building. Both show humans working undaunted at huge tasks—building a city and living in the Malaysian jungle.

During his initial fieldwork, Dentan was operating on all cylinders as a naturalist. Among his funding sources and institutional bases were the museums of natural history in New York and Chicago. He tells us, in his recent book, *Overwhelming Terror* (2008) that his political education came after returning from the field. Friends encouraged him while he was writing *The Semai* to pursue the theme of "nonviolence",

Plate 1.1 East Semai man felling a tree, 1962

(Photo credit: Robert K. Dentan)

which was then elevated to the subtitle—"*A Nonviolent People of Malaya*" (2008: 233). Of course, this became the dominant talking point about his book during the Vietnam War and even to this day. But, I would suggest that other observations resulting from his naturalist tendency might prove to be even more enduring. I am thinking, in particular, of what might be referred to as "adaptive mechanisms" such as the chameleon-like behaviour that Senoi exhibit in the presence of outsiders. Examples include the strategy for dealing with non-Semai

Plate 1.2 Workers building the Empire State Building in the 1930s

(Photo credit: Lewis Hine)

by which "... down-river groups cooperate (or appear to cooperate) with outsiders partly to cover for the up-river groups ... while up-river groups maintain a pose of impenetrable stupidity" (1968: 80–1). Even Dentan's attempt to understand the source of nonviolent behaviour among the Semai is cast in these terms, as a long-term adaptation to slave raids and other acts of aggression from outside. We see in these examples a parallel to what James Scott later referred to as "weapons of the weak" in his analysis of rural Malays, only, in this case, with a distinctly Senoi character (Scott 1987).

Let me turn now to Benjamin's arrival in Malaysia. What was in his box of tools, and what was his project? Benjamin's thesis topic was to be Temiar religion, a project he has continued to pursue through the recent publication of his book on the subject (Benjamin 2014). But, like Dentan, his research points to another passion. His first major paper, "Temiar Personal Names", was published in 1968, the same year as Dentan's book. It can be said that while Dentan's bias was toward nature, Benjamin's was toward language (Benjamin 1976, 1993, 2001, 2012). His tools consisted of a finely tuned set of linguistic categories, a range of perspectives on historical and social linguistics, and skills required for close analysis of grammar and language use. Like Dentan, his early work was given some direction by Rodney Needham; it was at Needham's suggestion that Benjamin undertook his detailed study of naming. What makes this work stand apart from Dentan's, however, was Benjamin's willingness from the start, to confront, head on, knotty theoretical issues in anthropology that were current in the 1960s. In fact, his article on personal names takes us directly into a tempest that had been brewing for some time at the intersection of British, French and American schools of anthropology, specifically between Rodney Needham and Levi-Strauss (Needham 1960) on one hand, and on the other, Homans and Schneider at Harvard and the University of Chicago (Homans and Schneider 1955).

This controversy, referred to by Benjamin as the "structure vs. sentiment debate" (Benjamin 1970) devolved upon the question of whether there is a correlation between the practice of prescriptive matrilateral cross-cousin marriage (where a man is required to marry someone who fits the category of his mother's brother's daughter) and a high level of social solidarity in societies where it is practised. The debate was sometimes characterized in more general terms as a difference in focus—the Americans on culture and the British on society. Oxford Professor Evans-Pritchard's view may be summarized as follows: Americans are interested in collecting cultural artifacts, while British social anthropologists are interested in culture insofar as it helps them understand the underlying principles by which societies operate (Evans-Pritchard 1962).

The philosophical underpinnings of the British position can be found in Wittgenstein's argument that common language obscures the underlying logic of the world; or rather, common language creates logical muddles because things that are fundamentally different are called by the same name. The philosopher's task, according to Wittgenstein, is to clear up these muddles (Wittgenstein 1958). The parallel assumption in social anthropology was that in order to understand the principles by which societies function, the social anthropologist must endeavour to look through and behind the flawed systems natives use to operate within their societies. For example, in the case of language, the aim is to uncover grammar behind speech; and for the social anthropologist to discover social logic beneath "muddled" systems of naming, kinship, and the like.

In his article on naming, Benjamin strives for synthesis. He concludes that the crucial problem of social anthropology is "the relation *between* [my emphasis] culture and society" (Benjamin 1968: 132). He expresses exasperation (with a touch of humour) at the complexities of the Temiar naming system, in which "names were changed almost daily—with capricious disregard for the ethnographer's difficulties" (Benjamin 1968: 99). Then, in his detailed analysis, he reveals that the Temiar use different systems when talking to outsiders, non-Temiars, and when talking among themselves. And, when talking among themselves, they use a rather complicated system or set of systems that includes personal names, referential names based on relations to their siblings and parents, and necronyms (death-names). Benjamin addresses the theoretical question raised by Needham and Levi-Strauss specifically in relation to the use of necronyms. He writes that "... death-names and social solidarity are different kinds of phenomena, one a fragment of culture, the other a feature of social interaction. It follows that the relation between them is not that of a causal-functional nexus; it is at best indirect, mediated by some sort of transducer mechanism." "The transducer," he suggests "is the individual member of society" (1968: 130).[1]

One thing that endured from this early work of Benjamin's, aside from the extensive and intensive description provoked by the debate of the day, is this notion of "transducer mechanism". Much has been gained, I believe, by applying this concept to the study, not only of solidarity within social groups, but the negotiation of boundaries between groups. In his recent work "On Being Tribal in the Malay World", for example, Benjamin stresses that being tribal "… is not the passive condition of a whole group of individuals, but the active agency of individuals" (Benjamin and Chou 2002). This approach aligns well with Dentan's observations on what I have referred to as adaptive mechanisms.

In 1978, in an unpublished but germinal paper presented at the Second International Conference on Austroasiatic Linguistics in Mysore, Benjamin said that he "turns everything on its head". The title of this paper, "The Anthropology of Grammar: Self and Other in Temiar", is listed among the references of a later-published work as being scheduled "to appear", but was apparently withdrawn (Benjamin 1993). In "The Anthropology of Grammar", Benjamin says that he assumes among other things that "languages are not bounded neutral structures, but leaky and power-dominated institutions", and that "grammar is not a neutral code of some kind, but an emergent from people's struggles to express their meanings". (Parts of this paper, including these particular points, appear in subsequent publications [Benjamin 1993, 2005, 2012].)

This was indeed a breath of fresh air when compared to the earlier discourse on culture and society. At this point, common language is no longer treated as the problem, but as a solution. The apparent contradictions and overlapping meanings in Temiar language are seen, not as muddles, but as mechanisms for emergent forms. Benjamin demonstrates how homophones, onomatopoeia and other tropes that occupy a central role in non-written languages, empower the language and its presumed flaws with the potential to create not only unique utterances, but unique ways of looking at and interpreting those utterances. His analysis uncovers in Temiar grammar precisely the kind of flexibility that enables individuals to function as transducers for social change and adaptation—namely, the potential for poetics and symbolic condensation that are, in turn, the basic building blocks of intelligence and imagination.

At about this time, in the early 1980s, things began to change dramatically for the Orang Asli. As the threat from Communist terrorists based in the jungle declined, the Orang Asli became a focus of government attention, which brought them unprecedented turmoil. They were subjected to resettlement and pressures toward acculturation, and their sanctuaries were subjected to appropriation and extensive deforestation. These developments are documented in the book by Dentan, Endicott, Gomes and Hooker, *Malaysia and the Original People: A Case Study on the Impact of Development on Indigenous People* (1997), which describes in detail how the economic and social anchors of the Orang Asli were pulled up and removed. It concludes that government policies "… appear to be transforming Orang Asli into a demoralized rural lumpenproletariat…." (1997: 159).

Early ethnographic work by Dentan and Benjamin revealing adaptive mechanisms now becomes especially relevant. The critical question becomes: How will Orang Asli adapt to these new challenges? Both Dentan and Benjamin addressed this question. The focus of Benjamin's work shifted from the theoretical debate between Oxford and Chicago to problems arising between Kelantan and Kuala Lumpur, or more generally to the problem of "Being Tribal in the Malay World" (Benjamin and Chao 2010). A corresponding change can be seen in what these anthropologists chose to look at and describe. In the earlier project of British social anthropology, their aim was to gather examples from marginal societies as a kind of laboratory to prove or disprove general theories. The new focus is on the margin itself. In Dentan's work, this change is expressed as a transition from his role as objective participant observer examining the position of humans in the natural world toward that of an active, non-indigenous participant attempting to alter some potentially destructive processes among humans. This new voice is evident in his work *Overwhelming Terror: Love Fear, Peace, and Violence Among Semai of Malaysia* (Dentan 2008).

My work with Orang Asli began in 1969 with a ten-month stay in Malaysia as a graduate student at the University of Malaya. I spent the first six months learning the Malay language with Professor Rama Subaya and studying Orang Asli language at the Gombak Hospital under the direction of Drs. Iskandar Carey and Gérard Diffloth. Then, over a period of about three months, I visited and studied in Jah Hut villages in Pahang. In 1985 and 1998, I returned briefly to complete and publish some of the earlier work.

From the beginning, my studies were in applied linguistics and action-oriented anthropology—more political than descriptive in nature. My work cannot be compared with Dentan's and Benjamin's in terms of breadth and depth of scholarship, but it offers examples of two themes that have emerged and benefited from their contributions as engaged scholars—namely, the role of language in cultural survival and the problem of adaptation for marginalized minorities to a radically changed environment.

Gérard Diffloth, who is a colleague of Benjamin and has done extensive work on Orang Asli language, was one of the advisors for my undergraduate honours thesis (Diffloth 1979). My project, conducted under his supervision at the Peter Dana Point Reservation in Maine, was the production of a primer for writing a Native American language—Passamaquoddy (Holaday 1968). This was a small part of a native literacy project being carried out by teams from Wesleyan and Harvard Universities. The motivation for this project, its passion in fact, was inspired by the political situation of Native Americans in the 1960s and their struggles for civil rights, land rights and cultural survival. My role was to introduce a systematic orthography in a form that could be used in reservation schools. There was no need for me to do extensive ethnography or in-depth study of the language. The fate of such projects was left to the native speakers. The post-colonial theory of the day predicted that such interventions would combat the self-deprecatory malaise that plagued colonial subjects (Fanon 1961). In the case of Passamaquoddy and Northeastern Algonquian, there is an excellent review of native literacy efforts and their effects written by a member of the neighbouring Maliseet tribe (Perley 2009).

I carried this research model, together with some rudimentary tools in phonetics and phonemics, to Malaysia in 1969 where I transcribed stories dictated by Batin Long bin Hok (Holaday et al. 1985 and 2003). Batin Long was recognized among the Jah Hut as a *puyang mna'*—a great shaman. It was his idea to record these stories. Telling stories came naturally to him as part of the work of teaching young shamans, a process that he referred to as "Jah Hut University". I had no specific agenda of my own in terms of linguistic or anthropological theory, aside from the notion that there was value in promoting native literacy. Later, however, reading Benjamin's "Anthropology of Grammar" together with Sol Worth's "From Visual Anthropology to the Anthropology of Visual Communication" (1981) gave sharper focus to my studies and renewed motivation for work in native literacy. I came to understand that it is not sufficient simply to eradicate self-deprecation, but necessary also to provide a context for renewed self-definition, that is, to find a venue for some form of publication. The prologue to the 2003 edition of the Jah Hut stories, titled "Self-Presentation and Visual Anthropology", summarizes my understanding of the process by which native speakers apply new media to their struggles for cultural and economic survival (Holaday et al. 2003). The film I made with Batin Long, his brother Dolah and his son On, "Metos Jah Hut", extends this model to visual communication (Holaday 1986).

On the second theme of adaptation to challenges and changes in the social and physical environment, Dentan's description of the "Temiar solution" to the predicament of being caught between Communist guerrillas and government security forces during the Emergency in the 1950s is most instructive (Dentan 1968: 80–1, 1997: 65). This "solution" involved a strategy of cooperation between upstream and downstream villages to placate both sides of the conflict and thereby secure the survival of the Temiar. The trope that animates this strategy— "upsteam/downstream"—is pervasive in Orang Asli discourse and has had a significant role in their survival in the past and will, no doubt, continue to do so in the future.

In 1970, while recording and transcribing the Jah Hut stories, I was fascinated by the fact that traveling up the Krau River from one village to the next was like a journey in time or to another world. Whereas downstream near Kuala Krau people wore sarongs and planted rubber trees, upstream they wore loincloths and hunted with blowpipes. I was aware that this might have had to do with the presence of trade and trade routes. Indeed, the work by Phillip Curtin on *Cross-Cultural Trade in World History* (1984) looks specifically at the area where trade routes crossed the Malay Peninsula within a few miles of Jah Hut settlements. But the actual mechanisms at work in the interior where the river systems meet remained obscure because of the lack of records and details of transactions. Only by living at and observing activity at these margins, as Dentan and Benjamin have done, have we begun to understand the origins and consequences of cross-cultural interaction for Orang Asli. Recent work by Gomes, *Looking for Money—Capitalism and Modernity in an Orang Asli Village* (1986), which was given direction by both Benjamin's and Dentan's work, combines historical and ethnographic methods to describe longstanding economic interactions between Orang Asli and the outsiders.

For the past 14 years, I have been a maple farmer and distiller of rum, and, in this capacity, consider myself to be a member of the "tribe" of small farmers in Vermont. It is from this point of view that I believe I might now suggest a further contribution to Orang Asli studies. When I started this venture, I declared that, this time, I would be "the native in the hills" and the subject of my studies, and, I must say, the learning curve has been steep. I am not claiming that the plight of Vermont's farmers is comparable to that of Orang Asli today. But the threat of loss, what Thoreau referred to "silent desperation", can be universal in its impact.

In Vermont, a movement has been under way for some time to counter and adapt to economic threats to small farming by encouraging local production of value-added products—cheese, bread, spirits—for sale at farmers' markets and beyond. This movement of social entrepreneurship has given new life to agriculture and, for that matter, to the cultural landscape in Vermont. My focus has been on rum, and as part of this project, I have been working with a University of Vermont professor, Dan Baker, and one of his students, Daniel Keeney (my young business partner), to source raw cane directly from smallholders in Honduras. Their cane made into rum and sold at Vermont markets would yield significantly higher margins through a direct trade arrangement than through existing commodity markets in Honduras.

I would suggest and encourage a similar strategy with Orang Asli. For example, *ubi kayu* (the source of tapioca), which grows easily in areas where jungle has been cleared, can be prepared and shipped directly to a distiller for processing into high-value products. I realize that such experiments are fraught with difficulties, and perhaps this one is unrealistic because of the particular circumstances of Orang Asli in Malaysia. In my experience, though, such experiments can work. I am convinced that it is through efforts of this kind that the descent into poverty described by Dentan et al. (1997) might eventually be turned around.

While the early work of Dentan and Benjamin has provided a solid foundation for further research on Orang Asli and comparative studies in relevant areas of anthropology and linguistics, it has also shown the way for applied efforts to improve conditions for the Orang Asli people.

NOTE

1.   The word "transducer" is defined by the *Britannica World Language Dictionary* as "Any device by means of which the energy of one power system may be transmitted to another system, whether of the same or a different type." In the context of social systems, the implication here is that the "individual member of society" acts as a transducer within and across social systems.

REFERENCES

Benjamin, G.

1968   Temiar Personal Names. Bijdragen Tot de Taal-, Land-, en Volkenkunde 124: 99–134.

1970   Review of Dentan, R. The Semai: A Nonviolent People of Malaya. American Anthropologist 72(3): 658–60.

1976   An Outline of Temiar Grammar. *In* Austroasiatic Studies, Part 1. P.N. Jenner, C. Thompson, and S. Starosta, eds. Pp. 129–87. Honolulu: University Press of Hawaii.

1993   Grammar and Polity: Cultural and Political Background to Standard Malay. *In* The Role of Theory in Language Description, W.A. Foley, ed. Pp. 341–92. Berlin: Mounton Gruyter.

2001   Orang Asli Languages: From Heritage to Death? *In* Razha Rashid and Wazir Jahan Karim, eds. Pp. 101–22. Penang: Malaysian Academy of Social Sciences.

2002   On Being Tribal in the Malay World. *In* Tribal Communities in the Malay World. G. Benjamin and C. Chou, eds. Pp. 7–76. Leiden: International Institute for Asian Studies (IIAS) and Singapore: Institute of Southeast Asian Studies (ISEAS).

2005   Consciousness and Polity in Southeast Asia: The Long View. *In* Local and Global: Social Transformation in Southeast Asia. Essays in Honor of Syed Hussein Alatas. Riaz Hassan, ed. Pp. 261–89. Leiden and Boston: Brill.

2012   Aesthetic Elements in Temiar Grammar. *In* The Aesthetic of Grammar: Sound and Meaning in the Languages of Mainland Southeast Asia. J. Williams, ed. Cambridge: Cambridge University Press.

Benjamin, G. and C. Chou

2010   Tribal Communities in the Malay World. Leiden: International Institute for Asian Studies (IIAS) and Singapore: Institute of Southeast Asian Studies (ISEAS).

Curtin, P.

1984   Cross-Cultural Trade in World History. Cambridge: Cambridge University Press.

Dentan, R.K.

1965   Some Senoi Semai Dietary Restrictions. Unpublished doctoral dissertation. New Haven: Yale University.

1967a   The Mammalian Taxonomy of the Sen'oi Semai. Malayan Nature Journal 20: 100–6.

1967b   Notes on Semai Ethnoentomology. Malayan Nature Journal 21: 17–28.

1968   The Semai: A Nonviolent People of Malaya. New York: Holt, Rinehart and Winston.

2002   The Semai: A Nonviolent People of Malaya—Field Work Edition. Belmont, CA: Wadsworth Group.

2008   Overwhelming Terror: Love, Fear, Peace, and Violence among Semai of Malaysia. Lanham, MD: Rowman & Littlefield.

Dentan, R.K., K. Endicott, A. Gomes and M.B. Hooker

1997   Malaysia and the "Original People": A Case Study of the Impact of Development on Indigenous Peoples. Boston: Allyn and Bacon.

Dentan, R.K. and Ong Hean Chooi
  1995   Stewards of the Green and Beautiful World: A Preliminary Report
         on Semai Arboriculture and Its Policy Implications. *In* Dimensions
         of Traditions and Development in Malaysia. Rokiah Talib and Tan
         Chee Beng, eds. Pp. 53–124. Petaling Jaya: Pelanduk.
Diffloth, G.
  1979   Aslian Languages and Southeast Asian Prehistory. Federation
         Museums Journal 24: 3–16.
Evans-Pritchard, E.E.
  1940   The Nuer. Oxford: Oxford University Press.
  1962   Social Anthropology and Other Essays. New York: The Free
         Press.
Fanon, F.
  1963   The Wretched of the Earth. New York: Grove Press.
Gomes, A.
  1986   Looking-for-Money: Simple Commodity Production in the
         Economy of the Tapah Semai of Malaysia. Unpublished PhD
         dissertation, The Australian National University.
Holaday, D.
  1968   Skijinuwi Agizuwe: A Passamaquoddy Primer. Unpublished BA
         thesis, Wesleyan University.
  1984   Making Media Fit: Short-term Adjustment to a New Communication
         Technology in a West Javanese Village. Unpublished doctoral
         dissertation, University of Pennsylvania.
  1986   Metos Jah Hut. 16mm film. Washington: The Human Studies Film
         Archive, Smithsonian Institution.
Holaday, D., Chin Woon Ping and Teoh Boon Seong
  1985   Tales of a Shaman: Jah Hut Myths as told by Batin Long bin
         Hok. Singapore: Times Books International.
  2003   Bes Hyang Dney and Other Jah Hut Stories. Subang Jaya,
         Malaysia: Center for Orang Asli Concerns (COAC).
Homans, G.C. and D. Schneider
  1955   Marriage, Authority, and Final Causes. New York: The Free Press.
Hymes, D.
  1972   Reinventing Anthropology. New York: Pantheon.
Needham, R.
  1962   Structure and Sentiment: A Test Case in Social Anthropology.
         Chicago: University of Chicago Press.

Perley, B.
  2009 Contingencies of Emergence: Planning Maliseet Language Ideologies. *In* Native American Language Ideologies: Beliefs, Practices, and Struggles in Indian Country. P. Kroskrity and M. Field, eds. Tucson: University of Arizona Press.

Scott, J.
  1987 Weapons of the Weak: Everyday Forms of Peasant Resistance. New Haven: Yale University Press.

Wittgenstein, L.
  1958 The Blue and Brown Books. New York: Harper & Row.

Worth, S.
  1981 Studying Visual Communication. Philadelphia: University of Pennsylvania Press.

chapter **2**

Continuity through Change: Three Decades of Engaging with Chewong: Some Issues Raised by Multitemporal Fieldwork

Signe Howell

MULTITEMPORAL FIELDWORK

Multitemporal fieldwork—the practice of returning to the same group of people on many occasions over a long period of time—has received relatively little anthropological attention, but in a recent publication (Howell and Talle 2012) we show how this practice can lead to an enhanced understanding of social and cultural values and practices. At the same time, we ask to what extent does this series of "ethnographic presents"—these diverse moments of ethnographic eye-witnessing and participant-observation—give us a privileged position for understanding how people react to, and how social life is effected by, new occurrences that result from interaction with the world beyond their own frontiers? And, does our long-term engagement result in a truer picture of the society? Multitemporal fieldwork raises analytical, methodological and epistemological questions that are worth considering. The practice is,

I suggest, particularly pertinent with regard to the understanding of vulnerable minority populations, such as the Orang Asli, whose ways of life have been seriously challenged during the last 30-odd years by initiatives originating from a number of outsiders with different agendas. In this chapter I will consider some advantages, as well as some quandaries, of multitemporal fieldwork and then present a description of Chewong society as it was during my first fieldwork and how my original understanding has both been confirmed and challenged by events on a number of subsequent visits.

As a result of logging, the creation of rubber and oil-palm plantations and other externally initiated economic activities, an increasing intrusion of bureaucratic demands by the state, the arrival of tourists and Christian and Muslim proselytizing, a number of sociocultural arenas have been affected in most Orang Asli communities. A new dependence upon a monetized economy has led to changes in economic activities which in turn show signs of affecting local political systems, including gender and intergenerational relations. All this has seriously confronted people's understanding of their own identity as individuals and as a social group. While they have been drawn into the larger society, they are also being alienated from it. How they react to and handle these challenges from what is increasingly becoming a global world becomes apparent as a result of repeat visits.

The early anthropologists who worked in Orang Asli societies have laid the foundation for our knowledge about the kind of life led at the time before they were pulled into the wider Malaysian society. Bob Dentan's and Geoffrey Benjamin's studies of the Semai and Temiar respectively are central to those of us who came a little later to these and other Orang Asli groups. Their work constituted an archive for us, and they presented us with a number of gate-keeping concepts (Appadurai 1986) that could not be ignored. Their publications on religion, kinship and the Orang Asli's egalitarian and peaceful way of life are seminal (Benjamin 1967, 1968a, 1968b, 2002, 2005, 2011; Dentan 1968, 1978, 1994, 2006, 2011). Both have continued their research in Malaysia over time and have observed both continuities and changes in the communities they know so well. While this has informed their recent writings, to my knowledge, neither of them has explicitly debated the methodological or epistemological consequences of repeat visits.

In multitemporal fieldwork a historical awareness of one's intellectual climate is necessary, as is reflexivity regarding changes in one's disciplinary engagement. I will return to this towards the end. Meanwhile, Clifford's characterization of Mauss' attitude to ethnographic fieldwork is of relevance. He says, "[Mauss] presented a generation of ethnographers with an astonishing repertoire of objects for study that put the world together: ethnography was a dipping of different nets in the teaming ocean, each time catching its own sort of fish" (1983: 130). From such a perspective, I suggest, the task of anthropologists is to contextualize the catches in relation to each other, both synchronically and diachronically. This is achieved by many return visits and by having periods of time in between to reflect upon one's most recent catch and ponder its significance in relation to one's existing knowledge—ethnographic, anthropological, personal. It enables one, inter alia, to investigate one particular significant practice and observe how it changes or continues over time, the depth and complexity of "total social facts" and the significance of key or dominant symbols. Hence my enthusiasm for multitemporal fieldwork. An added consideration is that the ocean is never identical each time one throws a net into it—and yet it is the same ocean.

In what follows I shall be considering social change and social continuity in one Orang Asli group, the Chewong. Chewong reactions to the invasion of their territory and how they have chosen to handle this is the main focus of my present-day research. Whatever interpretations I come up with about their current situation are informed by my continuing involvement with them over 35 years. A question I occasionally ask myself is how I would understand their present-day situation had I started my fieldwork with them as the first anthropologist at the time of my last visit. And, on what basis can I claim that because I have engaged sporadically with them over time this enables me to provide a more accurate analysis of their present situation than were I to arrive today? I cannot, of course, provide any definite answers to these questions, but they will be at the back of my mind as I discuss their current situation.

MY FIELDWORKS

My first fieldwork with Chewong, one of the smallest Orang Asli groups, began in the autumn of 1977 when I spent 18 months with them as part of my doctoral research. At that time they lived deep inside the rainforest of Pahang in central Peninsular Malaysia. Since then I have returned many times in order to keep in touch with the people and to observe how they were coping with the various external agents who slowly encroached upon their territory and whose activities were pulling them into the larger world around them. As I kept returning it became clear to me that I had acquired a historical perspective on their socio-cultural life and that this ought to be theorized, not least because my involvement with Chewong happens to have overlapped with a period of change which probably is the most dramatic they are likely to experience. Much literature on vulnerable populations, such as hunter-gatherers, tends to present a scenario of inevitable movement towards poverty, acculturation and disempowerment, and an assumption that individuals—given a chance—will seek to maximize personal benefit. But, Chewong actions demonstrate the complexity in people's understandings, motivations and choices, and that little can be predicted in the way they handle new situations (Howell 2002; Howell and Lillegraven 2013).

THEORETICAL CONSIDERATIONS

At the time of my first fieldwork, Chewong conformed, broadly speaking, to Sahlins' characterization of the "original affluent society" as having material plenty (according to their definition of their needs) and needing low physical exertion in order to satisfy most needs (1974). They also conformed—broadly speaking—to Woodburn's "immediate return society", which he characterized by a number of features that include an assertive egalitarian, non-competitive, ethos and economies that discourage saving and accumulation. Equality is achieved through direct and individual access to commonly held resources, and these values and practices discourage the accumulation of wealth and property and encourage sharing. This he contrasts to "delayed return societies" (Woodburn 1982). I found Woodburn's distinction of interest when starting to conceptualize change. Anthropologists need concepts with which to relate their ethnographic material, pegs on which to hang their interpretations. While his writings are of interest, they leave out a number of pertinent issues. In particular—and in contradistinction to Dentan and Benjamin—I miss a consideration of cosmology and ontology.

CHEWONG, 1977–2010

During my first fieldwork, Chewong lived in small impermanent scattered swiddens several days walk inside the forest. Chewong self-perception was—and still is at least amongst the middle to older generation—that of hunters and gatherers. Chewong ontological understanding, like those of most other Orang Asli groups, corresponds to that usually thought of as animism (Howell 1984, 1996, 2012b, forthcoming). As I have described in detail elsewhere, they see their forest environment as made up of many non-human, but conscious, beings with whom they interact on a daily basis by following a number of prescriptions and proscriptions that are predicated upon their cosmological understanding. I call these "cosmo-rules". The failure to observe them leads to illness or mishap of various kinds caused by some non-human personage or other. Behaviour is thus predicated upon knowledge that does not distinguish the social from the cosmological and that extends the boundary of their social world to include these animated beings. Equality, be this symbolic or social, has been—and continues to be—a positive value that permeates both cosmic and social structures. Indeed, it may be characterized as a dominant value and, as such, may be expected to be highly resistant to change (Howell 2010, 2012a). This manifests itself in an egalitarian social organization and in peaceful interaction; competition, anger and violence are foreign behaviour (Howell 1989, 2011). The forest and everything in it belongs to everyone, but, with the exception of produce collected for sale, all forest produce must be brought to the settlement and shared equally amongst those present. In particular, the treatment, cooking and eating of all food is highly circumscribed. The injunction never to eat alone (the *punén* cosmo-rule), but to share everything, discourages individual consumption

Plate 2.1 Social life in a typical settlement, 1978

(Photo credit: Signe Howell)

Plate 2.2 The fascination of what money can buy, 2010

(Photo credit: Signe Howell)

and accumulation. These values, whose meaning is constituted in their understanding of personhood and their relationship with the environment, manifest themselves further in an ideology and practice of immediate consumption of all food brought to the settlement. As they have entered the monetization of social life, this practice, I argue, is today extended into a behaviour of "immediate spending" of earned cash, and this acts as a brake on individual accumulation of wealth (Howell and Lillegraven 2013).

INVOLVEMENT IN THE MARKET ECONOMY

In 1977 only a handful of adult men could speak Malay, and people had minimal contact with the outside world. Today (2010), the vast majority have mastered the national language, and most are in regular contact with the larger Malaysian society. Chewong areas have been opened up to the outside world through logging, roads and the establishment of an Elephant Sanctuary which is a tourist attraction, all of which have led to increased interaction between the Chewong and outsiders. They are under heavy pressure from the state to "modernize" and assimilate into Malay society by adopting a standard rural Malay lifestyle. This entails settling in permanent villages, becoming cash-crop farmers, converting to Islam, and submitting to state institutions and control. Most Chewong are highly ambivalent about the changes, but many acquiesce, and changes in life-style are detectable. The reason for this seems to be a mixture of force, persuasion, feelings of powerlessness, and, not least, a fascination with "modern" consumer goods.

Despite their isolation, Chewong have been involved in trade, barter and occasional employment relationships with neighbouring Malays and Chinese for generations, but during the past three decades their reliance on a cash economy has increased rapidly, intensifying the relationship. Chewong happened to live partly inside the Krau Game Reserve, which was established by the British in 1926. Its boundaries are still respected today, but logging has taken place right up to them. As part of the attempt to "modernize" Chewong, by the end of the 20th century, government officials in the Department of Orang Asli Affairs (JHEOA; now called the Department of Orang Asli Development or

JAKOA) created a village on the fringe of the forest. Initially, a few wooden houses were built and communal latrines and piped water to stand-pipes provided; since then the village has expanded in size and number of houses. Today the houses are built of brick, each with its own water and electricity, and are placed in a long line facing the new road, no longer facing each other. Fruit and rubber gardens were established by the JHEOA in order to promote a cash economy. Several Chewong responded to the officials' requests and "gifts"—as much out of timidity as out of any actual desire to grow cash crops. But the orchards were soon abandoned and became overgrown. People preferred to harvest non-timber forest products for sale rather than become farmers and cultivate cash crops. By the mid-nineties, several families seemed to have settled in the gateway village. I predicted that more would do so and that the forest way life soon would be a thing of the past. On my return some years later I found to my surprise that the village was virtually abandoned (Howell 2002). People had moved back into the forest. I argued that by this removal from the village, "the Chewong have performed, and continue to perform, a cultural choice to abandon the experiment of settling down on the fringes of the jungle...." (2002: 262). I suggested that it was largely due to the women's dissatisfaction with their new way of life in the settled village. Despite their initial delight with shop-bought food and luxury goods, they began to dislike their enforced passivity. Now they were happily working in the forest and swiddens in the way they had done before. However, by 2008 and 2010 many women seemed happy to just sit around in the village, eating starchy food and, rather disturbingly, showing the first signs of obesity. During the period I have observed a constant flux in people's residence and work practice between a forest immediate return way of life and a more settled, cash-earning way of life.

Nevertheless, the extended gateway village is today larger than ever with more than one hundred inhabitants, many of whom appear to have settled more or less permanently and who engage in cultivating the same fields regularly. Cultivation is primarily done in order to sell, not consume, the produce. Several families have chosen to remain within the forest and can only be seen on the rare occasion when someone comes to sell forest produce. My several field visits from the late nineties until today have enabled me to perceive the fluidity of Chewong practices: that they did not make an either/or choice of settling in the village or remaining inside the forest. By and large, though, there is a clear pattern of increased economic interaction with Malays and Chinese, due partly to the villagers' strong and unrelenting desire for shop-bought food and modern commodities and partly to commands from the authorities.

Chewong's relationship with Malays and Chinese is marked by fear and timidity fuelled by centuries of experienced exploitation, which has led to feelings of profound distrust towards outsiders in general and Malays in particular. There is no shortage of events that confirm

Plate 2.3 A couple sets off for a hunting trip, 1978

(Photo credit: Signe Howell)

Plate 2.4 Hunter on motorbike returns with monkey, 2007

(Photo credit: Anja Lillegraven)

Chewong distrust and fear of outsiders. Slave raiding of aboriginal people continued up to the end of the 19th century (Endicott 1983). More recently, Malays and Chinese hire people to work, but fail to pay or pay much less than agreed. Chinese and Malays purchase jungle or agricultural produce, but pay well below the market price. The quality of public services offered is vastly inferior to that offered by Malays and Chinese in the neighbourhood. The Chewong are fully aware of this and regard their relationship with outsiders as profoundly unfair and exploitative. However, they rarely complain, but prefer the age-old Orang Asli practice of withdrawing if the situation is perceived as intolerable (Dentan 1968).

With increased monetization, Chewong are becoming involved in sustained work practices, systematically harvesting the forest and growing cash crops. These practices are undertaken at the expense of hunting, gathering and shifting cultivation, thus reducing the reliance on, and the more or less egalitarian exploitation by all, of the rainforest. Previously, the forest provided most of what was needed, and there was an endless supply of food for those who went in search of it. Today, Chewong, both inside and outside the forest, spend increasingly more time on cash generating activities. They tend to look for money to satisfy immediate needs. When they are out of rice or want a new T-shirt, they search for saleable forest products to obtain money to make the purchase. Any money left over is spent on whatever takes their fancy in the shop—immediate consumption. They do not save money unless they have a specific purchase in mind, such as the deposit or instalment payment on a motor-bike—demonstrating that they are not ignorant of planning, but that to save for a rainy day is far from their thoughts.

And yet, there are signs that this is changing, not only in the gateway village, but also inside the forest. Cultivation of rubber is becoming popular in the village and inside the forest as well. Small rubber fields are evidence of a slow but steady move towards a more settled way of life. Planting rubber is an investment in the future that requires the owners to stay in proximity to their fields in order to protect seedlings and later tap the rubber. Rubber plantations also require large areas of land for long periods of time, as opposed to the traditional shifting cultivation, a fact that opens the way for the introduction of the notion of private ownership of land. Having said that, the Chewong have no codified legal right to any land upon which they live or cultivate. They have been told that they may exploit the Game Reserve for produce for own consumption and may clear small swiddens, but to my knowledge, no documents exist that confirm these rights. So far, their clearings, whether inside or outside the Game Reserve, have not been challenged by the authorities.

EMERGING INEQUALITIES

As mentioned, the well-established practice of living from hand to mouth is today influencing the way most Chewong *spend* their money.

The new village shop and the nearby small town provide many opportunities to spend money on snacks, soft drinks, cigarettes, a new T-shirt or sarong. However, a combination of a deeply held egalitarian ideology and the ethos of immediate consumption of all surplus, has meant that no Chewong individual sees the virtue in long-term planning in order to maximize profit or accumulate wealth.

Thus, despite the opportunities for economic advancement under these changing circumstances, it is well-nigh impossible to enhance one's economic position above that of others. This may be attributed to their ontology, their root assumptions about the nature of things and their relationship within the total cosmological schema. Ultimately, it becomes a question of ethics, the ethics of forest life in which the cosmological and the social constitute one interwoven universe of meaning. However, new circumstances are not always easily accommodated into it. For example, the moral prescription of *punén*, which prohibits, inter alia, eating alone, is becoming difficult for people to observe. Unlike all produce caught or collected in the forest, which has to be displayed and shared amongst all present lest a person not included feels unfulfilled desire and thereby renders him/herself vulnerable to spirit attack leading to illness, money and purchases fall outside the *punén* cosmo-rule. By not including money in *punén*, Chewong are, in effect, establishing different "spheres of exchange" (Bohannan 1959); their economy is no longer fully "embedded in the social" (Polanyi 2001). At the same time, men in the gateway village still go hunting with their blowpipes, but they are more secretive about their catch, thus failing to observe *punén*. So we can observe a fragmentation into self-sufficient, more-or-less settled households that increasingly disregard the sharing injunction. The communal ownership of land in the vicinity of the gateway village, but not inside the forest, has been replaced by individually-owned plot.

Two kinds of inequalities may potentially emerge: that between the sexes and that between individuals and/or kin-based groups (for more details, see Howell 2012a; Howell and Lillegraven 2013). So far, nothing dramatic has happened, but with the arrival of money on a large scale, men have become the principal cash earners, and some men earn more money than others. It is noticeable that men are gradually taking on the role of decision makers in money and general household matters and that they spend the bulk of their earned income on goods of their choice, such as motor bikes, television sets and clothing. Most women in the village are becoming passive receivers of men's surplus earnings. There are some interesting exceptions. For example, one woman has refused to marry and is cultivating her own cash crop fields. Everything she earns belongs to her, and she is becoming relatively affluent. Whatever other women earn they also keep control over.

Although some individuals obtain more cash and commodities than others, this does not form a basis for authority or power any more than any other personal ability did in the past. An example will elucidate. The Department of Orang Asli Affairs, which has been responsible for most services to the Malaysian aboriginals ever since it was established by the British in 1952, appointed one man to be the headman of each group; the department assumed that this conformed with local practices. This man (never a woman) would be given some small insignia and a small annual stipend. It was also made an hereditary office. As far as Chewong were concerned, none of this made much sense, and 30 years ago the headman was not regarded in any way as a man of authority over the rest and neither is his son today. Despite having been given a more elegant house and, from time to time being summoned to a gathering of headmen, neither he nor the rest see his role as carrying any kind of privilege or responsibility. People are used to looking after themselves. I was happy for my earlier analysis of a thoroughgoing egalitarian ethos to be confirmed in this way. However, it is not impossible to envisage that this state of affairs will change, not from internal dynamics, but from external pressure and their response to it.

A further major change with unknown long-term repercussions is the establishment and rapid expansion of a National Elephant Conservation Centre next to the gateway village. Since the late 1980s, wild elephants have been brought here from all over the country when their natural habitat has been destroyed and turned into oil-palm plantations. Today the Centre is widely advertised as a tourist attraction (http://www.tourism.gov.my/en/Master/Web-Page/Places/Nature-n-Adventure/Kuala-Gandah-Elephant-Orphanage-Sanctuary-Pahang), and it attracts large numbers of Malaysian and foreign families. In 2009, 150,000 visitors were recorded, and the numbers are increasing. The facilities (for example, cafés, shops and adventure activities for children) are increasing, and the Chewong village is now right next door, having lost further land to the new car park. The pre-existing Chewong settlement was pushed out to make room for the village that was built for the employees at the Centre. A large tarmac road has been built through the deforested area up to the edge of the Krau Game Reserve where it divides towards the Elephant Reserve to the right and the "aboriginal village" to the left. At first no Chewong was employed at the Centre, but today several men (no women) have found regular paid work as guards or cleaners. The JHEOA has built a small house to exhibit and sell some Chewong artifacts and to provide a seating space for lectures about Chewong "cultural beliefs and practices". These lectures are given by the wife of an employee of the Elephant Reserve, who is also a teacher of Islam. Having listened to her a couple of times, I was dismayed to hear the numerous uninformed and prejudiced "facts" she provided with complete equanimity. She also sells the artifacts and collects money from dance or song performances that she organizes, but rumour has it that only a small portion of this is distributed to those who produced them. True to form, no Chewong confronts her about this.

CHANGE AND CONTINUITY

As the villagers enjoy more shop-bought food and consumer goods, they are learning that all this has its price in the form of regular hard work in order to provide sufficient produce to sell—whether forest or cultivated. They also have learnt that their highly valued freedom is under threat. There is thus a strong ambivalence concerning the new. There is no doubt that most Chewong would like more consumer goods and shop-bought food, but not at any price and preferably on their own terms. If they do not like what is going on in the gateway village—too many uninvited visitors and governmental demands—people abandon their houses and withdraw to the forest. However, these days most withdraw less deeply than in the past. All this may eventually lead to changes in their economic activities and their relations with each other. While new practices challenge old understandings, for profound changes to take place, it seems to me that Chewong will have to "disembed" (Polanyi 2001), that is, remove all economic practices from the broader socio-cosmological-constituted sociality. The exclusion of money from the *punén* rule is the first sign of such disembedding. It is, however, a process that is experienced as highly uncomfortable, the consequences of which people are reluctant to admit. Significantly, while the practice of immediate consumption and spending, deriving its meaning from cosmological knowledge, ensures continuity of the vital values of equality and autonomy in Chewong society, it also inhibits accumulation of wealth and, therefore, perpetuates (or rather gives rise to) poverty. Poverty was not an issue when I first went to live amongst Chewong.

In addition, many practices observed during my early fieldwork, such as shamanistic healing practices and singing (old and new Chewong songs) and telling myths and legends in the evening, have virtually ceased in the village. When I asked about this, I was told that the proximity to *gob* (Malays) made this very difficult. But television is a competitor for young people's attention, and older people seem to have resigned themselves to the loss of old practices. The daily interaction with the animated environment through the cosmo-rules has virtually vanished from young people's experience.

Although with varying degree of success, world religions have also entered the Chewong world, there are few signs that they are replacing the traditional metaphysics. In 2002 a large number of Chewong men, women and children converted to Islam, participated in Koran-reading gatherings (being read to since few could read) and dressed in Islamic clothing. I thought that this would be a permanent feature from then on, but just a few years later no trace of Islam could be discerned beyond the small unattended prayer house at the village entrance. Having achieved formal conversion, the missionaries left them to their own devices. Having spent the money they received for their conversion, the Chewong returned to their old ways. This interesting interlude would not have been caught by me had I not happened to be present at the operative moments. Christian evangelical missionaries appear to have more success. They return once a month to perform a Christian service, including Holy Communion, and they distribute food and clothing to the converted. They also provide medical services and, unlike their Islamic counterparts who insist on regular prayers and forbid food that the Chewong cherish (for example, wild pig, porcupine, monkeys, lizards), demand very little from the converts. But

having been present at such services and having talked to converted
Chewong, their understanding of Christianity remains narrow, and it
does not provide an existential base for how they orient themselves
in the world.

To what extent Chewong will be able to continue to live according
to previous values and practices that are vulnerable in the confrontation
with their more sophisticated neighbours is an uncomfortable question.
I will not predict, but I contemplate how my initial interpretations have
been confirmed or not through my experiences from recent visits. As I
keep returning I am confirmed in many of my earlier interpretations, but
I also face new uncertainties. It has been difficult to come to terms with
their strong desire for shop items and the lengths they are willing to go
in order to obtain these. I have also had to face my early romanticizing
of their way of life and my desire to ignore everything that I regarded
as an intrusion on this image. There are no simple answers, because,
despite my earlier interpretation of their situation that they were not
headed towards a familiar scenario of peripheral and underprivileged
existence suffering from acculturation, disorientation and consumerism
(2002), this is turning out to be more complex.

MULTITEMPORAL FIELDWORK: SOME LESSONS AND PERPLEXITIES

When asked, most anthropologists will say that repeated fieldwork over
a long period of time will give rise to enhanced understanding. This is
probably the case; one's language skills improve, one's access to people's
lives becomes ever more relaxed, one is able to contextualize events that
are "caught in the net"—new and familiar—and grasp complexities
more easily, but it is also the case that the more one observes and learns,
the more the picture become muddled. In my experience, clear patterns
are more easily discernible in the relatively early stages of fieldwork
than after many years. This does not mean the early perceptions are
wrong—or right—only that complexity muddles the issues, rendering
the perceived categories less clear-cut. But this complexity is, I think,
to be viewed positively. It implies that social and cultural life are
dynamic and cannot, and should not, be approached in simple terms.

Different contexts give rise to different meanings, and as we experience a multitude of contexts, we are enabled to envisage the many meanings that are not uniform but multiplex. Another way to put it is that through multitemporal fieldwork we learn the grammar and syntax of social life.

As the anthropologist becomes older and changes from student to teacher and from single to married with family of her own, she accompanies those she studied in their life stages. This brings its own kind of intimacy. In the case of my engagement with Chewong, long-term fieldwork has proved an exciting enterprise. Exciting because on each return visit I am warmly welcomed and included in daily life in a relaxed manner. Children who do not know me and whose reaction is one of panic upon being confronted by a non-Chewong in their midst, are calmed by older people by the words, "but she is not *gob* [Malay], she is Modn's daughter. She used to live with us deep in the forest, and she speaks our language." Words that warm, but also words that make me wonder how much I really am one of them.

One cannot study everything in one go. Repeated fieldwork enables one to focus on one particular practice and observe how it continues or changes over time, for example, shamanistic healing or gender relations. It also enables one to take up completely new topics, for example, leaving religious matters on the side in favour of economic ones (as I have done). Working in small-scale societies like the Chewong, where different strands of social life interweave, the chances are that most of what goes on has already been observed, albeit from the corner of one's eyes. Having read through my early field notes I was pleased to note how systematically I recorded events that fell outside my then main preoccupation of religion, such as the amount of game that was brought in every day, who had caught it and who shared it out. These notes have come in useful in my recent work.

Working over time in illiterate societies about whom very little or nothing had been written, the anthropologist becomes her own archivist (Parkin 2000: 107). At the same time, to be one's own archivist, as I would claim that I am, raises an added and awkward problem of comparison: the comparison of one's own numerous ethnographic presents. Of course, repeated fieldwork over a long period of time does not give rise to a seamless perception of history. Rather, it results in a series of ethnographic presents. The anthropologist drops in from time to time, picks up the threads, tries to understand what has happened in the intervening period and links it to the current situation and to relevant ones from the past. We return. We reflect on the experience of return. We take up old questions and look at them anew in the light of local as well as personal history, just as new events and issues are placed in the same trajectory.

Can I with confidence claim that my rendering of their way of life corresponds to their understandings? Despite the obvious presence of multiple voices, I have nevertheless feel certain that, at a general level, Chewong do not question the reality of their shared identity. Today, I feel fairly confident about my understanding of what makes them (or at least *made* them) tick. Although the Chewong lack many of the institutions that anthropologists tend to rely upon for analysis, such as a formal kinship system, relatively identifiable religion and rituals, social hierarchies—the absence of which led me to Eastern Indonesia in the hope of finding them there—I believe that I have managed to discern a pattern to their cosmology and social life which coincides with their own understanding. Their sporadic involvement with the outside did not challenge their ontology and epistemology, indeed, their metaphysics, when I first lived with them, but by now it is beginning to do so.

I wish briefly to consider the analytical question of dominant, or key, symbols and values, those that encapsulate the many strands of social life that are particularly significant and which crop up in a multitude of different contexts and upon which moral social action is predicated. Repeated fieldwork enables one to identify these with some degree of confidence. It also enables one to observe challenges to them. The following incident, which I have described elsewhere (2006), illustrates this. Between my leaving the field in mid-1979 and returning two years later, the men had taken up a new activity that, to my mind, challenged their animistic understanding and carried the seed to future inequalities. It concerned the collection for sale of a special species of rattan (*manao*) that fetched a high price. This rattan had previously not been collected for sale because, according to Chewong environmental classification, it was a species with consciousness (*ruwai*). However, a man's shamanic dream revealed that, rather than being a non-human conscious being, the rattan was the food for one such being. Hence, by providing some substitute offerings, Chewong might cut and sell it. Had I not been present at the moment when this was discussed, I would never have known about the epistemological dilemma. The solution confirmed the key idea of a potentially animated forest world at the same time as it demonstrated the flux of identity of such beings. By the 1990s this event was forgotten. In 1981 the collection for sale of this rattan had taken off in an astonishing way. Men saw that they could make relatively large sums of money and buy undreamt of wonders that did not have to be shared. In many ways this event pointed the way towards the future: the exclusion of women from new economic activities and the rise of personal property. This was the first sign that a new sphere of exchange was coming into existence with the resulting demise of the sharing injunction.

CONCLUSION

I have been involved with Chewong for 35 years during a time when they have gone from being "an original affluent society" to one that is having to cope with a number of new factors as a result of the intrusion of the modern world of Malaysia. What I have learnt is that, as powerful as these external forces are, they are not succeeding without some degree of collaboration from Chewong themselves. While several families have refused to move to the new village, many feel coerced to settle. The desire for rice, biscuits, oil and other shop food stuffs, for motorbikes, cell phones, clothes and finery must not be ignored as a contributing factor to their changing lifestyle. Certainly, they regret losing much of their previous way of life which they value, and they are concerned about the future, especially that of their children whose knowledge of forest exploitation is diminishing and who know little about the cosmology that made the forest a significant interlocutor for humans. But for the time being, many want to have their cake and eat it. As the relevance of their traditional forest-based ontology, epistemology and morality diminishes for those who grow up on the forest fringes, it is uncertain what will take their place.

ACKNOWLEDGEMENTS

My first fieldwork with the Chewong took place between September 1977 and June 1979 and was supported by the British Social Science Research Council. It formed the ethnographic basis for my DPhil thesis at the University of Oxford where I was supervised by Professor Rodney Needham. Subsequent field research visits (1981, 1990, 1991, 1997, 2001, 2002, 2006, 2008, 2010) were funded, inter alia, by the Suzette Tayler Travel Grant, Lady Margaret Hall, Oxford; by the Équipe de la Récherche d'Anthropologie Sociale: Morphologie, Échanches, Paris; and the Norwegian Research Council.

REFERENCES

Appadurai, A.
  1986 Theory in Anthropology: Center and Periphery. Comparative Studies in Society and History 28(2): 356–61.

Benjamin. G.
  1967 Temiar Religion. Unpublished PhD thesis, Cambridge University.
  1968a Headmanship and Leadership in Temiar Society. Federation Museums Journal 8 (New Series): 1–43.
  1968b Temiar Personal Names. Bijdragen Tot de Taal-, Land-, en Volkenkunde 124: 99–134.
  2005 Consciousness and Polity in Southeast Asia: The Long View. *In* Local and Global: Social Transformation in Southeast Asia. Essays in Honour of Professor Syed Hussein Alatas. R. Hassan, ed. Pp. 261–89. Leiden: Brill.
  2011 Egalitarianism and Ranking in the Malay World. *In* Anarchic Solidarity: Autonomy, Equality, and Fellowship in Southeast Asia. Monograph 60. T. Gibson and K. Sillander, eds. Pp. 170–201. New Haven, CT: Yale Southeast Asia Studies.

Benjamin, G. and C. Chou, eds.
  2002 Tribal Communities in the Malay World: Historical, Social and Cultural Perspectives. Leiden: International Institute for Asian Studies (IIAS) and Singapore: Institute of Southeast Asian Studies (ISEAS).

Bohannan, P.
  1959 The Impact of Money on an African Subsistence Economy. Journal of Economic History 19: 30–41.

Clifford, J.
  1983 Power and Dialogue in Ethnography. *In* Observers Observed:
        Essays in Ethnographic Fieldwork. G.W. Stocking, ed. Madison, WI:
        University of Wisconsin Press.
Dentan, R.K.
  1968 The Semai: A Nonviolent People of Malaya. New York: Holt,
        Rinehart and Winston.
  1978 Notes on Childhood in a Nonviolent Context: The Semai Case
        (Malaysia). *In* Learning Non-Aggression. A. Montagu, ed. Oxford:
        Oxford University Press.
  2008 Overwhelming Terror: Love, Fear, Peace and Violence among
        Semai of Malaysia. Lanham, MD: Rowman and Littlefield.
  2011 Childhood, Familiarity and Social Life among East Semai. *In*
        Anarchic Solidarity: Autonomy, Equality, and Fellowship in
        Southeast Asia. Monograph 60. T. Gibson and K, Sillander, eds.
        New Haven, CT: Yale Southeast Asia Studies.
Endicott, K.
  1983 The Effects of Slave Raiding on the Aborigines of the Malay
        Peninsula. *In* Slavery, Bondage and Dependency in Southeast Asia.
        A. Reid and J. Brewster, eds. Pp. 216–45. Brisbane: University of
        Queensland Press.
Howell, S.
  1984 Society and Cosmos: Chewong of Peninsular Malaysia. Oxford:
        Oxford University Press. (Paperback edition 1989, University of
        Chicago Press.)
  1989 To Be Timid Is to Be Human, To Be Angry Is Not to Be Human.
        In Societies at Peace: Anthropological Perspectives. S. Howell and
        R. Willis, eds. Pp. 45–59. London: Routledge.
  1996 Nature in Culture or Culture in Nature? Chewong Ideas of
        "Humans" and Other Species. *In* Nature and Society. P. Descola
        and G. Pálsson, eds. Pp. 127–44. London: Routledge.
  2002 Our People Know the Forest: Chewong Re-Creations of Uniqueness
        and Separateness. *In* Tribal Communities in the Malay World:
        Historical, Social and Cultural Perspectives. G. Benjamin and C.
        Chou, eds. Pp. 254–72. Leiden: International Institute for Asian
        Studies (IIAS) and Singapore: Institute of Southeast Asian Studies
        (ISEAS).
  2006 Chewong Women in Transition—Twelve Years On. *In* Orang Asli
        Women of Malaysia. A. Baer, ed. Pp. 61–90. Subang Jaya: Centre
        for Orang Asli Concerns.

2010   The Uneasy Move from Hunting, Gathering and Shifting Cultivation
       to Settled Agriculture: The Case of the Chewong (Malaysia). *In*
       Why Cultivate? Understandings of Past and Present Adoption,
       Abandonment, and Commitment to Agriculture in Southeast Asia.
       M. Janowski and G. Barker, eds. Leiden: KITLV Press.

2011   Sources of Sociality in a Cosmological Frame: Chewong,
       Peninsular Malaysia. *In* Anarchic Solidarity: Autonomy, Equality,
       and Fellowship in Southeast Asia. Monograph 60. T. Gibson
       and K. Sillander, eds. Pp. 40–61. New Haven, CT: Yale Southeast
       Asia Studies.

2012a Cumulative Understandings: Experiences from the Study of Two
       Southeast Asian Societies. *In* Returns to the Field: Multitemporal
       Research and Contemporary Anthropology. S. Howell and A.
       Talle, eds. Pp. 153–79. Bloomington: Indiana University Press.

2012b Knowledge, Morality and Causality in a "Luckless" Society.
       Social Analysis 56(1): 133–47.

n.d.   Seeing and Knowing: Metamorphosis and the Fragility of Species
       in Chewong Animistic Ontology. *In* Animism in Southeast Asia:
       Persistence, Transformation and Renewal. K. Århem and G.
       Sprenger, eds. London: Routledge. Forthcoming.

Howell, S. and A. Lillegraven
2013   Cash, Culture and Social Change: Why Don't Chewong Become
       Entrepreneurs? *In* Embedded Entrepreneurs: Market, Culture and
       Economic Action in Southeast Asia. E. Bråten, ed. Pp. 275–96.
       Leiden: Brill.

Howell, S. and A. Talle, eds.
2012   Returns to the Field: Multitemporal Research and Contemporary
       Anthropology. Bloomington: Indiana University Press.

Polanyi, K.
2001   The Great Transformation: The Political and Economic Origins of
       Our Time. Boston: Beacon Press.

Sahlins, M.D.
1974   Stone Age Economics. London: Tavistock.

Woodburn, J.
1982   Egalitarian Societies. Man 17: 431–51.

chapter **3**

Not Just Skin Deep: Ideas of Racial Difference in Genetic Studies on Orang Asli from the 1950s[1]

Sandra Khor Manickam

INTRODUCTION

This chapter deals with the blood-group studies carried out by medical doctors Ivan Polunin and P.H.A. Sneath in Malaya in the 1950s and connects the application of this new technology to earlier ways of classifying indigenous people. The first part of this chapter traces the development of classification schemes for indigenous peoples of the Malay Peninsula from the 1800s until the 1930s when indigenous people became firmly divided into three groups and separated from Malays. Following the background into the basis and history of the tripartite division of indigenous people, I then delve into the blood-group studies of the 1950s and examine the rationale behind using blood-groups as a basis for a seemingly more objective classification of indigenous groups. The chapter ends with an assessment of the results of blood-group anthropology, and it positions these studies as the precursor to DNA studies of Orang Asli, which have burgeoned in the 21st century.

KNOWING AND CLASSIFYING INDIGENOUS PEOPLE

The tripartite division of Malaysia's indigenous people, or Orang Asli, was not necessarily an obvious or objective classification even though it has been, as yet, the most long-lasting. The basic framework of the three-way division of indigenous people was presented by British anthropologist W.W. Skeat and linguist C.O. Blagden in their influential work, *Pagan Races of the Malay Peninsula* (1906). Yet, prior to and even during the publication of *Pagan Races*, there were competing theories of classification that went in and out of favour among Western scholars who were interested in and knowledgeable on indigenous people and Malays. As will become clear, determining who was indigenous and how many indigenous groups there were entailed gradually drawing intellectual boundaries between a conception of "native" Malays and of "indigenous" people who were seen as different from Malays.

Not surprisingly then, the beginnings of classifying indigenous people in the Malay Peninsula began in tandem with classifying Malays. An influential theory about the number of original peoples of the Malay Archipelago was put forth by colonial scholar and officer John Crawfurd in *History of the Indian Archipelago* (1820). Crawfurd hypothesized that there were two indigenous groups in the Malay Archipelago, the "brown" represented by the Balinese and the "black" represented by people from New Guinea. The latter category also included "Oriental Negroes" or "negritos" who were found in the hill regions of Kedah on the Malay Peninsula as reported by another British scholar, John Leyden (1811: 218; Manickam 2009: 69).

Greater familiarity with the Malay Peninsula came along with the establishment of the Straits Settlements in 1826 which comprised the British colonies of Penang, Singapore and Melaka. From these island and coastal bases, British colonial officers became more involved in the events in the Malay states on the peninsula and came to know better various segments of its inhabitants. In the process of arguing for the independence of one of the Malay states, Kedah, from the strong northern power of Siam, East India Company officer John Anderson inserted observations on the "aboriginal inhabitants" of the Malay Peninsula whom he said included not only "negrito" groups such as Semang, but also non-negrito groups, for instance, "Sakei", "Orang Bukit [People of the Hills]" and "Orang Laut [People of the Seas]" (1824: xxx–xxxi). Anderson's formulation changed the way the peoples of the Malay Peninsula were thought of in two crucial ways. Firstly, he excluded Malays from "aboriginal inhabitants", reinforcing the view of them as "native" but not "indigenous", and secondly, he expanded the "aboriginal" category to include people not classified as negrito (Manickam 2015: 38).

In this early period of classification, scholars used a range of determining factors to rationalize the inclusion or exclusion of people under the "aboriginal" or "Malay" heading. Outward physical characteristics such as skin, hair and eye colour, the character of the hair (variations between straight and curly), as well as stature were used to distinguish races along with other criteria such as language, culture and economic activity, which may sometimes be of greater importance than the physical characteristics. The expansion of the "aboriginal" category by Anderson is one example of where scholars highlighted the latter characteristics, resulting in the inclusion of non-negrito people as aboriginal. Malays were still distinguished from both negrito and non-negrito indigenous people by virtue of perceived differences in culture, religion and physical characteristics. Yet, with the development of the field of anthropology, to which the study of indigenous people of the Malay Peninsula was most frequently connected, there grew the emphasis on physical characteristics as the determining factors of racial classification (Turnbull 2008: 212). At least outwardly, scholars took to justifying their classifications based on physical attributes of indigenous people, a practice that privileged observations and measurements of the physical body as somehow objectively indicating similarity or difference from other bodies.

The tripartite classification of indigenous people was likewise justified on the basis of physical anthropological data even though other factors played roles in suggesting and reinforcing the classification. The physical anthropological data used to support Skeat's classification and the reports accompanying the data often did not give clear-cut indications as to racial grouping or affiliation. Instead, knowledge from the colonial and anthropological encounter, such as which individuals were included in which societies regardless of their physical characteristics, was often the overriding factor (Manickam 2012: 299). Nevertheless, Skeat insisted that any classification must be based on physical measurements without relying on criteria such as social standing or language in the deliberations. Indeed, he named each indigenous race based on the quality of hair associated with the particular race: either "woolly-haired" Negritos, "wavy-haired" Sakai or "straight-haired" Jakun (1902: 124–7).

Skeat's classification was partially based on that by physical anthropologist Rudolf Martin, who was hesitant in asserting a third indigenous race and preferred "mixed races" to Skeat's "Jakun" (Martin 1905; Skeat 1902: 124n1). The difference between Skeat's and Martin's ideas on the division of races is but one indication that Skeat's racial schema was not agreed upon by many scholars. Others had their own classifications, for instance anthropologists Nelson Annandale and H.C. Robinson who also conducted research on indigenous peoples. Specifically, they found it hard to distinguish between Sakai and Semang Negritos and expressed reservations at the validity of the Sakai category (Annandale and Robinson 1902: 413). R.J. Wilkinson, author of several books on Malays, indigenous people and Malaya, wrote in 1926 that there are "five distinct tribes or races of aborigines; the Semang, the Northern Sakai, the Central Sakai, the Besisi and the Jakun", which are distinguished by language, race and culture (Wilkinson 1926: 8). Another distinction between "tame" and "wild" aborigines, respectively indicating those who were more and less acculturated to Malay lifestyles, did not become an anthropological category even though Russian anthropologist N. Miklouho-Maclay suggested that it was an important distinction in 1878 (Miklouho-Maclay 1878: 211n1; Manickam 2012: 291). Despite other competing theories, by the end of the colonial period of British Malaya, the tripartite classification was dominant regardless of whether scholars found the classification to be sound based primarily on physical measurements, on observed lifeways or a mixture of both (Manickam 2015: 163–4).

TOWARDS NEW METHODS—BLOOD-GROUP ANTHROPOLOGY

In 1950s Malaya, a new form of physical anthropological measurement was added to the earlier list of outward bodily characteristics, that of blood groups. Blood-group testing had been conducted on a group of indigenous people in Malaya in the 1930s, but it was not until after the end of the Japanese Occupation (1941–45) and the resumption of British military command in Malaya, in the midst of preparing Malaya for some form of self-governance or independence, that these studies were continued and conclusions about the place of indigenous people within a wider humanity were made based on the findings (Green 1949: 130–2).

The interest in distinguishing people based on blood properties can be traced to the work of serologists Ludwik and Hanka Hirschfeld in Europe. In 1919, the pair published their findings on the testing of blood from soldiers in Salonika, Greece during the end of World War I. Earlier, in 1900, Austrian Karl Landsteiner discovered the ABO blood groups, and Hirschfeld himself conducted further research into its methods of inheritance (Hirschfeld and Hirschfeld 1922: 675–9; Mourant 1958: 1). In their 1919 article, the Hirschfelds described how blood groups could be of assistance in "the solution of the race problem". This problem was one of finding a way to distinguish differences within the human species based on blood. They suggested that scholars "make use of the properties of blood … to form an anthropological criterion for the discovery of hitherto unknown and anatomically invisible relationships between different races" (1922: 675, 677). Based on groupings of races (for example, "English", "French", "German", "Turk", "Jew", "Negro" and "Indian") the proportion of Group A to Group B blood was calculated, and the number called the Biochemical Racial Index was used as a means of categorizing races. Depending on the proportion of A and B in the overall sample, the Hirschfelds distinguished types: "European type" which had a higher percentage of A, "Intermediate Type" with a more even distribution of A and B, and the "Asio-African Type" of higher B (678). Biological anthropologist and historian Jonathan Marks calls racial serology "the first generation of human population genetics" (2012: S164). While the Hirschfelds did not rank the types, maintaining the index as a descriptor of different frequencies, other scientists super-imposed a ranking on the index, such that the European type was considered superior to the latter two.

In Malaya, one of the first known blood-group studies to be conducted on indigenous peoples was in 1931. In the 1949 publication of the *Bulletin of the Raffles Museum*, R. Green, Senior Bacteriologist at the Institute for Medical Research, wrote on the results of blood tests on samples taken from 117 Semai indigenous people in the state of Perak (Green 1949: 130–2; IMR 1951: 9, 33). The samples were taken already in 1931, but results of the test appear not to have been published until after the war.[2] The results showed a high frequency of blood type O, which was attributed to the "general conception" that blood-group O is usually the blood type of "island folk or [those who] have otherwise been isolated (sic)" (Green 1949: 130–2). Based on this frequency, connections were drawn between these indigenous people and other groups such as Tho and Muongs in mainland Southeast Asia and Tobas in Sumatra. Green reiterated, however, that "Blood grouping … is considered an accessory only to other anthropological factors, in assessing relationships between people" and he relied heavily on the pre-World War II work of anthropologists such as Ivor H.N. Evans, Father Paul Schebesta and H.D. Noone in explaining who the Semai were (Green 1949: 130–2).

This post-war phase of physical anthropology overlapped with, and was different from, the endeavours during the colonial period in significant ways. The measuring that took place from the 1800s to the 1930s primarily involved collecting measurements on outwardly accessible parts of the body such as the height of individuals, the length of bones in the legs and arms, and a variety of skull measurements in addition to skin, eye and hair colour. One of the hallmarks of this period of measuring was the assumption of the inferiority of indigenous peoples, and that taking bodily measurements, besides being a form of data collection such as making observations on lifeways, would also "show" such inferiority. The post-war phase is characterized by the beginnings of studying difference that was not just skin deep. The fact that the blood and cells of people could be studied and differentiated, and that those differentiations could again be grouped according to race, was a new technique of studying human difference which began to take the name of blood-group anthropology and that later scholars would call racial serology (Marks 2012: S164; Mourant 1947: 139–44). Unlike many scientists operating during the colonial period, the scholars writing about indigenous blood groups in post-war Malaya were not interested in ranking the groups according to their perceived inferiority or superiority vis-à-vis other groups. They were, however, interested in using blood groups as a marker of racial difference, and they approached blood groups much like they approached hair characteristics: as indications of a racial affiliation with those who had similar blood-group frequencies and racial divergence from others who had different blood-group frequencies. Significantly, the racial categories that they used were those in common usage, which were based on a mixture of external physical features and cultural ones. They did not propose that clusters of blood-group frequencies suggested entirely new groupings of races.

The main study of indigenous blood groups was conducted by Dr Ivan Polunin and P.H.A. Sneath in a series of articles from 1952 to 1954. Polunin was then part of the Department of Social Medicine and Public Health, University of Malaya in Singapore. Born in Britain to British and Russian parents, he came to Singapore in 1948 and settled there until his death in 2010 (See 2010; NUS Museum 2012). In 1950, Polunin was granted research funds from the University of Malaya "with a free hand to investigate diseases of Malayan aborigines" (Polunin 1952: 70, see Plate 3.1).

Along with Sneath, a British microbiologist stationed in Malaya at the same time, the two conducted research and wrote articles on the blood groups of aborigines that would later be used by the pioneer of blood-group anthropology, A.E. Mourant in his worldwide studies on blood-group distribution (Polunin and Sneath 1953; Sneath 1954; Mourant et al. 1958; Jones and Grant 2011). Mourant was, at the time, Director of the Medical Research Council Blood Group Research Laboratory in London and well-known for his work on blood groups. He discovered and co-discovered several blood factors and wrote extensively on blood groups of racial groups around the world (Wellcome Library, accessed October 2012). The collection of blood in Malaya, however, was not initially a matter of scholarly curiosity. Rather, it was intertwined with the history of post-war Malaya and

Plate 3.1 Ivan Polunin interviewing Orang Asli woman, 1953

(Photo credit: *Straits Times*, 23 Dec. 2010)

the development of health-care of the Malayan population. As such, the research on blood groups and its relevance to anthropology was a minor project related to the over-arching endeavour of determining the health of Malaya's people.

DRAWING ABORIGINAL BLOOD

After World War II, research into various diseases and aspects of health of the Malayan population resumed under the medical department of the Federation of Malaya and the Institute for Medical Research (IMR) in Kuala Lumpur. The IMR was founded in 1900 as the Kuala Lumpur Pathological Institute to study the diseases which affected Malaya's population before it became known as the Institute for Medical Research in 1901 (IMR 1951: 37–40). After the Japanese Occupation, the British reoccupied Malaya in September 1945, with the British Military Administration (BMA) governing Malaya until

March 1946 (Harper 1999: 62). During this time, the Nutrition Team of the BMA was based at the institute and tasked with ascertaining the nutritional levels and requirements in towns and rubber estates. In addition to this, inoculation against cholera, typhoid and rabies was also a priority, and great quantities of vaccine were prepared (IMR 1951: 75–6).

The Federation of Malaya was created in February 1948, with the Sultans retaining their sovereignty but a British High Commissioner appointed with overall authority. In June that year, a state of emergency was declared by High Commissioner Sir Edward Gent due to attacks by the Malayan Communist Party and associated groups against the British colonial government in Malaya (Andaya and Andaya 1989: 256–8; Leary 1989: preface). Throughout the late 1940s, research into diseases and public health initiatives continued, with reports of the Medical Department of the Federation of Malaya showing the efforts of intervention in public health by producing photographs of Malay school girls drinking milk and another of a man inoculating a young indigenous woman (MacGregor 1952: facing title page, facing p. 24). It was during the 10 to 15 years after the war that blood-group studies on Orang Asli were mostly carried out as one of a battery of tests on blood in order to determine if there were problems of nutrition and public health. Crucially, there were a few medical practitioners who believed in the value of blood types to anthropological studies, and they wrote on racial relationships and origins based on blood-type studies and older anthropological material.

The first mention of taking blood of indigenous peoples specifically for research purposes after the war was in 1950. In that year, the IMR began a hematological survey in Malaya primarily for public health reasons. It was an anaemia survey of rural communities that sought to determine the hemoglobin levels in various "social and racial groups", and to distinguish people who had iron-deficiency anaemia from those who suffered from nutritional megaloblastic anaemia (Struthers 1953: 30).[3] Approximately a thousand people were examined, with the subjects comprising "Malays, Tamils and Senoi and Negrito-Senoi aborigines" (Struthers 1953: 30). In 1951, the results of the report indicated that Indians and Negrito-Senois suffered from the most severe types of anaemia, and treatment was provided (Gross 1953: 19).

Further investigations into the blood groups of indigenous peoples from an anthropological perspective were carried out specifically by Polunin and Sneath. Under the University of Malaya grant and in association with the anthropological blood-grouping programme organized by Mourant, they attempted to answer many of the same questions asked by colonial anthropologists: what were the divisions of the indigenous peoples of Malaya and what were their connections to indigenous groups in places such as Africa and Australia. The two men conducted tests on four indigenous groups in Malaya and Borneo ("Negritos", "Malayan Senoi", "Aboriginal Malay" and "Land Dayaks") and they expressed interest in addressing how blood-group typing would add to determining racial groups, and the evolutionary question of how "races and subspecies would be produced" (Sneath 1954: 28). The people were tested for several blood-group systems, such as ABO, MNS, Rhesus and Kell, with the data concerning the ABO system analyzed in greatest detail compared to the other systems (Polunin and Sneath 1953: 221–2).

Old questions were asked with renewed vigour with the addition of new technology to possibly provide a different answer than what scientists came to before. Most notably, the question of the connections between Negritos of Malaya and other Negrito populations in Southeast Asia and Africa once again became a subject of interest. In 1820, Crawfurd considered that the Negritos of Southeast Asia might have been the descendants of a wrecked slave ship from Africa, but he also entertained the idea of a connection deeper in time that hinted at waves of human migration into the Malay Archipelago with Negritos being one of the earliest arrivals to the region (1820: 27–30). The Pan-Negrito theory, the concept that all indigenous peoples of Malaya were of Negrito origin and were connected to others with "negrito" physical characteristics, was dismissed by Skeat in 1906 as "absurd" (1906: 24–5). In the period immediately before the start of World War II, Negritos took centre stage in debates about human migration in the work of Paul Schebesta (1952), who studied African and Asian "Pygmies" or "Negritos" and explicitly connected the two Negrito groups in the two continents. Schebesta's engaging writings on Negritos led to a rekindling of interest among anthropologists in the subject (Manickam 2015: 179–80). In the 1950s, blood grouping, as the latest technique at the disposal of scientists, was applied to this question as well as other general questions concerning connections between the other two indigenous categories and peoples around the world.

Polunin and Sneath's blood-group anthropology results, published in 1953, did not remake racial boundaries nor draw completely new ones. While the tone of their writing indicated that they were open to discovering new categories, they only reinscribed old ones according to blood group. Despite the decline in the view that races could be ranked as superior and inferior during the 1950s, the use of physical characteristics as indicators of human connections and "race" remained, thereby connecting blood-group anthropology to pre-war racial scientists. Idealistically perhaps, Mourant, the authority on blood-group anthropology and director of the blood-group programme, wrote that blood-group classification gives scientists "objective criteria far removed from the traditional marks of 'race'" which were also "almost completely free from the effects of subjective judgments". "Though non-scientific racialism is by no means dead", Mourant added, "a scientific anthropology is coming into being" which will be established based partly on blood groups (Mourant 1954: 1). The main hope behind collecting anthropological material such as blood-group types and calculating gene frequencies was in order to "enable far-reaching conclusions to be drawn regarding the past migrations of the peoples concerned", indeed the aim of pre-war anthropology in Malaya (Mourant 1954: 139).

Though a scientific study of race that was free from prejudice was perhaps the hope and belief of many practitioners concerning this new method, the data were usually subject to agreement with the earlier anthropology. For Malaya, Polunin and Sneath's results were unsurprising in that they were mostly based on physical anthropological findings and categories from the colonial period. Yet, this is also the reason why the results are problematic. Other than the general finding of the prevalence of blood-group B in Asia, more specific data on individual groups were placed in the previous anthropological frame of reference with hardly any deviation. While purporting to investigate race through blood-typing, race was instead used as a taken-for-granted category that was laid over the data (Marks 2012: S164, S167). For indigenous people of Peninsular Malaya, Skeat's basic tripartite division between "dark-skinned and wooly-haired" Negritos, "wavy-haired"

Senoi and "lank-haired" Aboriginal Malays, though slightly altered in name to "Negritos", "Malayan Senoi" and "Aboriginal Malay", was used as a basis for collecting blood samples, and the data was compared between these already present categories (Polunin and Sneath 1953: 247, see Figure 3.1).

Possible connections, based on similar blood-group frequencies of other populations or "races", were posited, but only when such connections were seen to be reasonable or in keeping with the prevailing view of anthropological connections. Where the data coincided with pre-existing assumptions about connections, these results were taken as definitive, yet when the data disagreed with those assumptions, it was assumed to be random or unimportant. Again, the case of Negritos is particularly instructive. Polunin and Sneath noted the complete absence of the sickle-cell trait in Negritos of Malaya, and they cast doubt on the connection to Africans since this trait was supposed to be distinctive of Africans or African ancestry. This fact was highlighted as anomalous to older anthropological reasoning based on outward characteristics, or even that the blood-group data was "conflicting" (Polunin and Sneath 1953: 224). However, in a summary of their findings written by Sneath and published in another journal in 1954, the issue was revived again by his pointing out the similarities in frequency of one of the Rhesus genes between Malaya's Negritos and Africans. In vague terms, the similar incidence was said to support "the belief that the Negritos and Africans are descended from a *common stock* [emphasis added]". As to the lack of the sickle-cell trait, Sneath wrote that in any case "there is some doubt whether this trait is a safe criterion of African ancestry" (Sneath 1954: 28). Sneath thus appeared to selectively rely on the blood-group data where it was in agreement with former Pan-Negrito views. Likewise, the similarities between the Senoi ABO frequencies to those of people in India and Burma were taken to mean relationships between these groups, yet ABO similarities between Negritos of Malaya and people in Vietnam, India, Western Europe and people in Africa were seen as accidental because of the prevailing assumption that these groups did not share a more recent past (Mourant 1954: 112).

Despite the new technology, it was uncertain what the results of blood-group anthropology could have offered that would have been different from the older anthropology. While emphasizing "neutral"

Figure 3.1 ABO blood-group frequencies presented according to community

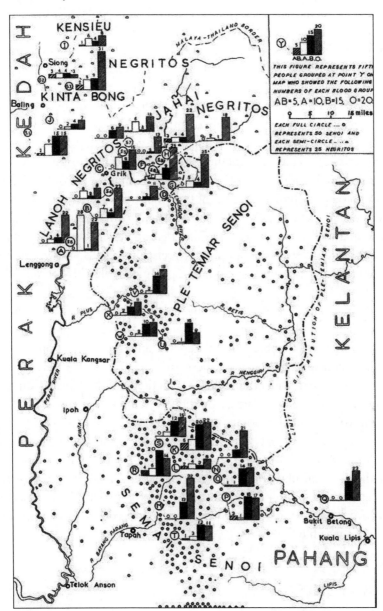

Source: Ivan Polunin and P.H.A. Sneath, "Studies of Blood Groups in South-East Asia", *The Journal of the Royal Anthropological Institute of Great Britain and Ireland* 83(2) (1953): 219.

characteristics unseen by the naked eye as a basis for racial classification, in a later paragraph Polunin and Sneath note that the "greater stability of the traditional measurements of physical anthropology [as compared to changeable blood-group frequencies] may make them more valuable than gene frequencies in the differentiation of some races" (Polunin and Sneath 1953: 247). Indeed, throughout their report, the older physical anthropological data was the defining and structuring feature of the blood-group data. Hence, it is unclear what place blood-group data was supposed to play in racial identification since, as they argued, "blood-group genes" were different from "genes determining physical characteristics", and each method would give different classifications (Polunin and Sneath 1953: 247). Moreover, similar to the older physical anthropology, differences, and not similarities, mattered. The ABO blood system was not the only blood system that was known at the time, yet it was preferred to other blood group systems such as M and N since the latter were more similar between populations and was dubbed by Mourant as having no "great anthropological value" (Mourant 1954: 141–2).

Polunin and Sneath's sympathy towards the peoples they studied is undoubted. Polunin himself continued working with and teaching about indigenous peoples in Singapore, and his dedication to their health is undisputed. Yet, how these two men saw indigenous people in relation to the wider humanity is another question based on their scientific beliefs and practices. In studying Orang Asli in the 1950s, it was unavoidable that scholars relied on pre-war physical anthropology since that was the most recent application of anthropological theories on Orang Asli. However, the goal of the project, to have a non-prejudicial racial classification based on neutral markers, did not take into account the cultural and political underpinnings of racial science which makes the dream of neutrality when it comes to classification nearly impossible.

CONCLUSION

The first half of the 20th century saw vast changes in the studies of indigenous people of Malaya by European anthropologists and colonial officials. Biological anthropological methods took over in emphasis from earlier studies focusing on indigenous languages. While the outward measuring of bodies took place in the early 1900s, from the 1930s onwards new ways of testing racial provenance became available in the form of blood-group studies which prefigured later, more comprehensive genetic studies of indigenous peoples in Malaya.

Such studies were conducted under immense political and social upheaval. In the thick of the Emergency, Polunin and Sneath were able to conduct tests on indigenous peoples in what could have been treacherous conditions. Yet, Polunin could write that "a good time was had by all", in reference to indigenous people poking fun at the "strange antics of the medical investigator" (Polunin 1953: 165). In fact, the upheaval caused by the Emergency, much like the rapid development during the colonial period which granted many anthropologists access to little known peoples, brought about new chances to study indigenous peoples. Many of the communities studied by Polunin were newly resettled by the BMA in order to deprive communist insurgents who were based in the jungle of indigenous people's help, to ensure that indigenous people were not swayed by contact with communists and to protect them from the fighting. Thus, the work of collecting blood samples was made easier due to the subjects being in accessible areas (Polunin 1953: 72–3).

Blood-group anthropology is of great importance as a bridge between the first phase of bodily measurements and racial theorizing from the 1800s–1930s, and the most recent spate of studies in the present. In the last 20 years or so, genetic studies on indigenous people of Malaysia and elsewhere have continued to excite the interest of biologists, pre-historians and politicians alike. These studies are undertaken by local and international researchers who collect biological material, subject the material to tests and computer simulations in order to calculate degrees of similarity or difference from other "populations" based on certain genetic markers (Ang et al. 2011; Hatin et al. 2012). Alan Fix's article (this volume) analyzes one such study where mtDNA was used to posit a theory of Orang Asli isolation after an initial migration out of Africa. As frequently argued by humanities scholars of science, such studies rarely debunk the assumption of racial difference and essentialization, with popular reports of such studies still maintaining that there are

inherent differences and characteristics between peoples whatever the
scientist may believe. Furthermore, in the case of Malaya, the initial
grouping of such studies already demonstrates a reliance on popular
racial-typecasting and historically-specific anthropological classification
that was formed during the colonial period and continually utilized until
the present (Manickam 2015: 188–90). Despite the absence (mostly)
of assumptions of inherent inferiority, the present-day studies, like the
blood-group analyses of the 1950s, nonetheless exhibit a reliance on
material that was formerly steeped in racial rankings.

NOTES

1. This chapter is partially based on a paper presented at the conference,
    Asia-Europe Encounters: Intellectual and Cultural Exchanges, 1900–50
    (7–8 Dec. 2012, Singapore), entitled "Drawing Blood at a Time of
    Emergency: New Studies of Orang Asli during Malaya's Decolonization".
    The author would like to thank Kirk Endicott for his many helpful
    comments on the chapter.
2. It is not known who exactly took the blood tests and the circumstances
    of the collection.
3. Iron-deficiency anaemia results in fewer or smaller red blood cells, while
    nutritional megaloblastic anaemia is due to deficiency in Vitamin B12
    and Folic Acid, resulting in larger than normal blood cells.

REFERENCES

Andaya, B.W. and L.Y. Andaya
    1982   A History of Malaysia. London: Macmillan.
Anderson, J.
    1824   Political and Commercial Considerations Relative to the Malayan
            Peninsula and the British Settlements in the Straits of Malacca.
            Prince of Wales Island: Printed under the authority of the
            Government.
Ang, K.C., J.W.H. Leow, W.K. Yeap, S. Hood, M.C. Mahani and B.M. Md-Zain
    2011   Phylogenetic Relationships of the Orang Asli and Iban of Malaysia
            Based on Maternal Markers. Genetics and Molecule Research
            10(2): 640–9.

Annandale, N. and H.C. Robinson
    1902   Some Preliminary Results of an Expedition to the Malay Peninsula.
            The Journal of the Anthropological Institute of Great Britain and
            Ireland 32: 407–17.

Crawfurd, J.
    1820   History of the Indian Archipelago, Containing an Account of the
            Manners, Arts, Languages, Religions, Institutions, and Commerce
            of Its Inhabitants. Edinburgh: A. Constable.

Genetics and Medicine Historical Network
    2012   Wellcome Library for the History and Understanding of
            Medicine, London. Arthur Ernest Mourant, 1904–94. Refer-
            ence code: GB 0120 PP/AEM. http://www.genmedhist.info/
            Records%20of%20British%20Human%20Geneticists/Mourant,
            accessed 31 Oct. 2012.

Green, R.
    1949   Anthropological Blood Grouping among the 'Sakai'. Bulletin of
            the Raffles Museum, Series B, 4: 130–2.

Gross, R.D.
    1953   Federation of Malaya: Report of the Medical Department for the
            Year 1951. Kuala Lumpur: Printed at the Government Press.

Harper, T.N.
    1999   The End of Empire and the Making of Malaya. Cambridge:
            Cambridge University Press.

Hatin W.I., A.R. Nur-Shafawat, M-K Zahri, Shuhua Xu, Li Jin, S.G. Tan,
Mohammed Rizman-Idid, Bin Alwi Zilfalil and The HUGO Pan-Asian SNP
Consortium
    2011   Population Genetic Structure of Peninsular Malaysia Malay Sub-
            Ethnic Groups. PLoS ONE 6(4): 1–5.

Hirschfeld, L. and H. Hirschfeld
    1922   Serological Differences between the Blood of Different Races:
            The Results of Researches on the Macadonian Front. The Lancet,
            18(Oct.): 675–9.

Institute for Medical Research
    1951   The Institute for Medical Research 1900–1950, Studies from the
            Institute for Medical Research, Federation of Malaya, Jubilee. Vol.
            25. Kuala Lumpur: Printed at the Government Press.

Jones, D. and B. Grant
    2012   University of Leicester, People—Bereavements: Emeritus Profes-
            sor P.H.A. Sneath—17th November 1923—9th September 2011.

http://www2.le.ac.uk/ebulletin/people/bereavements/2010-2019/
2011/09/nparticle.2011-09-23.0432474544/, accessed 1 Nov. 2012.

Leary, J.
  1989   The Importance of the Orang Asli in the Malayan Emergency
         1948–1960. Melbourne: Centre of Southeast Asian Studies,
         Monash University.

Leyden, John
  1811   On the Languages and Literature of the Indo-Chinese Nations.
         Asiatic Researches: or, Transactions of the Society, Instituted in
         Bengal, for Inquiring into the History and Antiquities, the Arts,
         Sciences, and Literature, of Asia 10: 158–289.

MacGregor, R.B.
  1950   Federation of Malaya: Annual Report of the Medical Department
         for the Year 1949. Kuala Lumpur: Printed at the Government
         Press.

Manickam, S.K.
  2009   Africans in Asia: The Discourse of 'Negritos' in Early Nineteenth-
         Century Southeast Asia. *In* Responding to the West: Essays
         on Colonial Domination and Asian Agency. H. Hägerdal, ed.
         Pp. 69–86. Amsterdam: Amsterdam University Press.
  2012   Situated Thinking, or How the Science of Race was Socialised in
         British Malaya. The Journal of Pacific History 47(3): 283–308.
  2015   Taming the Wild: Aborigines and Racial Knowledge in Colonial
         Malaya. Singapore: NUS Press.

Marks, J.
  2012   The Origins of Anthropological Genetics. Current Anthropology 53,
         S5: The Biological Anthropology of Living Human Populations:
         World Histories, National Styles, and International Networks:
         S161–S172.

Martin, R.
  1905   Die Inlandstämme der Malayischen Halbinsel: Wissenschaftliche
         Ergebnisse einer Reise durch die Vereinigten Malayischen
         Staaten [The Inland Tribes of the Malay Peninsula. Scientific
         Results of a Journey Through the Federated Malay States]. Jena:
         G. Fischer.

Miklouho-Maclay, N.
  1878   Ethnological Excursions in the Malay Peninsula—November 1874
         to October 1875 (Preliminary Communication). Journal of the
         Straits Branch of the Royal Asiatic Society 2: 205–21.

Mourant, A.E.
    1947   The Use of Blood Groups in Anthropology. The Journal of the Royal Anthropological Institute of Great Britain and Ireland 77(2): 139–44.

    1954   The Distribution of the Human Blood Groups. Oxford: Blackwell Scientific Publications.

    1958   Introduction. *In* The ABO Blood Groups: Comprehensive Tables and Maps of World Distribution. By A.E. Mourant, A.C. Kopec and K. Domaniewska-Sobczak. Pp. 1–6. Oxford: Blackwell Scientific Publications.

Mourant, A.E., A.C. Kopec and K. Domaniewska-Sobczak
    1958   The ABO Blood Groups: Comprehensive Tables and Maps of World Distribution. Oxford: Blackwell Scientific Publications.

NUS Museum
    2012   Exhibition: Camping and Tramping Through the Colonial Archive: The Museum in Malaya. http://www.nus.edu.sg/cfa/museum/exhibitions.php, accessed 1 Nov. 2012.

Polunin, I.
    1952   Anthropological Problems Encountered during a Disease Survey of Malayan Aborigines. Man 52: 70–1.

Polunin, I. and P.H.A. Sneath
    1953   Studies of Blood Groups in South-East Asia. The Journal of the Royal Anthropological Institute of Great Britain and Ireland 83(2): 215–51.

Schebesta, P.
    1952   Die Negrito Asiens, Vol. 1. Vienna: St Gabriel Verlag.

See, Boon Chan
    2010   Dr Ivan Polunin Dies: Well-Known Naturalist Polunin, 90, Preserved the Sights and Sounds of Singapore. The Straits Times, 22 Dec. http://www.straitstimes.com:80/Life%2521/LifeNews/Story/STIStory_616128.html, accessed Nov. 2012.

Skeat, W.W.
    1902   The Wild Tribes of the Malay Peninsula. Journal of the Anthropological Institute of Great Britain and Ireland 32: 124–41.

Skeat, W.W., and C.O. Blagden
    1906   Pagan Races of the Malay Peninsula, vol. 1. London: Frank Cass.

Sneath, P.H.A.
    1954   Anthropological Blood-Grouping in South-East Asia. Man 54: 28.

Struthers, E.A.
  1953 Federation of Malaya: Report of the Medical Department for the Year 1950. Kuala Lumpur: Printed at the Government Press.

Turnbull, P.
  2008 British Anthropological Thought in Colonial Practice: The Appropriation of Indigenous Australian Bodies, 1860–1880. *In* Foreign Bodies: Oceania and the Science of Race 1750–1940. B. Douglas and C. Ballard, eds. Pp. 205–28. Canberra: ANU E Press.

Wilkinson, R.J.
  1926 Papers on Malay Subjects: Supplement: The Aboriginal Tribes. Kuala Lumpur: F.M.S. Government Press.

Part Two

ORANG ASLI ORIGINS AND HISTORY

chapter **4**

Malaysia's "Original People": Do They Represent a "Relict Population" Surviving from the Initial Dispersal of Modern Humans from Africa?

Alan G. Fix

A recent genetic study has characterized Orang Asli as an isolated "relict population" based on their apparent retention of ancient mitochondrial DNA haplotypes dating from the original migration of anatomically modern humans from Africa some 44 to 63 kya (thousand years ago) (Macaulay et al. 2005). They suggest that the Malaysian Peninsula would have been forested during the last glacial period "which implies that this region acted as a glacial refuge where populations survived and genetic diversity was maintained" (2005: 1035). They go on to say that waves of migrants spreading across mainland Southeast Asia north of Malaysia resulting from farming dispersals did not reach the interior rainforest where the ancestors of the Orang Asli survived as small isolated populations.

The view that Orang Asli are survivors of a formerly widespread population persisting locally due to geographic isolation (geographical relict) or a population that continues to exist after the extinction of the former population (phylogenetic relict) (Darlington 1957) recalls the epigraph in the classic compendium of Orang Asli studies, Skeat and Blagden's *Pagan Races of the Malay Peninsula* (1906): "A land of old ... where fragments of forgotten peoples dwelt (Tennyson)".

However, the presence of "ancestral" mtDNA haplotypes among the Orang Asli does not necessarily mean that these populations have been isolated from all contact with other peoples since the founding colonization. This chapter will provide abundant genetic and historical evidence for interconnections between Orang Asli and other populations. Mitochondrial DNA is, after all, only one genetic locus (all the DNA of the mitochondrion is transmitted as a unit) and represents only the maternal ancestral line since all mitochondria are derived from the female gamete exclusively. Even so, the same study (Macaulay et al. 2005; see also Hill et al. 2006; Oppenheimer 2011) showed that other more recently evolved mtDNA haplotypes are shared by Orang Asli groups and other Southeast Asian populations. Similarly hemoglobin E and Southeast Asian ovalocytosis are prevalent in some Orang Asli as well as other Asians including parts of near Oceania (Fix 1995). These data argue against the long-term genetic isolation of the Orang Asli. Moreover, most modern Orang Asli groups speak languages of the Austroasiatic family forming part of this widespread Southeast Asian linguistic grouping, again indicating connections with other populations (Diffloth 1979).

The population history of the Orang Asli includes more than simply isolation in a glacial refugium. Sociocultural factors have structured patterns of mating and relationships between Orang Asli groups as well as with outside populations. The introduction of agriculture to the Peninsula some 4,000 years ago played an important role as migrants brought new genes and new selective environments. The engagement of some Orang Asli groups with outside traders also had an impact on gene flow.

This chapter will evaluate sociocultural models and data applicable to understanding the prehistory of Orang Asli populations and especially their connections with non-Peninsular populations. Archaeological and linguistic evidence relevant to Orang Asli prehistory has been recently reviewed by Bulbeck (2011; this volume) and Burenhult, Kruspe and Dunn (2011). Whatever the antiquity of particular mtDNA haplotypes found in their population, the Orang Asli have a long and complex history of interaction with outsiders.

RECONSTRUCTING ORANG ASLI ORIGINS

Despite its limited geographic extent, the Malaysian Peninsula shows a complex mosaic of human diversity, both biological and cultural. Much of this diversity is due to the relatively recent migration of Indonesian Malays and Chinese and Indians from British colonial days. The indigenes of the Peninsula, the Orang Asli, are also culturally and biologically differentiated. The traditional splitting of Orang Asli is into three subgroups: Semang foragers, Senoi swiddeners and Melayu Asli farmer-traders.

The classic explanation for the presence of these diverse populations in Malaysia was migrational; each Orang Asli group arrived sequentially as migrants from elsewhere just as did the more recent Malay, Chinese and Indian populations (see Carey 1976 for a summary of this literature). The Semang, of "Negrito" physical type and related to other Oceanic Negritos such as the Andaman Islanders and several Philippine groups, were the earliest arrivals. Some thousands of years later the Senoi, thought to be related to the Indian Veddas and/or Australian Aborigines (Skeat and Blagden 1906), entered as a second wave of colonization followed by the "proto-Malays" or Melayu Asli. Each wave displaced some portion of the previous population(s); each retained ancestral technologies and biological markers: Semang hunter-gatherers, pygmy-statured, dark-skinned with tightly curled hair; Senoi swidden farmers with lighter skin colour and wavy hair; Melayu Asli more intensive farmers and traders with even lighter skin colour and straight hair. On this view, differences existed among ancestral colonists and have persisted into present times. Thus the Orang Asli of today represent a layer cake built up of separate colonizations/invasions over many thousand years.

A more modern view of Orang Asli origins sees continuity of prehistoric Malaysian populations augmented by "successive population flows into Peninsular Malaysia" (Bellwood 1993). As applied to Thailand, the picture is: "layer upon layer of different peoples have come to Thailand, and their descendants remain" (Higham and Thosarat 2012). The driving force for these later waves of expansion is thought to be the population increase of agriculturalists labelled "demic diffusion" (Bellwood and Renfrew 2002).

An alternative to this emphasis on strict migrationism is to see Orang Asli populations as cultural and biological descendants of ancestral populations admixed by gene flow from other Southeast Asian populations (and to some extent with each other) but also evolving in situ to meet environment selective forces present in the Peninsula (Fix 1995).

EVOLUTION OF ORANG ASLI SOCIAL TRADITIONS

Such an alternative model to explain the origin and diversification of Orang Asli cultures and social patterns has been developed by Geoffrey Benjamin (1976, 1985). Benjamin proposed that the three traditions representing the modern Semang, Senoi and Melayu Asli differentiated from a common linguistic and cultural matrix within the last few thousand years. The stimulus for the separation of Semang from Senoi was the introduction of agriculture to the Peninsula. The actual date for this event (or process) is uncertain, but may be approximately 4,000 years ago (Bulbeck 2011: 236). Later, as trading contacts with outside non-Peninsular peoples developed, a niche for forest collecting for trade opened to be filled by the members of the Melayu Asli tradition.

Table 4.1 The three Orang Asli traditions

Tradition	Technology/Economy	Societal Pattern
Semang	nomadic foragers	exogamy, mobile conjugal families, extensive networks
Senoi	sedentary swiddeners	nodal kindreds, fission-fusion
Melayu Asli	sedentary farmers, collectors for trade	endogamy

The key insight in this model is that each of the three traditions are mutual responses to the others. Foragers displaced against farmers by exaggerating their differences, becoming hyper nomadic and adopting a societal pattern that was the antithesis of sedentism. Semang local groups are temporary associations in constant flux; exogamy is extreme, leading to wide-ranging kin ties. The Melayu Asli tradition strongly contrasts with the Semang. Local groups formed corporate groups in competition with other villages for trading partners, thus promoting local endogamy. The Senoi pattern is intermediate in that swidden cultivation implies sedentism (contrast with the Semang), but their more extensive agriculture requires less need for kin-based control of land. Senoi local groups are more stable than Semang and usually comprise a core group of relatives (nodal kindred); residence is ambilateral. Ties among settlements are promoted by consanguineous exogamy and there is a preference for marrying affines. These contrasts have been presented in much greater detail in Benjamin's work (which should be consulted).

Hopefully this brief synopsis will suffice to make the point that the social organizations and particularly mating patterns are quite different among the three traditions. These differences, I will argue, have important implications for understanding the biological history of the Orang Asli. It is important to remember, however, that these cultural patterns do not represent "ethnic groups" (Benjamin 2002), but rather enduring cultural and social models practised by (perhaps) varying groups of people. Although these traditions may be old, modern representatives (Semang foragers, Senoi farmers, Melayu Asli farmer-traders) are not necessarily members of a continuous stable biological population. Modern Orang Asli ethnolinguistic groups may lack long-term continuity as Mendelian populations.

BIOLOGICAL EVOLUTION OF ORANG ASLI POPULATIONS

In 1995 I concluded that the biological data available at that time were insufficient to reconstruct the population history of the Malaysian Peninsula (Fix 1995). The classic phenotypic "markers" characterizing

Semang, Senoi and Melayu Asli—skin colour, hair form and stature—
were shown to be highly variable among the three groups. Indeed, for
stature, measurements showed no difference between the "pygmoid"
Semang and the Senoi; both are short (see below for additional
discussion of Orang Asli stature). Genetic data for Orang Asli populations
were sparse, especially for Semang. Classical genetic markers (blood
groups, enzymes, etc.) also failed to elucidate Orang Asli origins and/
or affinities (Fix 2008). The small sample of mtDNA (Ballinger et
al. 1992), rather than sharply distinguishing the Orang Asli, simply
indicated a common origin for Southeast Asian populations.

   With the adoption of complete mitochondrial genome sequencing,
however, more detailed phylogeographic scenarios have been proposed
for many populations, including the Orang Asli (Macaulay et al. 2005;
Hill et al. 2006; Jinam et al. 2012). These studies have identified
mtDNA lineages that branched from the ancestral African root very
early, perhaps 44 to 63 thousand years ago (Figure 4.1).

   These "relict" mtDNA types localized to Orang Asli lead to the
suggestion that these mutations occurred among the first anatomically
modern human migrants traveling along a coastal route through
Malaysia to Australia and that Orang Asli (along with a few other
"Negrito" populations in the Andamans and Philippines) have survived
as a relict population in a "glacial refuge" (Macaulay et al. 2005).
Orang Asli thus provide key evidence for a coastal dispersal beginning
50 to 100 kya from East Africa along the Arabian Peninsula, India,
Southeast Asia to Sahul (New Guinea and Australia) (Stoneking and
Delfin 2010).

   On the hypothesis of a single, rapid coastal migration (Macaulay
et al. 2005), other basal mtDNA haplotypes might be expected along
the route from South India to Sahul. As Metspalu et al. (2006: 189)
state: "all of the three mtDNA domains along the SCR [Southern
Coastal Route] (South Asia, East Asia, and Sahul) harbour haplogroups
that stem directly from the M, N, and R trunks ... and demonstrate
coalescence times comparable to the initial expansion of M and N".
They suggest that the initial colonization was swift, spreading the same
founding haplotypes along the entire coast. That the Orang Asli should
carry stem haplotypes (M21a, M21b, M21c, N21, R21) should not
be surprising if their ancestors were members of the original (Asli)

Figure 4.1 Network of Asian mtDNA haplotypes. The L3 African root is in the centre. M and N haplogroups have diverged by mutation into numerous additional haplogroups (R, F, et al.). Haplogroups present in Malaysian Orang Asli are indicated by arrows.

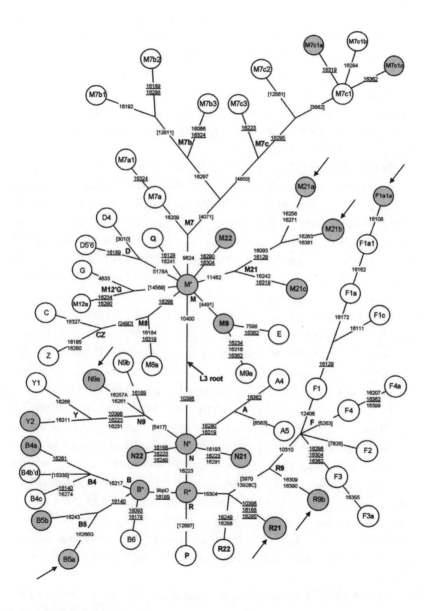

Source: Hill et al. 2006.

colonizing population. But then, on the hypothesis, all the rest of us are also descendents of this single wave out of Africa which over time spread to all parts of the world. The issue is not that any population possesses "ancient" genes. We all do; human cytochrome c is not very different molecularly from blue-green algae; "normal" human hemoglobin (Hb*A) is nearly identical to that of chimpanzees, and so on (King and Wilson 1975). The only argument for labeling Orang Asli a "relict population" (as opposed to possessing "relict" mtDNA haplotypes defined as close to the founding root haplotypes) would be that they have been genetically isolated (in a glacial refuge or similar geographic niche) since the founding colonization. This is demonstrably not the case for the Orang Asli.

Recall that the Orang Asli are subdivided into three groups: Semang, Senoi and Melayu Asli. Although only a tiny minority of the entire Malaysian population, the total population is many thousands. In 2000 it included 3,340 Semang, 44,723 Senoi and 44,790 Melayu Asli (Benjamin 2002). As with any inference, it is appropriate to wonder how representative of the population(s) is the mtDNA sample. The main Orang Asli study sample (Hill et al. 2006) comprised 260 apparently maternally unrelated individuals: 112 Semang (29 Batek, 51 Jahai, 32 Mendriq); 52 Senoi (51 Temiar and 1 Semai); 96 Melayu Asli (61 Semelai, 33 Temuan, 2 Jakun). Jinam et al. (2012) typed a further 51 individuals: Semang (22 Jehai) and 29 Melayu Asli (8 Temuan, 21 Orang Seletar). Additionally two hair samples over 100 years old from individuals from Malaysia labelled "Negrito" in the University of Cambridge museum were typed (Ricaut, Bellatti and Lahr 2006). The sampling fraction then is approximately 0.0034 overall although only about 0.0012 for the numerous Senoi. Notice also that the dialectally more diverse Senoi group, the Semai, are represented by a single sample. Moreover, potentially very interesting groups from a linguistic point of view not sampled in these studies are the Che Wong and the Jah Hut (Burenhult, Kruspe and Dunn 2011). Detailed comparisons among Orang Asli subgroups are thus somewhat limited. Nonetheless clear patterns emerge from the mtDNA data (Hill et al. 2006).

The most striking conclusion regarding the "relict" status of the Orang Asli is:

Phylogeographic analysis suggests at least four detectable colonization events that affected the Orang Asli.... Although this brings to
mind the traditional "layer cake" theory, the latter's assumption
of unchanged relics of earlier population waves is completely
unfounded. All three Orang Asli groups have local roots that reach
back to ~50,000 years ago, and all have been affected to a greater
or lesser extent by subsequent migrations to the Peninsula. (Hill
et al. 2006: 2488)

Furthermore, Semang genetic differences with other "Negrito"
groups such as those living in the Andaman Islands and the Philippines
"refutes the notion of a specific shared ancestry between the Negrito
groups" (Hill et al. 2006: 2488; see also Jinam et al. 2011). Hill and
co-authors nonetheless maintain that the Semang are "the most direct
descendants of the original inhabitants of the Peninsula and have only
minor subsequent gene flow from outside, probably in the recent past"
(Hill et al. 2006: 2488). I will have more to say about the possible
causes of this apparent genetic isolation below. It might be noted,
however, that the results of the analysis of hundred-year-old mtDNA
from museum hair samples show both "Negrito" haplotypes to be
B4c2, which is found from China, Southeast Asia and Indonesia; the
authors suggest that this haplotype rapidly spread across Southeast Asia
between the end of the last glaciation and the Holocene expansion of
agriculture (Ricaut, Bellatti and Lahr 2006). Even Semang isolation
seems incomplete.

Much more could be said concerning intrusive mtDNA haplotypes
into the Peninsula (see Oppenheimer 2011 for a recent summary),
however it should be clear from the preceding discussion that the Orang
Asli experienced episodes of gene flow over the millenia since initial
colonization. Other genomic and classical genetic data reinforce this
conclusion.

Although there are few autosomal SNP (single nucleotide
polymorphism) data available, they also demonstrate links to outside
populations. Reich et al. (2011) suggest that Semang (Jehai), a Philippine
"Negrito" group (Mamanwa) and Australians and New Guineans share
an ancient common ancestor, but have differing histories of gene flow
with other populations. The HUGO Consortium (2009) based on
42,793 autosomal SNPs found that all the Southeast Asian populations

(including Jehai and Kensiu Semang and Temuan Melayu Asli) as well as East Asian populations comprise a single monophyletic clade that is extremely well supported statistically. Interestingly, their phylogenetic tree constructed from the SNP data link both the two Semang groups close together but also the Temuan Melayu Asli in a tight branch.

Classical genetic loci (including blood groups, enzymes and structural proteins) were unable to resolve the origins and affinities of the Orang Asli (Fix 2000). Genetic trees purporting to show common descent (Cavalli-Sforza et al. 1994; Saha et al. 1995) were inconsistent with each other and led to unlikely historical connections; for example, in Cavalli-Sforza and co-author's big book of trees (1994), the Semai (Malaysian Senoi) clustered with the Zhuang, a Tai-speaking population of South China.

On the other hand, two malarial protective genes, hemoglobin E and Southeast Asian ovalocytosis, can provide insights into gene flow on the Peninsula (Fix 1995). Considering genes that are subject to natural selection is contrary to the usual requirement that only "neutral markers" be used in historical genetic analysis since the assumption is that the only relevant processes differentiating populations are fission, migration and genetic drift in isolation (Fix 2008). Branching trees are the appropriate graphic for non-recombining DNA (mtDNA, Y chromosome), languages and species but not necessarily for infra-specific populations of a species including all human populations. Gene flow and natural selection, however, are well attested evolutionary processes and to treat them as irrelevant or confounding is a mistake. As I suggest here, selected genes may amplify the signal of gene flow since their introduction to a favourable environment results in an increase of the allele.

The advent of agriculture in the Peninsula opened up the forests and provided a suitable habitat for mosquito vectors of malaria (Fix 1995). Thus human genes that provided some protection against malaria would gain selective value and increase in frequency. One such allele is hemoglobin E (Hb*E), one of many variant forms of human hemoglobin, which attains high frequency in many mainland Southeast Asian populations including Malaysian Senoi and Melayu Asli (Livingstone 1985). As an allele under selection, the frequency in any population is a function of the selective coefficients which is in turn due to the intensity of malaria. Thus shared gene frequencies does not indicate the degree of admixture between populations. However, hemoglobin mutations are exceedingly rare, and the incidence of Hb*E in contiguous populations surely represents diffusion of this adaptive allele via gene flow.

Hb*E provides a link (along with several mtDNA haplotypes) of the Orang Asli with mainland Southeast Asia, particularly Cambodia, Thailand and the hill peoples of Vietnam [Sedang with an allele frequency (q_E) of 0.355; Rhade, q_E=0.212]. The higher frequencies in these areas range from 0.13 to 0.35 (Livingstone 1985). For three Senoi samples, the range was 0.215 to 0.319 (two Semai and one Temiar groups); for Melayu Asli, Temuan and Jakun were much lower (0.015 and 0.017), while Semelai were somewhat higher (0.171). These differences represent to some degree differences in selective intensity but also chance effects in these small samples. The point, however, is that as agriculture diffused to the Peninsula perhaps 4,000 years ago, migrants came from populations where malaria and the genetic adaptation to malaria had already been established. Present-day high frequencies of Hb*E do not represent the proportion of migrants to the Peninsula; indeed, a trickle of migrants would be sufficient (see below for a model of this process). At the same time, ancestors of present-day Senoi and Melayu Asli could not have been sequestered in isolation.

The case of Southeast Asian ovalocytosis (SAO) illustrates the introduction of an adaptive allele to the Orang Asli from the other direction, from the islands in the south rather than from the north of mainland Southeast Asia (Fix 1995). While Hb*E is found primarily on the mainland, SAO, a red blood cell membrane mutation that produces an oval or elliptic shape, occurs sporadically in malarious areas from coastal New Guinea, Sulawesi and Sumatra (Minangkabau). As for Hb*E, there is good evidence for a protective role of SAO against malaria (Kidson et al. 1981). However, in contrast to Hb*E, higher frequencies of SAO are found in Melayu Asli (35 per cent in Temuan; 19 per cent in Jakun). Temiar and western Semai Senoi frequencies are approximately 7 per cent. Semai east of the Main Range in Pahang state show a higher frequency (21 per cent). Genealogical data show that the descendents of migrants from Selangor (presumably Temuan) account for a large percentage of the SAO individuals in this regional subpopulation (Fix 1995). Recalling the three traditions of Orang Asli discussed above, it would seem that the trading arrangements with outsiders characteristic of the Melayu Asli pattern included some genetic material. This example further undermines the notion of Orang Asli populations as long-term genetic isolates.

There are currently no data available for the other non-recombining portion of the genome, the Y chromosome. Just as mtDNA provides a picture of maternal genetic transmission, Y chromosome genes track the paternal contribution. This lack is particularly unfortunate in that one component of a model to be presented below cannot be tested.

FARMING AND MIGRATION TO THE MALAYSIAN PENINSULA

The genetic evidence indicates that considerable gene flow into the Peninsula occurred over the many thousand years since initial colonization (Oppenheimer 2011). Some of this contact may have been due to interaction among populations employing the widespread pre-Neolithic Hoabinhian tool tradition (Bulbeck 2011). Archaeological sites referred to this tradition are found from Vietnam to Sumatra. Shared technology may imply intermarriage and genetic exchange across this broad belt of Southeast Asia. The molecular dates assigned to some mtDNA haplotypes are consistent with such a scenario (Oppenheimer 2011).

The introduction of agriculture to the Peninsula, however, had a major impact on both sociocultural and genetic formations. According to one view, the new technology was introduced by a wave of farmers migrating south from the centre of rice domestication in China and displacing the resident foraging populations (Bellwood 1993; Higham 2002). This "demic diffusion" model (Cavalli-Sforza, Menozzi and Piazza 1993) or in its more recent formulation, the farming/language dispersal hypothesis (Bellwood and Renfrew 2002), was initially applied to the diffusion of agriculture from the Near East across Europe (Ammerman and Cavalli-Sforza 1971) and later extended to numerous other regions of the world. The dynamic for the wave of expansion of farmers is the supposed rapid rate of population growth produced by the new technology; growth leads to excess numbers of farmers each generation who must move on in search of new land. In Asia, this process resulted in the replacement of foraging populations across the mainland. Foragers survived only in the Peninsula (including a few groups in Thailand in the Isthmus of Kra). On this view, then, Senoi are descendents of agricultural migrants and Semang are the survivors of the indigenous hunter-gatherers of Malaysia. In its original formulation (Menozzi et al. 1978), the rapid growth of farming populations overwhelm the gene pool of foragers. The Senoi, as a wave front of advancing farmers, should be representative of mainland Southeast Asian farming populations.

Based on the mtDNA evidence, the demic diffusion hypothesis does not fit the Malaysian case. All three Orang Asli groups show significant proportions of founding mtDNA haplogroups, although a higher proportion of these "relict" haplotypes are found in the Semang groups (Hill et al. 2006).

I have proposed an alternative model that takes into account agricultural migrants to the Peninsula but as a "trickle" rather than an overwhelming wave of advance (Fix 2011). The model makes use of Benjamin's (1985) "three traditions" formulation (see above, Evolution of Orang Asli Social Traditions). Rather than a replacement of foragers by farmers, through a process of competitive displacement, both lifeways persisted and intensified the core socio-cultural patterns that locked each into their respective traditions. Foragers became hyper mobile and adopted or intensified extreme exogamous marriage practices and widespread kin ties that differentiated them from sedentary farmers whose marriage practices were more consistent with settled life (the Senoi less so than the even more localized Melayu Asli).

A further factor distinguishing foragers and farmers is malaria. It seems likely that the first farmers in the Peninsula opened up forest for swidden fields and as a consequence provided habitat for mosquito malarial vectors (Fix 1995). Malaria then became an important selective agent in farmer populations, favouring any human gene that might confer protection including hemoglobin E, SAO, Glucose-6-phosphate dehydrogenase deficiency, and the thalassemia(s) (the first three of which are found in Orang Asli farming populations). Foragers, whose mobile lifestyle, lower population density, and uncut forest habitat all preclude significant malarial incidence, would not be expected to harbour these genes (unfortunately, there are very few data from Semang populations) (Fix 1995).

The "trickle effect" model of initial Peninsular Orang Asli farmer-forager genetic relations (Fix 2011) reflects neither long-term isolation nor overwhelming waves of farmer colonists. Rather the model depends on small scale movements of agricultural peoples from the north who would continue to maintain genetic contact (intermarriage, gene flow) with their source populations while beginning to receive a trickle of in-migrants from resident foragers. This model does not require the huge demographic disparity between farmers and foragers that drives the demic diffusion wave of expansion. First farmers may begin to increase in population density but not at a sufficient rate to fuel colonizing waves. Again, an initial trickle is more plausible.

The model simulates the evolutionary processes of colonization, gene flow and natural selection to replicate the genetic distributions of indigenous and immigrant mtDNA and the evolution of Hb*E in the Peninsular farmers (Fix 2011). Recall that modern Orang Asli populations possess a mixture of "ancient" and "intrusive" mtDNA haplotypes (see Figure 4.1). Semang tend to harbour more founder types, while the Senoi (at least the small sample) are evenly divided between founder and migrant types (Hill et al. 2006). One haplotype is particularly common in Senoi, Flala, and is the result of several mutational steps from the founder root haplogroups (Figure 4.1). This derived haplotype is common in Vietnam and may represent one of the introductions by intrusive farmers. Modern Senoi populations also live in very malarious habitats and show high frequencies of malarial selected alleles such as Hb*E.

The model assumes initial migrants were derived from established farming populations already possessing Hb*E and that they also possessed derived mtDNA haplotypes such as Flala. A numerical computer simulation (see Fix 2011 for details) showed that under reasonable assumptions only some 20 to 30 generations were sufficient to produce the mix of founder/migrant haplotypes observed

in modern Senoi and for Hb*E to reach equilibrium frequencies
($q_E = 0.3$).

Surely given the several genetic signatures of non-Peninsular
populations among the present-day Senoi and Melayu Asli, they can
hardly be considered relict populations isolated in the Malaysian
rainforest. The Semang, however, seem to possess fewer haplotypes
shared with non-Peninsular people. It may be that since many Semang
are also phenotypically "Negrito", it is easier to imagine them as a
geographically isolated relictual population. Their supposedly very
distinctive set of features (shared with Andaman Islanders and
some Philippine groups) once thought to characterize the founding
migrants, perhaps also contributes to this view (but see Fix [1995]
for a counter argument). Benjamin (2013) has pointed out that the
characteristics making up the "Negrito" phenotype vary greatly
among all three groups of Orang Asli. Skeletal evidence contradicts
the unchanging (unevolving) persistence of an ancient "Negrito" type.
Early archaeological populations of Southeast Asia are not "Negritos".
David Bulbeck (2011) has shown that mean stature in pre-Neolithic
skeletons was considerably greater than among either present-day
Semang or Senoi (both are quite short); stature reduction occurred
over a considerable time. Presumably this change was adaptive in the
Peninsular environment, and various selective mechanisms have been
proposed to account for it (Migliano, Vinicus and Lahr 2007; Perry
and Dominy 2008).

Why is it, then, that several current Semang populations possess
mainly "archaic" mtDNA haplotypes? Geoffrey Benjamin (2013) has
recently addressed the question of how the Peninsular "Negritos"
could have maintained their distinctiveness. He cites Kirk Endicott's
(1984) suggestion that socio-cultural factors are the determinants.
The complementary but opposed Semang/Senoi social traditions have
reduced intermarriage sufficiently to keep their respective gene pools
somewhat separate. Of particular interest to the "geographic relict
population" issue is Benjamin's (2013) linking of the distribution of
Semang populations with trans-Peninsular portage routes utilized in
the Indianized period (beginning around 2,000 years ago). During this
period at least, Semang would have been "foraging" on the economic
activities of state-level trade while at the same time holding to their

nomadic tradition. Thus the barrier to gene flow was social rather than geographic.

A further factor especially relevant to the mtDNA maternally inherited haplotypes is the possibility of a unidirectional flow of forager women into the farmer population. This pattern has been documented for farmer-forager marital relations in Africa (Wood et al. 2005). As implemented in the trickle effect simulation, initial farming populations in the Peninsula exchanged mates with the northern groups from which they came and accepted women from the resident foragers. Thus forager mtDNA haplotypes were incorporated into the farming population leading to the ratio of "relict"/intrusive haplotypes observed in the modern Senoi sample, but, without a corresponding flow of women from farmers to foragers, foragers maintained the original founder mtDNA haplotypes.

The forager to farmer vector of female marital migration may depend on the extreme mobility demanded by the Semang tradition. Some evidence for sedentary forager-farmer intermarriage comes from pre-historic Thailand (Higham and Thosarat 2012). They describe a coastal settlement, Khok Phanom Di, occupied by sedentary hunter-gatherers for a very long time. Apparently there is archaeological evidence for contact between inland farmers and coastal foragers at several sites. More specifically, there is stable isotope ($^{87}Sr/^{86}$) evidence from skeletons recovered from Khok Phanom Di for the migration of women to coastal communities from inland sites (Bentley et al. 2007). These authors suggest that women "may have introduced new agricultural (and potting) skills" (Bentley et al. 2007: 312) to the forager community.

Farmer-forager-trader relationships in Southeast Asian prehistory were undoubtedly complex and varied (Morrison and Junker 2002), and there exist few data on long-term patterns of marriage among and between foragers and farmers. The Malaysian Orang Asli population represented by the Semang tradition has apparently maintained an extreme mobile foraging lifeway, in contact with the other traditions (including various historical state-sponsored trading activities), but avoiding social and genetic assimilation. This is not to say that they are unchanged relicts of prehistory; as already noted, the founding colonists were not "Negrito" in skeletal phenotype, and several common mtDNA haplotypes (B for instance) are not root forms. Furthermore, the autosomal DNA indicates shared Southeast Asian ancestry for "Negritos" as well as other Orang Asli.

FURTHER CULTURAL DIFFERENTIATION OF THE ORANG ASLI

According to the Benjamin model, the initial splits defining the three traditions represented in Orang Asli societies involved sedentary versus mobile strategies (Senoi/Semang) and opportunities for trade with outsiders (Melayu Asli). However, throughout history, contacts with other peoples caused cultural change and accommodation among the various Orang Asli groups. As Benjamin pointed out (2002), the mobile forager lifestyle made Semang well suited for portering goods across the trans-peninsular trade routes. Similarly many attributes of Semang and Senoi society and culture seem almost preadaptations for resisting incorporation into larger state polities (Benjamin 2002). Even the most salient and defining feature of most Orang Asli cultures, their extreme non-violence (Dentan 1968), most likely was a response to Malay slave raiding (Endicott 1983). Robert Dentan's (1975) thought-provoking title ("If There Were No Malays, Who Would the Semai Be?") further emphasizes the role of cultural contact and contrast in defining group identity and ethnicity.

Thus the modern Orang Asli groups seem less geographical (or phylogenetic) relicts, isolated from contact with the outside world, than socially defined populations. Through history, three traditions (Semang, Senoi, Melayu) differentiated (Benjamin 1985), each a socio-cultural niche occupied by people engaged in a nexus of cultural and migrational interaction. These lifeways influenced population size and density and patterns of gene flow (Fix 1995) resulting in a complex mosaic of genetic variability in their modern representatives. The commitment of the Semang to an extremely mobile lifestyle limited population size, thereby promoting genetic drift, and perhaps reducing in-migration and gene flow into their population. Nonetheless, all Orang Asli populations show a mixture of "ancient" and derived haplotypes and genotypes testifying to a long history of biological evolution on the Peninsula.

REFERENCES

Ballinger, S.W. , T.G. Schurr, A. Torroni, Y.Y. Gan, J.A. Hodge, K. Hassan, K.-H. Chen and D.C. Wallace
  1992   Southeast Asian Mitochondrial DNA Analysis Reveals Genetic Continuity of Ancient Mongoloid Migrations. Genetics 130: 139–52.

Bellwood, P.
  1993   Cultural and Biological Differentiation in Peninsular Malaysia: The Last 10,000 Years. Asian Perspectives 32: 37–60.

Bellwood, P. and C. Renfrew, eds.
  2002   Examining the Farming/Language Dispersal Hypothesis. Cambridge: McDonald Institute.

Benjamin, G.
  1976   Austroasiatic Subgroupings and Prehistory in the Malay Peninsula. *In* Austroasiatic Studies, Part 1. P.N. Jenner, L. Thompson and S. Starosta, eds. Pp. 37–128. Honolulu: University Press of Hawaii.

  1985   In the Long Term: Three Themes in Malayan Cultural Ecology. *In* Cultural Values and Human Ecology in Southeast Asia. K.L. Hutterer, A.T. Rambo and G. Lovelace, eds. Pp. 219–78. Ann Arbor, MI: Center for South and Southeast Asian Studies, University of Michigan Press.

  2002   On Being Tribal in the Malay World. *In* Tribal Communities in the Malay World: Historical, Cultural and Social Perspectives. G. Benjamin and C. Chou, eds. Pp. 7–76. Leiden: International Institute for Asian Studies and Singapore: Institute of Southeast Asian Studies.

  2013   Why Have the Peninsular "Negritos" Remained Distinct. Human Biology 85(1–3): 445–84.

Bentley, R.A., N. Tayles, C. Higham, C. Macpherson and T.C. Atkinson
  2007   Shifting Gender Relations at Khok Phanom Di, Thailand: Isotopic Evidence from the Skeletons. Current Anthropology 48: 301–14.

Bulbeck, D.
  2011   Biological and Cultural Evolution in the Population and Culture History of *Homo sapiens* in Malaya. *In* Dynamics of Human Diversity: The Case of Mainland Southeast Asia. N.J. Enfield, ed. Pp. 207–55. Canberra: Pacific Linguistics.

Burenhult, N., N. Kruspe and M. Dunn
    2011   Language History and Culture Groups among Austroasiatic-Speaking Foragers of the Malay Peninsula. *In* Dynamics of Human Diversity: The Case of Mainland Southeast Asia. N.J. Enfield, ed. Pp. 257–75. Canberra: Pacific Linguistics.

Carey, I.
    1976   Orang Asli: The Aboriginal Tribes of Peninsular Malaysia. Kuala Lumpur: Oxford University Press.

Cavalli-Sforza, L.L., P. Menozzi and A. Piazza
    1993   Demic expansions and human evolution. Science 259: 639–46.
    1994   The History and Geography of Human Genes. Princeton, NJ: Princeton University Press.

Darlington, P.J.
    1957   Zoogeography: The Geographical Distribution of Animals. New York: John Wiley.

Dentan, R.K.
    1968   The Semai: A Nonviolent People of Malaya. New York: Holt Rinehart and Winston.
    1975   If There Were No Malays, Who Would the Semai Be? Contributions to Asian Studies 7: 50–64.

Diffloth, G.
    1979   Aslian Languages and Southeast Asian Prehistory. Federated Museums Journal 24: 3–16.

Endicott, K.
    1983   The Effects of Slave Raiding on the Aborigines of the Malay Peninsula. *In* Slavery, Bondage and Dependency in Southeast Asia. A. Reid, ed. Pp. 216–45. St Lucia: University of Queensland Press.
    1984   The Association of "Negritos" and Foraging in the Malay Peninsula. Paper presented to the Conference on Ethnicity and the Control of Natural Resources, Ann Arbor, MI, 22–24 August 1984.

Fix, A.G.
    1995   Malayan Paleosociology: Implications for Patterns of Genetic Variation among the Orang Asli. American Anthropologist 97: 313–23.
    2000   Genes, Language, and Ethnic Groups: Reconstructing Orang Asli Prehistory. Indo-Pacific Prehistory Association Bulletin 19, Melaka Papers 3: 11–6.

2008   Genetic Dendrograms and Malaysian Population History. Structure and Dynamics, eJournal of Anthropology and Related Sciences 3(2): article 7. http://repositories.cfdlib.org/imbs/socdyn/sdeas/vol3/iss2/art7

2011   Origin of Genetic Diversity among Malaysian Orang Asli: An Alternative to the Demic Diffusion Model. *In* Dynamics of Human Diversity: The Case of Mainland Southeast Asia. N.J. Enfield, ed. Pp. 277–91. Canberra: Pacific Linguistics.

Higham, C.
2002   Languages and Farming Dispersals: Austroasiatic Languages and Rice Cultivation. *In* Examining the Farming/Language Dispersal Hypothesis. P. Bellwood and C. Renfrew, eds. Pp. 223–32. Cambridge: McDonald Institute.

Higham, C. and R. Thosarat
2012   Early Thailand: From Prehistory to Sukhothai. Bangkok: River Books.

Hill, C., P. Soares, M. Mormina, V. Macaulay, W. Meehan, J. Blackburn, D. Clarke, J.M. Raja, P. Ismail, D. Bulbeck, S. Oppenheimer and M. Richards
2006   Phylogeography and Ethnogenesis of Aboriginal Southeast Asians. Molecular Biology and Evolution 23: 2480–91.

HUGO Pan-Asian SNP Consortium
2009   Mapping Human Genetic Diversity in Asia. Science 326: 1541–5.

Jinam, T.A., L.-C. Hong, M.E. Phipps, M. Stoneking, Mahmood Ameen, Juli Edo, HUGO Pan-Asian SNP Consortium and N. Saitou
2012   Evolutionary History of Continental Southeast Asians: "Early Train" Hypothesis Based on Genetic Analysis of Mitochondrial and Autosomal DNA Data. Molecular Biology and Evolution 29: 3513–27.

Kidson, C., G. Lamont, A. Saul and G.T. Nurse
1981   Ovalocytic Erythrocytes from Melanesians are Resistant to Invasion by Malaria Parasites in Culture. Proceedings of the National Academy of Sciences 78: 5829–32.

King, M.C. and A.C. Wilson
1975   Evolution at Two Levels in Humans and Chimpanzees. Science 188: 107–16.

Livingstone, F.B.
1985   Frequencies of Hemoglobin Variants: Thalassemia, the Glucose-6-Phosphate Dehydrogenase Deficiency, G6PD Variants, and Ovalocytosis in Human Populations. New York: Oxford University Press.

Macaulay, V., C. Hill, A. Achilli, C. Rengo, D. Clarke, W. Meehan, J. Blackburn, O. Semino, R. Scozzari, F. Cruciani, Adi Taha, Norazila Kassim Shaari, J.M. Raja, P. Ismail, Zafarina Zainuddin, W. Goodwin, D. Bulbeck, H.-J. Bandelt, S. Oppenheimer, A. Torroni and M. Richards
  2005 Single, Rapid Coastal Settlement of Asia Revealed by Analysis of Complete Mitochondrial Genomes. Science 308: 1034–6.

Metspalu, M., T. Kivisild, H.-J. Bandelt, M. Richards and R. Villems
  2006 The Pioneer Settlement of Modern Humans in Asia. *In* Human Mitochondrial DNA and the Evolution of Homo Sapiens. H.-J. Bandelt, V. Macaulay and M. Richards, eds. Pp. 181–99. Berlin Heidelberg: Springer-Verlag.

Migliano, A.B., L. Vinicius and M. Mirazon Lahr
  2007 Life History Trade-offs Explain the Evolution of Human Pygmies. Proceedings of the National Academy of Sciences 104: 20216–19.

Morrison, K.D. and L.L. Junker, eds.
  2002 Forager-Traders in South and Southeast Asia. Cambridge: Cambridge University Press.

Oppenheimer, S.
  2011 MtDNA Variation and Southward Holocene Human Dispersals within Mainland Southeast Asia. *In* Dynamics of Human Diversity: The Case of Mainland Southeast Asia. N.J. Enfield, ed. Pp. 81–108. Canberra: Pacific Linguistics.

Perry, G.H. and N.J. Dominy
  2009 Evolution of the Human Pygmy Phenotype. Trends in Ecology and Evolution 24: 218–25.

Reich, D., N. Patterson, M. Kircher, F. Delfin, M.R. Nandineni, I. Pugach, A. Min-Shan Ko, Ying-Chin Ko, T.A. Jinam, M.E. Phipps, N.Saitou, A. Wollstein, M. Kayser, S. Paabo and M. Stoneking
  2011 Denisova Admixture and the First Modern Human Dispersals into Southeast Asia and Oceania. American Journal of Human Genetics 89: 516–28.

Ricaut, F.-X., M. Bellatti and M. Mirazon Lahr
  2006 Ancient Mitochondrial DNA from Malaysian Hair Samples: Some Indications of Southeast Asian Population Movements. American Journal of Human Biology 18: 654–67.

Saha, N., J.W. Mak, J.S.H. Tay, Y. Liu, J.A.M.A. Tan, P.S. Low and M. Singh
  1995 Population Genetic Studies among the Orang Asli (Semai Senoi) of Malaysia. Human Biology 67: 37–57.

Skeat, W.W. and C.O. Blagden
  1906   The Pagan Races of the Malay Peninsula. Two vol. London: Macmillan.
Stoneking, M. and F. Delfin
  2010   The Human Genetic History of East Asia: Weaving a Complex Tapestry. Current Biology 20: R188–93.
Wood, E.T., D.A. Stover, C. Ehret, G. Destro-Bisol, G. Spedini, H. McLeod, L. Louie, M. Bamshad, B.I. Strassmann, H. Soodyall and M.F. Hammer
  2005   Contrasting Patterns of Y Chromosome and mtDNA Variation in Africa: Evidence for Sex-Biased Demographic Processes. European Journal of Human Genetics 13: 867–76.

5

The Neolithic Gap in the Southern Thai-Malay Peninsula and Its Implications for Orang Asli Prehistory

David Bulbeck

INTRODUCTION

In his excavation report on the Gua Cha rockshelter, Sieveking (1954) described a sterile layer or "gap" separating the pre-Neolithic and Neolithic occupation layers. The implied abandonment of the site prior to the rise of farming could conceivably suggest a more general depopulation event. Bellwood (1997) pointed out that the re-excavation of the site by Adi (1985) cast doubt on the reality of this intervening sterile layer, and the recovered remains suggest population continuity in the face of rapid cultural change. Subsequently, Kealhofer (2003) misinterpreted the "gap" concept as supposedly marking a millennium-long hiatus in site occupation between the pre-Neolithic and Neolithic archaeological sequences throughout the Malay Peninsula, and also incorrectly attributed the concept to Bellwood (Bellwood 2005). In fact, there is something of a gap in the Peninsula's documented occupation sequence, but it actually separates the early and the late Neolithic. Further, the Neolithic record as a whole is consistent with Kealhofer's (2003) analysis of her phytolith data.

The basis for recognizing a Neolithic gap is a summation of the probabilities of site occupation during the Holocene, reaching back to 10,000 bp (before the present, 1950 CE). The geographic coverage of the dated sites is the southern Thai-Malay Peninsula from the Isthmus of Kra southwards (Map 5.1), or STMP for short.

This study area extends farther north than the Thailand/Malaysia border, which is generally used as the northern limit for studies that relate the archaeological record to Orang Asli ethnogenesis (for example, Benjamin 1987). However, two Orang Asli groups, the Ten'en and Tea-de, reside north of the border (Burenhult et al. 2011). Also, the Melayu Malays are the numerically dominant ethnic group in southernmost Thailand as well as Peninsular Malaysia, and their colonization of the Peninsula is closely intertwined with the fortunes of the Orang Asli in historical times (Benjamin 2002).

The Neolithic is correctly defined as the period when pottery and polished stone artefacts formed a component of the local material culture, prior to the availability of metals (Spriggs 2003). This definition allows independent investigation of when agricultural activities might have commenced in STMP, in contrast to the tendency of some scholars (for example, Higham 2013) to define the Neolithic as the period when they think farming entered a region. Bronze and iron metallurgy at the fortified site of Khao Sam Kaeo (Bellina-Pryce and Silapanth 2006; Murillo-Barraso et al. 2010) establishes 2500 bp as the transitional date from the Neolithic to the Early Metal Phase (EMP). Also, the term "protohistoric" is used here to cover the period circa 2000–1000 bp, for which there are sparse external written references to STMP as well as a small corpus of local inscriptions (Jacq-Hergoualc'h 2002). The better documented period from circa 1000 bp will be glossed as "historical".

As a final introductory point, the dates cited in this contribution are expressed in terms of their 95 per cent confidence interval bp. In the case of Carbon-14 dates, this is after calibration with the Oxcal programme for Intcal 09 (Bronk Ramsey 2013). The original dates and sources are presented in Bulbeck (2014).

Map 5.1 Southern Thai-Malay Peninsula: Aslian languages and sites mentioned in the text

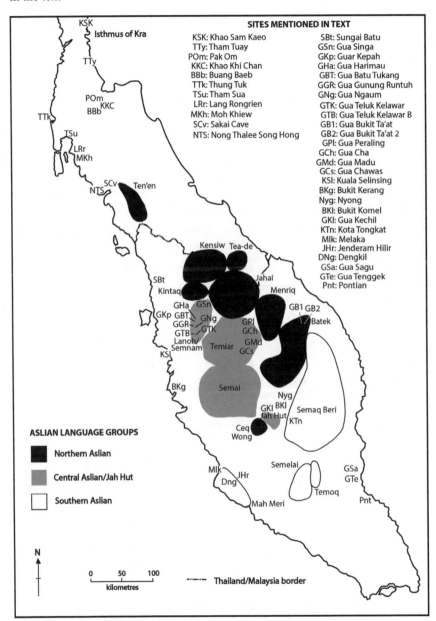

SITES MENTIONED IN TEXT

KSK: Khao Sam Kaeo
TTy: Tham Tuay
POm: Pak Om
KKC: Khao Khi Chan
BBb: Buang Baeb
TTk: Thung Tuk
TSu: Tham Sua
LRr: Lang Rongrien
MKh: Moh Khiew
SCv: Sakai Cave
NTS: Nong Thalee Song Hong

SBt: Sungai Batu
GSn: Gua Singa
GKp: Guar Kepah
GHa: Gua Harimau
GBT: Gua Batu Tukang
GGR: Gua Gunung Runtuh
GNg: Gua Ngaum
GTK: Gua Teluk Kelawar
GTB: Gua Teluk Kelawar B
GB1: Gua Bukit Ta'at
GB2: Gua Bukit Ta'at 2
GPl: Gua Peraling
GCh: Gua Cha
GMd: Gua Madu
GCs: Gua Chawas
KSl: Kuala Selinsing
BKg: Bukit Kerang
Nyg: Nyong
BKl: Bukit Komel
GKl: Gua Kechil
KTn: Kota Tongkat
Mlk: Melaka
JHr: Jenderam Hilir
DNg: Dengkil
GSa: Gua Sagu
GTe: Gua Tenggek
Pnt: Pontian

ASLIAN LANGUAGE GROUPS

Northern Aslian

Central Aslian/Jah Hut

Southern Aslian

N

0   50   100
kilometres

------- Thailand/Malaysia border

HOLOCENE SITE OCCUPANCY

In the methodology detailed by Bulbeck (2014), site occupancy during the Holocene is monitored by estimating the number of sites dated chronometrically for each of the 500-year intervals between the Pleistocene-Holocene junction (10,000 bp) and 1950 CE. Both Carbon-14 dates that can be calibrated and luminescence dates are included in the calculations. Please note that most Carbon-14 dates are published as radiocarbon years BP (before the present) but cited as calendar years bp (before the present) after calibration. To avoid confusion, "bp" is used throughout this chapter when referring to calendar years before 1950.

Sites can be categorized according to their "aspect" (general form) at the time referred to by the date. My recognized categories listed in Table 5.1 are in order of precedence; for instance, the Thung Tuk fortifications (Pailoplee et al. 2003) are classified as "Monumental" rather than "Maritime" despite their location on an offshore island. With the open-air categories, these can change over time. For instance, Khao Sam Kaeo was fortified (Monumental) during the 2500–2000 bp interval (Bellina-Pryce and Silapanth 2006) but at other times would be classified just as "Open". Site aspect is crucial for understanding changes over time in STMP's chronometric documentation, and so the charts showing the estimated numbers of sites per 500-year interval are assigned to bars according to their site-aspect composition.

Table 5.1 Site aspects recognized by Bulbeck, 2014

Aspect	Examples
Closed	Any cave or rockshelter deposit, rock art or archaeological object
Monumental	Open-air fortifications and megalithic cists
Maritime	Open-air estuarine sites and offshore islands; shipwrecks (none chronometrically dated for STMP)
Marine midden	Open-air middens built up from marine shell
Freshwater midden	Open-air middens built up from freshwater shell (none for STMP)
Open	Open-air sites not covered above

How this works can be shown with a pan-Holocene presentation of the estimated number of occupied sites per 500-year interval (Figure 5.1).

Figure 5.1 Estimated number of Holocene STMP sites occupied by 500-year interval

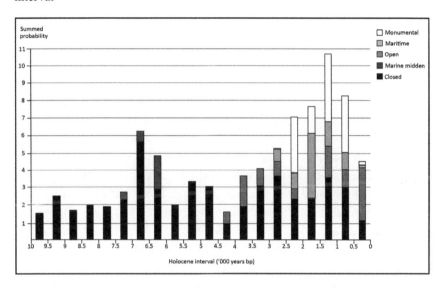

The results suggest an early period with between two and six documented sites (in round terms) in each 500-year interval between 10,000 and 4000 bp, and a late period of heightened site occupancy levels, peaking at over ten sites at 1500–1000 bp. There is a decline in chronometric documentation after 1000 bp, but this is because scholars can use the abundant chronological documentation (including local oral history) available for most sites during historical times, as well as the availability of tightly dated, mass-produced artefact types that provide a chronological anchor without the need to obtain a chronometric determination (for instance, Bulbeck 2003).

Documented occupation of closed sites (for example, rockshelters) fluctuates between approximately one and five sites per 500-year interval throughout the Holocene. Closed sites attract prehistorians because of their relative permanency in the landscape, but evidence for their occupation is susceptible to "taphonomic" loss (disintegration of material) with time (for instance, Williams 2011). This is particularly due to the degradation of charcoal and other plant matter beyond the stage where it can be used for dating (for instance, Adi 2000). This taphonomic effect would not however explain the low point in documented occupancy at 4500–4000 bp compared to earlier times. Accordingly, we may tentatively hypothesize that this interval was marked by a real decline or "gap" in the occupancy level of closed sites.

In addition to early (pre-4500 bp) occupation of closed sites, early habitation is documented by three inland, marine shell middens. Their dates after calibration (marine shell dates, corrected with Singapore's delta-R correction factor), 6669–7233 bp for Tham Sua, 6250–6523 bp for Bukit Kerang and 5935–6242 bp for Guar Kepah, relate to a time of high sea levels along the Peninsula at around 6500 bp. The shell contents cemented these middens into durable sites even after the coastline had retreated with the decline in sea level. The accumulation of these large middens at three separate locations, as well as on Sumatra's northeastern coast across the Melaka Strait, reflect the abundance of littoral resources associated with shallow flooding of the coastal plain (Bulbeck 2003). Marine shell middens would also have been created by coastal inhabitants at later times, but they were probably smaller and also susceptible to degradation and/or burial through the build-up of sediment along the coastal plain. An example of the latter is the *pulau kulit kerang* (marine shell islands) that make up the maritime site of Kuala Selinsing, dating to around 2000–1000 bp, which was covered by alluvial discharge from the Selinsing River (Nik Hassan 1991). Other early open-air sites in STMP have been discovered either through deep soundings into the coastal deposit that has preserved them (for example, Jenderam Hilir, Leong 1991) or, in the case of the Neolithic burial from Khao Sam Kaeo (Bellina-Pryce and Silapanth 2006), during the course of wide-scale excavation of this major site. We can be certain that the population was widely distributed across the landscape throughout the Holocene, but the archaeological record of their open-air activities before circa 4000 bp is not currently available (Bulbeck 2014), apart from the special case of a few marine shell hillocks dating to around 6500 bp.

After 2500 bp, contemporary with the start of the Early Metal Phase (EMP), there was a steady increase in the number and variety of chronometrically documented open-air sites, up to historical times beginning around 1000 bp (Figure 5.1).

A deeper understanding of the STMP chronometric record can be obtained by investigating changes to site usage over time. In this analysis, a multi-component site can be counted for each of its concurrent usages if they overlapped on the same 500-year interval. A relevant example is Gua Cha, part of which was evidently reserved for a Neolithic cemetery (Sieveking 1954), with one burial directly dated to 2366–2952 bp (Bulbeck 2014), and another part of which hosted intensive Neolithic habitation (Adi 1985), dated to 2494–3905 bp. My site usage categories and their order of precedence is presented in Table 5.2.

Table 5.2 Site usage categories recognized by Bulbeck, 2014

Usage category	Examples
Mortuary	Documented human burials and other ritual disposal of the remains of the deceased
Ceremonial	Ritual objects, buildings and activities other than the documented disposal of the remains of the deceased
Industrial	Specialist craft working including lapidary work and metallurgy
Transport	Boat remains; brick jetty at Sungai Batu
Gardening	Forest clearance in preparation for planting
Habitation	Any evidence of site occupancy not assignable to an above category

Habitation is the most strongly represented site usage category, and its chronometric profile (Bulbeck 2014) broadly resembles Figure 5.1. The second oldest, documented activity is the Mortuary category, presented at Figure 3.

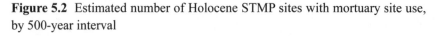

Figure 5.2 Estimated number of Holocene STMP sites with mortuary site use, by 500-year interval

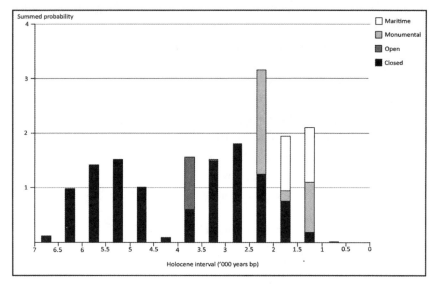

It shows that directly dated mortuary interments in STMP closed sites are essentially restricted to the 6500–4500 bp and 4000–1500 bp periods. The reappearance of the 4500–4000 bp gap is intriguing, and may reflect a transitional phase between the earlier burials with a limited number of burial goods and the later burials furnished with a wide array of Neolithic and EMP items (Bulbeck 2011). Of particular significance is the change in the use of closed sites at around 6500 bp to reserve a portion of them for use as cemeteries. This may reflect a combination of increased population size and the relocation of the main foci of habitation to open-air settings, allowing closed sites to be used for activities other than habitation. (Also, as noted for sites in general, open-air mortuary sites date back only to the fourth millennium bp, and are most numerous and abundant during the 2500–1000 bp period.)

The other four site-usage categories are chronometrically documented only for the last 3000 years bp (Bulbeck 2014), especially the gardening category (Figure 5.3).

Figure 5.3 Estimated number of Holocene STMP sites with gardening site use, by 500-year interval

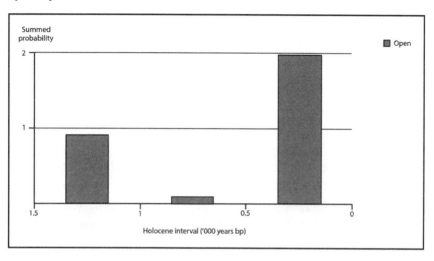

Plate 5.1 Archaeological excavation at Pulau Kelumpang, Perak, Malaysia

(Photo credit: David Bulbeck)

While the main conclusion to be drawn here is the underdeveloped state of research into the antiquity of gardening activities in STMP, the documented onset date of 1500 bp for gardening sites is consistent with the late dating available for crop remains. Pulau Kelumpang (Kuala Selinsing), whose central occupation period spans the second millennium bp, includes abundant rice remains in its anaerobic sediments, along with betel-nuts, coconuts and bottle gourds (Nik Hassan 1991). The Pontian boat, which contained rice on board (Evans 1927), is dated to 1411–1701 bp, and the rice remains from Gua Cha are dated to 678–1053 bp. Rice remains are also reported from Sakai Cave, but the reliability of their stratigraphic context is challenged by the very early dates of 8049–8972 and 8183–9441 bp for this level. The excavator suggests a mid-Holocene antiquity (Pookajorn 1996) but this will remain in the realm of speculation until the rice is directly dated.

The STMP dates can also be analyzed in terms of the category of material that provided the date. Again, the maximum contribution any site can provide to the count is 1 per 500-year interval per category, although the same site can be represented in multiple, contemporary categories if a variety of dating materials was employed. My material categories and their order of precedence are detailed by Bulbeck (2014).

The category of main importance here is "ceramic". In STMP's case, this category includes dates on charcoal extracted from ceramic objects and luminescence dates on pottery and bricks. The available dates demonstrate the presence of pottery in STMP by 3500 bp, but also suggest a particular importance of ceramic material culture during the 2000–500 bp period (Figure 5.4).

On current documentation, the presence of ceramics at other times would need to be assessed on grounds other than direct dates from ceramic objects. For instance, although Figure 5.4 may be used to argue that the oldest clear evidence for pottery in STMP dates to no earlier than 4000–3500 bp, reliance on direct dates would imply that ceramics mysteriously dropped out of the material culture during the third millennium bp.

Figure 5.4 Estimated number of Holocene STMP sites with ceramic dates, by 500-year interval

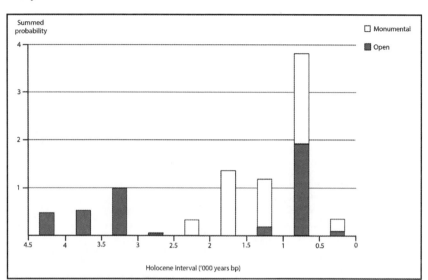

HOABINHIAN AND NEOLITHIC ANTIQUITY AND OVERLAP

The archaeological assemblages associated with the STMP inhabitants at the time of entry of the Neolithic are conventionally assigned to the "Hoabinhian". This is an umbrella term used for Southeast Asian lithic assemblages based on river cobbles flaked centripetally from their edges inwards, rather than creating "cores" with a distinct striking platform for the removal of flakes (Bulbeck 2003, 2011). STMP assemblages that post date 18,000 bp, the time of the Late Glacial Maximum (LGM), demonstrate a focus on flaked river cobbles, as can be shown by summarizing those assemblages that have been quantitatively described.

Before summarizing these assemblages, we should extend our chronometric coverage by including dates obtained on freshwater shellfish from STMP limestone rockshelters. While these dates cannot be calibrated, they can be assigned to broad intervals (Bulbeck 2014), allowing us to include site-habitation phases dated only by freshwater shellfish dates (column 3 in Table 5.3).

Table 5.3 Expanded coverage of the occupation of STMP Holocene closed sites

Period	Additional closed sites	Number of additional sites	Number of sites including Figure 5.1 sites
10–9000 bp	GGR, GCs, GPl, GTK, POm, GTB, GSn	7	9
9–8000 bp	GGR, GTK, GSn, GBT, GB1	5	7
8–7000 bp	GGR, GTK, GBT	3	5
7000–6500 bp	GTK, GB2, BBb, POm	4	10
6500–6000 bp	GTK, GBT, GNg	3	6
6000–5500 bp	BBb	1	3
5500–5000 bp	GB2	1	4
5000–4500 bp	GHa, POm, BBb	3	6
4500–4000 bp	–	0	1
4–3000 bp	GCs	1	4
3–2000 bp	GB1	1	4
2–1000 bp	–	0	3
1000–0 bp	–	0	3

Notes: Additional sites assigned to a period based on their freshwater shell BP dates (Bulbeck 2014). GGR = Gua Gunung Runtuh, GCs = Gua Chawas, GPl = Gua Peraling, GTK = Gua Teluk Kelawar, POm = Pak Om, GTB = Gua Teluk Kelawar B, GSn = Gua Singa, GBT = Gua Batu Tukang, GB1 = Gua Bukit Taat, GB2 = Gua Bukit Taat 2, BBb = Buang Baeb, GNg = Gua Ngaum, GHa = Gua Harimau.

Without interpreting the site numbers in the last column of Table 5.3 too literally, we can note a pattern of closed-site occupancy implied by the available data. Documented occupancy numbers peaked in the initial Holocene (10,000–9000 bp) before dropping in the early Holocene and later peaking again at 7000–6500 bp. Accordingly, the changes in site numbers might reflect initial dislocation of the inhabitants as sea levels rose, the landscape shifted from continental to peninsular (see Soares et al. 2008) and a mosaic vegetation of savannah and forest gave way to continuous rain forest cover (Kealhofer 2003), before the inhabitants successfully adapted to the changed conditions at 7000–6500 bp. After 6500 bp, documented occupation numbers at any time decreased to six sites or less, including the 4500–4000 bp gap (whose status as a distinct gap is even more pronounced after allowing for the inclusion of freshwater shellfish dates).

The statistical characteristics of dated Hoabinhian lithic assemblages (excluding hammers, anvils and utilized pebbles, whose statistics are presented by Bulbeck 2003) are presented at Table 5.4. Centripetally flaked river cobbles outnumber prepared cores wherever either is present, while flakes from the cobbles and cores account for the majority of the lithics. The unusually high proportion of flake tools compared to waste flakes at Moh Khiew evidently reflects Pookajorn's (1994) penchant to classify flakes as tools; most of the assemblage excavated from a separate test pit at Moh Khiew was classified as unutilized flakes (84 per cent), with only 6 per cent classified as utilized flakes (Chitkament 2006/07). After allowing for Pookajorn's classificatory idiosyncrasy, we can appreciate that there appears to have been little change in the basic characteristics of Hoabinhian assemblages from the terminal Pleistocene through to the late Holocene.

Table 5.4 also summarizes current evidence for the incorporation of Neolithic items in rockshelter assemblages. The scanty evidence of Neolithic items at Lang Rongrien as early as the Pleistocene-Holocene junction (circa 10,000 bp) looks too early as it is not corroborated by any other assemblage. However, the presence of Neolithic items by 7000 bp or soon after is difficult to doubt based on the evidence from Moh Khiew units 4–5, as well as the 86 potsherds from Gua Batu Tukang, from the same spits as the stone artefacts, associated with freshwater shellfish dates between 6000 and 9000 BP (Hassan 1998) and an overlying charcoal date of 3735–4089 bp. The apparent absence of Neolithic material culture from Gua Cha before the fourth millennium bp (Adi 1985), and the apparent disjunction between Hoabinhian and Neolithic levels at the undated site of Kota Tongkat (Bellwood 1997), appear to be the exceptions rather than the rule.

Table 5.4 Composition of STMP flaked stone assemblages (per cent)

Assemblage	Approximate age	Artefact number	UFC	BFC	Cores	FT	WF	Neolithic items
Gua Sagu spits 7–13	16,000 bp to mid-Holocene	30	10.0	20.0	0.0	0.0	70.0	Absent
Moh Khiew units 2–3	13–11,000 bp	12,441	1.1		0.0	68.1	30.8	Absent
Lang Rongrien units 5–6	12,000–8000 bp	182	8.8	1.6	3.8	14.3	67.6	Potsherd, 2 polished stone flakes
Gua Gunung Runtuh	12,000–7000 bp	397	20.4	6.3	1.6	1.4	55.4	Absent
Gua Teluk Kelawar	12,000–6000 bp	1465	5.9	2.3	0.3	2.5	88.9	Absent
Gua Tenggek	12,000 bp to mid Holocene	117	5.1	9.4	0.0	0.0	85.5	Absent
Gua Teluk Kelawar B	10,000–9000 bp	71	0.0	0.0	0.0	7.0	93.0	Absent
Gua Batu Tukang	9–4000 bp	86	3.5	1.2	0.0	5.8	89.5	Pottery
Gua Ngaum	7–6000 bp	91	8.8	4.4	0.0	19.8	67.0	Absent
Moh Khiew units 4–5	7–5000 bp	5920	0.4		0.0	57.6	42.0	Pottery, polished axes
Gua Cha Layers 3–4	7–4000 bp	544	4.4	8.1	5.5	3.7	78.3	Absent
Gua Kechil 14–34" deep	Mid to late Holocene	62	3.2	4.8	0.0	17.7	74.2	Pottery
Gua Sagu spits 1–6	Mid Holocene to 1000 bp	121	15.7	14.0	0.0	2.5	67.8	Pottery, mortars

Notes: Data from Bulbeck (2003), with the amendments that the Moh Khiew "cores" quantified by Pookajorn (1994) are predominantly flaked river cobbles (Chitkament 2006/07), and that the Gua Batu Tukang assemblage is associated with pottery (Hassan 1998). Approximate age based on the dates in Bulbeck (2014). UFC = unifacially flaked cobbles, BFC = bifacially flaked cobbles, FT = "flake tools" (retouched and utilized flakes), WF = "waste flakes" (flakes without recorded signs of retouch or utilization).

Dated evidence from other STMP sites also points to the onset of the Neolithic by 6500 bp. Pottery occurred at all levels in the Tham Sua shell midden above its basal, 6669–7233 bp date cited above (Anderson 2005). The Guar Kepah shell middens (now dated to 5935–6242 bp) contained pottery at all its levels and also yielded waisted ground adzes (Matthews 1961; Mok 2013). Khao Khi Chan, whose central period of use is dated to 5500–6500 bp, contained ground stone tools, while Buang Baeb contained polished stone adzes and tripod pots associated with freshwater shell dates between 7000 and 5000 bp and calibrated bone dates of around 5000 bp (see Srisuchat 1993). Finally, cultural phase 4 at Gua Peraling produced a polished stone adze and bases to complete pots, dated to 6005–7153 bp (Adi 2000). Gua Peraling is also of interest here for its very scanty pottery contents in its later levels (cultural phases 1–3). This indicates that the general availability of Neolithic material culture need not be reflected by the inclusion of Neolithic items in every rockshelter deposit.

Bellwood (1993, 1997) has argued that the "Ban Kao culture", named after the site of Ban Kao in mainland Thailand, was the source for the oldest Neolithic materials to reach Peninsular Malaysia at around 4000 bp. While there certainly are similarities between the burial goods at Ban Kao and at late Neolithic STMP burial grounds such as Gua Cha, these similarities appear to represent parallel inheritances from a pre-Ban Kao Neolithic tradition in Southeast Asia (Bulbeck 2011). As shown in Table 5.5, three of the supposed markers of the Ban Kao culture were present in STMP much earlier than at Ban Kao, and one putative marker is disputable in that the barkcloth beaters are ceramic at Ban Kao but made of stone in STMP.

ANTIQUITY OF HORTICULTURE IN STMP

A long history of plant exploitation is indicated by Bowdery's (1999) identification of the phytoliths (plant cell silica skeletons) at Gua Chawas, a site inhabited from around 12,000 bp onwards (Bulbeck 2014). Banana phytoliths were present throughout the sequence, while phytoliths from bamboo, and two tree species respectively useful for thatch and poison extraction, were identified at most levels. Bowdery

Table 5.5 Archaeological evidence contradicting the notion of a circa 4000 bp movement of the Ban Kao culture from mainland Thailand to the Peninsula

Putative Ban Kao culture marker	Approximate earliest documented presence in Southeast Asia	Approximate earliest documented presence in STMP	Representation at Ban Kao
Cord-marked pottery	8000 bp (Bacsonian)	6500 bp (Moh Khiew)	From 4000 bp
Tripod pots	5500 bp (Buang Baeb)	5500 bp (Buang Baeb)	Post 4000 bp
Pedestalled pots	5000 bp (Ha Giang)	3500 bp (Lang Rongrien)	Post 4000 bp
Polished axes	6500 bp (late Da But)	6500 bp (Moh Khiew)	From 4000 bp
Extended burials*	5000 bp (Ban Chiang)	3500 bp (Lang Rongrien)	Post 4000 bp
Stone barkcloth beaters	5000 bp (Ha Giang)	3000 bp (Gua Cha, maybe earlier at Gua Madu)	Ceramic rather than stone

Notes: Adapted from Bulbeck (2011), including calibration of the BP dates provided there, along with dating of the Lang Rongrien Neolithic burials (Bulbeck 2014). *Auetrakulvit et al. (2012) claim the presence of extended burials at Moh Khiew dated to the Pleistocene-Holocene junction, but this would need to be confirmed through direct dating of the remains.

(1999) does not comment on whether any of the banana phytoliths could represent one of the domesticated varieties that are believed to have originated in the New Guinea region during the early Holocene (Denham 2011), rather than a local wild species. Evidence for forest clearance, in the form of grass phytoliths, was recorded at the Pleistocene-Holocene junction (10,000 bp), but their number decreased later in the Holocene, including the Neolithic transition (about 7000 bp), before increasing after circa 2000 bp. The uppermost analyzed sample reflected intensified forest clearance, an increase in palm exploitation (Bowdery 1999) and the only evidence for rice and cane sugar phytoliths (Adi 2000). The two Orang Asli groups potentially associated with use of the rockshelter at this time are Semang foragers, who probably created the charcoal drawings on the site's walls, and the horticulturalist Temiar Senoi, who live in a village near the site. In either case, evidence for local horticulture would date to only the last millennium, even though the phytolith sequence indicates a human impact on the vegetation throughout the Holocene.

Of particular interest are the pollen and phytolith records extracted from the Nong Thalee Song Hong swamp in the southern Thailand lowlands (Map 5.1). Forested conditions in the swamp's catchment area are indicated throughout, with evidence for human impact most pronounced during the period of rising sea levels leading up to 7000 bp (Table 5.6). The STMP early Neolithic, now dated to around 7000–4500 bp, was associated with the strongest evidence for the betel-nut palm, possible coconut palm and domesticated rice, and the only banana in the sequence. The presence of banana and introduced rice phytoliths at just this level suggests these were domesticated varieties. Alternatively, minor crops are indicated by the pollen record after 4500 bp, but rice no longer appears amongst the cultigens.

Evidence for the use of domesticated plants also comes from the dental remains of Peninsular Malaysian prehistoric burials. The majority of the recorded teeth from the burials in the Guar Kepah shell middens bear traces of betel-nut staining, which suggests cultivation of the *Areca* palm for the use of its nuts as a mild stimulant. In addition, the teeth exhibit relatively little tooth wear,

Table 5.6 Summary of the Nong Thalee Song Hong vegetation sequence

Period	Disturbance/ forest burning	*Areca* pollen and/or phytoliths	Probable coconut phytoliths	Banana phytoliths	Rice phytoliths	Pepper, *Artocarpus, Garcinia* pollen
9000–6500 BP (10,000–7500 bp)	High	Present	Not stated	Absent	Wild rice	Absent
6500–6000 BP (7500–7000 bp)	Highest	Present	Not stated	Absent	Wild rice	Absent
6000–4000 BP (7000–4500 bp)	Low	Most pronounced	Present	Present	Introduced rice	Absent
4000–2000 BP (4500–2000 bp)	2 firing events	Present	Not stated	Absent	Absent	Present
2000–0 BP (2000–0 bp)	Low	Present	Not stated	Absent	Absent	Present

Source: Kealhofer (2003). Kealhofer's date estimates are expressed in years BP, so their approximate bp equivalent is also provided here.

and the jaws show quite high rates of periodontal disease, in a pattern consistent with a contribution of high-starch foodstuffs to the diet (Bulbeck 2005a). The available dating of circa 6000 bp for the middens provides an approximate if maximum age for the Guar Kepah burials. The Gua Cha Neolithic burials, which date to a later time (circa 3000 bp), resemble the Guar Kepah burials in their prevalence of betel-nut stained teeth, recorded on one-third of the individuals. Analysis of their oral pathology suggests that a portion of the population was using pottery to prepare easily masticated meals, although evidence for an agricultural component in the diet is not clear (Bulbeck 2005b).

Kealhofer's evidence for mid-Holocene introduced rice, in the context of the absence of dated rice from STMP archaeological sites until 2000 bp (noted above), parallels the findings of Diffloth (2011) from his search for Aslian reflexes (terms related to earlier forms) for rice. Only the Jah Hut Senoi have retained a reflex of the proto-Austroasiatic term for "husked rice" with its original meaning, although the Semai Senoi have retained a reflex that they apply to a common weed. The Semai term for husked rice is cognate with terms in Katuic and Khmuic (mainland Southeast Asian branches of Austroasiatic) for particular rice varieties, while the Temiar Senoi and Semnam Semang have retained a reflex of proto-Austroasiatic for "rice plant". This "... is a fair reflection of the various life-styles of societies where rice is not an indispensable element of the diet", and the "... Semai situation ... suggests a not-so-ancient shift from some kind of rice cultivation to a more jungle-oriented subsistence" (Diffloth 2011: 305). Accordingly, rice cultivation appears to have been introduced to STMP in the mid-Holocene, but to have continued at very low levels, even declining in its subsistence importance, until the last couple of millennia.

The onset of STMP horticulture may be expected to have triggered a transformation in settlement patterns. However, the shallow time depth of STMP open-air sites, apart from the special case of marine shell hillocks (Figure 5.1), has obscured any hamlets that might have related to small-scale cultivation during the critical 6500–4500 bp period. The only available indication is the indirect evidence of a decline in rockshelter occupation after 6500 bp and a shift towards reserving sections of closed sites for use as cemeteries. A period lasting millennia during which small-scale cultivation was combined with a predominantly foraging subsistence basis, as would appear to be the case for STMP, is supported by the evidence that foraging and low-level food production are entirely compatible with each other (Bulbeck 2013). Over the long haul, dependence on agriculture can be expected to have increased (Barker 2006), as reflected in the post-4000 bp increase in documented STMP site occupancy (Figure 5.1) and the transitional Neolithic-EMP open-air sites of Nyong and Bukit Komel (Adi 1989). The gap in the STMP chronometric record can therefore be interpreted as reflecting a period of relocation of much of the early Neolithic population to open-air hamlets, at a time before open-air sites can be readily detected.

LINGUISTIC AND GENETIC CONSIDERATIONS

Within the Austroasiatic language stock, the Aslian branch is most closely related to the Monic (Mon and Nyakur) languages of mainland Thailand and, at a further remove, the Nicobarese languages spoken on islands north of Sumatra (Sidwell and Blench 2011). These relations would be broadly consistent with a southward movement via STMP of a language ancestral to Aslian. As reviewed above, the archaeological evidence for the early STMP Neolithic is stronger in southern Thailand than Peninsular Malaysia, confirming the widely suspected association between the entry of an Austroasiatic language and the Neolithic cultural complex into the Peninsula. However, the Aslian languages are most diverse towards the south of their range, and most of the Northern Aslian languages represent a belated, northward offshoot (Bulbeck 2011; Burenhalt et al. 2011). Accordingly, the early Neolithic of southern Thailand would appear to have been associated with sister languages—now extinct—of Aslian, as would be consistent with the mitochondrial DNA (mtDNA) evidence.

Oppenheimer (2011) and Bulbeck (2011) recognize two mtDNA lineages, N9a6 and F1a1a, that appear to track Neolithic migration from mainland Southeast Asia to STMP in the middle Holocene. They agree in proposing a sea-borne entry into the Peninsula, avoiding Thailand north of the Isthmus of Kra and south of the Khorat Plateau, where both N9a6 and Flala are effectively absent. Where they disagree is Oppenheimer's emphasis on a relation with the arrival of early rice farmers from Indochina, without any specific linguistic associations, whereas Bulbeck associates Flala with the incursion of Austroasiatic languages. To be sure, the genetic evidence is hard to square with the linguistic affinity between Aslian and Monic. One possible resolution is that the common linguistic ancestor of Nicobarese (who do share these lineages), Aslian and Monic established itself in northern STMP, and that the N9a6 and Flala lineages were lost during the northward expansion of proto-Monic. Certainly, if N9a6 and Flala have any relationship with the movement of Austroasiatic into the Peninsula, then their geographic distribution rules out Ban Kao, in a location where those mtDNA lineages are absent, as any sort of predecessor of the STMP Neolithic. Further, their uneven distribution amongst Austroasiatic speakers (N9a6 most strongly present amongst the Jahai Semang, Flala amongst the Temiar Senoi, neither present amongst Monic speakers) would rule out large-scale immigration of early Austroasiatic speakers, consistent with Fix's (2011; this volume) "trickle" model of small-scale migration.

In any case, archaeological corollaries for early Aslian diversification would be restricted to Peninsular Malaysia. Burenhult et al. (2011) demonstrate a network of Semang forager languages and a separate network made up of the other Aslian languages, each network including languages from both the Northern and Central Aslian branches. Accordingly, there must have been two separate switches to Aslian by the ancestors of the Semang, succeeded by a loose network of social interaction that facilitated the exchange of lexical items across the proto-Semang range. Archaeological evidence for this network is provided by the tradition of charcoal drawings found in rockshelters distributed throughout the Semang range, whether involving Central Aslian (Mokhtar and Taçon 2011) or Northern Aslian (Adi 2000) speakers. In addition, where the archaeology detects a belated impact of the Neolithic, as at Gua Cha, this may reflect continuity of proto-Semang foragers still untouched by contemporary developments introduced by early Aslian-speaking settlers.

A large swathe of inland STMP, from the Ten'en haunts in the north to the Batek and northern Semaq Beri strongholds in the south, evidently persisted as a "forager's paradise" through to recent times. This points to a low overall rate of population growth and light pressure on territorial expansion by those groups that did practise horticulture as well as foraging. The clearest archaeological evidence for cumulative change during the Neolithic is the increased material prosperity represented by the funerary pottery buried at Khao Khi Chan and Buang Baeb (probably non-Aslian in their association) and, at a later date, the wide range of sumptuary goods interred at cemetery sites such as Lang Rongrien, Gua Cha and Gua Harimau (Bulbeck 2011). Gua Harimau additionally tracks the inclusion of early bronzes in rockshelter cemeteries with the transition to the Early Metal Phase, while Dongson drums (from Vietnam) and other ancient bronze regalia were also widely transported across STMP (Bulbeck 2003, 2004; Murillo-Barraso et al. 2010). The basis for this prosperity probably lay in the wide-scale trade of coastal produce inland and hinterland produce to the coast, as well as the exchange of foraged for farmed foodstuffs between groups that continued hunting and gathering and those that adopted horticulture. When iron metallurgy was locally established, the trade in ironware followed earlier established routes in superseding the inhabitants' previous use of stone tools for cutting and scraping tasks.

Benjamin (1987) notes the occurrence of numerous words in various Aslian languages that are of Austronesian but non-Malay derivation. His conclusion that one or more Austronesian languages, now extinct, were formerly spoken in STMP is supported by archaeological evidence. Locally produced wares at Khao Sam Kaeo and the nearby Tham Tuay rockshelter, dated to 2500–2000 bp, exhibit decorations similar to broadly coeval pottery from the Philippines, Sarawak and Cham-speaking parts of Vietnam (Bellina et al. 2012). An Early Metal Phase Austronesian presence is also suggested for southern Peninsular Malaysia, based on the reports of "red" (red-slipped) pottery in the upper (most recent) levels of Gua Kechil, Kota Tongkat and Gua Sagu. Early Austronesian infiltration is also indicated by the N21, N22, M7c1a and M7c1c mtDNA lineages recorded for the Semelai and/or Temuan Aboriginal Malays, but no other STMP populations, apart from a slight presence of N21 and M7c1c amongst the Melayu Malay (Bulbeck 2011). Accordingly, the historical expansion of the Malay language northward into STMP, initially focused on the coast but subsequently extending inland (Benjamin 1987, 2002), appears to have blanketed a pre-Malay Austronesian as well as an Aslian presence along the Peninsular coastal plain.

From at least 2500 bp, maritime sites and coastally located, fortified sites account for a substantial proportion of the STMP archaeological record (Bulbeck 2014). These sites substantiate Leong's (1990) model of a network of collecting centres, from the third millennium bp to historical times, for gold, tin and precious forest produce to be transported to coastal feeder points for onward shipping to STMP entrepôts. The entrepôts acted as entry points for technical expertise and religious beliefs from as far afield as South Asia and China, as well as exit points for STMP produce, as part of a maritime route that connected the Mediterranean and China by the late centuries BCE (Jacq-Hergoualc'h 2002; Glover and Bellina 2011). Benjamin (1987) had proposed an important role for the Mon in developing the STMP entrepôts, but in fact the oldest entrepôts —Khao Sam Kaeo and Sungai Batu (Bujang Valley) with its circa 1800 bp jetty and ritual buildings (Saidin et al. 2011)—predate the rise of the Mon to prominence. A succession of foreign powers claimed suzerainty over one or more STMP entrepôts, including the Mon (Wheatley 1983), Srivijaya based in southern Sumatra, the Cholas in southern India, and Ayudhya in mainland Thailand, before Melayu Malays established Melaka as the region's preeminent port and stamped their authority over local politics (Jacq-Hergoualc'h 2002; Andaya 2007). While the ethnicity of those who first established the STMP entrepôts may never be known, early Aslian and pre-Malay Austronesian groups almost certainly played a major role (Bulbeck 2004).

CONCLUSIONS

The Neolithic transition in the southern Thai-Malay Peninsula (STMP) dates to circa 6500 bp. This transition is most convincingly captured in southern Thailand in several rockshelter sequences and the Tham Sua shell midden. The phytolith sequence from Nong Thalee Song Hong also reflects the probable origins of arboriculture and rice cultivation in STMP at the same date. There was probably a relocation of much of the population to open-air hamlets at the time, based on an apparent decrease in rockshelter occupancy levels, and a shift towards the use of rockshelters as burial grounds. This hypothesized relocation is not reflected in the open-air archaeological record because the recovery of such sites has a maximum time depth of circa 4000 bp (apart from the special case of marine shell hillocks). As a result, documented site occupancy levels actually register a 4500–4000 bp "gap", before the combination of slow population growth and improved visibility of open-air sites produced STMP's better documented, late Neolithic to Early Metal Phase archaeological sequence. The entry of the Neolithic and early Austroasiatic speakers into STMP may well have been a coupled event, but only if a circa 6500 bp dating is accepted for this event.

REFERENCES

Adi Haji Taha
    1985   The Re-excavation of the Rockshelter at Gua Cha, Ulu Kelantan, West Malaysia. Federations Museum Journal 30.
    1989   Archaeological, Prehistoric, Protohistoric and Historic Study of the Tembeling Valley, Pahang West Malaysia. Jurnal Arkeologi Malaysia 2: 47–69.
    2000   Archaeological Excavations in Ulu Kelantan, Peninsular Malaysia. Unpublished PhD thesis, Australian National University, Canberra.
Andaya, B.W.
    2007   Malacca. *In* Historic Cities of the Islamic World. C.E. Bosworth, ed. Pp. 309–18. Leiden: Brill.
Anderson, D.
    2005   The Use of Caves in Peninsular Thailand in the Late Pleistocene and Early and Middle Holocene. Asian Perspectives 44(1): 137–53.

Auetrakulvit, P., H. Forestier, C. Khaokhiew and V. Zeitoun
  2012   New Excavation at Moh Khiew site, Southern Thailand. *In* Crossing
         Borders: Selected Papers from the 13th International Conference
         of the European Association of Southeast Asian Archaeologists,
         Volume 1. M.-L. Tjoa-Bonatz, A. Reinecke and D. Bonatz, eds.
         Pp. 60–70. Singapore: NUS Press.

Barker, G.
  2006   The Agricultural Revolution in Prehistory: Why Did Foragers
         Become Farmers? Oxford: Oxford University Press.

Bellina, B., G. Epinal and A. Favereau
  2012   Caracterisation Préliminaire des Poteries Marqueurs d'Echanges en
         Mer to Chine Méridionale à la Fin de la Préhistoire [Preliminary
         characteristics of the pottery markers of exchange in the South
         China Sea at the end of prehistory]. Archipel 84: 7–33.

Bellina-Pryce, B. and P. Silapanth
  2006   Weaving Cultural Identities on Trans-Asiatic Networks: Upper
         Thai-Malay Peninsula—An Early Socio-Political Landscape.
         Bulletin de l'École Française d'Êxtreme-Orient 93: 257–93.

Bellwood, P.
  1993   Cultural and Biological Differentiation in Peninsular Malaysia:
         The Last 10,000 years. Asian Perspectives 32: 37–60.
  1997   Prehistory of the Indo-Malaysian Archipelago, rev. ed. Honolulu:
         University of Hawai'i Press.
  2005   Mind the Gap. Asian Perspectives 44(2): 247–8.

Benjamin, G.
  1987   Ethnohistorical Perspectives on Kelantan's Prehistory. *In* Kelantan
         Zaman Awal: Kajian Arkeologi dan Sejarah di Malaysia. Nik
         Hassan Shuhaimi bin Nik Abdul Rahman, ed. Pp. 108–53. Kota
         Bahru: Perpaduan Muzium Negeri Kelantan.
  2002   On being tribal in the Malay world. *In* Tribal Communities
         in the Malay World: Historical, Cultural and Social Perspectives.
         G. Benjamin and C. Chou, eds. Pp. 7–76. Singapore: Institute of
         Southeast Asian Studies.

Bowdery, D.
  1999   Phytoliths from Tropical Sediments: Reports from Southeast Asia
         and Papua New Guinea. Bulletin of the Indo-Pacific Prehistory
         Association 18: 159–68.

Bronk Ramsey, C.
  2013   OxCal 4.2., https://c14.arch.ox.ac.uk/oxcal/OxCal.html, accessed
         7 September 2013.

Bulbeck, D.

2003   Hunter-Gatherer Occupation of the Malay Peninsula from the Ice Age to the Iron Age. *In* The Archaeology of Tropical Rain Forests. J. Mercader, ed. Pp. 119–60. New Brunswick, NJ: Rutgers University Press.

2004   Indigenous Traditions and Exogenous Influences in the Early History of Peninsular Malaysia. *In* Southeast Asia from Prehistory to History. I. Glover and P. Bellwood, eds. Pp. 314–36. London: Routledge Curzon.

2005a   The Guar Kepah Human Remains. *In* The Perak Man and Other Prehistoric Skeletons of Malaysia. Zuraina Majid, ed. Pp. 383–423. Penang: Universiti Sains Malaysia.

2005b   The Gua Cha Burials. *In* The Perak Man and Other Prehistoric Skeletons of Malaysia. Zuraina Majid, ed. Pp. 253–309. Penang: Universiti Sains Malaysia.

2011   Biological and Cultural Evolution in the Population and Culture History of *Homo sapiens* in Malaya. *In* Dynamics of Human Diversity: The Case of Mainland Southeast Asia (Pacific Linguistics 627). N.J. Enfield, ed. Pp. 207–55. Canberra: The Australian National University.

2013   The Transition from Foraging to Farming in Prehistory and "Ethnography". World Archaeology 45: 557–73.

2014   The Chronometric Holocene Archaeological Record of the Southern Thai-Malay Peninsula. International Journal of Asia-Pacific Studies 10(1): 112–62.

Burenhult, N., N. Kruspe and M. Dunn

2011   Language History and Culture Groups among Austroasiatic-Speaking Foragers of the Malay Peninsula. *In* Dynamics of Human Diversity: The Case of Mainland Southeast Asia (Pacific Linguistics 627). N.J. Enfield, ed. Pp. 257–75. Canberra: The Australian National University.

Chitkament, T.

2006/07   Lithic Analysis of Moh Khiew Rockshelter (Locality I) in Krabi River Valley, Krabi Province, Southwestern Thailand. Unpublished MA thesis. Tarragona: Universitat Roviri I Virgili.

Denham, T.

2011   Early Agriculture and Plant Domestication in New Guinea and Island Southeast Asia. Current Anthropology 52(S4): S379–95.

Diffloth, G.

Austroasiatic Word Histories: Boat, Husked Rice and Taro. *In* Dynamics of Human Diversity: The Case of Mainland Southeast Asia (Pacific Linguistics 627). N.J. Enfield, ed. Pp. 295–313. Canberra: The Australian National University.

Evans, I.H.N.

1927 Notes on the Remains of an Old Boat from Pontian, Pahang. Journal of the Federated Malay States Museum 12(4): 93–8.

Fix, A.

2011 Origin of Genetic Diversity among Malaysian Orang Asli: An Alternative to the Demic Diffusion Model. *In* Dynamics of Human Diversity: The Case of Mainland Southeast Asia (Pacific Linguistics 627). N.J. Enfield, ed. Pp. 277–91. Canberra: The Australian National University.

Glover, I.C. and B. Bellina

2011 Ban Don Ta Phet and Khao Sam Kaeo: The Earliest Indian Contacts Re-assessed. *In* Early Interactions between South and Southeast Asia: Reflections of Cross-Cultural Exchange. P-Y. Manguin, A. Mani and G. Wade, eds. Pp. 17–45. Singapore: Institute of Southeast Asian Studies.

Hassan, Z.

1998 Urutan Kebudayaan Prasejarah Lembah Lenggong, Hulu Perak, Perak pada Zaman Holosen [Prehistoric Holocene cultural sequence in the Lenggong Valley of the Hulu Perak administrative district of Perak State]. Unpublished MA thesis, Universiti Sains Malaysia, Penang.

Higham, C.

2013 Hunter-Gatherers in Southeast Asia: From Prehistory to the Present. Human Biology 85(1): Article 2. Available at http://digitalcommons.wayne.edu/humbiol/vol85/iss1/2.

Jacq-Hergoualc'h, M.

2002 The Malay Peninsula: Crossroads of the Maritime Silk Road (100 BC–1300 AD). V. Hobson, trans. Leiden: E.J. Brill.

Kealhofer, L.

2003 Looking into the Gap: Land Use and the Tropical Forests of Southern Thailand. Asian Perspectives 42(1): 72–95.

Leong Sau Heng

1990 Collecting Centres, Feeder Points and Entrepôts in the Malay Peninsula, c. 1000 B.C.–A.D. 1400. *In* The Southeast Port and

Polity: Rise and Demise. J. Kathirithamby-Wells and J. Villiers, eds. Pp. 17–38. Singapore: Singapore University Press.

1991   Jenderam Hilir and the Mid-Holocene Prehistory of the West Coast Plain of Peninsular Malaysia. Bulletin of the Indo-Pacific Prehistory Association 10: 150–60.

Matthews, J.

1961   A Check-List of "Hoabinhian" Sites Excavated in Malaya, 1860–1939. Singapore: Eastern Universities Press Ltd.

Mok, O.

2013   At Guar Kepah, Last of Country's Stone Age Sites. The Malay Mail online, http://www.themalaymailonline.com/malaysia/article/at-guar-kepah-last-of-countrys-stone-age-sites, accessed 7 December 2013.

Mokhtar Saidin and P. Taçon

2011   The Recent Rock Drawings of the Lenggong Valley, Perak, Malaysia. Antiquity 85(328): 459–75.

Murillo-Barroso, M., T.O. Pryce, B. Bellina and M. Martinón-Torres

2010   Khao Sam Kaeo—An Archaeometallurgical Crossroads for Trans-Asiatic Technological Traditions. Journal of Archaeological Science 37: 1761–72.

Nik Hassan Shuhaimi bin Nik Abdul Rahman

1991   Recent Research at Kuala Selinsing, Perak. Bulletin of the Indo-Pacific Prehistory Association 11: 141–52.

Oppenheimer, S.

2011   MtDNA Variation and Southward Holocene Dispersals within Mainland Southeast Asia. *In* Dynamics of Human Diversity: The Case of Mainland Southeast Asia (Pacific Linguistics 627). N.J. Enfield, ed. Pp. 81–108. Canberra: The Australian National University.

Pailoplee, S., B. Chaisuwan, I. Takashima, K. Won-In and P. Charusiri

2003   Dating Ancient Remains by Thermoluminesence: Implications of Incompletely Burnt Bricks. Bulletin of Earth Sciences of Thailand 3, available at http://www.geo.sc.chula.ac.th/geonew/BEST/volume3/Number1/researchPaper/2-Pailoplee%20et%20al.pdf, accessed 8 September 2013.

Pookajorn, S.

1994   The Geology Setting and Excavation Report of Moh Khiew Cave. *In* Final Report of Excavations at Moh Khiew Cave, Krabi Province; Sakai Cave, Trang Province; and Ethnoarchaeological

Research of Hunter-Gatherer Group, Socalled Mani or Sakai or Orang Asli at Trang Province. S. Pookajorn, A. Waiyasadamrong, S. Sinsakul, M. Wattanasak and Y. Chaimanee, eds. Vol. 2, pp. 306–47. Bangkok: Silkaporn University, Faculty of Archaeology.

1996   Human Activities and Environmental Changes During the Late Pleistocene to Middle Holocene in Southern Thailand and Southeast Asia. *In* Humans at the End of the Ice Age: The Archaeology of the Pleistocene-Holocene Transition. L.G. Straus, B.V. Erikson, J.M. Erlandson and D.R. Yesner, eds. Pp. 201–13. New York: Plenum Press.

Saidin, Mokhtar, J. Abdullah, A.J. Osman and A. Abdullah

2011   Issues and Problems of Previous Studies in the Bujang Valley and the Discovery of Sungai Batu. *In* Bujang Valley and Early Civilisations in Southeast Asia. S. Chia and B. Watson Andaya, eds. Pp. 15–26. Kuala Lumpur: Department of National Heritage, Ministry of Information, Communication and Culture, Malaysia.

Sidwell, P. and R. Blench

2011   The Austroasiatic Urheimat: The Southeastern Riverine Hypothesis. *In* Dynamics of Human Diversity: The Case of Mainland Southeast Asia (Pacific Linguistics 627). N.J. Enfield, ed. Pp. 315–43. Canberra: The Australian National University.

Sieveking, G. de G.

1954   Excavations at Gua Cha, Kelantan, 1954. Part 1. Federations Museum Journal 1 and 2: 75–143.

Soares, P., J.A. Trejaut, J.-H. Loo, C. Hill, M. Mormina, C.-L. Lee, Y.-M. Chen, G. Hudjashov, P. Forster, V. Macaulay, D. Bulbeck, S. Oppenheimer, M. Li and M.B. Richards

2008   Climate Change and Post-Glacial Human Dispersals in Southeast Asia. Molecular Biology and Evolution 25: 1209–18.

Spriggs, M.

2003   Chronology of the Neolithic Transition in Island Southeast Asia and the Western Pacific: A View from 2003. The Review of Archaeology 24: 57–80.

Srisuchat, A.

1993   Comments on the Results of Carbon-14 Dating Applied to Archaeological Finds from Excavated Sites in Thailand. *In* An Application of Technology and Science in Archaeological Work in Thailand. T. Srisuchat and A. Srisuchat, eds. Pp. 41–54. Bangkok: Krom Sinlapakon.

Wheatley, P.
  1983   Nagara and Commandery: Origins of the Southeast Asian Urban Traditions. Research Papers Nos. 207–8. Chicago: University of Chicago, Department of Geography.

Williams, A.N.
  2011   The Use of Summed Radiocarbon Probability Distributions in Archaeology: A Review of Methods. Journal of Archaeological Science 39: 578–89.

6

The Importance of Tools in Orang Asli Prehistory

A.S. Baer

INTRODUCTION

We look into the past to find our roots and to make sense of the world. For western Southeast Asia, two large patterns emerge in its history, both based on human ingenuity. One pattern is the interaction of people with the natural environment. The other involves cultural interactions. During thousands of years of human existence in the region, both types of interactions have changed—have evolved—and they continue to evolve. They are dynamic.

The interaction with the environment started with the needs of the first pioneers to find food and shelter. They also needed to avoid predators and parasites as best they could, learn the geography and ecology of their new homeland, and adapt their tool technologies in order to survive and thrive. The fact that the Asian mainland expanded during the ice-age centuries and later greatly contracted also had far-reaching consequences. This included human dispersals that put the pioneers' genetic signature on a wide swath of Southeast Asia when their descendants ventured north toward Indochina or east toward Australia (HUGO 2010; see also Bulbeck and Fix, this volume).

Language developed in tandem with ecological and geographical knowledge, but language skills also evolved as social interactions became more complex over time, enabling people to cope in their local group and cope with strangers. Indeed, the overlapping themes of long-term cultural and ecological adaptation stand out as the foundation for understanding Southeast Asians today. A major, but sometimes overlooked, factor in this cultural and ecological complex is the bamboo and rattan tool kit. A review of archaeological findings and other published reports can help us to understand the role of tools in long-term survival on the Thai-Malay Peninsula.

Many stories are possible about human history on the peninsula, but any reliable story must focus on the Orang Asli. Their ancestors may not only be the first people of the peninsula but of Southeast Asia in general. In this view, the cultures and biology of western Southeast Asians derive importantly from pre-farming people of the peninsula, based on the pioneering way of making a living by foraging (White 2011); the forager tool kit went along with this change. The idea that farmers swept into Southeast Asia from China or Taiwan is popular, but alternative ideas merit consideration and may be fruitful.

The earliest date of pioneering on the Thai-Malay Peninsula is some 70,000 years ago at Kota Tampan in northern Malaya, based on findings of stone tools. The next earliest date is minimally 43,000 years ago, based on stone-tool findings at Lang Rongrien in southern Thailand. Because the Niah Cave artefacts of Sarawak date to about 46,000 years ago and a similar age has been reported for the human occupation of Australia, it is likely that pioneers reached the peninsula long before that time.

One hereditary marker of this pioneering group (mitochondrial DNA, mtDNA) shows high diversity today in the Thai-Malay Peninsula and nearby areas. Moreover, the existence of ancient mtDNA lineages in Orang Asli on the peninsula suggests a longer human history there than to the east or the north. This basic genetic signature in Southeast Asia is also suggested by the diversity in the majority of DNA (nuclear DNA) in Orang Asli.

People first arrived on the Thai-Malay Peninsula during the ice age when the ocean retreated and the continental, underwater shelf of western Southeast Asia became land. This shelf, called Sundaland, stretched east to Borneo and Bali, north toward the Philippines, and on to Vietnam. The people who first settled Sundaland spread far and wide, initially in a surge or pulse that radiated northward and also to the land's edge to the east, first exploring, then colonizing. The Sundaland crossing may have taken less than a thousand years because the Asian pioneers had no mountains or deserts to cross before reaching Bali. Some traversed the lowlands of what is now the Java Sea. Splinter groups heading toward Indochina, or Palawan, could also travel through lowlands. It was an easy expansion.

Once the major pulse ended, most of the now dispersed Sundaland groups expanded closer to home, including the interior of the Thai-Malay Peninsula. For the next 20,000 or 30,000 years there was convergence and divergence all over Sundaland by land and sea, as populations expanded and adapted to their local habitats. For example, the Iban of Borneo have ancestral DNA from the mainland, shared with northern Orang Asli (Baer 2011; Simonson et al. 2011). Notably, while the Iban speak an Austronesian language today, northern Orang Asli speak Austroasiatic languages, showing that languages can be unreliable predictors of biological history.

After 15,000 years ago, the Sundaland area started to change to an amazing extent, gradually at first but at a faster pace later. By at least 8,000 years ago, the sea had invaded much of Sundaland as the climate warmed when the ice age melted away, eventually shrinking Sundaland by half and producing the islands, such as Borneo, that exist today. Some three million square kilometres of land was drowned, initiating strong monsoon conditions from the South China Sea. As a result, coastlines expanded and rivers gained shorter access to the sea. This inundation tended to isolate scattered groups, but voyages did take place on the shallow Sunda seas. In fact, Southeast Asia provides the earliest evidence of seafaring in the world, given that people reached eastern Indonesia, New Guinea, and also Australia by at least 45,000 years ago. One experimental bamboo raft modeled on ancient technology reached Australia from Timor in six days (Bedorarek 2000).

In general, the evidence suggests that the first people on the Thai-Malay Peninsula and its environs engendered the rich biological heritage of western Southeast Asians and were the foundation for the region's cultural complexity.

THE ORANG ASLI TOOL KIT

For long over a million years, the human line has been using rocks as tools. The *Homo sapiens* pioneers in Southeast Asia undoubtedly arrived there with a learned tradition for using such tools. Tools are cultural resources that improve the human ability to interact both with nature and society. Early colonists on the Thai-Malay Peninsula used a versatile tool kit to obtain and prepare food, construct shelters, and generally survive. It consisted of bamboo, rattan, resins, wood, bark, shells, rocks, bone, and anything else that was useful.

In a sense, language is a basic human tool. Fire can also be a tool, as in burning off a swidden field (Maloney 1995; Kealhofer 2003; Taylor et al. 2007; Hunt et al. 2012). More conventionally, tools include weapons such as spears, instruments (needles), digging sticks, and facilities such as fish weirs and traps (Torrence 2001). Archaeologists have found rocks that functioned as tools in caves and other sites on the Thai-Malay Peninsula. Tools that were less durable than rocks were undoubtedly also used by early people, but let us look at the rock category first.

At Kota Tampan in the Lenggong Valley in Perak, quartz cobble tools, sharpened on one side, are reported to have been manufactured on an ancient lakeshore and at nearby sites, starting more than 70,000 years ago (Zuraina Majid 1990). The Bukit Bunuh site nearby, dating to about 40,000 years ago, was an open-air area where cobbles were worked on rock anvils with hammer-stones to produce tools, including flake tools (Saidin 2006). Notably, above Lenggong are numerous salt licks which attract game animals (Davison et al. 1995). In ancient times Lenggong may have been a convenient place to produce cobble tools for hunting at the salt licks.

People, apes and monkeys have all used hammer-stones to crack open edible nuts or hard-shell clams. The food source is smashed on a flat stone, an anvil. But only people excel at making many other forms of rock tools. At Lang Rongrien, a cave near the west coast of southern Thailand, the earliest stone tools were small, sharp rock flakes. Later tools were made from large river cobbles usually knapped on both sides, called bifacials; many of them had heavily worn edges. Findings at Lang Rongrien have been dated from more than 43,000 up to 12,000 years ago (Anderson 1980). Multi-purpose cobble tools were used widely on the peninsula and nearby areas. They were easy to make, hand-sized, and easy to carry anywhere.

Besides rocks, animal bones have been found near hearth sites at Lang Rongrien. They testify that large game such as deer and elephant were butchered there, but smaller animals were more commonly caught, including tortoises. The deer was a species known to live in open environments and rather dry forests (Anderson 2005; Mudar and Anderson 2005), which were fairly common there during the ice age.

Moh Khiew is another early human site in southern Thailand close to the coast, with its lowest excavated cave level dated to perhaps 25,000 years ago. This level had both unifacial and bifacial stone tools, some for hunting game. Other tools showed by microwear analysis that they were used to work wood, or perhaps bamboo, although bamboo was not mentioned in the site report (Pookajorn 1996). Both large and small animals were hunted, based on bones found in the cave—from wild water buffalo, wild pig, tapir, and primates, down to squirrels. Even bones of otter and sun bear were found. Later cultural levels in the cave showed evidence of a wide range of hunted animals but also evidence of marine molluscs. Between 6,000 and 4,000 years ago, people using the cave still made cobble and flake tools but also had polished stone adzes and axes and bone tools. Pottery fragments were found in this top-most excavation layer.

Inland from Moh Khiew is Sakai Cave. Findings there go back no more than 9,000 years. The animals hunted were small, and stone tools were not ground smooth at that time. In the upper, more recent levels of the excavation, polished adzes, pottery, and shell beads were found, but bone tools were found at all occupation layers at this site.

Sometime after the height of the ice age, perhaps 10,000 years ago, the rock tool kit on the peninsula began to include "sumatraliths", elongated unifacial cobbles, but flakes, hammerstones and bifacials also still occur in the so-called "Hoabinhian" tool assemblage. These tools have been found at Lang Rongrien, Moh Khiew, and at cave sites in central Malaya. The Gua Cha rockshelter in interior Kelantan, dating from 10,000 to 3,000 years ago, contained bones of monkey, gibbon, pig, deer, sun bear, cattle, squirrel, fruit bats, rats, and even rhinoceros. Carbonized rice occurred at Gua Cha about 2,200 years ago but not earlier (Adi 1991). The last rock-based tool kit is called Neolithic and dates to perhaps 5,000 years ago. It includes ground stone tools and pottery and may be associated with early agriculture.

Rocks have also long been used for other purposes. Quartz crystals have been used in healing and natural rock walls have been used as surfaces for artwork (Matthews 1959; Tan and Chia 2010; Saidin and Taçon 2011). Utilitarian uses include cooking stones in fire pits and stones to build weirs to trap fish in shallow pools upstream. In fact, unmodified rocks have many uses that are "invisible" to archaeologists. Some archaeologists have written that the Sunda area had a monotonous technology because of its simple stone tools, but they did not consider the scope of bamboo in tool kits. Notably, the total tool kit of foragers and swiddeners is known to be widespread in Southeast Asia, largely based on bamboo and rattan.[1]

Let us consider for a moment the requirements of a reliable tool kit for living in a tropical woodland or forest. Beyond ensuring food and shelter, it should provide fire for cooking, protection from dangerous animals, and night-time warmth, and it should facilitate water travel. Fortunately, Southeast Asia has an abundance of materials other than rocks that can be used as tools, from porcupine quills for punching holes to giant bamboo used to make rafts or water-carrying tubes for household use. Food can also be roasted, boiled, or stewed in green bamboo tubes.[2] Some writers refer to a "bamboo age", rather than a "stone age", for Southeast Asia history before the later metal age. One observer noted that bamboo is indispensable to the Temiar for house building, household utensils, vessels, tools, weapons, fences, baskets, water-channeling pipes, rafts, musical instruments and ornaments (Noone 1936; see also Higham 2013: 24; White 2011: 27–32).

Bamboo is an optimal technology for many desired outcomes. It is easy to harvest. Like small trees, bamboos can be bark-ringed by a cobble tool and then snapped off. The same technique was used in early times at Lang Rongrien on deer antlers: ring and then snap. After harvesting a bamboo clump, the stumps can be burned to stimulate the growth of new shoots. When a bamboo stem (culm) is smashed with a rock, splinters are produced that are sharp-edged and useful as knives or dart shafts (West and Louys 2007). Such splinters have long been used to cut the umbilical cord at birth. Today inventive people even make bicycle frames out of bamboo because it is as strong as steel as well as being a sustainable resource. Old stories of people being created inside bamboo stems and being freed with outside help dramatize the importance of bamboo to many people in Southeast Asia.

Malaya has over 30 native species of bamboo. They range in size from pencil-thin creepers to stems as large as a young tree trunk. A conspicuous use of bamboo on the peninsula is the blowpipe, emblematic of Orang Asli tool kits today (Endicott 1969). It has a strong outer tube and a thin inner one. The most valued inner tubes come from a bamboo species that grows only in the highlands of Malaya; it has an internode length of about eight feet, which provides a smooth bore for blowpipe darts. Semai blowpipes are measured as five forearms long, from the elbow to the tip of the fingers. Women's and children's blowpipes are generally shorter.

Plate 6.1 Jah Hut men making bamboo rafts

(Photo credit: Colin Nicholas)

Plate 6.2 Temiar man making snare of bamboo and rattan

(Photo credit: Colin Nicholas)

Likewise, bamboo "stampers" are used by Orang Asli as percussion instruments during singing fests. Bamboo flutes and zithers are also popular. Both blowpipes and stampers were important developments, one for physical survival and the other for cultural cohesion. Once invented, they probably spread rapidly among forager groups (Noone 1954). Other bamboo tools included snares, fish traps, fish spears, and scaffolding on trees to reach bees' nests to harvest honey. Some spring traps for game have a wooden shaft and a bamboo blade (Evans 1916).[3] Fire is made by friction devices of wood or bamboo and twine.

All such items can be made from materials readily at hand; no repair van or moving van is needed.

Bamboo has also been used by Orang Asli as a noise maker to scare off harmful animals, by placing a bamboo tube on a fulcrum in a stream. As the canted vessel fills up, it falls over onto a well-positioned rock, making a resounding "clonk", and then tips backward to fill up again. To make a "scare" against birds visiting a swidden of ripening crops, bamboo tubes are used in something like a wind-chime on a post. Also, music can be made by wind organs or windmills

Plate 6.3 Temiar man with rattan fishtrap

(Photo credit: Colin Nicholas)

Plate 6.4 Semelai women with fish cages in dugout canoes

(Photo credit: Rosemary Gianno)

positioned high in the trees.[4] Another use of bamboo, akin to the action in blowpipes, is to provide tubing for piston-driven air compression, such as in the aeration of metallic materials in fire pits to purify iron or copper or aeration of kilns to produce pottery. Several accounts suggest that such air-compression technology is ancient on the peninsula, as well as elsewhere in Southeast Asia.[5] Bamboo piston bellows are still being used by Orang Asli.[6] And there is now experimental confirmation that simple flaked cobbles can be used to make complex bamboo tools (Ofer Bar-Yusof et al. 2012). In short, bamboo technology is versatile, the raw material is plentiful and portable, and it does not require sophisticated processes to make tools. Rattan has many of the same attributes.

Climbing palms (rattans) have various uses (Ave 1988). For example, because they have thorns on their stems, when built into conical animal or fish traps by Orang Asli, the thorns impale the prey inside the trap. The technique may be ancient in Southeast Asia and out to Melanesia (Balfour 1925).[7] Thorny rattans are also used as fish hooks and as rasps or graters (Evans 1937).[8] Some rattans are used as rope. One species of rattan has crystals of resin in its fruit, called dragon's blood; it is still used by Orang Asli but was once sold as a red dye and as a medicine (Morris 1996). Other resins were used as glues for hafting projectile points to spears and arrows, and crafting blowpipes and their darts. Resins are also used as incense and as boat caulk and hull sealant.

Northern Orang Asli once used bows and arrows but later switched to blowpipes. Both types of projectiles, arrows and blowpipe darts, have a longer effective range than hand-held spears. Forests were once less dense in the north of the peninsula and bows were more useful in such open forests. Blowpipes are superior in dense forests where visibility is poor and many prey animals are high above one's head. The light blowpipe darts can travel in a straight line for at least 25 metres, an aid in aiming at partially hidden animals high above the ground. Arrows can travel just as far but are heavier and have an arc trajectory, a disadvantage compared to darts in a rainforest (Zahorka 2006). During the ice ages, however, open forests were fairly common on the peninsula, giving an advantage to bows in many places. Some 19th-century bows were two metres long and made of split bamboo; the arrows had iron heads (Mikluho-Maclay 1878). Others were made from tree saplings, such as *langsat*, a section being cut off and split lengthwise (Schebesta 1926). A split half was then shaved to make it the correct thinness for easy bending and notched at the ends. The metre-long arrows, in some cases, had two or three short-clipped hornbill feathers, which "whistled" in flight, disorienting and dazing game such as wild boar (Schebesta 1926).[9] Bows were used by Orang Asli into the 1950s but are not used today.

Making a bamboo blowpipe seems a more demanding task than making a bifacial cobble tool. The knapper must knock off flakes from the cobble in careful order and correct positions. This can take about 30 decision steps. Likewise, about 30 steps lead to the manufacture of a blowpipe and quiver full of poisoned darts. The main difference is that the knapper can sit still to work while the blowpiper must go hither and yon to obtain materials, but the mental work might be the same in the two cases. Blowpipe making is not as difficult as one might imagine, if only one has the right materials. In this view, blowpipes could have been made as early as cobble tools, or even as early as a set of bow and arrows.

However, blowpipes, as a closed-forest adaptation, were perhaps more advantageous recently, particularly in the last, wetter 10,000 years. The technology likely spread quickly from the Thai-Malay Peninsula with its long-jointed bamboo to areas of Southeast Asia where blowpipes were made laboriously by reaming out wood because the proper bamboo species was lacking. Some southerly Orang Asli groove two halves of wood and bind them together with rattan covered with latex (Williams-Hunt 1952). Nevertheless, the question remains as to which came first, bows or blowpipes. Early blowpipes have long disintegrated, as have bows and arrow shafts. Archaeologists have not found stone arrowheads on the peninsula, except for possibly two at Mon Khiew, but have found possible spear points, more accurately described as bifacial, slightly tapered axe-like heads. Bone arrow tips have, however, been found at the Gua Cha rockshelter, and the pointy cobble flakes at Lang Rongrien could have served as arrow tips (Anderson 1997). In more recent times, Orang Asli made arrow tips from sharpened forearm bones of siamang (Howell 1984).

A possible cross-over technology between bows and blowpipes is the use of bertam palm-frond midribs as arrow and dart shafts. And, as in blowpipe darts, arrow tips coated with a naturally occurring poison from the sap of the *ipoh* tree that causes cardiac arrest are effective hunting devices on small animals and even on larger game. Orang Asli blowpipe darts are often tipped with a mixture of *ipoh* sap and of strychnine, obtained from a vine (Kopp et al. 1992).[10] Notches on poisoned blowpipe darts and on arrow tips are designed to break off once they embed in a prey animal, even when the shaft is dislodged, a technological improvement over un-notched tips. Batek Orang Asli char the tips of their blowpipe darts to make them easy to be broken off in a prey animal, rather than notching them. Besides midribs or splinters, arrows could have also been made from straight tree branchlets with fire-hardened, sharp tips. Hard wooden arrow tips, two inches long, were coated with poison and were detachable; they could bring down large game, even rhinoceros (Wray 1892). Wooden spear points can also be fire-hardened.

Twine was available in ancient times, made from rattan or by rubbing strands of inner tree bark on one's thigh. Twine may have been used as bowstrings and, well, twine in general.[11] Resins were also used as torch materials, as a source of incense, as glue and in other applications.[12] Coconut shells can serve as ladles. Pounded derris root became useful for stunning fish in fish drives. Bark cloth was made from the stripped inner bark of certain trees. Finally, human shelters of bamboo, tree bark, rattans, palm leaves and poles provide a habitat

Plate 6.5 Batek woman weaving pandanus mat, using bamboo hair comb as tool

(Photo credit: Thomas Kraft)

for tropical people to live in harmony with nature, unlike cubicles in an office tower nowadays.

Mobile foragers had many uses for nature's resources. Consider, for instance, how they might carry things, such as infants and bulky foodstuffs when they moved camp. Bark cloth is generally flimsy, but when several layers are folded together, they are useful as infant slings, as early Orang Asli photographs show. Carrying bulky food items by hand is possible, but a container is preferable. Such items can be bundled, covered with banana leaves, and secured by knotted rattan or twine; they can be hoisted on a wooden bar carrier. Quickly-made bark baskets held together with resin and rattan probably preceded basketry, but the archaeological record has not reported any. Bark canoes, also made by Orang Asli until recently, are more easily constructed than dugouts for river travel (Abbot 1907; Davison 1989; Kiew 1989). Notably, the tool kit of swidden farmers who also fish and hunt need not be different from that of mobile foragers. A dibble stick for planting seeds in a swidden is like a stick used to dig yams out of the ground. A half coconut shell is a food ladle and also a canoe bailer.[13]

Much has yet to be learned about early tools and technology on the Thai-Malay Peninsula. Scanning electron microscopic studies have shown that cut marks made on bone by cobble tools differ from those made by bamboo knives. The knives leave a distinctive residue on the bone, but such studies are rare in Southeast Asia. Ancient Asians in arid or cold regions may have favoured stone tool kits but those in tropical forest areas had less need for stone tools because they had bamboo. While students at one California university call their Archaeology Department "Stones and Bones" because of its focus on these items, such a department in Southeast Asia might well focus on the "bamboo and rattan age", if more attention were paid to perishable items of local tool kits.[14]

Eventually metals were added to Southeast Asian tool kits, but dates are uncertain. Bronze items show up in coastal sites in central Thailand at least 4,000 years ago. Bronze and iron appeared on the Thai-Malay Peninsula 1,000 to 3,000 years ago, at different times in different places. Imported six-inch nails were sometimes forged by Orang Asli into arrowheads or fish-spear tridents.

PREHISTORY AND ORANG ASLI

We can never know enough about history, but we can understand the history of the Thai-Malay Peninsula on a human scale. We can be sure that early foragers, swidden farmers, coastal fishers and traders adapted to new situations that arose over time. We can be sure that these situations arose because of changes in climate, geography, food sources, social networks and technologies. Not the least important was bamboo technology.

Our knowledge of the early uses of bamboo is far from complete. Nevertheless, enough is known to show that digging up the past in caves reveals only a small part of Orang Asli technology, or of Southeast Asian technology in general, all of which uses bamboo as a key component of a tool kit. Bamboo seems to encourage human ingenuity. It is no coincidence that Southeast Asia has many useful species of bamboo. This species variety helped bamboos become a foundation of Southeast Asian life in the past and, with luck, will continue to grace human life in the future as well.

The good news is that Southeast Asia still has sustainable bamboo. The bad news is that predatory palm oil plantations are a menace to the survival of bamboo, forests and people.

NOTES

1. Bamboo bridges and other bamboo technologies in Borneo are described in Wallace (1869), pp. 59–61.
2. While clay cooking pots have been dated in China to about 20,000 years ago, pottery shows up on the peninsula only much later, perhaps because bamboo cooking tubes not only were serviceable but also because pottery is fragile and heavy to carry around.
3. Other hunting devices include pit traps and bird liming.
4. The Semelai used wind bamboos near ladangs (swiddens) to scare away ghosts "... and must have been effective as I myself have yet to see a ghost in a Semelai ladang" (Williams-Hunt 1952: 30).
5. The bellows for a Jakun iron forge once used a hollow wooden cylinder (Lake and Kelsall 1894).
6. A Semai fire piston is described in Wells (1940), p. 219. Orang Asli usually employ fire saws that use rattan-friction on soft wood.

7. More recently, Semelai Orang Asli were known to have 19 kinds of traps, including deadfalls, pitfalls and snares, as well as thorn-lined fish traps (Gianno 1990).
8. The interiors of bamboo blowpipe tubes were smoothed by pulling a thorny rattan through their length.
9. Not all Asian bows use arrows, however. In Pakistan Chiral bows have two strings an inch apart with a leather sling in the middle. A stone shot from the sling can kill a squirrel at 50 yards (Moorhouse 1984).
10. African foragers were using poisoned arrows 40,000 years ago (Balter 2012).
11. Some twined bowstrings may not stay taut in a wet forest, but bowstrings made of twisted *terap* bark fibres used by Orang Asli even strengthen when wet. Likewise, anchor lines are made with *terap* ropes.
12. Fossil resins and gums have been found in Pahang, Perak and Kedah but have not been analyzed.
13. Open-sea fishing for tuna in Southeast Asia dates to 42,000 years ago, using bone fish hooks (O'Conner et al. 2011).
14. Bamboo stems, some burnt, were found in caves in Thailand dating to 10,000 or more years ago (Yen 1997).

REFERENCES

Abbot, W.
1907 Bark Canoes among the Jakuns and Dyaks. Journal of the Straits Branch of the Royal Asiatic Society 49: 109–10.

Adi Taha
1991 Gua Cha and the Archaeology of the Orang Asli. Bulletin of the Indo-Pacific Prehistory Association 11: 363–72.

Anderson, D.
1980 Lang Rongrien Rockshelter. Philadelphia: University of Pennsylvania Museum.
1997 Cave Archaeology in Southeast Asia. Geoarchaeology 12: 607–28.
2005 The Use of Caves in Peninsular Thailand. Asian Perspectives 44(1): 137–53.

Ave, W.
1988 Small-scale Use of Rattans in a Semai Community in West Malaysia. Economic Botany 42(1): 105–19.

Baer, A.
    2011   Iban DNA. Borneo Research Bulletin 42: 317–9.
Balfour, H.
    1925   Thorn-Lined Traps and their Distribution. Man 21: 33–7.
Balter, M.
    2012   Ice Age Stone Tools Hint at 40,000 Years of Bushman Culture.
           Science 337: 512.
Bedorarek, R.G.
    2000   Crossing the Timor Sea by Middle Palaeolithic Raft. Anthropos
           95(1): 37–47.
Davison, G.
    1989   Orang Asli Rafts. Malaysian Naturalist 42(4): 20–1.
Davison, G. et al.
    1995   The Malaysian Heritage and Scientific Expedition to Belum:
           Temengor Forest Reserve. Malaysian Nature Journal 48: 135–46.
Endicott, K.
    1969   Negrito Blowpipe Construction on the Lebir River. Federation
           Museums Journal 14: 1–36.
Evans, I.
    1916   Notes on the Sakai of the Kerbu River. Journal of the Federated
           Malay States Museums 7: 75–89.
    1937   The Negritos of Malaya. Cambridge: Cambridge University
           Press.
Gianno, R.
    1990   Semelai Culture and Resin Technology. New Haven: Connecticut
           Academy of Arts and Sciences.
Higham, C.
    2013   Hunter-Gatherers in Southeast Asia: From Prehistory to the
           Present. Human Biology 85(1–3): 21–43.
Howell, S.
    1997   Socicty and Cosmos. Chicago: University of Chicago Press.
HUGO Pan-Asian SNP Consortium
    2011   Mapping Human Diversity in Southeast Asia. Science 326:
           541–5.
Hunt, C. et al.
    2012   A 50,000 Year Record of late Pleistocene Tropical Vegetation and
           Human Impact in Lowland Borneo. Quaternary Science Reviews
           37: 61–80.

Kealhofer. I.
    2003 Looking into the Gap, Land Use and the Tropical Forest in Southern Thailand. Asian Perspectives 42(1): 72–95.

Kiew, B.I.
    1989 The Making of an Orang Asli Bark Boat. Malaysian Naturalist 42(4): 3–4.

Kopp, B. et al.
    1992 Analysis of Some Malayan Dart Poisons. Journal of Ethnopharmacology 36: 57–62.

Lake, H. and H. Kelsall
    1894 A Journey on the Sembrong River from Kuala Indau to Batu Pahat. Journal of the Straits Branch of the Royal Asiatic Society 26: 1–23.

Maloney, B.
    1998 A 22,000 Year Old Record of Past Environmental Change from Trang, South Thailand. Bulletin of the Indo-Pacific Prehistory Association 17: 54–5.

Matthews, J.
    1959 Rock Paintings Near Ipoh. Malaya in History 5(2): 22–5.

Mikluho-Maclay, M.
    1878 Ethnological Excursions on the Malay Peninsula. Journal of the Straits Branch of the Royal Asiatic Society 2: 205–21.

Moorhouse, G.
    1994 To the Frontier. New York: Harcourt, Brace.

Morris, K.
    1996 Forest Materials for Market: Rattan and the Semaq Beri of Ulu Tembling. Akademika 48: 93–112.

Mudar, K. and D. Anderson
    2007 New Evidence for Southeast Asian Pleistocene Foraging Economies. Asian Perspectives 46(2): 298–334.

Noone, H.D.
    1936 Report on the Settlements and Welfare of the Ple-Temiar Senoi of the Perak-Kelantan Watershed. Journal of the Federated Malay States Museums 9(4): 1–83.

Noone, R.
    1954 Notes on the Trade in Blowpipes and Blowpipe Bamboo in North Malaya. Federation Museums Journal 1–2: 1–18.

O'Conner, S. et al.
  2011   Pelagic Fishing at 42,000 Years before Present and the Maritime Skills of Modern Humans. Science 324: 1117–21.

Ofer Bar-Yusof et al.
  2012   Were Bamboo Tools Made in Prehistoric Southeast Asia: An Experimental View from South China. Quaternary International 269: 9–21.

Pookajorn, S.
  1996   Human Activities and Environmental Changes During the Late Pleistocene to Middle Holocene in Southern Thailand and Southeast Asia. *In* Humans at the End of the Ice Age. L. Strauss et al., eds. Pp. 291–313. New York: Plenum.

Saidin, M.
  2006   Bukit Bunuh, Lenggong, Malaysia. *In* Uncovering Southeast Asia's Past. E. Backus et al., eds. Pp. 60–4. Singapore: Singapore University Press.

Saidin, M. and P. Taçon
  2011   The Recent Rock Drawings of the Lenggong Valley. Antiquity 85: 459–75.

Schebesta, P.
  1926   The Bow and Arrow of the Semang. Man 53–54: 88–9.

Simonson, T. et al.
  2011   Ancestry of the Iban is Primarily Southeast Asian: Genetic Evidence from Autosomal, Mitochondrial, and Y Chromosomes. PLOS One 6(1): e16338.

Tan N.H. and S. Chia
  2010   "New" Rock Art from Gua Tambun, Perak, Malaysia. Rock Art Research 27(1): 9–18.

Taylor, J. et al.
  2001   Late Quaternary Peat Formation and Vegetation Dynamics in a Lowland Tropical Swamp: Ne Soon, Singapore. Palaeogeography, Palaeolimnology, Palaeoecology 171: 269–87.

Torrence, R.
  2001   Hunter-Gatherer Technology. *In* Hunter-Gatherers. C. Panter-Brick et al., eds. Cambridge: Cambridge University Press.

Wallace, A.R.
  1869   The Malay Archipelago. London: Macmillan.

Wells, C.
1940 North of Singapore. New York: R. McBride.

West, J. and J. Louys
2007 Differentiating Bamboo from Stone Tool Cut Marks in the Zooarchaeological Record. Journal of Archaeological Science 34(4): 512–8.

White, J.
2011 Emergence of Cultural Diversity in Mainland Southeast Asia: A View From Prehistory. *In* Dynamics of Human Diversity. N. Enfield, ed. Pp. 9–46. Canberra: Pacific Linguistics.

Williams-Hunt, P.
1952 An Introduction to the Malayan Aborigines. Kuala Lumpur: Government Press.

Wray, L.
1892 Ipoh Poison on the Malay Peninsula. Journal of the Anthropological Institute of Great Britain and Ireland 21: 476–81.

Yen D.E.
1997 Hoabinhian Horticulture? *In* Sunda and Sahul. J. Allen et al., eds. Pp. 567–99. London: Academic Press.

Zahorka, H.
2006 Blowpipe Dart Poison in Borneo and the Secret of its Production. Borneo Research Bulletin 37: 223–32.

Zuriana Majid
1990 The Tampanian Problem Resolved. Modern Quaternary Research in Southeast Asia 11: 71–96.

Part Three

ASLIAN LANGUAGES

chapter 7

The Language of Eating and Drinking: A Window on Orang Asli Meaning-Making

Niclas Burenhult and Nicole Kruspe

1. INTRODUCTION

For the ethnographer and field linguist alike, understanding one's object of inquiry involves painstaking examination and characterization of indigenous distinctions, big and small. Whether at the micro-level of meaningful sounds, or the macro-level of over-arching cosmological concepts, the teasing out of these distinctions—typically under trying circumstances—is a prerequisite for any successful interpretation of the representational levels and systems that interest us. At every level, however, language provides the primary inroad into the subject matter. This volume is dedicated to two scholars whose indefatigable pursuit of such distinctions has created the foundations of our current understanding of the rapidly vanishing identities and worldviews of the Orang Asli. The editor of the volume is in their company. For these scholars distinctions in language have not only been mere vehicles of analysis but eminent objects of study in their own right.

In the spirit of Geoffrey Benjamin, Bob Dentan and Kirk Endicott, we make in this chapter a first probe into the lexical domain of eating and drinking as it is construed in the Aslian languages, a branch of the Austroasiatic language family spoken by a majority of the Orang Asli of the Malay Peninsula. Fundamental to human experience and representation, the domain of ingestion has received increased linguistic attention in recent years. Setting out from our own primary field data from several Aslian languages, collected over the past 25 years (archived at www.lu.se/rwaai), we examine the form, meaning, and history of eating and drinking vocabulary and show that Aslian harbours unusual lexical strategies for ingestion. We place particular focus on ingestion events as expressed in the class of verbs. Moreover, in this seemingly restricted and mundane domain, we unpack semantic principles of wider significance to Aslian meaning-making, which speak directly to cultural distinctions within the Orang Asli sphere. In particular, we uncover a clear distinction in semantic categorization strategies between foragers and non-foragers.

2. BACKGROUND

2.1 The Linguistics of Eating and Drinking

Ingestion is central to human experience and a domain certain to be universally represented in language and thought. In fact, eating and drinking are such basic functions that they might seem to be good candidates for universal lexical expression in the world's languages. However, although all languages seem to target the domain lexically, there is increasing evidence of considerable diversity in how word meanings delimit the domain, and how they divide it up (Newman 2009a). At the one extreme, some languages have a single word which denotes both eating and drinking, and in some instances other activities of consumption as well, such as smoking (Aikhenvald 2009; Wierzbicka 2009). At the other extreme, some languages divide up ingestion into a number of different categories, with distinct words for different kinds of ingestion determined for example by the manner in which something is ingested or, less in evidence, by what is ingested (Rice 2009). Despite this semantic diversity, current wisdom asserts that the basic and universal character of ingestion makes it an important source domain for metaphorical imagery and involves widespread figurative extension to other experiential domains (Newman 2009b: vii). For example, words for eating are frequently mapped onto experiences like internalization (English: *swallow one's words*), emotional or intellectual satisfaction (English: *be consumed with passion*), psychological torment (English: *eaten up with anger*), and so on. Thus, the domains of cognition and emotion have a strong tendency to become targets of such ingestion imagery. Other more concrete examples of extension include physical destruction and sexual intercourse (Newman 2009c).

2.2 The Aslian Languages

Aslian is a small geographically and typologically outlying branch of the Austroasiatic language family, comprising some 18 languages, which are divided into three main sub-branches—Northern, Central and Southern—and the isolate Jah Hut (Dunn et al. 2011). Peculiar to this branch is a relatively well-documented societal and biological diversity unmatched not only within the family, but across mainland Southeast Asia more generally. Less well known is the linguistic diversity that the Aslian languages harbour, and the potential insights this can provide into the subsistence modes, the world views, the ethnographies, and the histories of their speakers. In a framework developed by Benjamin (1976, 1985), a three-way division within Aslian was postulated, where Northern Aslian languages aligned with the mobile foraging of the Semang, Central Aslian with swidden horticulture of the Senoi, and Southern Aslian with the collection of forest produce for trade of the Malayic cultural tradition. These categories however are not watertight, and several groups display considerable admixture cross-cutting the categories (Burenhult et al. 2011), for instance the Central Aslian speaking Semnam foragers, and the Southern Aslian speaking Semaq Beri foragers. Our previous research into Aslian genealogical relationships, using modern techniques (Dunn et al. 2011) but inspired by Benjamin (1976), essentially supported Benjamin's findings of a tripartite branching of the Aslian languages. In this study into Aslian semantic typology, we reveal how linguistic categorization strategies correlate with cultural distinctions, in this case foragers versus non-foragers, cross-cutting the genealogical subgroupings.

The Aslian languages are typologically peculiar in a number of ways. However, the feature of most concern to this study is their unusual penchant for very detailed meanings encoded in single words, especially verbs, and in domains presumed to be fundamental to human experience. This is a recurring feature across various verbal domains and emerges as a systematic and global principle of lexicalization (Matisoff 2003: 48–50; Kruspe et al. 2014: 466–7; Wnuk, forthcoming). For example, instead of having a word meaning "to carry" or "to transport", many Aslian languages have distinct, formally unrelated words for different manners of carrying: "carry in one's hand", "carry on one's back", "carry on one's shoulder", "carry on one's head", and so on. Another example is the domain of motion, which in most Aslian languages is divided up lexically according to the substrate and direction of motion: "walk along a river", "walk along a hillside", "walk up a hillside", "walk along crest of a ridge", etc. Even an activity like "looking" can be cut up into distinct one-word concepts like "look right in front", "look upwards", "look downwards", "look sideways". This semantic principle appears quite extreme from a cross-linguistic perspective, and its causes and effects on language in general remain largely unexplored.

3. THE ASLIAN INGESTION LEXICON

3.1 Semantic Encoding: Matter, Manner, and More

Lexicalization of ingestion can take a variety of forms and conflate different components of meaning. For example, in English and many other languages, the properties of the ingested substance account for the basic lexical distinction between *eat* (solid food) and *drink* (fluid). Many languages make further distinctions on the basis of the manner in which the substance is ingested, for example English *nibble*, *gobble*, *sip* and *swig*. Other conceivable components of semantic encoding include the location of ingestion (for example, at the table vs. in the open air), the instrument of ingestion (for example, an implement vs. the hand), or the force or actor of ingestion (*eat* vs. *feed*), although such lexical distinctions are less in evidence. Languages also vary greatly as to the semantic extension of their ingestion terms. Some have a single verb which covers both eating and drinking, and sometimes also activities like smoking, or having sexual intercourse, in which case the term might be better translated into English as "ingest", "consume", "enjoy", or similar (Aikhenvald 2009). Others, conversely, make more fine-grained distinctions, lexicalizing for example, the difference between ingesting separate types of solid food as in the Athapaskan languages (Landar 1964; Rice 2009; see Berlin 1967 for Mayan Tzeltal). The semantic range of English *eat* may in such cases be divided up and covered by more than one term.

As noted, a characteristic feature of the Aslian languages is their penchant for fine-grained semantic distinctions in the verbal lexicon (Kruspe et al. 2014: 466). The domain of ingestion is no exception, and two major semantic components are relevant in accounting for the rich Aslian ingestion vocabularies: (1) the categorial identity of the ingested substance (the "matter", 3.1.1), and (2) the way in which a substance is ingested (the "manner", 3.1.2). Furthermore, occasional terms encode additional components such as location, or cultural mores (3.1.3).

3.1.1 Verbs encoding categories of ingested matter

The simplest and most commonly attested lexical distinction noted for verbs of ingestion is a basic one between properties of the ingested substance where *eat* is for solid food and *drink* is for fluids. This is the case in a number of Aslian languages like Semelai (Southern Aslian) which has *ca* "to eat" and *jʔɔh* "to drink", Jah Hut (isolate) *caʔ* "to eat" and *wəh* "to drink" (Kruspe field notes 2002), and Ceq Wong (Northern Aslian) *caʔ* "to eat" and *ʔuh* "to drink" (Kruspe 2010). The Central Aslian languages Temiar (*ca:ʔ* "to eat" and *ʔɔ:k* "to drink") and Semai (*cɒ:ʔ* "to eat" and *ŋɔ:t* "to drink") also appear to follow this basic pattern (Benjamin pers. comm.; Diffloth pers. comm.).

Mah Meri (Southern Aslian) lacks a monolexemic (one-word) term for "to drink"; the verb *cado* is a fusion of *ca* "to eat" + *do* "liquid", suggesting a more generic meaning of consume, rather than eat (compare with the corresponding term in Mayali, an Australian language, Newman 2009: 4). In fact, this appears to be reflected in extended senses of the verb to mean "consume" or "destroy", see 3.3 below.

Another major organizing principle present in some Aslian languages—and one that is far less familiar to a speaker of English, Malay, Temiar, or Semelai, for example—is the encoding of different food categories in the ingestion verbs. The first indication in the literature of such distinctions was provided for Batek by Endicott (1974). In such languages, a small set of verbs express ingestion of a corresponding set of generic food categories represented by nouns. This pattern of encoding culturally defined generic categories of foodstuffs in basic eating verbs is hitherto unattested elsewhere among the world's languages, unrepresented for example in the contributions in Newman (2009a).

The Northern Aslian language Jahai, spoken by subsistence foragers in the upper parts of Perak and Kelantan and adjacent parts of southern Thailand, is a case in point. Here, four generic food categories—*bap* "starchy food", *tʔaʔ* "leafy greens", *bɔh* "ripe fruit", and *ʔay* "edible animal"—are closely matched by a set of four ingestion verbs. Each verb encodes the ingestion of members of a particular generic category: *gey* "to eat starchy food", *hẽw* "to eat leafy greens", *but* "to eat ripe fruit", and *muc* "to eat animal". There is no general verb corresponding to "to eat", so the eating verbs always involve implicit reference to which category of edibles is involved. However, the "eat starchy food" verb *gey* serves as a stand-in generic if the eaten matter is not known, or if a meal consists mainly of starchy food (tubers and rice being the most basic and common staples). But it is unthinkable to use this verb generically if the meal is known to consist of only animal tissue, for example.

With almost no exception, each eating verb associates with all the members of the respective food category and closely shadows the distinctions maintained in those categories (Levinson & Burenhult 2009: 161–4). This becomes especially clear in cases where an eaten species is classified differently depending on its state of maturity. Thus, you *but* a ripe banana (categorized as *bɔh*), but you *gey* a cooked unripe banana (categorized as *bap*). The semantic correspondence between food nouns and eating verbs in Jahai was a crucial piece of evidence in the development of the new theoretical and descriptive concept "semplates", semantic configurations which organize lexicon across form classes (Levinson & Burenhult 2009). In this chapter we document for the first time very similar semplates in closely related languages.

It is interesting in this context to note the categorial treatment of those few food items which do not belong to any of the four general food categories. These are often new introductions into the Jahai nutritional regime. While failing to subsume under those categories, such food does associate obligatorily with the eating verbs. The "eat ripe fruit" verb *but* is used for ingestion of honey, chocolate, and other sweets; the "eat leafy greens" verb *hɛ̃w* for noodles.

Another illuminating indication of the closely matched semantics in eating verbs and food categories is provided by the "eat edible animal" verb, *muc*. While this verb generally denotes the ingestion of any type of animal, one of its readings presupposes a dietary adherence to the Jahai food taxonomy in that it applies to all the species subordinate to the *ʔay* "edible animal" food category, all of which represent wild game or fish. Thus, to *muc* also means to willingly and habitually eat any of those animals. If you have permanent dietary restrictions which significantly reduce your ability to eat these items, such as those prescribed by Islamic law, you cannot *muc*. Indeed, one of the most commonly expressed hallmarks of ethnic identity among the Jahai, as opposed to the Malay-speaking Muslim majority of the peninsula, is the practice of "animal-eating".

The closely related Northern Aslian language Batek Deq has very similar food categories and associated ingestion verbs—*ciʔ* "to eat starchy food" and *bap* "starchy food"; *rɛɲ* "to eat game and mushrooms" (Endicott pers. comm.) and *ʔay* "game"; *hãw* "to eat vegetable foods" and *tʔaʔ* "palm cabbages" and *sayo* "vegetables"; and *lɔ̃t* "to eat ripe fruit" and *ploʔ* "fruit" and *lɛŋ lwɛy* "honey". Endicott (1974: 36–7), informed by a wordlist from Geoffrey Benjamin, was the first to discuss this parallelism (also referred to in Lye 2004: 60; cf. Kruspe field notes; Burenhult field notes). Thus, Batek Deq appears also to lack a generic verb for eat, like Jahai and Semaq Beri.

In a northern variety of Semaq Beri, a Southern Aslian language spoken by hunter-gatherers in Terengganu (Kruspe 2014), there is also a set of ingestion verbs that map onto culturally-specific food groups, first noted by Kuchikura (1987: 63). The verbs and corresponding food groups are: *ɲca* "to eat starchy foods" and *mãm* "starchy foods";

crɛt "to eat edible animal, fungi or cooked forest greens" and *ʔay* "edible animals, fungi and cooked forest greens"; *glɔt* "to eat ripe fruit" and *buah* "ripe fruit eaten raw" (from Malay *buah* "fruit"); *mamãh* "to eat raw vegetables" (from Malay *mamah* "to masticate") and the corresponding fourth group "raw vegetables" which has no label, although a subgroup are called *ʔulam* "raw accompaniment" (from Malay *ulam*).

Introduced foods are incorporated into existing categories and select for the corresponding verb, for example cassava, rice, and flour and derivative products like noodles, bread and cakes are in the *mãm* category and select the verb *ɲca* "to eat starchy food", and introduced vegetables like pumpkin, beans, cabbage and eggplant, and cow's milk are incorporated into the *ʔay* category and select *crɛt* "to eat edible game, fungi or cooked forest greens". There are few substances which do not fall into one of these groups, the exceptions being "honey" and *dak tuh* "breastmilk", and the introduced cultivars *tboʔ* "sugarcane" and *jagoŋ* "corn". Honey selects a verb based on the way in which it is prepared and eaten, for example *ɲca* "to eat a starchy food" is used for cooked bee larvae, which is classed as *mãm*, but with a manner verb (see 3.1.2) as in *blɛk* "to lick" for extracted honey boiled with young *Bayas* or *Langkap* palm fronds, which is then eaten off.

If one eats a starchy food in combination with an accompaniment from the *ʔay* class, it is described as *ɲca mãm* "to eat starchy food", but in all other cases, the speaker must select the verb appropriate to the category, and are observed to self-correct when inadvertently using the wrong term. The combination of a verb and an inappropriate entity is marked and indicates an extraordinary situation.

There is no word for meal, nor are there prescribed meal times; people will eat early in the morning if they have food when they wake up, otherwise they only eat when food becomes available. The Semaq Beri describe *mãm* as the minimal component that constitutes a meal, for the purpose of staving off hunger. A "real" meal includes an accompaniment of animal *ʔay*, which causes one to feel truly sated, rather than simply full, and speakers often say they have not really "eaten" if they have only consumed a meal of starchy food [Dentan (1970: 18) for Semai, Howell (1989: 230) for Ceq Wong for similar sentiments, and Kruspe field notes for Semelai]. Although meat is highly-prized, it is rarely eaten alone. When a hunter returns with game, regardless of the time of day, rice or tubers are prepared to accompany the meat (Kuchikura 1987: 63–4; Kruspe field notes 2008–11).

The Semaq Beri are a disparate group spread over a vast area from northeast Pahang and adjoining Kelantan and Terengganu, to areas south of the Pahang river. In a southeastern variety, also spoken by people who were traditionally foragers (Kruspe field notes), the attested eating verbs are *mĩʔ* "to eat starchy food", *crɛt* "to eat edible animals" and *glət* "to eat ripe fruit". Investigation is ongoing, but there only appears to be labelled food categories for edible animals (*ʔuʔɔʔ*) and ripe fruit (*bwah*), and not for starchy foods. It is unclear if there is a separate verb for the consumption of vegetables, and whether they constitute a separate class.

Preliminary observations suggest that similar semantic principles apply to the basic ingestion verbs in Semnam, a Central Aslian variety spoken by former foragers in the middle Perak valley. Thus, the verb *buut* "to eat leafy vegetables" maps on to the food category *bəəy* "leafy vegetables", *hilɨ̃t* "to eat fruit" to *kmɔɔʔ* "fruit", and *tuuɲ* "to eat animal" to *ʔnteʔ* "animal, game" (Burenhult and Wegener 2009: 295ff). However, the generic verbs *gɛɛy* "to eat" and *ʔɔ̃ŋ* "to drink" encode a distinction similar to that in English (solid food vs. fluid) and do not associate with more detailed classifications of ingested matter. That is, Semnam *gɛɛy*, unlike its cognatic Jahai equivalent *gey*, does not encode ingestion restricted to starchy food, a category for which there is no overarching term in Semnam.

It is noted that generally Aslian verbs do not encode distinctions about the kind of fluid being ingested, perhaps because traditionally after weaning the only beverage available was water; however, distinctions are found as in Ceq Wong *gak* "to drink vine sap", and Semelai *jmɛʔ* "to drink alcohol", the latter being the only group known to distill alcoholic beverages.

It is noteworthy that systems of food category-encoding eating verbs are only recorded in languages whose speakers are or were traditionally subsistence foragers: Jahai, Batek, Semaq Beri and Semnam. They remain unattested in other Aslian languages, including Ceq Wong, Semai, Semelai, Jah Hut and Mah Meri. Interestingly, however, the food categories as such may have very close parallels in these languages, as shown early on for Semai by Dentan (1970), and for Ceq Wong (Howell 1989: 170; Kruspe field notes).

3.1.2 Verbs encoding manner of ingestion

Aslian languages have a wealth of ingestion terms that encode specific techniques, including delivery of food to the mouth and mastication. Although associated with a limited set of ingested items, such techniques are typically unrestricted in relation to food categories of the kind described in 3.1.1. For example, some languages have a verb dedicated to ingesting by chewing the ingestible substance out of fibrous or crusty material that is then discarded, such as sugarcane, stringy tubers like the edible piscicide *Dioscorea piscatorum*, and honeycomb (Jahai *kpah*; Semaq Beri *kpat*). Another verb denotes sucking digestible matter out of a hard casing, such as molluscs or crustaceans from their shell, or marrow from a bone (Jahai, Kentaq and Batek Deq *sksɔk*, Semnam *sooʔ*, Mah Meri *cɔcɔp* and Ceq Wong *krɔɲ*). The preceding Ceq Wong term contrasts with *sɔk* "to suck liquids through an instrument". Other verbs denote ingesting any type of loose matter from a cupped hand (Jahai *həp*, Semnam *suoop*, Semelai *hʊp* and northern Semaq Beri *mĩk*); or biting off parts of crunchy or crispy food items, such as stalks, biscuits, or chocolate bars (Jahai *raɲip*, possibly from Malay *rangup* "crisp"); sucking until dissolved (Ceq Wong *but*); gnawing (Jahai *kɔc*, Ceq Wong *raɲ* and Semaq Beri *ruɲ*), and licking or lapping up (Jahai, Batek Deq and Ceq Wong *kal*, Semelai *lek* and Semaq Beri *blɛk*).

Some verbs denote eating techniques that are restricted to certain food types, thereby mapping implicitly onto the food categories described in 3.1.1. For example, the Jahai verb *bɨc,* Semnam *ɲɨɨc* and Semaq Beri *muc* denote eating that avoids stones or seeds of members of the generic food class "(ripe) fruit" of those languages. Ceq Wong *gɔt* "to swallow" is used for consuming small, whole ripe fruit, including the seed, and also medicine in tablet form. Jahai *lẽk,* Semnam *tic,* Ceq Wong *tɨs* and Mah Meri *kuntãy* denote eating by tearing off pieces of meat with one's teeth (from the bones or a larger piece of meat) and are restricted to food items subsumed by the generic class "edible animal", while Ceq Wong *tɔɲ* denotes biting off pieces of large starchy food like pieces of cassava or larger fruits and cassava bread, and *ɲwɛ̃h* "to chew on starchy foods". Semelai *mrataratah* and Mah Meri *latah* "to eat game or fish without a starchy food accompaniment" are loans from Malay *meratah* "to eat only one thing".

There are also verbs specifically for ingesting liquid foods, such as sipping or slurping hot liquids like the gravy from a stew, or slurping up hot noodles [Semaq Beri *timok*; Mah Meri *hirop* (from Malay *hirup* "to inhale, slurp"); Jahai *huc*].

Some languages have special verbs for ingesting substances which are then expelled, like Semaq Beri *suɲɛ̃l* "to chew tobacco" and Ceq Wong *mɛ̃h* "to masticate food for an infant". Chewing betel has a special verb form in Batek Teq *myã̃m*, while other languages simply use the generic verb "to eat", or the verb "to eat starch" for this activity.

Another large class of manner verbs is that which encodes the characteristics of the ingestion event in terms of the speed or intensity of the act of consumption, or the quantity of food consumed. These meanings are independent of the type of food eaten, and the technique involved. Jahai examples include *khɔp* "to gobble down", *cbɔt* "to devour", *sksɛ̃k* "to swallow quickly", and *jɲɔ̃ŋ* "to eat a lot, to glut". Batek and Semaq Beri encode magnitude with *bagɔt* "to eat a lot". Other examples are Semaq Beri *ratuɲ* "to chew vigorously (as on tough flesh)", *jɲɔ̃ŋ* "to suck vigorously", *bhan* "to eat voraciously", Semelai *ksep* "to eat a little at a time", and Mah Meri *pɔkɔt* "to eat clean" and *kõc* "to gulp down (fluids)". In Mah Meri there are also two verbs, now rarely heard, which indicate the size of a meal, *teŋkereʔ* "to eat a light meal", and *tkancak* "to feast". Semelai *bjujay* or *rbobɔɲ*, which express gobbling or eating up on one's own, are imbued with negative connotations.

Verbs of drinking may encode manner in terms of bodily posture (Ceq Wong *pijɔr* and Semaq Beri *gakgɛk* "to drink with the head tilted back"), and are restricted to the consumption of fluids. The Mah Meri term *dəbɔk* means "to drink in a manner that fouls the drink", for example with one's mouth over the bottle.

Aslian languages also have ingestion terms specific to ingestion by infants, for example "to suckle" (Mah Meri *mũʔ*, Jah Hut *bʔbuʔ*, Ceq Wong *buʔ*, Semaq Beri *mõm*), or "to eat pre-masticated food"

(Ceq Wong *mɔ̃k*). Often there are also special verb forms used when speaking to small children (Ceq Wong *gĩʔ* and Mah Meri *mam* "to eat"), or special imperative forms used to cajole infants (Semelai *ʔʔɔh!* "Drink!" and Ceq Wong *mɔʔ!* "Suckle!").

3.1.3 Other distinctions

In the Southern Aslian languages Semelai and Mah Meri location is also a relevant distinction in the domain of ingestion, reflecting a general worldview that the forest or areas outside of one's immediate place of residence are fraught with danger. To eat "in the wild" is a marked event, yet only in Semelai is this lexicalized in a unique verb *bbtir* "to eat a meal outdoors away from one's residence".

Across the Aslian sphere there are wide-ranging proscriptions in relation to the acquisition, handling and consumption of food. In many languages this is evident linguistically in avoidance terms for naming animals and other potential foodstuffs; see, for example, Lye (2004: 113–4) for Batek. In Southern Aslian this avoidance terminology extends to the articulation of ingestion, for instance in Mah Meri one should eat before setting out for the sea or forest, and the verb *ʔaʔam* "to eat" replaces the usual *ca*.

In Semelai, a special avoidance language (*cʋkʋp bsener*), based on word substitution, is used when speakers enter the forest to prevent various misfortunes such as violent storms. Many terms are often also used around the home, by some for an extra sense of security, for others the enjoyment of wordplay. It is the only Aslian avoidance language known to include verbs, and among them are numerous ingestion verbs. The semantic distinctions in the everyday language are maintained in the avoidance language, such as separate verbs for ingesting solids versus liquids, and smoking, a situation counter to that in some Australian languages for example, where such distinctions are removed. For some verbs there are multiple terms, because certain locations were associated with heightened danger warranting their own variants. *Ca* "to eat" is expressed as *bchɔr* from *chɔr* "to peck, of birds" or *bcher* "to have stomach pains" or the unanalyzable *grphɔp* (*g<rp>hɔp*) from *ghɔp* "to be hot". *Jʔɔh* "to drink" is replaced by *srdɔc rwaŋ* (*s<r>dɔc rwaŋ* cool<CAUS> inner.chamber) "to cool the inner chamber", and "to drink alcohol" is *crlew gnŋlɒŋ* (*c<r>lew g<nŋ>lɒŋ* bathe<CAUS> swallow<NMZ>) "to bathe the throat" from *clew* "to bathe, (avoidance term)".

Ingestion verbs also feature in the formation of avoidance terms, like *ca jkləlk* (*ca jk<k>lək* eat smoke<HAVE>) "to smoke", expressed as *ʔɲuk* "to suck, smoke homegrown tobacco" or *mrɔkɔk* "to smoke cigarettes" in everyday Semelai. Likewise, two avoidance terms for *ca pinaŋ* "to chew betel nut" are *ca br-ca* (eat MID-eat) literally "to eat (the) eaten", and *ca cmlaŋ* (eat be.red<NMZ>) "to eat the red one". Within our sample, however, we have only documented this feature in Semelai.

Another distinction found in Southern Aslian is the presence of dysphemistic forms for some ingestion verbs, used either to express displeasure or disgust at the consumer (Mah Meri *tdarah* "to eat"; Semelai *mmbarʔi* "to eat", *mmhəl* "to smoke", or at the consumed item Semelai *carɔʔ* "to eat").

The incidental distinctions discussed in this section, location and avoidance language, and dysphemism, while restricted to the Southern branch in our current data set, serve to illustrate some of the kinds of highly specific and culturally-anchored meaning-making that may be encountered within the domain of Aslian ingestion verbs.

3.2 Etymology: The Story of **ca:ʔ*

The history of languages can be explored by tracing the origins of words and their change in form and meaning through time, across their respective language families. Using such evidence, proto-forms are reconstructed. This approach provides valuable clues to the origins and development of current Aslian eating vocabulary. Thus, on the basis of existing Aslian words, a form **ca:ʔ* "to eat" has been reconstructed for Proto-Aslian, the ancestor of all Aslian languages, estimated to have been spoken 4,000–4,500 years ago (Diffloth 1975: 6; Dunn et al. 2013). This Proto-Aslian form is, in turn, ultimately derived from a Proto-Austroasiatic form **ca:ʔ* (Sidwell & Rau 2014: 345), reconstructed in eight of their eleven branches of Austroasiatic, and believed to belong to the very oldest layer of the Austroasiatic language family (Diffloth 2011: 118). The reflexes of the Proto-Aslian form in present-day Aslian languages are given in Table 7.1.

Table 7.1 Reflexes of the Proto-Aslian form *ca:ʔ* and their meanings across Aslian languages and subgroups

Language	Subgroup	*ca:ʔ* reflex	Recorded meaning
Ten'en Maniq	Northern	–	[cognate unattested]
Kensiw		ciʔ	"eat"?
Kentaq		ciʔ	"eat"?
Batek		ciʔ	"eat starchy food"
Menriq		ciʔ	"eat"?
Jahai		ciʔ	"ignite"
Ceq Wong		cəʔ	"eat"
Lanoh	Central	–	[cognate unattested]
Semnam		–	[cognate unattested]
Temiar		ca:ʔ	"eat"
Semai		cɒ:ʔ	"eat"
Jah Hut	Jah Hut	caʔ	"eat"
Semaq Beri N	Southern	ɲca	"eat starchy food"
Semaq Beri S		–	[cognate unattested]
Semelai		ca	"eat"
Mah Meri		ca	"eat"

As can be gleaned from Table 7.1, the descendant forms have undergone some systematic sound changes and diversification concomitant to the different subgroups of Aslian. Indeed, such changes form part of the very identification and definition of the subgroups. For example, in the Northern Aslian languages, the long *a:* of the proto-form has developed into a short *i* or *ə*; in Southern Aslian the *a:* has lost its length and the final glottal stop has been dropped; Jah Hut has lost the vowel length but retained the final glottal stop; two Central Aslian languages have retained both vowel length and the final consonant, Temiar displaying a reflex identical to the reconstructed Proto-Aslian form.

The exact meaning of the Proto-Aslian form *ca:ʔ* is unknown. However, most present-day reflexes are recorded as having a meaning close to a generic "to eat" or "to ingest solid food", and it is not unreasonable to posit a similar meaning for the proto-form (Diffloth 1975: 6; Sidwell & Rau 2014: 345). For some of the languages, the recorded meanings are distinct: the Northern Semaq Beri and Batek exponents are glossed as "to eat starchy food", showing that in these languages the form has undergone a semantic narrowing from a superordinate level "to eat" to denote a subordinate type of eating defined by a food category. The Jahai exponent has a meaning "to combust", "to ignite", having undergone a semantic shift away from ingestion to combustion according to a well-documented pattern of extension of eating vocabulary to denote material destruction (Newman 2009c), see 3.3 below. But note that while the present meaning is likely to be the result of extension historically, it is no longer an example of extension since the meaning has been altered completely and no longer applies to ingestion.

Cognates of *ca:ʔ* are unattested in four Aslian varieties: Ten'en Maniq (Northern Aslian), Lanoh and Semnam (Central Aslian), and a southern variety of Semaq Beri (Southern Aslian). In Ten'en Maniq the most general (but possibly not fully generic) term for "to eat" is *hãw* (Wnuk pers. comm.), a form which has cognates in other Northern Aslian languages meaning "to eat leafy vegetables" (see 3.1.1). In this case, the form has presumably undergone semantic widening from a subordinate level to a superordinate one, thus replacing the *ca:ʔ* reflex (which is still present as *ciʔ* "to eat" in the closely related varieties Kensiw and Kentaq). In Semnam and Lanoh the generic eat terms are *gɛɛy* and *gɛy*, respectively; a term that is attested in Central Aslian Semai as *gɔ:y* "to sit" (Dunn et al. 2011, Appendix [www.lu.se/rwaai]). This term from the domain of bodily postures seems to have undergone a semantic shift to ingestion, again replacing the *ca:ʔ* reflex completely. Jahai (Northern Aslian) has a cognate form *gey* "to eat starchy food" while lacking a generic "eat" term and reserving the *ca:ʔ* reflex for combustion senses, as described above.

Assuming that the original meaning of Proto-Aslian *ca:ʔ* was a generic "to eat" or "to ingest solid food", we have here observed patterns of semantic change in the form of narrowing or lexical loss that have affected a subset of the Aslian languages, including members of the

Northern, Central and Southern branches of the family. Conspicuously, though, these patterns are restricted to languages spoken by subsistence foragers, and those whose basic system of eating verbs is modeled semantically on different food categories. It is tempting to hypothesize that forager-specific semantic systems based on food categories have provided a rigid framework in which inherited Aslian eating vocabulary has had to undergo particularly forceful processes of semantic change. This would be in line with a general tendency for rapid replacement and change of basic vocabulary in many of the Aslian languages spoken by foragers (Burenhult et al. 2011; Dunn et al. 2011). One caveat: detailed semantic analyses of eating vocabulary are still lacking for several Aslian varieties; for example, our current glosses of cognates in forager languages like Kentaq, Kensiw and Menriq are provisional and may change as new data are collected.

3.3 The Semantic Extension of Ingestion Verbs

As noted in 2.1, there is a theoretical expectation that basic ingestion verbs are significant sources of extended meanings and figurative and metaphoric language (Newman 2009a). Cross-linguistically, ingestion verbs are well documented as a source for expressing events that focus either on the experiencer's act of consuming, the benefits of consumption or the consumption or destruction of the ingested entity. To some extent these cross-linguistic patterns hold true for Aslian languages as well, but what is harder to determine is to what extent they are truly figurative, and not just an extension of the core meaning to a more general "consume". While some of the examples here are clearly figurative like *ca kʰoy* (eat head) "to be taken advantage of financially" (Mah Meri), in others the consumption is perceived as actual within the speakers' worldview, for example the consumption of the soul by an evil shaman is perceived as actual by the Semelai.

   In our current data set, semantic extension is almost exclusively restricted to the generic eating verb, and appears overall to be restricted to quite specific subdomains, and in some cases in set expressions. Further, the attested extensions are almost exclusively based on the adverse effect on the consumed entity, for example *ko=ca bulan* (3UA=eat moon), literally "Someone has eaten the moon" to describe the moonless phase before a new moon (Semelai), or the blinding effect of a light *ʔu=cəʔ kaʔ mẽt* (3SG=eat LOC eye) "It strikes (it) in the eye" (Ceq Wong).

The agent of destruction may be animate or inanimate as the preceding examples demonstrate. Commonly attested agents range from fire (Semelai and Mah Meri *ca ʔus* "to be consumed by fire"), meteorological phenomena like a lightning strike, or the sun burning, or causing something to shine, and illness like the effects of a common cold *mrəɲ haʔ təŋ la=ki=ca=la=hawar* (be.itchy LOC ear because=3A=eat=AG=phlegm) "(My) ears are itching because (this) phlegm is affecting (them)", customary law (Semelai), and the grasshopper that causes tooth decay *ʔu=cəʔ blalaŋ* (3SG=eat grasshopper) "(I) have tooth decay", or tight elastic, and chaffing nappies (Ceq Wong). The verb *ca* may also be used to describe the effectiveness of an instrument in working on a surface, the only clear case of agent-based extension, for example a blade cutting as in *mə=daʔ ki=ca la=wɒy* (REL=NEG 3A=eat AG=knife) "the one the knife can't affect" the Semelai avoidance name for the Malayan Pangolin (*Manis javanica*), or a pen writing (Mah Meri). In Mah Meri *ca* also means "to suit or match", for example with colours or couples. Very similar extensions have been noted in Central Aslian Semai (Means & Means 1986: 24; Tufvesson pers. comm.).

The one instance of semantic extension with an ingestion verb other than a generic "eat" verb is Ceq Wong *gɔt* "to swallow", which also means "to drown", and is used to express the adverse effect one suffers when breaking a taboo. The extension of "swallow" to "drown" is again a cross-linguistically attested one (Newman 2009a).

A remarkable fact about the present data is that extended usage of ingestion verbs is limited in the languages in which it occurs and is entirely absent in other languages. For example, we are unable to find a single example of extended usage of eating verbs in Jahai and Semaq Beri, two of the languages for which we have the most extensive documentation and expertise. Why should this be so? It may not be a coincidence that the languages for which we have recorded extended uses all have and employ a generic eat verb (Ceq Wong, Mah Meri, Semelai). Those without extended uses do not have such a generic verb (Jahai, Semaq Beri) but have instead a more fine-grained basic system of eating distinctions modeled on food categories.

Possibly, the more detailed semantics of such distinctions do not lend themselves as well to semantic extension. It is noteworthy that their application within their subdomain of ingestion is rigidly restricted too: the verbs associate very closely with particular biological taxa and in some cases states of maturity or manner of preparation of the members of those taxa. It is unthinkable to extend the usage of such a verb to members of a food class for which it is not intended. On the other hand, we observe a general absence of figurative language and conceptual metaphor in these languages, so it may be a pattern that is not restricted solely to ingestion verbs (Burenhult field notes).

One final factor to consider here is that the semantic extension may not be an internal development, but is in fact the result of language contact. These constructions may be modeled on similar uses of Malay *makan* "to eat, consume, wear away; to take effect (of weapons)". Indeed this is the probable source of the Batek term *makan* "to be sharp". However returning to the point made previously, such a development may only be possible where a language has a generic eat verb on which to build this extension.

4. SUMMARY AND CONCLUSIONS

This chapter has examined the lexical representation of ingestion events in Aslian languages, as expressed in the class of verbs. Here we summarize our main findings.

First, the domain of ingestion has offered important insights into lexicalization processes in Aslian. In what emerges as an increasingly clear and distinct Aslian pattern, monolexemic (one-word) verbs encode fine-grained semantic distinctions and divide up the domain into great numbers of categories in each language. This is concordant with similar semantic specificity observed in other domains across the family. The languages display distinct eating verbs for ingesting solids versus liquids, or smoking, as well as rich sets of single-word terms for expressing manners of intake and mastication, and adverbial qualities such as the quantity consumed or speed of ingestion.

Second, two distinct over-arching semantic types or strategies emerge from the data, associating with different subsets of Aslian languages and attendant properties.

1. One type—epitomized by Jahai and Semaq Beri and with parallels in Batek and Semnam—has a basic system of three or four classificatory eating verbs which encode high-level specificity focused on the categorical membership of the consumed item. These verbs denote ingestion of food categories, typically meat, vegetables, starch and fruit. The languages tend not to have a generic "eat" verb superordinate to the food category verbs (but note the possible exception of Semnam, see below). A reflex of the Proto-Aslian eating verb *ca:ʔ* is either retained and then has a narrowed or altered meaning (as in the case of Batek, Jahai and Northern Semaq Beri) or it has been lost altogether (as in Semnam and a southern variety of Semaq Beri). The food category verbs co-exist with a large number of additional eating verbs which encode manner of eating; in some cases these verbs are subordinate to the basic food type verbs in that they associate with the same food categories, in others they cross-cut those same categories. Extended meanings of eating verbs in the form of figurative usage and metaphorical imagery have not been documented in these languages. This type correlates exclusively with languages whose speakers have traditionally been engaged in mobile subsistence foraging, over-riding language-genealogical boundaries (Jahai and Batek are Northern Aslian, Semnam is Central, Semaq Beri is Southern).

2. The second type—represented by Ceq Wong, Mah Meri, Semelai, and probably other languages like Jah Hut—has a superordinate ingestion category in the form of a generic verb meaning "to eat" or "to ingest solid food". A large number of additional and more specific ingestion verbs are event-focused without specific reference to the participants, i.e. they encode different manners of eating; these types of distinctions also occur in languages of Type 1. Food category verbs are undocumented. A reflex of the Proto-Aslian eating verb *ca:ʔ* is retained and consistently represents the generic "eat" verb in these languages. The languages show evidence of marginal extension of the "eat" verb to other domains, in accordance with a cross-linguistically expected pattern. This

type correlates exclusively with languages whose speakers are not mobile subsistence foragers but engage in mixed swidden horticulture and collecting for trade. As in the case of Type 1, it over-rides language-genealogical boundaries (Ceq Wong is Northern Aslian, Mah Meri and Semelai are Southern).

The Central Aslian languages are comparatively understudied as far as eating vocabulary is concerned and it is not clear if they would fit into one or the other category, or form an intermediate third type. Central Aslian Semnam, spoken by a group which shares societal features with both foragers and non-foragers and for which we have only limited primary data, gives the impression of having both a generic term (albeit not a reflex of *ca:ʔ*) and a basic system modeled on food types and may thus represent an intermediate of sorts.

   The food category-encoding verbs and the attendant lack of generic "eat" verbs is a hitherto rarely observed strategy for basic semantic distinctions in the domain of ingestion. Our observation that these systems cross-cut language-genealogical boundaries and coincide with a forager mode of subsistence offers a cultural clue to why such systems exist. The answer may lie in the composition of meals. The peninsular foragers, like many other hunter-gatherers, are "immediate return" societies (Woodburn 1982). Food resources are typically consumed directly, or shortly after they have been foraged, and they are rarely if ever stored for later consumption, nor elaborately processed (Woodburn 1982: 432). This has obvious implications for meal habits: meals do not occur according to a regular daily schedule, and they do not typically involve elaborate combinations of different foodstuffs (cf. Rousseau 2006). Many if not most meals involve opportunistic ingestion of a single resource. This means that there is no culturally salient type of ingestion event for which a general concept or label "eat" seems necessary; instead, each ingestion event can readily be conceptualized as something more specific. Possibly, this is what paves the way for more fine-grained systems of distinctions, such as those based on the culturally salient food categories.

   The ethnographic literature on the Orang Asli provides ample evidence of differences in food ideology and preferences between foragers and non-foragers. For example, Dentan (1965: 249–325) describes for the non-foraging Semai a preferred meal which combines a starchy staple with condiments in the form of meat, fish, mushrooms, or vegetables. Indeed, a meal which does not involve such a combination is considered incomplete. The foraging Batek, on the other hand, do not have such preferences but pursue and consume particular food categories and species according to availability, especially those which are seasonal (Endicott & Bellwood 1991: 163).

However, the forces of language contact should not be ruled out as a potential factor as well: as we have shown in previous work, peninsular foragers exhibit distinct patterns of lexical exchange and development not shared by other Aslian speakers (Burenhult et al. 2011). It is not unthinkable that their contact situation has also resulted in the streamlining of semantic strategies and principles beyond exchange of individual lexical items.

Whichever cultural underpinnings are at work, we believe we have identified a hitherto unrecognized pattern of lexicalization of the domain of ingestion. While seemingly at odds with the fundamentality of "eat", lacking for example the theoretically anticipated semantic extensions of the domain, the pattern is concordant with other domains as observed in Aslian languages. The endangered Aslian-speaking cultures have once again proved to be a fertile microcosm for exploring human meaning-making across linguistic and cultural boundaries.

ABBREVIATIONS AND CONVENTIONS

AG "agent"; CAUS "causative"; HAVE "possessive"; LOC "locative"; MID "middle voice"; NMZ "nominaliser"; REL "relative clause marker"; SG "singular"; 3A "third person agent"; 3UA "third person unidentified agent"; = "clitic"; < > "infix"

ACKNOWLEDGEMENTS

We would like to thank Kirk Endicott for inviting us to contribute to this volume, and for his comments and editorial assistance. Our contribution has also benefitted from discussions over the years with Geoffrey Benjamin, Bob Dentan, Lye Tuck-Po, Sylvia Tufvesson and Ewelina Wnuk. We are gratefully indebted to the communities, without whose acceptance and cooperation our research would not be possible.

Burenhult's research was supported by the Swedish Research Council (421-2007-1281), the Volkswagen Foundation (DOBES) and The European Research Council (the European Union's Seventh Framework Programme, Grant agreement no. 263512); Kruspe's research was supported by the Research Centre for Linguistic Typology, La Trobe University, the Hans Rausing Endangered Languages Program, Volkswagen Foundation (DOBES) and The Bank of Sweden Tercentenary Foundation (Riksbankens Jubileumsfund P13-0381). The Bank of Sweden Tercentenary Foundation (Riksbankens Jubileumsfond In:1-0066-1) funds the Austroasiatic archive RWAAI (www.lu.se/rwaai). We also acknowledge the support of our sponsors at Universiti Kebangsaan Malaysia, and the EPU and JAKOA for permission to conduct research.

The authors appear in alphabetical order and contributed to this chapter equally.

REFERENCES

Aikhenvald, A.
  2009 "Eating", "Drinking" and "Smoking": A Generic Verb and Its Semantics in Manambu. *In* The Linguistics of Eating and Drinking. J. Newman, ed. Pp. 91–108. Amsterdam: John Benjamins.

Benjamin, G.
  1976 Austroasiatic Subgroupings and Prehistory in the Malay Peninsula. *In* Austroasiatic Studies vol. 1. P.N. Jenner et al., eds. Pp. 37–128. (Oceanic linguistics, Special Publication, 13.) Honolulu: University of Hawai'i Press.
  1985 In the Long Term: Three Themes in Malayan Cultural Ecology. *In* Cultural Values and Human Ecology in Southeast Asia. K.L. Hutterer et al., eds. Pp. 219–78. Ann Arbor MI: Center for South and Southeast Asian Studies, University of Michigan.

Berlin, B.
   1967   Categories of Eating in Tzeltzal and Navaho. International Journal
           of American Linguistics 33: 1–6.
Burenhult, N., N. Kruspe and M. Dunn
   2011   Language History and Culture Groups among Austroasiatic-
           Speaking Foragers of the Malay Peninsula. *In* Dynamics of Human
           Diversity: The Case of Mainland Southeast Asia. N.J. Enfield, ed.
           Pp. 257–75. Canberra: Pacific Linguistics.
Burenhult, N. and C. Wegener
   2009   Preliminary Notes on the Phonology, Orthography and Vocabulary
           of Semnam (Austroasiatic, Malay Peninsula). Journal of the
           Southeast Asian Linguistics Society 1: 283–312.
Dentan, R.K.
   1965   Some Senoi Semai Dietary Restrictions: A Study of Food
           Behaviour in a Malayan Hill Tribe. Unpublished PhD dissertation,
           Yale University.
   1970   Labels and Rituals in Semai Classification. Ethnology 9(1): 16–25.
Diffloth, G.
   1975   Les Langues Mon-Khmer de Malaisie: Classification Historique
           et Innovations [The Mon-Khmer Languages of Malaysia:
           Historical Classification and Innovations]. Asie du Sud-Est et
           Monde Insulinde 6(4): 1–19.
   2011   Kuay in Cambodia: A Vocabulary with Historical Comments.
           Phnom Penh: Tuk Tuk editions.
Dunn, M., N. Burenhult, N. Kruspe, S. Tufvesson and N. Becker
   2011   Aslian Linguistic Prehistory: A Case Study in Computational
           Phylogenetics. Diachronica 28: 291–323. Doi: 10.1075/28.3.01
Dunn, M., N. Kruspe, and N. Burenhult
   2013   Time and place in the prehistory of the Aslian languages. Human
           Biology 85: 383–99.
Endicott, K.
   1974   Batek Negrito Economy and Social Organization. Unpublished
           PhD dissertation, Harvard University.
Endicott, K. and P. Bellwood
   1991   The Possibility of Independent Foraging in the Rain Forest of
           Peninsular Malaysia. Human Ecology 19(2):151–85.
Haspelmath, M. and U. Tadmor, eds.
   2009   World Loanword Database. Munich: Max Planck Digital Library.

Howell, S.
 1989   Society and Cosmos: Chewong of Peninsular Malaysia. Chicago: University of Chicago Press.

Jenner, P.N., L.C. Thompson and S. Starosta
 1976   Austroasiatic Studies, 2 vols. (Oceanic linguistics, Special Publication, 13.) Honolulu: University of Hawai'i Press.

Jenny, M. and P. Sidwell, eds.
 2014   The Handbook of Austroasiatic Languages, 2 vols. Leiden: Brill.

Kruspe, N.
 2009   Ceq Wong Vocabulary. *In* World Loanword Database. M. Haspelmath and U. Tadmor, eds. wold.clld.org/vocabulary/26. Munich: Max Planck Digital Library.
 2014   Semaq Beri. *In* The Handbook of Austroasiatic Languages. M. Jenny and P. Sidwell, eds. Pp. 475–516. Leiden: Brill.

Kruspe, N., N. Burenhult and E. Wnuk
 2014   Northern Aslian. *In* The Handbook of Austroasiatic Languages. M. Jenny and P. Sidwell, eds. Pp. 419–74. Leiden: Brill.

Kuchikura, Y.
 1987   Subsistence Ecology among Semaq Beri Hunter-Gatherers of Peninsular Malaysia. Hokkaido Behavioral Science Report Series E, No. 1. Sapporo: Hokkaido University.

Landar, H.
 1964   Seven Navajo Verbs of Eating. International Journal of American Linguistics 30: 94–6.

Levinson, S.C. and N. Burenhult
 2009   Semplates: A New Concept in Lexical Semantics? Language 85: 153–74.

Lye, T-P.
 2006   Changing Pathways: Forest Degradation and the Batek of Pahang, Malaysia. Lanham, MD: Lexington Books.

Matisoff, J.A.
 2003   Aslian: Mon-Khmer of the Malay Peninsula. Mon-Khmer Studies 33: 1–58.

Means, N. and P.B. Means
 1986   Sengoi-English English-Sengoi Dictionary. University of Toronto and University of York: The Joint Centre on Modern East Asia.

Newman, J., ed.

2009a The Linguistics of Eating and Drinking. Amsterdam: John Benjamins Publishing.

Newman, J.

2009b Preface. *In* The Linguistics of Eating and Drinking. J. Newman, ed. Pp. vii–xii. Amsterdam: John Benjamins Publishing.

2009c A Cross-Linguistic Overview of "Eat" and "Drink". *In* The Linguistics of Eating and Drinking. J. Newman, ed. Pp. 1–26. Amsterdam: John Benjamins Publishing.

Rice, S.

2009 Athapaskan Eating and Drinking Verbs and Constructions. *In* The Linguistics of Eating and Drinking, J. Newman, ed. Pp. 109–52. Amsterdam: John Benjamins Publishing.

Rousseau, J.

2006 Rethinking Social Evolution: The Perspective from Middle-Range Societies. Montréal: McGill-Queen's University Press.

Sidwell, P. and F. Rau

2014 Austroasiatic Comparative-Historical Reconstruction: An Overview. *In* The Handbook of Austroasiatic Languages, M. Jenny and P. Sidwell, eds. Vol. 1. Pp. 221–363. 2 vols. Leiden: Brill.

Wierzbicka, A.

2009 All People Eat and Drink: Does This Mean That "Eat" and "Drink" Are Universal Human Concepts? *In* The Linguistics of Eating and Drinking, J. Newman, ed. Pp. 65–90. Amsterdam: John Benjamins Publishing.

Wnuk, E.

n.d. Semantic Specificity in Maniq Verbs of Perception. Unpublished PhD thesis, Max Planck Institute for Psycholinguistics, Nijmegen. Forthcoming.

Woodburn, J.

1982 Egalitarian Societies. Man 17(3): 431–51.

Part Four

ORANG ASLI RELIGIONS

chapter 8

Landscape of Ghosts: Semelai Shamanism and a Cosmological Map

Rosemary Gianno

INTRODUCTION

In 1980, during my first meeting with Kak Hakek, a Semelai shaman (*puyɒŋ*), while he was explaining the significance of *kijay* incense resin, and the tree (*Triomma malaccensis* Hook f.) from which it comes, he sketched, unsolicited, a map of paths through the Semelai cosmos that situated the tree between this world and the after-world (Map 8.1a). He explained that during the *b-blyan,* a trance ritual, the shaman's soul might follow that path in its search for the missing soul of a seriously-ill person.[1]

The *b-blyan* establishes the shaman as a cosmic traveller with alien contacts. The trance ritual is cognitively structured as a journey through a conventionalized sequence of named loci, that is to say, a topogeny (Fox 1997). Moving through a dreamed landscape, encountering a succession of spirit personages, the shaman enacts a heroic narrative in his attempt to rescue the soul of a person who is teetering between life and death. Kak's ability to draw a map based on his cosmological knowledge and soul journeying allowed him to answer my questions, while demonstrating his credentials as a powerful shaman. His map

Map 8.1a Kak's map

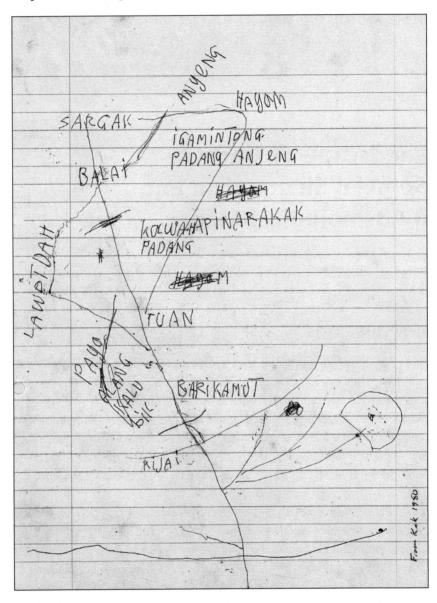

graphically provided a stage, outside of the ritual, where he could narrate what he did and where he sought out spirit-helpers while eluding dangerous spirit agents.

However, when I searched in the map for the loci that comprise the main path of the curing ritual, many were difficult to find, and most of the features in the map do not figure in the main sequence of the ritual. The *b-blyan* main path or drumbeat topogeny, nowadays the only one followed, barely appears in the map. Apparently what Kak had done is to combine in one map cosmological schemas found in the curing ritual, funerary ritual and two magical incantations. Side paths that diverge from the main path in the *b-blyan* are central to the map. The scant overlap between the ritual and map suggests that Kak had attempted to combine distinct Semelai cosmological narrative schemas that fit together uneasily (Wessing 2010).

SEMELAI CULTURE AND SOCIETY IN CONTEXT

Semelais (5,026 persons in 2000 [COAC 2012]) speak a Southern Aslian Mon-Khmer language that incorporates many grammatical and lexical Malay borrowings. Their homeland in eastern Negeri Sembilan and southwestern Pahang, before massive deforestation, was comprised of low-lying, swampy tropical rainforest. As a pioneering, swiddening, rice-cultivating people with incipient political ranking, and oriented toward forest product trade, Semelais fit within Benjamin's "Malayic traditions" grouping (Benjamin 2011). Trade to downstream communities created some surplus to support incipient social hierarchy and differentiation. Travel for trade and interaction with ethnic others helped them develop a worldview oriented toward the outside world.

Much of the richness and distinctiveness of Semelai culture derived from their interactions with the lowland rainforest, wetlands and wildlife that surrounded them. Now, with that environment largely degraded or destroyed and replaced by oil palm estates and rubber lots, their subsistence economy has diminished significantly, and socio-economic inequality is growing. Nevertheless, they retain their Semelai language and cultural identity.

PROHIBITIONS

Semelai customary law outlines the rules people must follow in relation to particular other beings and forces in the world in order to avoid sickness, misfortune and death. They make a major distinction between *pantaŋ* ("taboos"), on the one hand, and *dusaʔ* ("sin") and *papaʔ* ("in a state of sin"), on the other.

Breaking Taboos

Pantaŋ are the rules that one should follow relative to sentient beings, including plants and animals, in an animistic cosmos, within which one feels relatively powerless. For example, while one can play with (even torture) a land leech, one cannot laugh at it; such a transgression could precipitate a deadly thunderstorm and flood. Semelais seem to relate to *pantaŋ* as to the law of gravity: one ignores them at one's peril. The transgressive act does not make one a bad person, just not very smart.

Sinful Behaviour

Dusaʔ, in contrast, are transgressions of rules concerning other human beings. The idea is in accord with a cosmology that sharply distinguishes human beings from other beings. The prototypical sinful act is addressing one's parent-in-law by name, believed to cause uterine prolapse in women and swollen testicles in men. But a state of sin (*papaʔ*) is caused by many transgressions against other people, including ridicule or laughter, stealing and murder. While breaking a taboo potentially brings illness or chaos, committing a sin taints the person in the supreme deity's eyes, condemning that person to prolonged suffering, in life or in death.

SOULS, GHOSTS AND SPIRITS

Bayaŋ

Semelai souls are seen as bounded corporeal spirits while Semelai ghosts and spirits are, reciprocally, free, unfettered, potentially dangerous souls. The spiritual essence or soul of a living being in Semelai is a *bayaŋ*, which also means "shadow", implying that the soul reflects the form and size of the body. During dreams, the soul is thought to detach from the body and to travel in the spirit world. Its capture by spirits causes sickness. Death results in permanent soul detachment and creates a spirit or ghost.

Semelai spirit typology is formalized and public. There are three major, mostly non-personalized, types: *kmũc, pʔreʔ* and *skɔʔ*, each associated with a spatially defined cosmological domain.

Kmũc

Kʰbəs kmũc means "to die a natural or good death", that is, from old age or sickness. The ghosts created by such a death are called *kmũc*. Dying *bayaŋ* follow the *kmũc* forest path to the *balay jamwan* ("feasting hall"), where they join their deceased kin, become *kmũc* and then go on to *sərgaʔ* ("paradise"). (See details below.) *Kmũc* are the least feared spirits since they dwell far from the living in their own community and rarely cause trouble.

Pʔreʔ

Kʰbəs pʔreʔ means "to die with 'blood coming out' (*mhãm krwɒl*), accidentally, unnaturally", for example, from a tiger attack, a falling tree, falling from a tree, murder, but also drowning and epidemic disease (cf. Gianno 1990: 116).[2] Immediately after death, *pʔreʔ* go to a place variously called *pʔreʔ, pʔreʔ* country, *pʔreʔ* forest, *pʔreʔ* city, or *lawot darah* ("sea of blood") (see Map 8.1b). Then, some said, they follow a red wind thread made from their blood to the *balay* where they briefly reunite with their deceased *kmũc* kin before returning to this world.

High flying, *pʔreʔ* are the most mobile and feared spirits. In incantations they are called *sitan* (Malay *setan*, Arabic *shaitan*, English "satan"). *Sitan* are associated with thunderstorms. *Pʔreʔ* attach threads between the victim and perpetrator of an impending accident. Violating certain taboos could cause *pʔreʔ* to send a tiger or crocodile after the violator. For example, while in the forest, if one notices some blood but with no known source, it should not be acknowledged.

Map 8.1b Kak's map (edited)

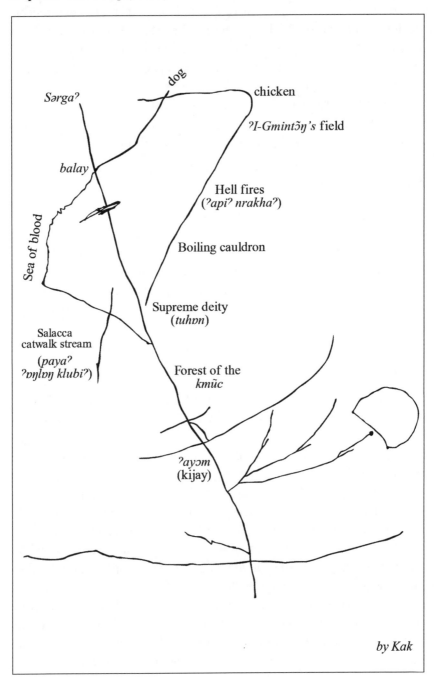

dog

Sərgaʔ

chicken

ʔI-Gmintɔ̃ŋ's field

balay

Hell fires
(*ʔapiʔ nrakhaʔ*)

Sea of blood

Boiling cauldron

Supreme deity
(*tuhɒn*)

Salacca
catwalk stream
(*payaʔ
ʔɒŋlɒŋ klubiʔ*)

Forest of the
kmũc

ʔayɔm
(kijay)

by Kak

Skɔʔ

Skɔʔ haunt the forest in this world, especially prominent features such as large trees, rocks and pools of water. They are the "owners" of the forest. *Skɔʔ* seem not to have died at all; they were just always there. Some said they were people lost in the forest or that they died in the flood that created Tasek Bera. They therefore had never travelled to the after-world.

Skɔʔ are often blamed for illnesses. They are thought to either invade a person's body in order to eat the soul. If a person in the forest is craving a certain food, especially game, this will cause the victim's soul to resemble that animal to *skɔʔ,* who will then try to trap it, cage it and eventually eat it. *Skɔʔ* are not evil, but when they cage the soul, to be slaughtered later, that person experiences soul loss. The shaman investigates that possibility in a *b-blyan* and then tries to rescue the soul before it is eaten. People whose souls are eaten by *skɔʔ* die *kmũc*.

HEALERS

Semelais have diverse approaches to diagnosing and treating illnesses. Semelai magico-religious specialists combine the idea that illness results from soul loss with the idea that harmful spiritual agents can invade the body. As one man said, "It's not just that souls travel, it's also that sickness enters." Generally, Semelais use magical spells to counteract spirit intrusion and shamanic journeying to retrieve souls. Semelai healers today consider biomedicine effective in treating illnesses from germs (*kuman*), while they themselves specialize in spirit-related sickness.

Magicians

While most Semelais know some incantations (*jampiʔ*), *bɔmɔ̃* are magicians who have acquired and memorized many of them. Their recitation can repel harmful spirits or attract beneficial ones. Incantations to repel spirits, such as *matiʔanak* ("malevolent spirits of women who died in childbirth"), are believed to work by naming the agent, its characteristics, and its origins in order to more clearly and concretely define it, thus neutralizing its effect. Harmful spells constitute sorcery. A *bɔmɔ̃*'s magical practices do not involve his soul. There are many more magicians than shamans.

The *tŋpuŋ* (< *tpuŋ* "flour") is a more powerful magical treatment for a person with a lingering illness. Rice flour is mixed with water, producing a pasty ball. The watery blandness of the rice flour works as a boundary weakener. The ball is fumigated with *kijay* incense. *Tŋpuŋ* is considered more efficacious than *jampi?* because of the many spells whispered beforehand into the ball with the prospect that at least one will work. The ball is then rolled over the head, torso, and any painful area, to extract the invading spirit.

Shamans

Puyvŋ (soul-journeying shamans) minister to individuals in the *b-blyan* ritual. In Semelai, *srɛŋ* denotes an ability to experience efficacious dreams during sleep or trance, in which one's soul leaves the body and can see what is normally unseen. The souls of those who are *srɛŋ* are believed able to travel in the spirit world in an intentional and controlled way, interacting and communicating with spirits. Shamans can fly, but only on a horse, unlike a witch, which can fly without a horse. They can also observe others remotely.

Individuals become *srɛŋ* because a spirit familiar confers it upon them. For males, the spirit familiar becomes his spirit wife, for females, her spirit husband. Being *srɛŋ* is a two-edged sword, however. Because of the shaman's soul's relatively unbound mobility and liminality, it is feared that shamans could potentially harm their enemies through witchcraft. Therefore, the *b-blyan*'s relatively rigid and controlled liturgy can be interpreted as a method for containing and channelling the shaman's powers and making the shaman's travels transparent. Becoming a shaman amounts to public acknowledgment of one's soul-journeying abilities, while vowing to use them to heal others. In dreams and the *b-blyan*, the shaman's soul travels intentionally in the spirit world and develops relationships with otherwise unseen agents that can assist in healing. Shamans must also have extensive knowledge of incantations and mythic narratives. While very few Semelai shamans are left, a *b-blyan* I attended in January 2012 included one shaman, five drummers and perhaps as many as a hundred other attendees.

The *puyɒŋ,* in contrast to the *baten* (highest ranked political office, chief), is not an inherited office, although descent from a *puyɒŋ* may enhance one's credentials. I know of only one case at Tasek Bera, ethnohistorically, where the *baten* was also a *puyɒŋ.* It takes initiative and success in healing to achieve the status of *puyɒŋ. Puyɒŋ* are quasi-members of the political establishment, participating in some judgments and fines, such as violations of marriage rules. *Puyɒŋ* can be intimidating. But shamanic power is not unmitigated; Semelai shamans mostly demonstrate potency through healing. Therefore, if patients do not improve, criticisms may be expressed and perceived shamanic power diminished.

TRANCE CURING RITUAL

The purpose of the *b-blyan* is for the shaman to find the missing soul and return it to the patient before it reaches the land of the dead. The curing ritual usually takes place in a house. During the ceremony, the shaman sits cross-legged facing east with his eyes closed, the patient lying before him, and drummers to his side (see Plate 8.1).

He wears a cloak (*bajuʔ*) made from fan palm shoots over his shoulders, and in one hand holds a whisk, which is shaken and sometimes slapped against the other hand, made from the same shoots and seven *cpɔt* (*Bonnaya* sp.) leaves. A "wind string" (*taliʔ ribut*) made of fan palm shoots spans the room, west to east, forming a catwalk for the shaman's soul. The house is not completely dark. *Kijay* incense is burned continuously during the ritual.

When the shaman goes into trance, his soul, following the wind string out of the house, searches for the patient's soul along a main pathway (*tɛŋ,* meaning "vehicle"), with optional branching side paths. Each locus in the journey is also called a *tɛŋ,* and is signalled by a particular drumbeat rhythm (*nkpok*) and song. The ritual transports the shaman's soul to the succession of loci where anthropomorphic spirits of plant and animal species, deceased shamans, culture heroes, various ghosts, artefacts and geographic features (such as mountains and seas)

Plate 8.1 Shaman and drummers

(Photo credit: Rosemary Gianno)

are found. These spirit-guides can provide sacred knowledge or healing substances to aid the *puyŋ* in his work.

The topogenic main path of the ritual, its "backbone" as it were, consists of anywhere from 30 to 83 different loci. These are the different points in the topogeny, each marked by a distinctive drumbeat.

Because the liturgy is primarily a complicated series of drumbeats, an experienced and knowledgeable senior *taron* ("drummer") is required. Drummers often have to study to achieve this proficiency. For example, one *taron* tape-recorded an older, more experienced drummer playing the basic rhythm of each drumbeat so that he could practise them. Semelais make a point of saying that, in the past, a drummer had to be secured for a *b-blyan* before the shaman, suggesting primacy. The drumbeats are said to lead the shaman even though, in practice, it is the shaman who decides, for example, whether to take a particular side road. Although I never attended a *b-blyan* that used a side path, drummers I spoke with indicated that the shaman informed them beforehand what side paths, if any, to follow. The coordination between the shaman and drummers is a major way that the *b-blyan*'s meaning is shared beyond the shaman, and a way that the liturgy becomes conventionalized and sociocentric, while leaving room for some innovation by individual shamans.

Singing is also central to the *b-blyan*, but, perhaps, less overtly. While "to sing" in Semelai is *ɲaɲiʔ,* shamanic singing in a *b-blyan* is *m-rawet.* The drumbeats honour each spirit at each locus visited, while the true name of the spirit there must be sung. At each intersection with a side path, the shaman inquires as to the soul's whereabouts. Sometimes the shaman acquires a healing song or soothing dew from a particular spirit-guide. The shaman vocalizes his experiences, which vary with each *b-blyan*, in song. The drum rhythms are conventional and public, as anyone can pick up a drum and follow along. Hood (1978: 203–65) presents possible scenarios for *b-blyan* main path loci.

The ritual is liturgy-centred (as opposed to performer-centred) in that it is "dominated by orderly sets of ritual procedures which coordinate the actions of practitioners and congregants" (Atkinson 1989: 14). However, because it is only the shaman who sings (there is no chorus), because the songs use poetic language and alternative vocabulary, and because his singing is often overpowered by the drums, the shaman's songs may not be understood or even heard by others. The audience at a *b-blyan*, at least based on my experience, is consequently not very engaged, because they generally have little to do and do not necessarily recognize what is transpiring as it is happening. Most either play cards outside of the main room or fall asleep. Shamans themselves sometimes use a stand-in for part of the night. There are also five breaks at specified loci in the *b-blyan* sequence when the drumming stops and the shaman emerges from his trance. A *tŋpuŋ* (flour extraction ritual) is performed before the drumming resumes.

However, if the *puyɒŋ,* after the *b-blyan*, narrates his experiences, it is far more interesting. He describes how his soul flies on a horse, with the wind, out of the house toward the east, and returns at dawn. He follows the efficacious sound of the drums (*rnẽŋ*), which, as the barking of dogs, leads to the errant soul. The *Bonnaya* sp. leaves form his umbrella, shielding him from the sun and catching the wind, while the fan palm leaves look and sound like the rattling of chains (*rantay*)

to spirits to frighten them away. The shaman's soul is also guided by
the *kijay* incense, an avatar of his spirit wife. The vapour, seen as
stinging insects by obstructing spirits, can chase them away.

The structure of the *b-blyan* allows some agency. Particular
shamans have their own sequence of loci that they habitually use, adding
songs they receive from their spirit-guides, but they must coordinate
these changes with the drummers beforehand. Within the performance,
both the misplaced soul and the shaman have agency and can make
different choices. As mentioned above, individual shamans decide
whether or not to take a particular side path. What transpires in the
b-kkmũc, one of the side paths, for example, is contingent. Whether
the soul uses one set of roots or another to descend to the *kmũc* forest,
whether the soul steps on a gourd near the *balay*, indicates whether
the soul will likely return to this world. Consequently, the narrative
and diagnosis, often relayed during breaks or the next day, vary. But,
at the same time, society, through the drumbeats, has contained the
shaman's movements.

B-blyan Side Paths

There are several optional side paths that branch from the main path at
specified loci. These include the *b-kkmũc* (going to *kmũc*), *b-bboŋsoŋ*
(going to the *bosoŋ/boŋsoŋ* sea), *b-ssraw* (going to the *sraw* sea)
and *b-sskɔʔ* (going to the *skɔʔ*). Each topogenic side path takes the
shaman through a specific cosmological region where the patient's
soul may be found. After journeying through a side path, the shaman
then returns to the main path and continues along it to its terminal
locus.

The *B-kkmũc* Side Path

Taking the *kmũc* forest path is considered the most dangerous for the
shaman as it constitutes a near death experience. The road, deep and
well-trodden by the very ill and very old of all species, goes downslope
toward the sunset. It is not associated with a specific disease. *Kmũc* is
normally bypassed because the shaman's spirit guides usually do not
indicate that the soul is there. Even though shamans rarely go there,

there is detailed knowledge of *kmũc*, perhaps because its proximity to death makes what experience *puyɒŋ* and the very sick have had there all the more meaningful and memorable.

According to Kak's variant of the *b-blyan*, *kawɔŋ* ("argus pheasant") stands at the junction of this path with the main path and can be questioned. I compiled this list of *b-kkmũc* path loci (cf. Hood 1978: 436–7 for a slightly different list):

ʔAyɔm (*Triomma malaccensis* tree) [See Map 8.1b]
Ralɔŋ Ga-boŋsuʔ (*Ga-boŋsuʔ*'s infant coffin)
Gpəl (*Canarium littorale* tree)
Kmalaw (*Parinari oblongifolia* tree)
Kdondoŋ (*Canarium* sp. tree)
Pikʰɔm (a short rattan-like palm)
Baŋkoŋ (*Artocarpus* sp. tree)
Jlutuŋ (Dyera costulata tree*)*
Srɒy kmũc (*Shorea acuminata* tree)
Payaʔ ladaŋan (*Pandanus* sp. stream) [See Map 8.1b]
Relek (*Phrynium* sp. herb) *(lerek* in Malay)
Cʰɔŋ traŋ (Clear Hill)
Pawoh (*Irvingia malayana* tree)
Crŋlɒŋ (unidentified secondary forest tree species)
Bandon (a vine) with *tawɔ* (gibbon)
Dŋdɔŋ galaŋ (log athwart the path) [See Map 8.1b]
Pagar sasaʔ (swidden fence)
Tmakaw sraja kʰayal (a strong tobacco)
Tlagaʔ kmũc (*kmũc* well)
Balay jamwan (feasting hall)

As a shaman travels deeper down the *kmũc* path leading to death, he must have the spiritual power to resist its seductive force. Because a *kmũc* accompanies the soul, the shaman has to wrest the soul away somehow. When the shaman finds the pair, he circles around them and blocks the path, unleashing the stinging insects. He could also transform into a tiger or bear. The *kmũc* is chased back to *sərgaʔ*, and the soul either returns on its own to this world or is captured by the shaman and placed in his cloak.

B-bboŋsoŋ, *B-sŋgugut* and *B-ssraw*

These *b-blyan* side paths represent seas associated with particular diseases. The patient's symptoms may suggest to the shaman where to look for the missing soul. *B-bboŋsoŋ* (going to *bosoŋ*) begins with *kɔjɔr*, identified variously as a bird or chevrotain anthropomorphic spirit, who can be questioned about the lost soul. *Bosoŋ* was identified as jaundiced fever but also as a childhood swelling of the body, face and eyes. Whether the path leads just to *lawot bosoŋ* (sea of *bosoŋ*) or also to *lawot sŋgugut* (sea of dysmenorrhea) and *lawot sraw* (sea of childhood fevered seizures) varied among consultants (cf. Hood 1978: 439). Each of these bodies of water and surrounding land is inhabited by the animal species believed to cause each illness. Therefore, eating an animal that inhabits the sea or its shores, the animals of which constitute *boŋsoŋ*'s topogenic loci, is believed to cause the patient's soul to languish there and require rescue.

KAK'S MAP

Kak (pronounced Kãʔ) was perhaps 40 years old when he sketched the map for me in 1980 (see Maps 8.1a and 8.1b). He had been a lead drummer before becoming a shaman. He was charismatic, but also feared, and widely regarded as effective and knowledgeable. He travelled to Malay villages to treat clients there as well. In 1980, he and his family were the only Semelais at Tasek Bera who lived apart, at their swidden, not in a village. I consulted with Kak regularly until his death in 2005.

Kak's map shows the paths leading from this world to the afterworld. Only a small section of the main path of the *b-blyan,* which is represented in the ritual by the different drumbeats, appears in Kak's map. That is because his map was specially drawn to show the location of the *kijay* tree at the place where the *kmũc* side path departs from the main path of the *b-blyan* and crosses from this world into the forest of the *kmũc* and the world of the dead. The central path in the map is actually the *b-kkmũc* side path within the *b-blyan* ritual. The section of the *b-blyan*'s main itinerary that is depicted in Kak's map surrounds the junction of the main path with the *b-kkmũc* as well as the junction with the other side paths just described above.

According to Kak's exegesis of the map, passage to the after world begins with the *kmũc* ("ghosts of natural death") forest path that proceeds from the bottom toward the upper left. A second line near the bottom runs perpendicular to the first, marking the beginning of the journey in the spirit world. The three lines fanning out on the right lead to the *lawot boson* ("sea of a jaundiced fever or swelling disease"), the *lawot sygugut* ("sea of dysmenorrhea") and the *lawot sraw* ("sea of childhood fevered seizures"). The contours of one of those are drawn.

Further along the main path, a line labeled *kijai* crosses it. *Kijay* is the tree (known as *ʔayɔm* in the context of the *b-blyan*) that produces the incense and stands on the border (*smpadan*) between this world and the *bari kamot* ("*kmũc* forest"). The next short crossing line in the *kmũc* forest path is the pandanus stream. The first junction is with a path on the left to the *lawot darah* ("sea of blood") for *pʔreʔ* ("ghosts of accidental death"). Continuing on the *kmũc* forest path, *tuhɒn* (the supreme deity) stands at the second fork in the road and sends people who sinned (*bdusaʔ* or *papaʔ*) down the *troŋ ʔapiʔ nrakʰaʔ*, "hell fires path". Continuing on the *kmũc* forest path, a thicker line marks the *dŋdɔŋ galaŋ* (log athwart the path), followed by the *balay* (the *kmʉc* feasting hall). Beyond that is *sərgaʔ*, home of the *kmũc*.

The soul of a person who died violently also follows the *kmũc* path until it turns off at the junction with the *pʔreʔ* path and then eventually returns to this world as a dangerous spirit. The souls of sinners, on the other hand, are sent through hell by *tuhɒn* and eventually reach *sərgaʔ*. Only those souls who have found themselves in locations in the spirit world visited by the main path of the *b-blyan* or its side paths (including the *kmũc* path, which is the central path in Kak's map), can be rescued by the shaman before reaching the after-world. Therefore, Kak's map includes different paths to the after-world, only one of which is included in the curing ritual.

Journeys to the Land of the Dead

Ordinary death and dying

As mentioned above, the souls of people dying of natural causes
proceed along the *kmŭc* path, which passes through the forest of the
kmŭc. The narrative presented here closely adheres to the sequence
of *b-kkmŭc* loci listed above. Souls stop to rest at the *Ɂayɔm/kijay*
tree, where they smoke tobacco, chew betel nut, and beat the tree's
buttresses. To enter the *kmŭc* forest, souls must climb down the
exposed tree roots. There are actually two sets of roots: *rɛs clakaɁ*
("bad luck roots") and *rɛs Ɂris* ("living roots"). If the soul uses the
former, it cannot return to this world, while those who follow the
latter can return.

The extreme pleasantness of the *kmŭc* forest seduces the soul into
following the path. So many human (and animal) souls have traversed
this road that it has become a long, wide and deep trench; they disappear
into it up to their ears. The first leg passes through a primary forest with
fruiting trees, birds, a small stream with wild pandanus and lots of fish
(much larger than in real life), where people stop, smoke and fish. The
fish are eaten by those who are dying. There are also some wild but
harmless animals like the gibbon, which eats the *bandon* (unidentified
vine) fruits. If a soul mistakes the bark of the roots of the *jlutuŋ* tree
for wild boar skin and eats it, the person will die. The trees in this
forest have better fruits than the same species in this world have. While
relek leaves in our world are small, they are huge there and can be
used as a head covering in the rain. *Pikʰɔm* fruits are much bigger and
more abundant. There are tailorbirds there, larger than life, and souls
are startled when they hear their clanging call. If they are going to die,
they run toward *sɔrgaɁ*, if not, they retreat toward this world. *Pawoh,*
the tallest tree, is filled with birds and leans with its crown extending
into *sɔrgaɁ*. Souls stop there to smoke or chew betel nut and make bird
snares. *Pawoh* fruits, tasteless in this world, are sweet there. If they
hang low and appear ripe, the soul eats them and the person dies; if
they are unripe or rotten, the person will live.

Beyond this primary forest lies a secondary forest, with trees
such as *cɔc* (*Commersonia bartramia* [L.] Merr.) and *stew* (*Trema*

orientalis [L.] Blume) in fruit. As the path exits the *kmũc* forest a large log lies across it. If the supreme deity shrinks it, the soul can continue. If he makes it as high as the sky, the soul heads back. Successive loci are a wattled swidden fence (if *kmũc* open it, the person will die), cultivated tobacco and gourds (if the soul steps on a gourd, causing it to pop, the person could be startled back to life), a bathing pond, and lastly the *balay jamwan* ("feasting hall"). The person's deceased relatives wait there and prepare. At this point, there is little breath left, but if the soul does not eat, the person could still recover. The further down the *kmũc* path a soul goes, the less likely it is to return.

The path to the after-world has been trodden by so many that it is as deep as a trench ... or a grave.[3] Victims of ordinary deaths are buried in cemeteries away from human habitation. In the death rituals the body's journey from its home through the fields and forest into its new home in the cemetery metaphorically parallels the passage of the *kmũc* through the *kmũc* forest and on to the *balay*. The forest is the liminal space between life and death in this world and the after-world. The aim of Semelai activity surrounding death is to facilitate the transition of the nascent *kmũc* down to the *balay,* which is to say, the grave. The ritual sequence echoes the shamanic topogeny through the structural features of the grave itself, which correlate with loci at the end of the *b-kkmũc* path. Therefore, I was told, the log athwart the *kmũc* forest path is really the *tŋũl* (logs placed in a quadrangle around the grave mound). The wattled fence is the planks placed diagonally over the body to shield it from dirt. And the tobacco and gourds are the seven cigarettes and water container left on the grave. The transition from *bayaŋ* to *kmũc* occurs when the last breath is taken and the deceased begins to eat the food at the *balay*/grave. The *tŋũl* are structurally analogous to *bnul* (the outer perimeter beams of a house or *balay* floor). Add to that the construction of a roof and the deposition of grave goods, which include broken or old everyday necessities, which appear new or unbroken in the spirit world, such as a lighted kerosene lamp and dishware, and the grave incorporates the essential features of a house or *balay*. And to the extent that those who die *kmũc* are buried together, they form a community.

Violent death

The souls of victims of violent, accidental death (*pʔreʔ*) turn off at the *pʔreʔ* path, which soon crosses the *payaʔ ʔɔŋlɔŋ klubiʔ* (*Salacca* sp. bushes catwalk stream). The thorns stand up as *kmũc* go by, turning them back to the *kmũc* path, but lie down when *pʔreʔ* approach. The *pʔreʔ* go on to the sea of blood and then on another path to the *balay.* From there they return to the ordinary world, where they behave as dangerous spirits menacing living humans.

However, while *pʔreʔ* are said to reside in a distant place that forms a binary pair with the, perhaps, more distant *kmũc*, *pʔreʔ* are actually very much in this world, flying around and causing trouble. Semelais had difficulty trying to reconcile these competing assertions. However, using standard incantation formulae, by locating the origin of a threat, a foundation is laid for the threat to be named, thereby containing an otherwise dangerous, unbound spirit and defining away its power. Therefore, knowing the cosmographical origin of *pʔreʔ* provides the basis for incantations to disempower them. Therein may lie the utility of maps of the afterlife. The distinction between the two kinds of ghosts underlies and gives greater reality to their theory of what causes accidents and how to prevent them.

The mortuary rites for those who died accidental deaths were traditionally minimal and dramatically different from those for victims of natural deaths. In the past, Semelai cemeteries were only for *kmũc*; those who died *pʔreʔ* were buried where they were killed, immediately and without grave goods, in very shallow graves. However, in the 1970s, two children tragically died *pʔreʔ* in a house that caught fire. They were buried in the local cemetery, but no one could remember exactly where. Since then, a separate section for accidental deaths has been set aside in cemeteries.

There is now a vigil for *pʔreʔ* deaths (often from motorcycle accidents) as well, in accordance with the idea that *pʔreʔ* visit the *balay* (feasting hall) briefly before returning to this world. In the funeral procession, the shaman enters the cemetery first, burning *pʔreʔ* repellant plant matter, and exits last, placing a thorny branch across the path, while saying an incantation to prevent *pʔreʔ* from following mourners home. Small cement markers with inscribed names now identify their graves. Grouping *pʔreʔ* graves together furthermore suggests a community. While the treatment of those killed by accidents has improved, the distinction between them and those who died normal deaths remains.

Death of sinners

Finally, the deity directs the souls of sinners onto the hell fires path. There the soul must walk along a sword blade over a *kawah* ("cauldron of boiling water"). There is also a grass field (*padaŋ*), which is set afire by *ʔI-Gmintoŋ* for those who committed incest. The soul then encounters a chicken that flaps its wings to cool the soul if it had been good to at least one chicken during its lifetime. Similarly, a dog will get a drink for the soul who has been good to at least one dog and will urinate on the others. The path then reconnects with the *kmũc* forest path at the *balay*, from where the soul proceeds to *sərgaʔ*.

THE B-BLYAN AND THE MAP NARRATIVES

Kak's map places the after-world (*sərgaʔ*) at a significant distance from this world on a two-dimensional plane that descends gradually toward the west. While Malay *surga* is "paradise", Semelai *sərgaʔ* is said to be unknown because no one living has been there. But it can be inferred that there are a lot of *kmũc* there. Some called it a *bandar* ("town"). The border between this world and the after-world, imagined as an escarpment, is meaningful but not a Rubicon, for it is crossed and re-crossed by detached souls, ghosts and shamans. While creating a duality (this world and the after-world), the border marks a midpoint in a continuum. The paths, as metaphors for illness, span and transcend the liminal, forested space between health (the quintessence of life) and death. Proximity to death is imagined spatially. Those who are ill or injured may have crossed the border, approaching death, or they may not have. Since most people die *kmũc*, and from a variety

of ailments, it makes sense that the route is elaborated. And, because
it is when people are still ill or injured, not (yet) dead, that healing
may be effective, knowledge of the paths before arrival at (complete)
death is critical.

CONCLUSION

I have endeavoured here to interpret and analyze the cultural and
social meaning of a Semelai cosmological map. Kak's map connects
the landscape of illness, as experienced in the *b-blyan,* with the
landscape of death, suffering and accident. It graphically traces paths
between this world and the after-world as well as the shaman's ability
to retrieve lost souls. Given that little of what the shaman experiences
during the *b-blyan* is easily comprehended by non-shamans, narrative
mapmaking helps him communicate important salient knowledge and
ideology. Analysis suggests that the complexity in Kak's map is due to
his attempt to reconcile distinct cosmological narratives. There appear
to be at least three that are analytically distinguishable embedded in
the map:

- The *b-blyan* is part of a sociocentric cosmological schema.
  It subsumes Semelais within a sentient cosmos that includes
  anthropomorphic spirits, many representing other species. This
  shamanic narrative provides an avenue for grappling with
  sickness and a path leading to natural death.
- A magical cosmological model structures many prohibitions
  (*pantaŋ*) and incantations (*jampi?*). A narrative for accidental
  or bloody death provides a bleak destiny for these souls. This
  contrasting narrative of death is reinforced by a separate set
  of mortuary practices intended to protect the living from the
  dangerous ghosts and is invoked in magical incantations to
  prevent further misfortune.
- The anthropocentric cosmological model is concerned with
  punishments and rewards for behaviour toward other people.
  One's sins cause the supreme deity to send one's soul through
  nrakʰa? on its way to *sərga?*. This model is clearly sociocentric
  and transcendental.

Creating maps of paths leading to remote places and powerful personages, whether empirical or not, lends greater reality to those places and authority to the mapmaker. It is therapeutic to have an authority diagnose the illness and enact healing procedures. The narrative allows the patient to be rescued. The convention of drawing pathways of illness and death lends cosmic dimensions to these conditions as well as avenues for shamanic action. The shamanic narrative of death (the *b-kkmũc*) is usually ignored in the *b-blyan*, while, within the context of mortuary practices, the pathways to death take precedence. All of this is culturally reproduced by incantations, shamanic rites, mortuary rites and the discourse of the supreme deity's punishment of sins, in addition to the maps.

Kak's relationship with his map is reciprocal (cf. Wood 1993). He derives authority from his ability to map life and death. But, similarly, the map derives its power from him because Semelais, and others, including me, who sought his help, perceived him as an authority.

But as Semelai society gives narrative power to the shaman, it also takes it away. It provides a formal status for those who can communicate and interact with the spirit world and gives them potentially great power. But then it circumscribes and curbs that power through the *b-blyan* itself and the threat of witchcraft accusations. The shaman in Semelai society truly lives in tension and instability, betwixt and between goodness and evil, spirit and material, seen and unseen, help and harm, life and death.

ACKNOWLEDGEMENTS

The fieldwork upon which this analysis is based was funded by the National Science Foundation, Sigma Xi, the Institute for Intercultural Studies, the National Geographic Society, the Wenner-Gren Foundation, Marion and Jasper Whiting Foundation, a Keene State College sabbatical and Faculty Development Grants. The research was sponsored and supported by the Jabatan Botani, Universiti Malaya, the Muzium Negara, the Institute for Environment and Development (LESTARI), Universiti Kebangsaan Malaysia, the Jabatan Hal Ehwal Orang Asli

and Wetlands International. I would also like to thank Robert Wessing
for discussions of contrasting Southeast Asian cosmologies. Chelsea
Nickerson prepared Map 8.1b for publication.

NOTES

1. I had just begun an ethno-archaeological investigation of the collection
    and trade of resins among Semelais at Tasek Bera.
2. Paradoxically, women who died in childbirth, even though they are
    believed to become *mati?anak* (a kind of malevolent spirit), are buried
    with those who died *kmũc*.
3. A Semelai story recounts how, in earlier times, the corpse was left in the
    rafters of an abandoned house, suggesting that burial may not be ancient.

REFERENCES

Atkinson, J.M.
> 1989   The Art and Politics of Wana Shamanship. Berkeley and Los
>   Angeles: University of California Press.

Benjamin, G.
> 2011   Egalitarianism and Ranking in the Malay World. *In* Anarchic
>   Solidarity: Autonomy, Equality and Fellowship in Southeast Asia.
>   K. Sillander and T. Gibson, eds. Pp. 170–201. New Haven, CT:
>   Yale University Southeast Asia Studies.

COAC
> 2012   Orang Asli Population Statistics. C. Nicholas, ed. Subang Jaya,
>   Malaysia: Center for Orang Asli Concerns.

Fox, J.J.
> 1997   Place and Landscape in Comparative Austronesian Perspective.
>   *In* The Poetic Power of Place: Comparative Perspectives on
>   Austronesian Ideas of Locality. J.J. Fox, ed. Pp. 1–21. Canberra:
>   Research School of Pacific and Asian Studies, The Australian
>   National University.

Gianno, R.
> 1990   Semelai Culture and Resin Technology. Volume 22. New Haven,
>   CT: Connecticut Academy of Arts and Sciences.

Mohamad Salleh Hood
    1978   Semelai Rituals of Curing. Unpublished PhD dissertation, St Catherine's College, Oxford University.

Wessing, R.
    2010   Porous Boundaries: Addressing Calamities in East Java, Indonesia. Bijdragen tot de Taal-, Land- en Volkenkunde 166(1): 49–82.

Wood, D.
    1993   What Makes a Map a Map? Cartographica 30(2 & 3): 81–6.

chapter 9

Sono-Visionary Intimations: Reflections on Temoq Shamanic Epistemology

Peter Laird

"*Ɂhai Ɂatok Ɂhai suar ɛlɛŋ*".
"I'm there I visions see".

Puyvŋ (shaman) Paq Loong (1982)

Temoq shamanism is a complex and intricate domain of thought and action expressed through all night ritual healing performances.[1] The discussion focuses on how Temoq shamanic trance-like visionary knowledge and experience is expressed in ritual through, first, the shaman's singing in an altered state of consciousness, and, second, the discourse about ritual language and meaning created during formal interviews focused on recorded and transcribed performances. The Temoq recognize several types of consciousness in ritual from wide awake (*wawoh*) to unconsciousness (*titoit*). Between these two limiting conditions lies a range of named altered states from light reverie to deep rapture. The Temoq shaman's singing and visionary encounters, usually accompanied by intense drumming, is state-specific, meaning that changes in state of consciousness are expressed through changes in the shaman's singing style and body language. For example, in light reverie the shaman's loud singing can be characterized as clear sighted epic narrative, whereas in a deep state of rapture his quieter lyrical singing is focused on "inner" experience as he becomes almost overwhelmingly enchanted by the profound beauty of creation, a condition which can inadvertently lead to his death.

Unfortunately textual transcription and translation tend to flatten out Temoq shamanic singing, as it does for most oral traditions, into a uniform and steady English which discards most of the richness and virtuosity of the original recording, even if some of the poesy and prosody is faintly evident. However, some words can be tracked through the epistemic layers of the shaman's singing, one being *suar* ("visions") which may be understood in different but complementary ways according to whether the emphasis is on language per sé or on altered consciousness. Suar lies at the core of the shaman's sung performance and clearly illustrates the epistemological armature that makes sense of the varying relationship between the shaman's language, experience, and altered consciousness during the progress of a ritual performance.

The discussion focuses on the ritual world of *puyɒŋ* (shaman) Paq Loong, with whom I intermittently collaborated for a period of ten years. Paq Loong's healing performances were noted for beautiful singing, resplendent imagery and deep mystical insight. He was a very successful healer who made journeys to the very edge of the habitable world to bring back, in company with his guardian and familiar spirits, the "seeds" of the blooming tropical rain forest. Steeped in the social, emotional, spiritual and psychological life of community members, Paq Loong's virtuosity inhabited a vast universe stretching from the edge of the snake encircled world to the deepest recesses of human suffering and well-being [Laird n.d.(a)].

THE TEMOQ

The Temoq are one of 19 Orang Asli ethnolinguistic groups. They live in southeast Pahang, Peninsular Malaysia and, along with the Semelai, Smaq Bri and Btsisi, form the Southern Aslian branch of the Aslian

(Austroasiatic) language-speakers of Peninsular Malaysia. Having been declared extinct several times by government officials, they are as of August 2014 still living in several small communities on the Menentang River and tributaries of the Jeram and Bera Rivers. Never populous, the Temoq probably number fewer than 100 individuals and in the past few decades have become absorbed into the neighbouring Semelai group for census and administrative purposes—thus their "extinct" status.

During the 20th century the Temoq were forest product collectors and swiddeners, augmented by regular hunting, fishing and gathering of tubers, fruit and medicines (Laird 1978). Recently massive rain forest clearing and the establishment of oil palm plantations have largely destroyed the basis of the traditional economy. Some Temoq have responded to the new challenges by seeking education and a modern Malaysian life style. Several have gained tertiary qualifications in, for example, accounting and architecture. Others have retreated further into what remains of the forest to pursue their traditional way of life. Increasingly relegated to the logged forest margins or interiors of oil palm plantations, the Temoq, like other very small Orang Asli groups, face severe challenges to their long-term survival as a distinct and unique people.

Traditionally Temoq lived in small matrifial housing clusters, ideally a core family with in-marrying sons-in-law, in dispersed swiddens, eschewing village life as too noisy and stressful. But today most Temoq live in five small villages.

Each settlement until recently was protected by one or more shamans. Even Temoq who aspire to modernity still seek out shamanic healing, despite availing themselves of modern medical treatment. Unlike modern medicine, shamanic healing can provide a spiritual dimension to human suffering by situating illness and affliction within a wider moral framework that includes the life sustaining powers of the rain forest and its denizens, which are invoked by the shaman during a performance.[2] More significantly, the Temoq believe that one cause of affliction is sorcery, thus demanding shamanic intervention irrespective of modern medical treatment. Shamanic curing is more than just a supplement to modern medicine, as I will show below.

RITUAL PERFORMANCE: *SMYUM TENG KIJAI* (MAY 1982)

The following synoptic account of a ritual performance by shaman Pak Loong provides a background to the discussion of Temoq shamanic epistemology. Paq Loong was a specialist in over 100 cosmic regions and habitats, each embodied in a song and drum rhythm from which he created many different itineraries and hence performances. Shamans collectively journey to over 150 regions, in more or less mutually exclusive itineraries, which overall define the Temoq shamanic ritual cosmos.

The longest performance is the seven night *Teng Gaduq* (Mother Rite) where the shaman travels to the very edge of the living world to collect the seeds that become the rain forest blossoms and fruit. Thus the *Teng Kijai* performance discussed below is just one example of an extensive repertoire that could take him to within earshot of the deep reverberant sound of the giant earth encircling snake [Laird 2011; n.d.(b)].

During the morning of 22 May 1982 Paq Loong announced that he wished to perform (v int. *brsmyum*) a healing ritual (*smyum*) that evening for an elderly married couple and a middle-age married woman. During the afternoon women went into the forest to collect *palas* palm (Licuala sp.) shoots and *ceput* plants (Elattariopsis sp.). The *palas* palm shoots were rendered into strips and woven into the shaman's headband. A single shoot was unfolded, stripped and fashioned into the shaman's *labung* (whisk). The *ceput* plants were macerated and mixed with water, producing a bowl of green flecked liquid, *daq ceput* (*ceput* water). Women also heated hill rice in a metal pan to produce *bertih* (parched rice). Men provided the *kijai* (Trigonochlamys sp.) resin, which is burned to purify and cleanse ritual *halat* (accoutrements) and the patient's body as well as create clouds of fragrant incense smoke during the performance. The *rebana* (drum), normally played by men, accompanied the shaman's journey. The *perasap* or *perbaran* (censer), usually an enamel plate but sometimes a palm leaf container, was charged with glowing coals from the household hearth by both male and female ritual attendees throughout the performance.

At about 12.45 a.m. Paq Loong indicated that he wished to begin, and he positioned himself on a mat facing east. The bowl of *ceput* water, parched rice and the censer were placed in front of him, into which he incanted spells appropriate to each item. He fumigated his headband with *kijai* incense, dipped it in *ceput*, and placed it on his head. Following this he incanted into the parched rice and began the *bertih* divination to determine if the disease-spirits were amenable to extraction. The *bertih* was thrown over the patient several times and the residual grains left in his hand were placed on the floor and sorted into pairs. An even outcome indicates success while odds bodes trouble. This was repeated several times. He then picked up his whisk, rubbed his hands through the tassels, and held the whisk over the censer. After this divinatory procedure, the lamp was removed, and he

Plate 9.1 Temoq shaman dancing with a spirit boat *lancang*

(Photo credit: Peter Laird)

began to *brcaman* ("liturgize"), calling on his guardians and familiars to awaken and join the ascending entourage. After a few strophes the *tarun* (drummer) began playing the *kanjar* melody which followed the striding gait of the shaman's travelling soul.[3]

Moving into the heavens at the beginning of the performance the shaman's travelling soul heads for *Tuan Putri Bungsu*'s (tutelary sylph) cloud-mountain pool via a series of intermediary familiars and guardians embodied in specific *teng* ("songs") noted in Table 9.1. Simultaneously, the skyward imagery is used to create the illusion of the ritual house as a microcosm to trick the disease-spirits into experiencing the illusion as literal and "out there". Thus the billowing clouds of kijai smoke are "cloud-mountains", the house floor structure is the earth's under-girding, the perimeter beams are the earth encircling cosmic snake, and the fringing thatch is the sky vault's distant horizons. The *balai* (ritual house) becomes the earth, and, although unsaid, the green flecked body of the patient becomes the earth's "topography". The performance is projected to the spiritual centre (*axis mundi*) around which the living earth revolves. The axis mundi is imaged as the plume of kijai smoke rising from the censer and mingling with a stream of falling bird lice that become *pa'jih* (disease-agents) when they strike humans. The shaman is imaged as travelling in a spiral around this sacred and numinous centre.

A synopsis of Teng Kijai in Table 9.1 contains a row for each of the six *teng* or "songs" of the Teng Kijai performance and five columns containing information on *teng* title and metrics, familiar spirit and habitat, core healing and aetiological image, drumming rhythm, and finally the number and duration of disease-spirit extractions. Each *teng* begins with travelling and the *kanjar* (striding) drum rhythm and then changes to the drum melody associated with the guardian or familiar as the shaman approaches their habitat or domain. Near the end of a *teng* the drumming will usually change back to *kanjar* as the shaman moves away from the visited *bandar* (habitat) or *negeri* (region).

The six *teng* represent the itinerary of the shaman from his initial ascent to the heavens via a *kijai* tree inhabited by his familiar *Putri Aiyum* in the first *teng* to his final destination at the wispy pandanus fringed cloud-mountain pool of *Putri Bungsu*, where she washes the subtle form of the afflicted in the sixth *teng*. *Teng* are typically named

Table 9.1 Synopsis of *teng kijai* performance (1,396 utterances)

Teng (Song)	Familiar Spirit (gunig) / Habitat	Core Healing and Etiological Images	Drumming Rhythm	Disease-spirit Extraction
Kanjar 35.26 mins 251 Utterances	Travelling upstream to a kijai (resin) tree from which the shaman ascends into the heavens. Gunig is Putri Aiyom.	Garland way – lined with flowers and framed by distant vistas and thunderstorms. The cuttings and trimmings of creation become disease-agents.	Travelling gait of walking purposefully on level ground and uphill	1: 6 mins (Paq Banai) 2: 5 mins (Maq Banai)
Langsir 56.51 minutes 385 Utterances	Wreathed hornbill (Aceros undulatus) guardian who transports the shaman a great distance to the cloud-mountains.	When the shaman utters "ek ek" he has enwrapped himself in the hornbill's cloak soul to make the jump to their preening perch. The falling lice become disease-agents.	Rapid wreathed hornbill wing beat rhythm	1: 10 mins (Maq Banai) 2: 5 mins (Maq Alias) 3: 8 mins (Paq Banai) 4: 8 mins (Paq Banai)
Dusun 31.48 mins 212 utterances	Sacred groves ("rain forest") planted by shamanic creator ancestors.	Sacred groves heavy with fruit and singing birds, and buffeted with mists and strong winds. Focus on creator ancestors who planted the verdant earth. Cloud poisons.	Gusting wind style	1: 10 mins (Paq Banai)

Table 9.1 (*cont'd*)

Rangut 28.57 mins 204 utterances	Female jambu fruit dove (Ptilinopus jambu) familiar. A manifestation of creator ancestor Maq Sidi with whom Paq Loong expressed a deep sense of mystical affiliation.	Fruit dove imaged flying upstream and downstream collecting twigs, building nest, laying eggs, and the tap tap of hatching chicks. Preening jambu fruit dove casting out lice which become disease-agents. When the shaman briefly possesses rangut he utters a cooing sound.	Jambu fruit dove wing beat rhythm	1: 8 mins (Paq Banai)
Lilin 27.09 mins 197 utterances	Female (menkedur lilin) helmeted hornbill (Rhinoplax vigil).	Cannonading sounds of "wooden tops" as distant but highly visible helmeted hornbills strike their casques. Preening helmeted hornbills casting out lice which become disease-agents.	Helmeted hornbill wing beat rhythm	1: 7 mins (Paq Banai)
Kolam 21.48 mins 147 utterances	Tuan Putri Bungsu's cloud-mountain bathing pool.	Mist shrouded fragrant pandanus fringed cloud-mountain healing pool inhabited by Tuan *Putri* Bungsu the shaman's tutelary. Focus on cooling, cleansing and toxin neutralization. Refreshing and spiritually revitalizing.	Bathing / splashing rhythm	No extractions

after the familiar or guardian spirit of the region through which the shaman journeys. The shaman visits his *gunig* or familiar spirits to elicit their help in the healing of the patient. Often the shaman will take on the form of the *gunig* and utter its call, such as the ek ek, ek ek of the wreathed hornbill in the second *teng* and the hoo'ooooooooooooooooo of the female *jambu* fruit dove in the fourth *teng*. The vocalizations of all familiars momentarily "possessed" by the shaman are considered to contribute to the patient's healing. Importantly, it is the shaman who possesses the familiar, who enwraps himself in the cloak soul of his *gunig*, and not the familiar who possesses the shaman, as is the case with Temoq *berjin* spirit possession rites. Familiars help in various ways. For example, the *jambu* fruit dove's cooing ministers directly to the afflicted, even though her preening also produces lice which are *pa'jih* (disease-agents). The shaman's brief possession of the wreathed hornbill allows him to traverse yawning chasms between huge cloud-mountains and arrive safely at their distant perches, where he images the birds preening and casting out lice which also become

Plate 9.2 Drummers and *kelundang* player accompanying the Temoq puyɒŋ Paq Loong on his journey to the land of the bearded pigs

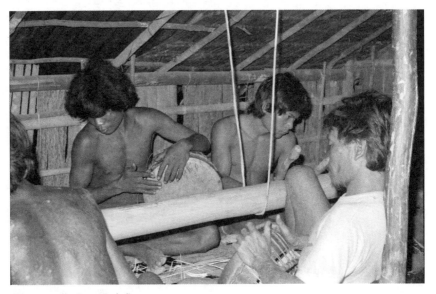

(Photo credit: Peter Laird)

Plate 9.3 Temoq shaman talks to *minan* held firmly under his right thumb

(Photo credit: Peter Laird)

pa'jih. The imaging of familiars and their behaviours and habitats expresses a fundamental dimension of Temoq thinking about healing and illness: both affliction and healing come from the same sources. The same imagery is expressed in the dual nature of the *axis mundi*, which graphically merges striated *kijai* incense plumes with a falling stream of lice cast out by preening birds.

Each *teng* has its own drum rhythm and playing style, as outlined in column four of Table 9.1. Percussion plays a central role in shamanic ritual, for without music the shaman cannot travel or enter the deep state of rapture necessary for beguiling the disease-spirit, inducing an altered state in himself and all assembled, and invoking his familiars with their characteristic gaits and vocalizations. The original Temoq shamanic musical instrument is the *kelundang*, a type of log idiophone made from a trimmed and tuned *meranti*, *kelai*, or *pelawan* tree trunk, suspended from the roof, and struck with wooden strikers. However, nowadays a drum with a wooden frame and a monkey skin membrane provides the usual accompaniment to the shaman's performance. Rhythms and playing styles express the archetypal energies of familiar spirits and the movements of the shaman's travelling soul. For example, the wreathed hornbill drum rhythm is a single pitch fast beat with an alternate beat every few seconds indicating a wing movement. This playing style is termed *klepuh* (flying). In contrast the playing style for the last *teng* is in part *klecuk* (splashing) which suggests the cradling action of the tutelary *Tuan Putri Bungsu* cleansing and washing the patient's afflicted soul. The drummer must assiduously follow the shaman's journey, changing drum rhythm and playing style as the shaman encounters new familiars and realms, dangerous beings, and challenging cosmological obstacles. If the drummer does not accurately reflect the region through which the shaman is travelling, it is said that the shaman may become lost, endangered, or even die. So the drummer, pictured as travelling in front of the entourage led by swarms of buzzing bees, must be constantly aware of the shaman's wider visionary narrative in order to stay on track.

Disease-causing agents range from lice cast out by preening birds to glowing shards of lightning or "brimstone", the trimmings and cuttings of ancestral creation, and celestial fisher folk. Although there are many types of disease-agents, once inside the body of the afflicted, all disease-agents are primarily addressed and referred to as *minan*. The disease-spirit is a complex being, and its multifarious identity, behaviour, and toxic effects on the body of the patient are evoked by an extensive vocabulary of pathological terms encompassing both soma and psyche. For example, there are 27 different expressions used to define the afflicted condition of the patient's blood alone. Fever and lassitude are two common effects of *minan*'s actions. In the patient's body *minan* conceals itself in blood clots and releases toxins while consuming the patient's blood and flesh. The disease-spirit is considered to "get high" on the patient's blood and flesh, so the shaman must redirect its rapture from the patient's body to the cosmos. *Minan*'s behavioural repertoire includes stabbing, spearing, bloating, stirring and spasms. The shaman applies *ceput* water with his whisk to cool the patient, neutralize toxins, and render *minan* more amenable to extraction.[4] The shaman also speaks to *minan*, asking it to desist from further harming the patient. The shaman must put the disease-spirit into a deep state of reverie or trance, as this is considered necessary in order to extract it from the patient with the *palas* palm whisk from which it is pulled off and held in the tight clasp of the shaman's hand until expelled. Only when the disease-spirit is convinced that the microcosmic house, with billowing incense "cloud-mountains", is the macrocosm from whence it came, will it vacate the patient's body. Often the inert and disabled shiny black leech shaped disease-spirit, in a state of labile "rapture", is shown to all before being sent back to its origins with a quick flick of the shaman's whisk. The ritual house is also an acoustic microcosm, where all the beings that participate in the performance have a sonological presence created by the shaman's vocal imagery of ancestral voices and bird and animal calls.

During the course of the performance (Table 9.1), eight disease-agents were extracted from two patients, with an additional extraction from a third patient. Extraction duration lasts from when the disease-agent is extracted by the shaman's whisk and held in his hand until it is placed back in the whisk and expelled in a weakened state back to its origin in the heavens. Examining *Teng Langsir* we see that four disease-agents were extracted, with the longest extraction event lasting ten minutes. All told 31 minutes out of a Teng Langsir duration of 56 minutes were devoted to the extraction and expulsion of disease-agents. Extractions in all *teng* (except the last) took more or less one third to one half of the *teng* length. However interaction with the disease-agent begins well before extraction because ideally the disease-agent will only be amenable if the microcosmic illusion is sufficiently "real" to convince it to leave the patient's body and jump into the tassels of the whisk. The whisk tassels dancing up and down over the patient's body and shedding *ceput* water are part of the shaman's deception and are imaged as rain streaming down from clouds.

The core images that define the distinctive character of each *teng* in Table 9.1 by no means exhaust the broader cosmological imagery within which each habitat is nested. The snake encircled cosmos with the world mountain or world tree at the centre defines the horizontal limit of the earth. Between the world mountain and the outer rim of the world lies one or seven oceans. The sky is a huge dome of glowing blue rock on which ancestral beings live. Between the sky dome and earth drift many types of clouds, and weather conditions varying from wild thunderstorms to fragrant breezes wafting up from the rain forest canopy. The world is alive and vibrant, and the constant movement of wind, clouds, foliage, trees and living beings is strongly imaged in all of Paq Loong's performances and is embodied in drum rhythm playing styles. In this upper realm also live celestial fisher folk, who, plying their *lancang* (boats) on aerial currents, bring misfortune to humankind through mistaking humans for prey. Humans live at the bottom of a vast atmospheric ocean. The fisher folk cannot clearly see the human realm, so, for example, smoke drifting through a thatch roof is seen by them as a turbid waterhole and playing children as schooling fish. Debris thrown overboard also becomes *pa'jih* (disease-spirits).

All shamanic "songs" include the repetitive naming of deities and ancestors who created all living forms and were the first shamans. Many terms both singular and compound are used to name these ancestors. Some names highlight the wider historical context of Temoq religion, ranging from *Perman,* which is most probably derived from *Peruman*, one of the many names for *Siva*, and *Allah* from Islam. Shamanic genealogies stretch back to *Paung Perman* where paung is possibly the circa Angkorian Khmer *poñ*, a high status title that could be glossed as "shaman-king" (Michael Vickery, pers. comm. 1986). Interestingly at the very edge of the world, near *Pulau Plei* (Island of Fruit Trees) lie *gambar temung* or stone likenesses of guardian spirits, spirit helpers and familiars.

Each *teng* or song is composed of alternating content and gestural frames typically, but not always, in different strophes or verses as described below. For example, the shaman will focus on travelling along the *terung asik* (ecstatic path), then switch to magnificent visionary earthscapes created by the ancestors, then take on the cloak soul and "become" momentarily, for example, a *jambu* fruit dove, dusky leaf monkey, cicada, flying fox, or frog *gunig* (familiar). He may then use his whisk to minister to the patient with ceput water and kijai incense while convincing the disease-spirit to leave the patient's body. Beautiful singing not only ministers to the patient through melodious sound, but also evokes in the patient an enchanted wonderment of a vibrant colourful living earth. Simply put, Paq Loong healed by extracting disease-spirits, and, more significantly, by evoking overwhelmingly beautiful images that merged with a deep state of reverie (trance) created by sustained drumming. This had a powerful transformative effect on the patient as well as other participants.

The shaman intentionally constructs an "as if" world where incense clouds "are" mountains, house perimeter beams "are" the world encircling snake and so forth. Yet, the source of the metaphorical world lies beyond the ritual house in the experience of the travelling shaman's soul, and despite extracting the disease-spirit and relieving the suffering of the patient, both of which are equally "real", efficacy lies in the extra-corporeal relations the shaman has with the numinous denizens of the earth revealed through an altered state of consciousness. These beings are formally thanked in the *putus smyum* performance where elaborate platforms topped by bamboo tubes filled with healing waters are punctured at the end of the performance, bathing people in a cascade of fragrant waters (Laird 2013).

SUAR: SONO-VISIONARY INTIMATIONS AND THE *PUYɒ*'S JOURNEY

Paq Loong's journey, along with his entourage of guardian and familiar spirits, bees, drummer, and the astral forms of participants, is epistemologically primary, being the source of the shaman's imagery used to create the metaphorical illusion in the ritual house. Yet the journey to the heavens is also a sea of tropes expressed in a nocturnal shadow language of "as if". Everywhere Paq Loong looks he sees the "footprints" and "traces" of ancestral creativity, and whatever path he seeks to follow is a song line "left behind" by the shamanic ancestors. His beautiful compositions are inscribed in the very fabric of the world, and it is this ancestral *tulis* (inscriptions, tracery) that he is able to see and transform into his sung journey.

Blazing like the "fires of hell" (TqM *api neraka*), the shaman's infernal vision (*cermin*), radiating from his forehead, reveals and clears the way far ahead. Puyɒ Paq Loong "liturgizes" (*brcaman*) in the sixth song (strophes TI-9 and TI-10) of his four night twenty-one song journey to the Land of the Bearded Pigs (*Negeri Nangoi*):

eh ai *tampak gemilau lagi*	eh ai behold the shimmering glow,
cermin ulun tandang gunung	my "vision" travels the mountain
tandang nengerik lagi	travels the earth, further,
nengerik di suar dari Bijak oh eh	earth "envisioned" by *Bijak* oh eh
nengerik suar dari Perman	realms "envisioned" by *Perman*
mentujuh rasup	seven crossbeams (world snake) TI-6:9
tujuh benor lagi	seven girds (world snake) further
ah...................	*ah........................*
layar langgam lagi	drifting earthscapes
layar nengerik	drifting lands
lagi layar gunung	again drifting cloud-mountains TI-6:10

Beginning with the image of the shaman's "third eye" (*cermin*) brightly illuminating a shimmering earthscape, strophes TI-6:9 and TI-6:10 embody images of broad visionary sight surveying the cosmos and discerning misty lands, realms, and the snake begirt earth itself, across which drift a magnificent cloudscape. *Suar* is clearly used metaphorically where house floor structure is the cosmic snake. However at the beginning of TI-6:9 *suar* refers to his revelatory visionary experience of the earth bequeathed by ancestors *Bijak* and *Perman* and only then moves to metaphor to express his experience.

The Temoq mountain journey shaman is a traveller through an ever receding cosmorama of towering mountains, blue-green vistas, and distant glowing horizons revealed by visionary sight. These vast pellucid spaces revealed by the travelling shaman's visionary in-sight and hearing belie the actual experiential nature of the shaman's imaginal journey which takes place within non-linear dimensions, and atemporal duration. When we move closer to the shaman's cosmological imagery we see that it is somewhat misplaced to give a geometrizing gloss to what is experienced as the "face of creation"— the work of *Maq Kerinduan*, the shaman's "beloved divine feminine". As we shall see, the shaman's "vision" is not so much a geometrizing experience of self and other, as a profound spiritual and aesthetic encounter with the primal powers of creation. Thus the shaman's cosmological imagery is a processional reality that suffers significant distortion and warping if we attempt to reduce it to a mapping exercise or ersatz cosmography.

Having acquired a *cermin* (TqM. "mirror"), or visionary sight, at the beginning of his spiritual quest from his tutelary spirit, the Temoq shaman is able to gain access to the primordial habitats and regions traversed by the creator shamanic ancestors at the beginning of time. He is able to discern the *suar* they left behind, and it is this experience that forms the archetypal ground of his shamanic "liturgizing" (*brcaman*) that takes place within a ritual performance (*smyum*).

The following dialogue recorded on 24 November 1982 with *puyɒŋ* Paq Loong, research collaborator Datang bin Joho, and several others, is part of an extended interview of a transcribed *Teng Kijai* healing ritual, including audio track, performed on 22 May 1982 [Laird n.d.(b)]. Most interestingly Paq Loong in true dialogical fashion reached into my experience and my background to explain a point of meaning in Temoq shamanic experience.

> Peter Laird (verbally repeating audio recording): "*tinggal suar lagi Malim sekarang dulu?*" (*suar* left behind by shamans past and present?)
>
> *Puyɒŋ* Paq Loong: "Shamans past and present—not me during this era—no! —Peter—shaman's past and present ages ago on *Jalan Kesati* (Sacred Way) (knocking on floor)—ah—at the very beginning."
>
> Peter Laird: (paraphrasing audio recording) "*tinggal lagi suar Malim?*"
>
> Puyɒŋ Paq Loong: "he left behind the *suar*—I *suar* this country— *tinggal suar* (shaman knocking floor with knuckles to emphasize point of "placing" or leaving behind something).
>
> Peter Laird: "Shaman ancestors?"
>
> Puyɒŋ Paq Loong: "Shamans of former times left behind the *suar.*"
>
> Peter Laird: "Is *suar* like a picture?"
>
> Puyɒŋ Paq Loong: "It's not a picture."
>
> Peter Laird: "Then what's *suar?*"

Puyɒŋ Paq Loong: "This is what I *suar*—if I *suar* a country like Peter's—I view from afar—and pausing awhile—oh I am enchanted by Peter's country where exist *suar* and things left behind."
Interjection from K: "A place that's beautiful!"
Puyɒŋ Paq Loong: "A place that's beautiful, a place that's spacious...."

Further on in response to a question about the *gunung* (mountain), Datang bin Joho asks *Puyɒŋ* Paq Loong: "So where is the mountain?" Shaman Paq Loong: "It's only a *suar*—it's not a real mountain—it (the *suar*) was left behind (bequeathed) by people (creator ancestors/shamans) ages ago."

Suar is a key ontological precept for understanding the nature of the created cosmos, and a pivotal epistemological term for appreciating the shaman's imaginal experience. *Suar* is a difficult term to understand for it is predicated on a state-specific phenomenology only experienced, in principle, by the shaman in an altered state of consciousness. As a Temoq friend pointed out to me, a simple example of *suar* would be to see images in clouds, an imaginary exercise common in Anglo-American culture. However, shamans state that *suar* does not simply mean visual image but covers a wider range of both visual and acoustic phenomena. The cloud image is however apposite—with his *cermin* the shaman "sees" the animate forms of the world in clouds. Indeed, the world mountain (TqA. *bnum*, TqM. *gunung*) is nothing less than a towering cumulonimbus cloud. The cloud mountain climbing shamans *suar* the cumulonimbus clouds as the world *bnum* (mountain) drifting between the earth and sky vault at the *pusat dunia* (earth's navel).

Suar is an epistemological bridge between the essential nature of "being" revealed by the ancestors and a way of knowing creation beyond the normal powers of mortal discernment.[5] The shaman's night journey into the numinous nether regions of this earth is a re-creation of the original world creating journey made by the shamanic ancestors. The fashioning, singing, trimming, shaping, making, carving, painting, planting, daubing, ordering, arranging, and envisioning itinerary of the ancestors gave form to the spatial and temporal cosmos as the Temoq experience it today. The shaman follows their path, and on the world mountain he "sees" the *lekam* (footprints/spoor) and the *tulis* (traces/handiwork) of the original ancestors who still reside in the heavens. Trudging up and down the billowing hills and vales, and periodically flying across chasms between clouds in the garb of cicadas and hornbills, he follows the ancestral tracks, and where they stopped, he stops and pauses.

Shamanic poesis ontologically merges with the immanent poesis of continually emerging creation. Hence, the identity of the shaman is epistemologically indeterminate, and this very indeterminacy allows for the creation of an imaginal reality that undividedly reaches from the inner condition of the patient to the very edge of the vessel within which all existence is countenanced. The imaginal autonomy of the shaman's sono-visionary experience collapses objectivity, subjectivity and intentionality. The objectivity of the world dissolves into a transphenomenal revelation of the tropical rain forest preternaturally shimmering under the stony sky vault, and the subjectivity and intentionality of the shaman's healing journey into the discarnate harmonies and rhythms of the cosmos itself. The true shaman does not sing in ritual, rather he is the discarnate voice of creation itself. It is this epistemological indeterminacy of the vocalizing agent (shaman and familiars), associated with several different types of altered consciousness, that presents a challenge to interpretation and translation.

SUAR, IDENTITY AND SHAPE SHIFTING

Suar is rarely mentioned in reference to familiars and guardians but almost always to their habitats and abodes. The lineaments of creation are "as if", but the presence of familiars, wreathed hornbills, Malayan sun bears, tiger cats, dusky leaf monkeys, frogs, cicadas, and many others, are given, as noted, a powerful sonological presence in ritual when the shaman enters their outer forms, vocalizes their calls and becomes, if only momentarily, the form of the being he possesses. The shaman can even dissolve his subtle form into mists and clouds so as to hide himself from malevolent beings and travelling shamans from other communities.[6]

The following discussion of *Teng Rangut* (*jambu* fruit dove), the fourth *teng* in the *Teng Kijai* performance (Table 9.1), exemplifies the interplay of language, identity and revelatory experience. This beautiful fruit dove can be heard in the morning and evening and is the emanation or embodiment of *Maq Sidi*, a world creating female shamanic ancestor. As Paq Loong said to me, the *jambu* fruit dove is *Maq Sidi* in her guise as a *gunig* or familiar. The deepest level of identification is when Paq Loong enwraps himself in the *baju* or cloak soul of *rangut* and utters her cooing call. *Rangut* is a divine numinous presence and embodies the creativity of all living things.

In the *Teng Kijai* performance from which this description of *rangut* is drawn, *rangut* imagery spans strophes 4.3 to 4.68 in a 204 strophe *teng*. The evocation of *rangut* begins with the shaman singing that he can see *rangut*'s nest far ahead. In 4.8 he sings of the far distant nest and states that it is the *sentana* (abode) of *rangut*, buffeted by strong winds. Rangut's *sentana* was first created by *Maq Sidi*, *Maq Pandai* and other shamanic ancestors. The nest was *suar* (envisioned) by these ancestors, and he sings that the *hator* (design or arranging) and *celis* (trimming or snipping) processes are still evident in the structure of the primordial nest. Ancestral creativity is an ongoing process as is the presence of these beings in the very fabric of the earth's creative processes. Shaman Paq Loong then images *rangut* building her nest, a nest whose archetypal design was bequeathed by *Sidi* and the ancestors. This is an image of life and creativity at its most intense.

A little further on Paq Loong amplifies the numinosity of the imagery by locating it at the centre of the earth where it becomes a classical *axis mundi* integrating the plume of *kijai* incense from the censer with a downward streaming column of lice emanating from *rangut*'s preening. Here we see the deep aetiological connection between health and affliction discussed previously.

eeeeeeeeeeeeeeeeeeeeeeeeeeeeeeeeeeeh *patah rantiŋ oi tujuh teŋkoh* *buat peŋaraŋ telor ana?* *buat sentana seraῦ oi lah* 4.16	eeeeeeeeeeeeeeeeeeeeeeeeeeeeeeeeeeeeh snapping off twigs *oi* in sprays of seven making a nest for her eggs building an airy abode *oi lah* 4.16
buat sentana ralaῖ sudah *di tambaŋ sidi* *di hator malim* *di hator bijaʔ lagi* *sentana pandaῖ* *sentana juaris sudah lagi* 4.17	building a scraggy dwelling bequeathed by Sidi arranged by shamans woven by Bijak further the seer's dwelling the ancestral abode 4.17
bagi di celis sudah *patah rantiŋ ujuŋ bandar* *sudah gunah dayaŋ lagi* *di tambaŋ sidi* 4.18	appears as if trimmed snapping off twigs in the region's far reaches a mournful spirit maiden Sidi's doing 4.18

In strophe 4.52 below Paq Loong sings out hoo'ooooooooooooooo three times signifying that he has taken on the garb of the *jambu* fruit dove, that is *Maq Sidi*, and merges with her inner being—a powerful image of mystical union. In the two strophes preceding *rangut*'s call Paq Loong sings of being in deep reverie with the images of shamans past and present who experience the numinous power of *rangut*'s abode. Paq Loong exclaims a loud vocalization and then enters *rangut*'s *baju* (cloak soul or outer form). In strophes 4.52 and 4.53 on the following page Paq Loong images the plaintive call of the *gunig* (spirit guide) as she surveys her seasonally dry and leafless habitat.

We can see that the ritual image of the female *jambu* fruit dove, frequently seen and heard in the forest, embodies seasonality, reproductive behaviour and vocalizations. She is imaged at her creative peak, as are all familiars, and is projected to the numinous centre of the world. The shaman's cooing vocalization also places him at the sacred centre of *rangut*'s *sentana*, ministers to the patient, influences the disease-spirit, and attests to the shaman's ability to call upon the unseen powers of the tropical rain forest. Yet his language is never more than intimations of an unseen reality that only occasionally attains presence in vocalizations, disease-spirits and the persuasive power of metaphor. As Rumelhart (1993: 80) states, "Although we often have strong intuitions about what is *literally* true and what is only *metaphorically* true, the judgements are not always easy...." (author's italics). The same could be said for the power of the microcosmic illusion and the travelling shaman's experience.

CONCLUSION: HORIZONS OF KNOWING

The Temoq once inhabited an extensive lowland tropical rain forest that constituted the landscape of shamanic spiritual life and ritual performance. Incorporating hundreds of natural species transformed by a rich religious imagination into ancestors, guardians, familiars,

yooooooooooooh eeeeeeeeeeeeeeeeeeeeh haî heywan lagi malim sekaraŋ dulu di tambaŋ tiŋgal sentana dayaŋ 4.50	yooooooooooooh eeeeeeeeeeeeeeeeeeeeh hai in reverie shamans past and present bequeathed the spirit maiden's abode 4.50
yooooooooooooooooooooooooooh haî lah 4.51	yoooooooooooooooooooooooooooh hai lah 4.51
hoo'ooooooooooooo hoo'ooooooooooooooo hoo'oooooooooooooooo 4.52	hoo'ooooooooooooo hoo'ooooooooooooooo hoo'ooooooooooooooooo 4.52
eeeeeeeeeeeeeeeeeeeeeeeeeeeh bagi di celis sentana pandaî lagi bagi di hator sentana bijaʔ lagi sudah 4.53	eeeeeeeeeeeeeeeeeeeeeeeeeeeeeh Pandai's dwelling as if trimmed Bijak's dwelling as if arranged 4.53
eeeeeeeeeh ah tampak mərusuh dusun kesaû dayaŋ lagi oheh di tambaŋ gunuŋ lagi 4.54	eeeeeeeeeh ah behold the plaintive spirit maiden the spirit maiden's leafless groves oheh on the cloud-mountain 4.54

helpers, healers and medicines, their creative powers enjoined shamans to heal individuals and communities. Their empowering presence also added a redemptive dimension to the shaman's skyward journeys.

The shaman's ritual persona is complex and ever changing. His envisioning of the earth is a processional reality of ever receding horizons and defies any sense of formal geometry or epistemology. The shifting between form and substance, of presence and absence, waking consciousness and deep trance, and the sea of tropes through which he moves, leads to a state of epistemological indeterminacy. This is expressed by the language of metaphor and "as if", a numinous shadow language of sono-visionary intimations cresting into epic clarity and brisk gestures, and then troughing into the silent stillness of overwhelming beauty. Indeed if the latter state persists for more than a few minutes, anxious assistants will attempt to call the shaman back by singing and even grabbing the whisk out of his hand and shaking it over his back and head.

Paq Loong's deep and profound identification with the primal powers of creation unmistakeably demonstrates that beyond the anthropological labels of religion and *kepercayaan* (M. beliefs) lies a powerful stream of mystical insight equal to anything found in other religious traditions. That this visionary experience is given form by sung poetry of great beauty and depth also attests to Paq Loong's compositional virtuosity in which each new performance invokes a primordial shadow world fusing therapeutic and "biospheric" processes into a powerful event that heals human beings, the earth, and not least, disease-spirits.

NOTES

1. Temoq shamanism is situated in what I define as the Southern Aslian Shamanic Complex, which includes the neighbouring Semelai, Smaq Bri, and several formerly Aslian and now Malay dialect-speaking Jakun. Shamanic spirit journey itineraries are unique to specific shamans and hence to the communities in which they practise. Each

community is a node in a shamanic network that extends beyond the Temoq to neighbouring ethnolinguistic groups. I surmise that the Southern Aslian Shamanic Complex probably once covered a much larger area extending to the Btsisi (Southern Aslian speakers) who live adjacent to the Straits of Malacca.

2.   This is quite apart from the more than 60 traditional plant medicines used to treat a wide range of conditions from infections to headaches and childbirth.

3.   It is difficult to translate Temoq ideas about non-visible dimensions of the body and its various subtle manifestations. Basically the body (*kepan*) has several subtle forms including *bayang* (shadow), *baju* (upper cloak sheath soul) and *sarong* (lower cloak sheath soul), and *semangat* (manikin soul). These terms form expressions such as "*bayang semangat*", "*sarong baju*", "*sarong bayang*", "*sarong semangat*" and "*baju bayang semangat*". These "souls" travel in the entourage, and at the end of a *teng* the shaman asks them to bivouac in one place and not to scatter and endanger the patient. At the end of a performance they are requested to return to the body. Soul imagery is not consistent in any simple classificatory sense, for *baju* and *sarong* are also used to refer to the invisible sheath counterpart of the patient's body in the ritual house. Another example is *semangat*, which is also imaged in ritual as a yellow clump of pollen carried under the hind legs of a bumble bee flying upfront of the entourage. Finally, people report that when the *bayang* joins the entourage they have the sensation of sleepiness induced in part by drumming.

4.   The placebo response, as in modern medicine, no doubt plays a significant role in Temoq shamanic healing. See http://programinplacebostudies.org/.

5.   *Suar* does not mean illusion or mirage for which the term *sangka* is used when the shaman mistakenly "sees" a far distant phenomena that turns out to be something else on getting closer.

6.   From a shamanic perspective each Temoq community functions like a small autonomous political unit, and a performance entourage bears striking resemblance to a royal procession. Intercommunal shamanic warfare resulting in, for example, the blinding of Paq Loong in one eye by an invisible dart sent by a shaman in another community, is openly discussed. This is one of the reasons that shamans tend to specialize in mutually exclusive itineraries so as to reduce the chance of meeting a shaman who is performing on the same night in another community.

REFERENCES

Laird, P.F.
  1978   Temoq Shamanism and Affliction: A Preliminary Investigation.
          Unpublished PhD thesis, Monash University.
  2011   Beguiling Minan: The Language, Gesture, and Acoustics of
          Disease-Spirit Extraction in Temoq Shamanic Ritual. Shaman
          19: 69–111.
  2013   The Architecture of Thankfulness: The Role of Bathing Platforms
          in Temoq Shamanic Ritual. Paper presented at the 11th Conference
          of the International Society for Shamanistic Research (ISSR),
          Guiyang, China.
  n.d.(a) Temoq Shamanism: Songs of Life and Healing in a Malaysian
          Rain Forest Society.
  n.d.(b) Smyum Teng Kijai: A Temoq Shaman's Ecstatic Journey to the
          Cloud-Mountains.
Rumelhart, D.E.
  1993   Some problems with the notion of literal meanings. *In* Metaphor
          and Thought. A. Ortony, ed. Pp. 71–82. Cambridge: Cambridge
          University Press.

10

Folk Beliefs vs. World Religions: A Malaysian Orang Asli Experience

Juli Edo and Kamal Solhaimi Fadzil

Thank God, there will be Jehai in heaven!

Chen 2010

INTRODUCTION

The Department of Orang Asli Development (JAKOA 2012) estimated the Orang Asli population for 2010 to be 178,197 people. Of this, 51,437 or 29 per cent were Semai. The Semai communities are largely distributed in the states of Pahang and Perak, with Selangor home to about 1,000 Semai people.

In 2011, approximately 23 per cent of the 53,299 Orang Asli[1] in Perak were Muslim, 18 per cent had converted to Christianity, 5 per cent had embraced Bahai, and less than 1 per cent followed other world religions such as Buddhism, Hinduism and Taoism (JAKOA Perak pers. comm.).

Using the Semai village of Mendang as a point for discussion, this chapter explores the impact of world religions on the Orang Asli. Inhabited by 300 people comprising 55 households, Mendang is a

251

252 Juli Edo and Kamal Solhaimi Fadzil

small village. The people there practise different world religions as well as folk religion and are divided based on their different religious affiliations: folk belief (animism), Islam and Christian denominations (for example Gospel Hall, Methodist and *Roh*).

The penetration by these world religions has greatly impacted their identity and cohesion, particularly the maintenance of social solidarity and the collective pursuit of native customary rights and development.

MENDANG VILLAGE AND EARLY PROSELYTIZATION

Mendang village was first settled by Semai people in 1947,[2] just before the Malayan Emergency was declared by the British in 1948. Prior to British colonization of Malaya, or even before the emerging of the ancient Malay kingdom in Perak, the Mendang area was a Semai inherited territory or customary land, known as Gaib. On the eastern side of Gaib was another Semai territory, known as Talang. In pre-World War II colonial Malaya, the eastern part of Talang was occupied by the Chinese, mostly vegetable, groundnut and tapioca growers. They had established a small township known as Nyatoh (now Air Kuning). In addition, there was another large Semai territory located on the south eastern side of Gaib, known as Krikal (now Kelubi). When the British introduced land laws in the early 1900s, Gaib was gazetted as a Malay reserve with a big chunk of its western part converted into wet rice, or paddy, fields. Although the area had been designated a Malay reserve, the Semai maintained their presence in Gaib, especially around the eastern part of the territory. Later, they established several villages in the area, which continue to exist to the present day. Talang was designated under two different land statuses. The eastern part of Talang became state land where a Temporary Occupation Licence (TOL) was given to Chinese growers, while the western side was converted into a forest reserve, known as the Keroh Forest Reserve. Despite being a protected area, Mat Arip, a Semai leader, continued to occupy western Talang. In 1937, all members of Mat Arip's group were jailed for a week by the British for allegedly encroaching on the forest reserve (see

Juli 1988). While dwelling in the Talang area, Mat Arip established close relations with a group of Chinese from Nyatoh, who later formed the local Kuomintang chapter, an important anti-Japanese resistance force that was to become an important ally to British forces during the Japanese Occupation (1942–45). Around the time that Mat Arip made friends with the Chinese at Nyatoh, Krikal was converted into state land for the purpose of tin ore mining.

Gaib, gazetted as a Malay reserve in the early 20th century, was occupied by Javanese-Malay people who practised wet rice cultivation. Shortly after the Japanese surrendered in 1945, the British colonial administration banned the Malayan Communist Party (MCP). As a result, the MCP turned their struggle into an insurgency against the colonial government. In 1947, communist insurgents attacked the Javanese-Malay village in Gaib, forcing villagers to abandon the village and run for their lives. Towards the end of 1947 the British summoned Mat Arip, a Semai leader whose group practised swidden agriculture in the vicinity of west Talang (or Keroh Forest Reserve) and requested that he move his group into the lower part of the abandoned Mendang village (Kampong Krob) and settle there permanently.[3] Much later, the British ordered another Semai group within the vicinity of Gaib, in which Mathias was an elder, to move to Kampong Kmil, located in the upper part of the area.

Mat Arip was appointed headman for the "new" settlement at Mendang. Under Mat Arip's leadership, the villagers took up wet rice cultivation, and they performed the annual rituals related to land, fruits and plants, healing, and so on. These rituals express gratitude to the land guardian spirits of the area for giving the people a good life, health and bountiful harvests. Mat Arip was not only a headman, he was also a good friend of the British. Most of the time he was busy accompanying British officers, especially Major P.D.R. Williams-Hunt and R.O.D. Noone, on their visits to Orang Asli villages in Perak and Pahang, persuading other Orang Asli to support the government in their fight against the insurgents. For the same reason, he also frequently travelled to Taiping, Ipoh, Tapah and Telok Anson in Perak; Kuala Lipis, Bentong and Kuantan in Pahang; and Kuala Lumpur and other towns in which the aborigines protection offices were located.

In 1948, Chinese farmers from Nyatoh asked the people of Mendang to work in their gardens. Four villagers, including a husband and wife, accepted the offer, as they were jobless and needed money to support their families. At that time, they had not yet started farming because the government needed to complete their land survey of the area to delineate the boundary between Semai and Malay territory. The Semais who agreed to work in Nyatoh, however, were kidnapped by insurgents only four days after starting work there. Two men were able to escape, but the husband and wife remain missing to this day. Mat Arip brought this matter to the British attention. The British, however, asked Mat Arip to investigate the matter in a subtle way, as they wanted him to identify the members of the secret insurgent nest. Through his Kuomintang network, Mat Arip managed to ascertain that his people were kidnapped by an armed wing of the MCP led by a wealthy businessman, locally known as Bah Atak. Mat Arip conveyed this information to the British. This led to the deployment of a big military operation to apprehend Bah Atak. It involved a combination of an air strike and ground troops; a platoon of the Gurkha regiment was dispatched for the mission. In that operation, Bah Atak was killed in the airstrike, while the rest of his men were either killed or detained by the Gurkha forces. The British appreciated Mat Arip's role in dealing with the insurgents, and they then appointed him as a mediator to liaise between the Orang Asli and the colonial authority. The British aimed to have the Semai on their side, and they believed that the involvement of local people such as Mat Arip in the psychological warfare would aid their struggle against the MCP and would help win the hearts of the local Semai as well as those of other Orang Asli communities.

In the early 1950s, the British asked Mat Arip to persuade the Semoq Beri people of Maran town (in the state of Pahang) to move into a settlement scheme as part of measures to address the Malayan Emergency (see Juli 1998). He was there for a few months and came back to Mendang at the end of 1950. While he was in Mendang, the villagers were subjected to two air strikes launched by the British on 28 and 29 March 1951.[4] In the first attack, seven bombs were dropped, and during the second attack, the village was strafed by machineguns. In those attacks, a villager received a head wound when he was hit by a bombshell. Moreover, these aerial attacks destroyed their chicken coops and barns behind their houses. After the attack, Mat Arip went to Telok Anson town to report the matter to the District Officer (DO) and asked the DO to explain why the British attacked the village. He was told that attacks were based on a report made by a group of Javanese-Malays who wanted to reclaim Mendang. The report claimed that the Semai of Mendang were assisting and hiding communist insurgents, sheltering them in small houses built at the backyards of the main houses. The accusation was of course false. Thus, Mat Arip realized why the British air force targeted their coops and barns. The British sent a paramilitary troop to investigate the matter and found no evidence that the people of Mendang were assisting or protecting members of the MCP, so the British allowed the Semais to remain in Mendang. On 21 April 1951, the Officer in Command Police District (OCPD) of Telok Anson and Major P.D.R. Williams-Hunt came to Mendang to apologize for the attacks, and they gave Mat Arip $300 to organize a feast in the village. A few months after that, Mat Arip was once again required by the British to go back to Maran in Pahang, and this time he had to stay there for over a year.[5] Because of that, Mat Arip decided to bring along his family, and he handed over the headmanship of Mendang to Mathias, an elder of Kmil village.

The Mendang people started wet rice cultivation during the time Mathias was headman. The Semai of Mendang thus shifted from shifting cultivation and hunting and gathering to a peasant type economy. Mathias remained as head of the community until the mid-1960s, when he divorced his wife. Because his main tie to Mendang was through his wife, Mathias stepped down as headman and handed over the position to his brother-in-law, Pandak, who also came from Krikal. Mathias afterwards left Mendang for Teaw Menchag, a Semai village near Kampar town.[6] There, he joined fellow villagers collecting and selling jungle produce, such as rattan, and cutting small trees, to be sold to mining companies. It was tough work, and Mathias always felt he lacked the necessary energy to follow his friends working in the jungle. While at home, Mathias often frequented a coffee shop in Kampar, owned by a Chinese man known as Bah Kaka that was a favourite among the Semai. There, he met a middle-age Indian man, who was also a regular customer. After knowing one another for some time, they became close friends. The Indian man offered Mathias all kinds of aid and support—such as used clothing, minor medical aids, advice and consultation on all matters—and became his spiritual guide. The man was an active member and later a committee member of the Gospel Hall (GH) church. After a long relationship and exchange of ideas (and perhaps persuasion and preaching) between the two, Mathias agreed to visit the church, and he accepted the congregation's offer to distribute those goods to the local Semai community of Teaw Menchag and whoever else was in need. Soon after that, Mathias joined the Gospel Hall church. Immediately after he embraced the religion, Mathias became one of the missionary volunteers whose role was to introduce GH's preaching to other Semai villages. However, to avoid conflict, Mathias' mission was aimed at Semai villages which had not been visited or influenced by other churches. In one of his missions to a village named Chawang, near Sungkai town, Mathias met a young girl whose family decided to embrace GH. He married the girl and stayed in the village for a few years. Later, Mathias and his family moved to several other villages before finally settling down in Teaw Menchag in the early 1970s. However, Mathias soon realised that he was no longer an influential figure in Teaw Menchag as the villagers were not receptive to his preaching of GH. A number of the villagers had already joined other churches, particularly, Catholicism.

Interest in Catholicism had begun during the late 1960s after the death of a man named Uda in a road accident. The deceased's funeral was conducted by the church, and he was buried in a Christian cemetery. In addition, Father Lee of the Catholic church offered free English education to Semai children and adults, gave food and presents to children during Christmas and assisted the people in various petty matters. These services attracted the people to accept Catholicism and, in doing so, to sideline Mathias and the GH.

In the mid-1970s, a year after his second child was born, Mathias divorced his young wife. He and his two children continued to live in Teaw Menchag for a few years before moving back to Mendang. His brother-in-law Pandak was still the headman of Mendang. Pandak, who was also a shaman, continued to practise the *ngengulang*[7] ritual every year, a major event in Semai religion. We speculate that Mathias, whose sister was married to Pandak, may have influenced the latter to convert to Christianity. In any case, towards the end of that decade, Pandak also embraced Christianity. He continued to hold the headmanship until he died in the early 1990s, although he had abandoned all traditional rituals related to Semai religion. As a faithful Christian in Gospel Hall, he attended Sunday services and celebrated Christmas together with Mathias.

THE CHRISTIANS

Today 28 Mendang families identify themselves as Christians. Out of this number, 13 families belong to the Methodist church, 9 families follow *Roh* and 6 families belong to Gospel Hall, although this number is declining due to a lack of local leadership. The origin of Gospel Hall in the village is closely related to the life history of Mathias, as described above.

The Methodist group began to penetrate the community in the mid-1990s. Initiated by two Semai women missionaries from the Methodist church in Gopeng, the movement was then assisted by Long, a female Semai preacher from Teaw Menchag. After about three years of missionary work, they successfully converted many families to the Methodist church. However, towards the end of the decade, Long was influenced by another Christian missionary group, locally known as *Roh*.

Roh in the Malay language means soul or spirit. Unable to confirm the reference to Roh, we speculate that the soul or spirit among this group refers to the Holy Spirit (translated in Malay as *Roh Kudus*). One attraction of the group is the ability of the preacher or priest to fall into a trance and heal people using verses from the Bible. More than his sermons, the ability of the priest to perform faith healing drew widespread support among the villagers. Long, formerly a Methodist preacher, joined the *Roh* flock along with a male Chinese priest. Over time, more members of the Methodist group have started converting to this new Christian group.

The various Christian denominations conduct their own Sunday services, held at different locations and times. Most Christian services are held at the house of the local preacher, who leads the prayers. For the Gospel Hall group, however, their priest is not a local member of the village and is always absent from local prayer.

Before a local preacher was appointed, the Methodists in Mendang had to celebrate Christmas a day early. This was because on the first day of Christmas, the priest would typically be busy conducting prayers in other settlements with Methodist churches. For many years, then, there were two days of Christmas celebrations in Mendang, one by the Methodists followed by those of the Gospel Hall and Catholic churches.

THE MUSLIMS

Islam came to Mendang primarily through marriage. The first villager to embrace the religion was Alang, the elder sister of Mat Arip (the first headman). In the early 1950s, Alang divorced her first husband and then married a Semai man from Cenderiang who had earlier

Plate 10.1 Children going for prayers at the Gospel for the Poor church, Kampung Tual, Lipis, Pahang

(Photo credit: Kamal Solhaimi Fadzil)

Plate 10.2 Pastor Razali meditating on his sermon for Saturday prayers, Gospel for the Poor church, Kampung Tual, Lipis, Pahang

(Photo credit: Kamal Solhaimi Fadzil)

Plate 10.3 Pastor Razali delivering his sermon at the Gospel for the Poor church, Kampung Tual, Lipis, Pahang

(Photo credit: Kamal Solhaimi Fadzil)

converted to Islam. Although her husband was a Muslim, in the beginning Alang did not embrace the religion. The couple lived ordinary Semai lives or as non-Muslim Semai until her husband died in the mid-1970s. From their union, they were blessed with two children, a son and daughter. Their son died at an early age, but the daughter, Chumin, went to a government school, eventually qualifying as a nurse. She worked at the Orang Asli Hospital in Gombak until her retirement in 2002. Although her father was Muslim, Chumin was not raised as a Muslim. She became a Muslim when she married a Jakun man, who was a Muslim. From this union they produced two children and raised them as Muslims. However, Chumin's marriage was not meant to be, and by the 1980s they separated.

About five or six years before Alang died in 2000, she became determined to become a true Muslim. Assisted by her grandchildren who were Muslims (mostly converted to Islam through marriage), she began learning Islam in earnest. She was assisted particularly by Ipang, her grand-daughter who lived in Kampar. Ipang moved to Mendang to make sure her grandmother learned the proper practice of Islam. While in Mendang, Ipang's husband died. Soon after, Alang passed away as a Muslim and was buried in the Muslim cemetery near Mendang. In 2002, Chumin retired and returned to Mendang. In 2009, one of Alang's daughters from her first marriage, Teh, converted to Islam. Teh, a single mother, embraced Islam as a result of constant missionary activities organized by the state. Today, three single mothers who are Muslims live in Mendang. They receive substantial support from the state and the surrounding Malay communities.

SEMAI RELIGION

Although the last 50 years have seen the encroachment of world religions into Mendang social space, today 50 per cent of Mendang inhabitants remain faithful to the traditional Semai religion. They hold onto their traditional religion because they believe that if they convert to other religions and do not follow Orang Asli traditions and if they stop speaking the Semai language, they will ceased to be Orang Asli. Thus

Semai religion, as the major component of Semai cultural traditions, plays an essential role in Semai identity.

At the heart of Semai religion is the belief that the world is filled with spirits, many of which are dangerous to humans. Belief in these spirits entails the need for an expert, called a *hala',* to handle the supernatural elements. Semai religion involves all forms of shamanism[8] and can be described as a shamanistic religion.

Like those who practise world religions, the villagers of Mendang who continue to follow the traditional religion are divided amongst themselves. The traditional religionists today are divided into two groups. These are, first, the moderate Semai who want to remain as Semai, while, at the same time, being willing to adjust to the demands of modernization, and, second, the orthodox group, who hold steadfastly to Semai shamanism. They both continue to hold onto the traditional practices and beliefs that many illnesses are caused by the actions of people who cast spells and use black magic. Illnesses can also be caused by the loss of one's soul or *ruwai*. A person may lose their soul when the soul fails to return to the body or is taken by a malevolent spirit. This group remains suspicious of other members of the community, who they see as potential threats to their wellbeing. Hence, they remain constantly engaged in tense interpersonal relations with other members of Mendang.

Nonetheless, previous studies by prominent scholars such as Robert Dentan (1968), Geoffrey Benjamin (1976), Kirk Endicott (1979), Signe Howell (1984), Marina Roseman (1991), and others, show that indigenous Orang Asli religions are effective in maintaining social order and promoting unity and justice among members of the community.

IMPLICATIONS

In the 1970s the state introduced a national ideology referred to as *Rukunegara*. The first of five *Rukunegara* principles is "Belief in God". The creation of this ideology thus placed the Orang Asli in a particularly delicate position, whilst paving the way for proselytization from those who practise theistic faiths, particularly from among practitioners of world religions.

The ensuing pressure to conform to the national ideology and the pulls from different religions have deeply affected social relations within Mendang. On the surface, the people of Mendang look like a cohesive community. However, in reality they remain a divided society. The division within the community is not just between groups but also within the groups. On the broad level, the community is divided into Muslims, Christians and those who practise the traditional religion. But scratch beneath the surface and we are confronted by internal divisions. Thus, for example, the Christians are divided into different church affiliations, while the traditional practitioners are divided into moderate and orthodox. This situation has greatly hindered the struggle for indigenous rights and community development within Mendang.

THE STRUGGLE FOR INDIGENOUS RIGHTS

The majority of the people of Mendang have abandoned many traditional cultural elements due to the influence of modernization and world religions. These modern influences, which have wrought much change, have largely been introduced through formal education. Today many Orang Asli, like the people of Mendang, maintain cultural features that mark them off as indigenous peoples, including their languages and fundamental values and customs, many related to kinship and marriage. In reality, however, traditional values that uphold these customs have eroded. The impact of modernization, nationalism and the spread of world religions over the last five decades has gone beyond superficial change. Orang Asli themselves are deeply divided on the importance of traditional practices and beliefs and on how to represent themselves as a collective whole.

The Perak Orang Asli Foundation proposed in 2002 that a *Jis Ngengulang* celebration be introduced as a state holiday, similar to the practice of *Gawai* in Sarawak and *Sava Kaamatan* in Sabah. These holidays are harvest celebrations. However, before the state government had the opportunity to act on the proposed *Jis Ngengulang,* Christian

Orang Asli groups registered their opposition to a ritual that was deemed to celebrate the "free spirits" of the traditional religion. Later, the state government also opposed the proposal as un-Islamic. However, this is a difficult argument to accept coming from the state, because Malaysia recognizes Chinese New Year, Deepavali, Thaipusam, and so on, all of which are based on belief systems that are not Islamic, as state or national level celebrations.

Although on the surface the Orang Asli people appear to share a common struggle over issues related to land rights and representation, their unity is like that of soccer fans. When they come together in solidarity for the World Indigenous Day celebration or join in the struggle for land claims, they appear united. However, like soccer fans, once the whistle has blown, everyone goes back home to their individual villages, lives and personal faiths. Thus, representing indigenous identity through the use of traditional customs and symbols is to reduce them to mere political markers. Their meanings and values within the traditional worldviews are lost in translation. The ambiguities and contradictions between the worldviews of members of different faiths denies the real meaning of the cultural elements or symbols, reducing them to empty shells devoid of meaning.

MOVING FORWARD AS ORANG ASLI

Modernization creates expectations in people. Orang Asli, like the neighbouring Malays, want development, and they expect it to "take-off". However, in reality, the development that Orang Asli experience can be described as *pembangunan tengah tiang* ("half-way development"). What this means is that development does not go all the way. Just like passengers on an aircraft, they have already taken off from the old airport (the traditional way of life) and are moving forward towards a new and promising future (leaving behind the old way of life). However, they have not yet arrived at their final destination. But, without any way of knowing where their final destination will be, they become anxious and vulnerable. They do not know because they lack the tools that can help them navigate these changes. A local Orang Asli activist, Achom Luji, expressed the view that the Orang Asli are unable to complete their flight because they lack three key resources: *ilmu* ("knowledge"), *duit* ("financial capacity") and *kuasa* ("political representation").

Orang Asli today remain in limbo—confused, uncertain and divided on who they are. The choice they face can be described as having to choose among three distinct pathways. They can choose, first, the path created by the state which is centred on Islamization and is meant as a way of integrating them into Malay society (*muij gop* or "becoming Malay"); second, the pathway promoted by churches which is meant to create modern Christian Orang Asli; and, third, the old path followed by the elders from previous generations, now somewhat neglected and overgrown. To follow the last pathway, however, the Orang Asli will have to clear the undergrowth and bushes, perhaps even to build a new pathway that will enable a group of traditional but moderate Orang Asli to construct a way of life that is adapted to modern conditions, while preserving their cultural life, norms, value system and language.

CONCLUSION

The experience of Mendang with world religions is just one example of a social phenomenon that is today pervasive among Orang Asli communities. One religion can be effective in maintaining order, promoting unity and providing guidelines to achieve better living and justice. However, if too many religions exist in a small society like Mendang, it creates disunity and instability, putting their people at a difficult crossroad. As the saying goes, "too many cooks spoil the broth". In Mendang and other villages like it the political space created by state policies enabled world religions to move in, turning Orang Asli villages into contested sites for the different faiths, thus causing the sorts of ambiguity and contradictions that promote divisions between and within the different communities, rather than paving the way towards internal cohesion and indigenous solidarity.

With the current trends and internal contestations between religious groups, the future of Orang Asli as a unique community remains in question. Although we regard Orang Asli as a distinct category of

Malaysian citizens, our argument should not be construed as romanticism or over-generalization, ignoring the diversity among different Orang Asli groups as well as the complexities of how modernity impinges on the different groups in different ways. There is no singular Orang Asli experience or Orang Asli group.

However, the observations made in this chapter are meant as a catalyst to encourage new areas of research in Orang Asli studies. We suggest that more work should be done to focus specifically on how world religions impinge on Orang Asli communities. As world religions find new ways to make inroads into Orang Asli settlements, one of which today is through economic development, there is a serious need to redirect our focus in exploring the impact of development among the Orang Asli to include the role of world religions. There are many questions to ask, and we can start with these. How do contesting faiths divide communities? Why must they divide? Do conversions to world religions affect local notions of landscapes and land rights? How has Orang Asli identity adapted to religious change? For instance, if a Semai converts to Islam, has he become a Malay? Do conversions mean a transformation of selfhood? How has this affected social organizations in communities? Does conversion mean an end to local rituals, such as traditional healing practices, harvest rituals and the *bela kampong*[9] rituals? To take a page out of the Comoroffs (1986), to have a more nuanced appreciation of Orang Asli experiences with world religions, we need to start looking at the multiple discourses that developed out of these encounters.

ACKNOWLEDGEMENTS

We dedicate this chapter to the memory of Mat Arip Kulop and Mathias and thank their families and the JAKOA for support in our research.

NOTES

1. The Orang Asli groups in Perak consist largely of the Semai people, with the rest consisting of Temiar, Lanoh, Kintak and Jahai peoples.

2. Based on Mat Arip's notes.
3. The term upper and lower part of a village or area is made in reference to the movement of the sun. Hence, where the sun rises (east) is referred to as *atas* or "upper", and where the sun sets (west) is *bawah* or "lower".
4. Based on Mat Arip's notes.
5. Mat Arip came back to Perak in 1952 and stayed in Kampar town, then moved to Teaw Menchag. Much later, he moved permanently to a neighbouring village, Sahom (see Juli 1990).
6. Dentan had carried out his doctoral fieldwork in this village in the 1960s.
7. The purpose of the ritual is similar to the Gawai of Sarawak and Sava Kaamatan of Sabah, which is to convey gratitude to the land guardians for a good harvest in the past season and to pray for a better harvest in the coming season.
8. Shamanism among the Semai involves the use of *mahkluk ghaib* or translucent beings as spirit familiars to assist in healing as well as rituals that provide protection and well-being for the indigenous community. These rituals protect the villagers as well as crops from malevolent spirits. The translucent beings often are referred to as *gunig* ("spirit guides"), *keramat* and *mai dengrik*, both reference to land guardians, and others, generally known as *nyaniik* (see Juli 1998: 67–75).
9. *Bela kampung* refers to a cleansing ritual performed to ensure the village is free from threats by malevolent spirits.

REFERENCES

Chen, P.C.Y.
    2010   Reaching an Unreached People Group: The Jehai of the Temenggor Forest. Selangor, Malaysia: Akitiara.
Comaroff, J. and J. Comaroff
    1986   Christianity and Colonialism in South Africa. American Ethnologist 13(1): 1–22.
Dentan, R.K.
    1968   The Semai: A Nonviolent People of Malaya. New York: Holt, Rinehart and Winston.
Endicott, K.M.
    1979   Batek Negrito Religion. Oxford: Clarendon Press.
Howell, S.
    1984   Society and Cosmos: Chewong of Peninsular Malaysia. Singapore: Oxford University Press.

JAKOA
    2012   Annual Report. Department of Orang Asli Development. Kuala Lumpur, Malaysia.

Juli Edo
    1988   Claiming Our Ancestors' Land: An Ethnohistorical Study of Seng-oi Land Rights in Perak, Malaysia. Unpublished PhD thesis, Australian National University, Canberra, Australia.
    1990   Tradisi Lisan Masyarakat Semai. Bangi: Penerbit Universiti Kebangsaan Malaysia.

Metcalf, P.
    1982   A Borneo Journey into Death: Berawan Eschatology from Its Rituals. Philadelphia: University of Pennsylvania Press.

Mehrdad Arabestani and Juli Edo
    2011   The Semai's Response to Missionary Work: From Resistance to Compliance. Anthropological Notebooks, Slovene Anthropological Society 18(3): 5–27.

Nicholas, C.
    2004   The Orang Asli and the Contest for Resources: Indigenous Politics, Development and Identity in Peninsular Malaysia. Copenhagen: IWGIA.

Nobuta Toshihiro
    2009   Living on the Periphery: Development and Islamization among the Orang Asli in Malaysia. Subang Jaya, Malaysia: Center for Orang Asli Concerns.

Roseman, M.
    1991   Healing Sounds from the Malaysian Rainforest: Temiar Music and Medicine. Berkeley: University of California Press.

Part Five

SIGNIFICANCE OF ORANG ASLI CULTURES

chapter 11

Order and Challenge in Education and Therapy: The Influence of Temiar Beliefs and Practices

Andy Hickson and Sue Jennings

INTRODUCTION

There is ample literature supporting the idea that the Temiars, like their neighbours the Semai, are peaceful people (Benjamin 1967, 2014; Dentan 1968, 1988, 2008; Roseman 1991). The authors, who lived in the Temiar community for over 12 month's fieldwork (1975–76) and have made subsequent visits up to the present time, have been witnesses to this non-violent way of life. We also observed that there is a fear of chaos and destruction from a relentless landscape and weather that needs to be appeased. There is also a total horror at blood-shed; even when the blood is from a minor injury, it causes fear and fright. Fear of strangers is also present, "stranger danger", particularly when faced with non-Temiar or non-Orang Asli people.

Having lived a non-violent ethos with the Temiars has had a profound effect on the way we both work in education and therapy. In this chapter we discuss how the Temiar non-violent way of life has influenced our professional practices. Our understanding of Temiar beliefs and practices comes from our lived experience of staying with the Temiars and from the publications of Geoffrey Benjamin, Robert Dentan and others, both before and after our fieldwork. The debate concerning Temiar dream control is on-going and will not feature in this chapter. There is an excellent overview (Domhoff 1985), and Benjamin (1974, 1987, 1989, 2014) summarizes all the literature, together with fair comment.

The focus here is on how Temiar children traditionally grow up to be non-violent adults who flee from potential violence rather than fighting back. The striking thing about Temiar disagreements is the peaceful way they resolve them. It is very public: people meet, discuss issues and decide on ways to reconcile disagreements. Usually it involves drawing an individual's attention to their behaviour. Disputes are often concerned with lack of cooperation or the sharing of food. Issues are not discussed in private; the thin walls in Temiar houses makes it impossible in any case. However, one does not see people whispering together about other people. If there is whispering, it is telling others that there is danger lurking from thunder or tiger or foreigners.

Something affecting the whole community will often be resolved by a speech from an older member of the community or a shaman. For example if it is felt that young people are being too noisy and boisterous, an elder will make a speech to the whole community as he sits in the doorway of his house. He will remind everyone that noise and extrovert behaviour will provoke unwelcome attention from the thundergod.

Whereas Temiar have their own ways of dealing with disputes and unacceptable behaviour, there is more tension when they have disputes to settle with the outside world and with non-Temiar. Since the Temiar believe that outcomes need to be "fair" to all concerned, the inequality in loss of land-rights and deforestation has left them in an unequal position with no room for negotiations. Only recently have Temiar become politicized and found lawyers to negotiate external conflicts.

Our specific professional interest lies in how Temiar-style conflict resolution can be applied creatively in community groups such as day-centres and clubs and in educational settings (Hickson 1994, 2011) and *curatively* in therapeutic work with children and adults (Jennings 1995, 1998, 2011, 2012).

There are some cultures in the world that appear to deal with the problems of violence among members by structuring feelings of anger and aggression; other cultures suppress these feelings. Orang Asli groups in Malaysia such as the Temiar and Semai are talked of as being non-violent cultures. "Most of the time Semai children see no physical violence except the overwhelming violence of thunder squalls and floods" (Dentan 1999: 4). In contrast many children in the UK "suffer severe physical punishment: most children are hit by their parents, up to a third of younger children more than once a week" (Calouste Gulbenkian Foundation 1995: 10).

The "Semai do not deliberately punish aggression in children" and "the absence of punishment means that the would-be aggressive child has no model to imitate" (Dentan 1968: 61). Temiar children learn that "fear and flight are valued, not hostility and aggression ... and are taught that illness comes from harsh words" (Roseman 1991: 180). The majority of the Orang Asli could be regarded as economically poor, and many have few formal qualifications. However research shows that in the UK, low income families and people with few formal qualifications (or parents with unskilled/semi-skilled/manual occupations) are generally more likely than high income families to physically discipline their children (Cawson et al. 2000: 19).

Since we did our fieldwork there have been major discoveries in neuroscience which have led to new understanding of brain function, attachment and the nature-nurture debate. The human brain is often referred to as the triune brain (Maclean 1985; Cozolino 2002, 2006). This "three part brain" is composed of the reptilian or reactive brain, the mammalian brain, and the executive function brain. Although very simplified, it is a useful metaphor for understanding certain aspects of Temiar behaviour. The reactive brain is where the fear responses of Temiar children develop; small infants and children have their ears

Plate 11.1 Temiar creative workshop

(Photo credit: Andy Hickson)

covered by parents or grandparents during a major thunderstorm, while the adults mutter "fear, fear". Since fear is projected onto the outside world, either onto thunder or tiger or strangers, it frees them to be loving and nurturing parents, bringing up their children to be non-violent. In the mammalian part of their brains children develop strong bonds with both parents. The close parent-child bonds are reinforced by the parents adopting teknonyms after the birth of a child, being called mother or father of the named child. The constant massage and nursing of new-born babies also reinforces the security of attachment through this part of the brain, which is also shared by other primates. The dichotomy of fear and protection are constantly demonstrated and shared at a family, extended family and also community level.

During the 1990s specific neurons were identified that would respond when certain physical actions were performed by other people. They are called "mirror neurons" because they fire in response to witnessing specific movements. The discovery of mirror neurons in the brain has shed light on what drives communal activity such as dancing, cooperation and sharing. Mirror neurons reflect actions from people in proximity to babies and infants and demonstrate that role-modelling is an active and reflective process. "Mirror neurons lie at the crossroads of the processing of inner and outer experience, where multiple networks of visual, motor, and emotional processing converge" (Cozolino 2006: 187).

We can observe how the close proximity of Temiars living their non-violent ethos and projecting violence and fear onto thunder and non-Temiar enables them to maintain their love and respect and child-centred way of life.

Below are several examples of actual practice with children, teenagers and older people that show how a Temiar-influenced approach can create both stability and change.

ANDY'S PERSPECTIVE

I was first introduced to the Temiars, as a teenager, by Geoffrey Benjamin. In this respect Geoffrey was a great influence on the way I was to grow up. Living with the Temiars was a life-changing experience. It changed me as a person and has guided much of the way I work in schools and colleges using social theatre to creatively deal with issues of violence and bullying.

So, the Temiar way of life was a huge influence on my life personally and professionally. In a professional context the Temiars have influenced my social theatre programmes for dealing with bullying and violence in schools and the community. On a personal level I grew up very fast in the jungle. By the age of 14 years I was participating in many aspects of Temiar adult life and affairs: learning to build bamboo houses without a single nail, hunting in the jungle with a blowpipe and making dugout log canoes. One of my favourite activities in the jungle was learning about Temiar dance and shamanic practice. Returning to England at age 15 was an extremely difficult transition for me. As a family we moved from London to rural Warwickshire where I re-entered the British schooling system. I went from being a respected adult back to being a schoolboy. This was a miserable year for me; I felt powerless and insignificant.

The "adult" Temiar experience and then becoming a child again back in England and feeling that I had lost many of my rights fuelled my sense of wanting justice, equality and respect for all, particularly young people. These personal Temiar influences helped me develop my social theatre practice. In all the social theatre programmes I developed I wanted the young people involved to experience and be involved in projects as if they were adults. I applied the same conditions for young people as if I had been working with adult groups. I had expectations that they would use their own initiative and energies in a positive way directed towards the benefit of the group and projects as a whole. I also treated the young participants with the same respect as I would have treated a group of adults.

As mentioned, the Temiars have a reputation for being amongst the most peaceful people in the world. During my time with them I never witnessed an act of physical violence amongst the Temiar, whether it was between adults, young people, friends, family or strangers. This is

Plate 11.2 Creative workshop in Britain

(Photo credit: Andy Hickson)

not to say that the Temiar never argued or disagreed, but they found alternative ways to violence, including, interestingly, the occasional threat of violence to deal with their disagreements.

The foundations of social theatre are based around the principles of creativity and theatre and are used to explore and educate people about a variety of issues. Social theatre may be defined as theatre with specific social agendas; "theatre where aesthetics is not the ruling objective; theatre outside the realm of commerce, which drives Broadway/the West End, and the cult of the new, which dominates the avant-garde" (Thompson and Schechner 2004: 12). My social theatre programmes take on many forms, the most common being the use of live performances on issues of violence where the audience form part of the action along with the actors. A standard social theatre programme could look like this:

1.   Actors perform a short play to an audience on an issue or issues of violence.
2.   Audience members are invited to comment on the piece.
3.   Audience members take on roles of the protagonist/s in the play and demonstrate alternative ways of being.
4.   The new characterizations from audience members within the framework of the play lead the actors to improvise around their own characters, thus showing how people can feel, behave and interact in different ways.
5.   The process is repeated with everyone having a chance to demonstrate how they think characters can behave in situations and thus enable them to make positive life changes.

Through this process of "role-play", audience and actors achieve a catharsis and an understanding of alternatives without fear of retribution or ridicule.

The social theatre that I practise is influenced by Temiars on several levels. Social theatre programmes offer us the possibility of caring about what happens to other people whilst also offering alternative paths for action. This develops an openness in dialogue and interactions and a respect for the others' points of view, such as we might see in Temiar life where difficulties and problems are discussed openly in communal houses and in front of people rather than behind closed doors. Benjamin (1994) describes how Temiars balance, with some difficulty, the profound concern for communality while avoiding interference with the wishes of an individual.

The social theatre play can represent a slice of real life much like the open discussion of a dream in Temiar culture can. Within the play, actors and audience are encouraged to "feel" and "interact" as if they were the characters themselves living the dream (the play). When staying with Temiars I am often asked about my dreams the night before, and several interpretations are usually offered by my Temiar friends.

Finding non-violent solutions to difficulties is an important aspect of social theatre as it is in Temiar life. I have developed a creative programme that looks at how to stop bullying without becoming a bully oneself, in other words, without bullying back. "The Senoi prefer withdrawal to conflict, and they are not afraid to admit when they are afraid" (Domhoff 1985: 17).

The careful use of non-violent language plays an important role in the development of a non-violent way of life. This aspect of social theatre is often difficult for westerners to grasp, but can be seen in what I call the language of violence, when we talk about beating the bullies, stamping on violence and fighting for peace. Such expressions are contradictory, confusing and send out conflicting messages to people. Temiars are careful not to use inappropriate words in situations. For example, to use the word for eating meat, *rec*, for eating a durian fruit, rather than *caa*? ("consume food"), would be an insult. If you said to someone that they *rec* durian rather than *caa*? durian, you would be insulting them.

Punan (*selantab* in Temiar) is a word used in the context of sharing, whether it be the sharing of food, luxury items or community interaction. It is a word often used by adults to promote sharing in children, the lesson being that if one does not share with others, then one will cause them pain. A person who is in pain is a vulnerable person and therefore will be liable to have some kind of accident or some kind of emotional depression. *Punan* refers not only to the refusal to give food (cause), but also to the resulting vulnerability (effect) of the person who did not get their share of the food. The concept of *punan* and making others feel unhappy or depressed forms part of the concept of bullying that I work with in schools: "to make someone unhappy, especially in frustrating his desires, will increase the probability of his having an accident.... The Semai say that *punan* accidents result somehow from the fact that the *punan*'s victim's heart is 'unhappy'" (Dentan 1968: 55). Dentan and Robarchek argue that *pehunan* inhibits violence and aggression. Robarchek suggests that in the West, the "normal" response to frustration is aggression, whereas with the Semai, when frustration does occur, "the resultant emotion in the frustrated party is not anger but is rather a fear of the danger to which one has become vulnerable" (1977: 769).

The Batek, another Orang Asli people who live nearby, have a similar concept called *ke'oy*. This is described as a serious condition arising when someone has been mistreated by other people in some way. It is an "affliction of the heart", "an emotional depression usually accompanied by physical symptoms such as fever". "This is regarded as a serious disease which can lead to death" (Endicott 1979: 109).

I promote a "whole school approach" to dealing with bullying which again can parallel this idea of *punan*. It "makes it clear that a system of sanctions so markedly other-directed can serve admirably as a means of infusing the whole community with a moral concern for one's fellows" (Benjamin 1967: 337). This can be observed in how Temiar communities care, share and interact with each other. The whole school approach suggests that for a programme dealing with bullying the whole school community need to be involved and have an input.

Depression in the UK is often not taken seriously, at least not as seriously as physical (visible) sickness. Bullying was often seen as a "rite of passage" that people should go through to make them stronger, to build their characters. The problem is that some people suffer bullying so badly that they want to take their own lives (on average 15–20 young people commit suicide every year in the UK due to bullying).

A social theatre piece can be described as developing the Temiar "middle" voice that Benjamin talks about: "The Temiars ... have developed a distinct middle voice, in which subject and object become one, because 'the individual's empirical self or felt subjectivity is thus portraying as a dialectical composite of Self and Other'" (quoted in

Jennings 1995: 115). This caring, sharing and empathetic way of living can be mirrored in my use of role-play where we help develop empathy by showing that everyone has the potential to be a bully, just as we all have the potential to be victims of bullying and that we can all take on the role of the "other" as ourselves to help find solutions in a caring, sharing dynamic.

Let us explore a Temiar influenced social theatre programme in more detail. I first used Temiar related material for a creative anti-bullying programme in 1994. I created a social theatre piece about an English boy, Geoff, who was suffering from bullying at school. I should point out that this story is not a Temiar story but contains Temiar characters and is based loosely on some of the authors' perceived Temiar ideals.

In the play Geoff tells his sister a story of when Temiar land was taken over by the loggers. In the play the audience are introduced to Temiar characters, beautiful lively forests and crystal clear waters. Then came the ghost man:

> 'Look just clear off snake' said the ghost man (a logger). 'I'm having all these trees round here'. Tagou Relai was quite upset, this was no way to behave. Why did this strange ghost-like man have to be so greedy? Couldn't he use a tree that was unoccupied? There were lots of trees, more than enough for everybody. (Hickson 1994: 7)

The help of a Temiar shaman (*halak*) named Tengah is requested:

> 'She is vulnerable Geoff, her *rewaay* (head soul) strength has been used to protect yours. Help her Geoff by helping yourself, stay with positive people and find a way to stand your ground. Fear breeds fear. Once fear has been planted it spreads easier than butter on hot toast'. (As Geoff) 'What can I do?' (As Tengah) 'Find a way to cool off the toast. This is a path you have to find yourself. Yourself. Yourself. Goodbye Geoff and remember; don't let the reservoir run dry....' (Hickson 1994: 7)

The play ends without providing any answers. Afterwards the audience are encouraged, through the use of role-play, to show us how Geoff could have improved things for himself.

This play proved to be one of the most popular shows that I have created and had over ten national tours across the UK and to Japan. Many children took on the role of "Geoff" in role-playing situations dealing with bullying; the other characters were used as witnesses, bystanders and bullies. There was an emphasis on the internal and the responsibility we have as humans to ourselves (Hickson 1996, 2002, 2009, 2011), something that we can take control of in our own lives and those we directly affect. This was reflected in the spiritual aspects of the performances.

Audience members suggested and demonstrated ideas that could help Geoff overcome bullying. This process allowed the group to witness and experience a whole range of strategies for dealing with bullying without any fear of retribution or ridicule. The process also encouraged empathy, sharing and caring.

Evaluations of my social theatre programmes run with young people in the UK have demonstrated that group members gain insights around the subject of bullying, including its definition and its relationship to power; they gain confidence and competence as creative workshop facilitators; and they have increased their skills as peer supporters by developing such skills as active listening, empathy and general groupwork.

SUE'S PERSPECTIVE

Living with Temiar people with three children (8, 12 and 13 years old) changed my whole outlook on child-rearing. Participating in a child-centred community as a lived experience influenced both my personal and professional life. And certainly my research began to include child-rearing as the context for understanding group activities, including trance and dance.

Dramatherapy and Therapeutic Theatre

For many years Western European therapy has been dominated by Freudian psychoanalytic thought and practice with an emphasis on verbal communication and interpretation. Having been a professional dancer and actor, my main interest lay in whether the arts, and theatre in particular, could be more helpful for people with mental health issues, as well as children with emotional or behavioural difficulties. I was already convinced that theatre contributed to mental health and social stability, as reflected in the early writings about ancient Greek theatre (Taplin 1989).

Rather than using role-play to act out a specific personal difficulty as happens in psychodrama, I was developing a group process whereby participants worked through a myth or story or play text that at some level would have connections with themselves. The "remoteness" of a text would paradoxically bring people "closer" to themselves. Over the years a framework has emerged called "embodiment-projection-role", with which to structure a dramatherapy session (see details below) (Jennings 1990, 1998, 1999, 2011).

When I settled into fieldwork with the Temiars, it was apparent that they had their own "mental health" rituals which worked for both the community and individuals. They said that the séances with singing, dancing and trancing kept the head soul of the village strong. The séances were certainly a time for everyone to come together; even small babies were carried in slings while their mothers played bamboo stompers to accompany the singing. The stompers are two lengths of bamboo that are beaten in duple rhythm on a log by a group of women, who echo the singing of the shaman or other singer. Rhythm permeates the dance sessions. The houses are built off the ground on stilts, and the flooring is made from split bamboo which has a bounce to it. The sessions could be for fun and playfulness or for more serious healing ceremonies (Jennings 1995). Séances of a particular kind were practised at the end of the mourning period as a transition back to normal life again.

How does this translate into actual practice of a dramatherapist in my own culture? Firstly, there is an emphasis on physical movement, voice and rhythm; secondly, there is a transition from everyday reality to dramatic reality, which could be described as a light state of trance; thirdly, there is a democracy of therapy in which facilitator and participants work together to achieve their goals; and, fourthly, there is a focus on group creativity and individuals within the group.

A typical session

I have been asked into a primary school where the abrupt resignation of the head teacher and accompanying departure of half the staff have left chaos and uncertainty amongst remaining staff, pupils and parents. The therapeutic team move in for a week to work with the whole school of 90 pupils. We have decided on the story of Noah's Ark to work towards calm after the storm.

1. Embodiment (warm-up): pupils move as different animals, large and small, fierce and friendly.
2. Embodiment (rhythm and voice): pupils choose an animal and find a partner who is the same; they march together to a drum beat and learn and sing "The animals marched in two by two...."
3. Projection: everyone chooses an animal to draw and colour. They show and share pictures in small groups. They think about similarities and differences.
4. Group discussion: what are the difficulties of living on this boat together? How will the Noah family deal with so many animals?
5. Role: in small groups, they create a scene of Mr and Mrs Noah and their children when one of the animals becomes difficult (each group decide what their difficulty is).
6. Role: they share all the scenes, compare and contrast.
7. Emergence: they play a physical game to come out of roles and return to a quiet state.

This session has gone through the three stages of embodiment-projection-role (Jennings 2011, 2013a) and has allowed the exploration of the school's difficulties through distanced roles and scenes (Jennings 2013b). Participants are addressing issues of peaceful co-existence and being encouraged to express their own opinions and ideas. Everyone is listened to, and everyone's contribution is respected.

Second example

An intensive programme was planned for nine children aged between 8 and 11 who had been excluded from school or who had severe behavioural and emotional difficulties. Adult volunteers assisted each child in the group. The six days were divided into two days of physical and rhythmic activities (embodiment), two days of painting and modelling (projection) and two days of drama and stories (role) [hereafter EPR]. Through the pairing with an adult each child was able to explore risky actions, such as standing on each other's backs or shoulders, within the safe context of being "held", rocked or cradled, or working in a circle with a large parachute that connected everyone together.

However, the sessions did not progress as planned, as any attempt to introduce any drama work or masks was immediately rejected, and the children became very disruptive. They did not want to engage in any role activities. But a return to the physical and sensory sessions immediately calmed everyone down.

Some less experienced staff commented that EPR did not work, as the children would not play roles. However, there was one role that all the children coveted, that was preparing and serving food and dressing up in a chef's hat and apron. With my Temiar guide sitting on my shoulder I reflected and then shared with staff what could be happening.

1. It was very significant that the children in particular wanted to stay with the rhythm and drumming work.
2. They requested repeats of the face and hand massage.
3. They enjoyed taking physical risks when supported by their adult partner.
4. They enjoyed "messy play" with finger paints and clay.
5. They wanted to be a part of the food preparation, serving and also sharing.
6. They enjoyed sitting with the adults and talking.

I suggested that these activities (especially 1–4) belonged to the very early stages of child development and that being involved with food is one way of satisfying emotional hunger.

The team agreed that we would all observe the children's behaviour more closely for the remainder of the programme and would share our observations. It was quite apparent that the children all wished to work with the physical and sensory activities, especially rhythmic play. In fact the children were all functioning at an emotional age of about two years old. Therefore it made complete sense that they could not play roles, not that they would not.

Using my Temiar model, I looked again at the embodiment stage of development and noted that there were three distinct stages: sensory play, rhythmic play and dramatic play. These start during pregnancy and continue at least half way through the first year. Before they are born, Temiar babies experience massage, singing, dancing and bamboo rhythms, and these continue after birth once the post-partum time is over. During this secluded time the midwife has moved into the same space as mother and baby, helping with massage, rocking, feeding and advice. The housing itself with sprung bamboo flooring means that every step has a bounce to it, and when not being held and rocked, small babies are put in sarong hammocks that are attached to a spring. Looking first at the Temiar focus of pregnancy, childbirth and early months, I then compared it with western ideas of attachment theory (Bowlby 1965; Gerhardt 2004) and realised that Temiar children are very securely attached to their parents, physically and emotionally. The attachment is also expressed by the belief that children have a weak head soul and are reliant on the head souls of the parents. In fact the parent-child triangle is brought together through food avoidance, changes of name, physical contact, rhythmic movement and song and protection of head souls.

In the dramatherapy sessions I plan a model of "active attachment" whereby a child works with a significant adult in close physical proximity, including massage and messy play, rhythmic movement, drumming and songs and dramatic playfulness through games and pretence.

Third example

My attachment to older people, especially those with dementia, has been encouraged by the artistry of my own mother, who lived

into her 90s. (She was a professional dancer and sculptor's model
for the Vimy Ridge war memorial.) Also my Temiar mother, who
adopted me from the outset, was a tremendous influence. She was
treated with great respect in the community and was also a very
experienced midwife. A substantial amount of my fieldwork data
came through talking with fellow women and joining in their
activities, at a time when there was little information about the role
of women in Orang Asli societies, a situation that has since changed
considerably (see, for example Baer 2006; Endicott and Endicott
2012). Quite simply, if we were family, then there was no danger
from strangers. We were brought into a network of relatives
with accompanying expectations, roles and obligations. But most
importantly, older people were treated with respect, and their advice
was listened to.

There is a care home in Penang, Malaysia where the 70 female,
elderly and frail residents are dressed in uniform cotton pyjamas
and are in the same room with closely packed metal beds. (There
is a similar ward for male residents.) There are no activities, and a
couple of televisions are permanently on but too far away to see or
hear. I take 16 professional volunteers to work with Shakespeare's
A Midsummer Night's Dream as therapeutic theatre. We have beautiful
fabrics, cotton, chiffon and silk, cream for massage, a variety of
musical instruments, and various objects for storytelling. Initially we
work in small groups doing massage and telling the story of the play,
playing with clothes, fans and flowers. The whole ward becomes the
magic forest, and the volunteers play all the fairy roles and the lovers.
Residents are very alert and excited and watch every action, and they
offer to hide the fugitives! Despite the arrival of food and the delivery
of red envelopes (during special days people deliver gifts of money
in red envelopes to friends and family members), everyone is focused
and obviously enjoying themselves.

We work with a second group in an open recreation space with
older people who are more mobile and less confused. We tell the
story again, think about the forest and play with fabrics and textures.
People want to be the fairies and work the magic potions. One
Oberon in his 80s cannot wait to put the spell on Titania, who is also

in her 80s, but she is not having it and tells him he is a waste of space (in Hokkien), that she is keeping the little Indian boy, so Oberon can get lost! This is a very powerful, even though amusing, instance of a woman being empowered through the text to communicate and confront!

CLOSING REFLECTIONS

The above examples in education and therapeutic work illustrate how Temiar experiences have empowered ritual and drama work with a range of child and adolescent groups as well as older people. Our work brings us in contact with thousands of participants each year, and it is both humbling and inspiring to see genuine change being brought about in people of all capabilities. The Temiars' major contribution to what we do has been first and foremost to change the way we think about other people and their potential, leading to a true democracy of attitude and application. They have also helped us to separate the idealized idea from the practical and rational. The Temiars are able to manage their lives in ways that both enhance individuals and groups; traditionally they are child-centred and value love over violence.

We have both benefited in ways that we are still discovering—the role of trance in theatre and therapy and the conflation of self and other. Trance is a relative concept, and the degrees of "entrancement" can indicate the level of engagement and focus in participants. It also places enormous responsibility on the facilitator to create the "safe space". Future work needs to be developed with therapists on the relationship between shamanism, healing and therapy. The space between self and other in Western culture is comparatively wide when compared with Temiar culture. Finding ways to help narrow the Western self/other dichotomy will go a long way to help create empathetic relationships between people where we can care as much about others as we do about ourselves. In this way the Temiars will indirectly, the authors believe, help develop many caring, nurturing and peaceful relationships in the UK and beyond.

ACKNOWLEDGEMENTS

We would like to thank our Temiar families, especially Johnny, Adoi, Manan and Andros. We dedicate this chapter to the guiding spirits of Abilum, Tengah, Busu, Dalam and Minono.

REFERENCES

Baer, A., ed.
  2006   Orang Asli Women of Malaysia: Perceptions, Situations & Aspirations. Subang Jaya, Malaysia: Center for Orang Asli Concerns.

Benjamin, G.
  1967   Temiar Religion. Unpublished PhD thesis, Cambridge University.
  1974   Indigenous Religious Systems of the Malay Peninsula. *In* The Imagination of Reality. A.L. Becker and A.A. Yengoyan, eds. Pp. 9–27. Norwood, NJ: Ablex.
  1987   Notes on the Deep Sociology of Religion. Department of Sociology working paper no. 85. Singapore: National University of Singapore.
  1989   Achievements and Gaps in Orang Asli Research. Akademika 35: 7–45.
  1994   Danger and Dialectic in Temiar childhood. *In* Enfants et Sociétés d'Asie du Sud-Est. J. Massard-Vincent and J. Koubi, eds. Pp. 37–62. Paris: L'Harmattan.
  2014   Temiar Religion 1964–2012: Enchantment, Disenchantment and Re-enchantment in Malaysia's Uplands. Singapore: NUS Press.

Bowlby, J.
  1965   Child Care and the Growth of Love. London: Penguin.

Calouste Gulbenkian Foundation
  1995   Report of the Commission on Children and Violence. London: Calouste Gulbenkian Foundation

Cawson, P., Wattam, C., Brooker, S. and Kelly, G.
  2000   Child maltreatment in the United Kingdom: a study of the prevalence of abuse and neglect. Executive summary. London: NSPCC.

Cozolino, L.
  2002   The Neuroscience of Psychotherapy. New York: W.W. Norton.

2006   The Neuroscience of Human Relationships. New York: W.W. Norton.

Dentan, R.K.
1968   The Semai: A Nonviolent People of Malaya. New York: Holt, Rinehart and Winston.
1988   On Reconsidering Violence in Simple Human Societies. Current Anthropology 29(4): 624–9.
1999   Teaching Kids Fear and Nonviolence. Buffalo, NY: Buffalo Education.
2008   Overwhelming Terror: Love, Fear, Peace and Violence among Semai of Malaysia. Lanham, MD: Rowman and Littlefield.

Domhoff, G.W.
1985   The Mystique of Dreams: A Search For Utopia Through Senoi Dream Theory. Berkeley: University of California Press.

Endicott, K.
1979   Batek Negrito Religion. Oxford: Clarendon Press.

Endicott, K.M. and K.L. Endicott
2012   The Headman Was a Woman: The Gender Egalitarian Batek of Malaysia. Subang Jaya, Malaysia: Center for Orang Asli Concerns.

Gerhardt, S.
2004   Why Love Matters: How Affection Shapes a Baby's Brain. Hove, UK: Routledge.

Hickson, A.
1994   Creative Action Methods in Groupwork. Bicester, UK: Winslow Press.
1996   The Groupwork Manual. Milton Keynes, UK: Speechmark.
2002   Pause for Thought: Action or Stillness with Young People. *In* Communicating with Children and Adolescents: Action for change. A. Bannister and A. Huntington, eds. Pp. 33–54. London: Jessica Kingsley.
2009   Social Theatre: A Theatre of Empowerment to Address Bullying in Schools. *In* Dramatherapy and Social Theatre. S. Jennings, ed. Pp. 131–40. Hove, UK: Routledge.
2011   How to Stop Bullying. Milton Keynes, UK: Speechmark.

Jennings, S.
1990   Dramatherapy with Families, Groups and Individuals. London: Jessica Kingsley.

1995   Theatre, Ritual and Transformation: The Senoi Temiars. Hove, UK: Routledge.

1998   Introduction to Dramatherapy: Ariadne's Ball of Thread. London: Jessica Kingsley.

1999   Introduction to Developmental Play Therapy: Playing for Health. London: Jessica Kingsley.

2011   Healthy Attachments and Neuro-Dramatic-Play. London: Jessica Kingsley.

2012   Theatre of Resilience: Ritual and Attachment with Marginalised Groups in Ritual Theatre: The Power of Dramatic Ritual. *In* Personal Development Groups and Clinical Practice. S. Schrader, ed. Pp. 200–16. London: Jessica Kingsley.

2013a Creative Activities for Developing Emotional Intelligence. Buckingham, UK: Hinton House.

2013b 101 Activities for Social and Emotional Resilience. Buckingham, UK: Hinton House.

Maclean, P.D.

1985   The Triune Brain in Evolution: Role of Paleocerebral Functions. New York: Plenum Press.

Roseman, M.

1991   Healing Sounds from the Malaysian Rainforest. Berkeley: University of California Press.

Robarchek, C.A.

1977   Frustration, Aggression, and the Nonviolent Semai. American Ethnologist 4(4): 762–79.

Taplin, O.

1989   Greek Fire. London: Jonathan Cape.

Thompson, J. and R. Schechner

2004   Why Social Theatre? The Drama Review 48(3): 11–6.

chapter **12**

Semai Ecological Epistemologies: Lessons for a Sustainable Future

Alberto G. Gomes

INTRODUCTION

There is no doubt that the greatest challenge to humankind is the increasing degradation of the natural environment. Global warming has become one of the most pressing concerns, as its effects on climate and the rise of sea levels are being felt around the world and are predicted to intensify in the years to come. Such concerns have stimulated critical reflections on the relations between humans and the environment, and a growing number of scholars have stressed the need for a "paradigm change" from the current ecologically damaging growth-focus economic model to one that is ecologically sensitive or environmentally friendly (Gomes 2012). Some have also contended that a change in the economic paradigm itself, while crucial, is not adequate alone to create an ecologically sound society. Such economic paradigmatic shift must be accompanied by a change in normative principles and values: from views, attitudes, perceptions and conceptions that devalue or are negative toward nature to ones that are ecologically sound and friendly. Here is where religion and cosmology fit in. In an article published in 1967, Lynn White traced the roots of the ecological crisis to the Abrahamic traditions of Judaism and Christianity which advocate the transcendence of God (divinity) above nature and the dominion of humans over nature. White (1967) argued that this Judeo-Christian theological conception in relation to nature propagated an anthropocentric imperialist or utilitarian attitude towards the natural environment, which in turn has brought about environmental destruction and degradation through over-exploitation and pollution. Such "sky-focused" religions, according to White (1967), stood in stark contrast to "earth-based" religions practised by most, if not all, indigenous peoples, many Asian cultures, and European cultures in ancient times. White (1967: 1205) notes:

> In Antiquity every tree, every spring, every stream, every hill had its own genius loci, its guardian spirit. These spirits were accessible to men, but were very unlike men; centaurs, fauns, and mermaids show their ambivalence. Before one cut a tree, mined a mountain, or dammed a brook, it was important to placate the spirit in charge of that particular situation, and to keep it placated.

One does not need to dwell on the past to look for such ecologically sound cosmologies. In every nook and corner of this world one can find indigenous peoples subscribing to such religions and cosmologies. As Anderson (1996: 166) observes, "All traditional societies that have succeeded in managing resources well, over time, have done it in part through religious or ritual representation of resource management." As indigenous peoples have been marginalized by the forces of modernity, so have their epistemologies which have been neglected and devalued vis-à-vis modern scientific knowledge systems (Berkes 2012). It is these marginalized epistemologies that I contend will need to be recovered, resuscitated, recuperated and reinstated in our endeavour for ecological salvation. Such epistemologies ought to be considered as the foundations for paradigmatic and normative change. This chapter will focus on one indigenous people, the Semai of Malaysia, and it describes specific aspects of Semai religious beliefs and rituals that are linked to their ecological ontology.

THE SEMAI OF MALAYSIA

The Semai are an aboriginal (officially known as *Orang Asli*) people of Peninsular Malaysia with a total population of about 45,000. They live in relatively small settlements along roads and rivers in the forested and forest fringe parts of the central section of the Main Range, the mountains and hilly ranges that run along the spine of the Peninsula. They speak an Austroasiatic language referred to by linguists as Senoic-Semai, and it is primarily on this ethno-linguistic criterion that they are classified by anthropologists and government officials as belonging to the Senoi group, one of the three ethnic categories of Orang Asli in Malaysia. The majority of Semai practise a type of animistic religion unique to them, but today many of them have adopted Christianity or Islam as a consequence of proselytizing. Anthropologists generally describe the Semai as swidden horticulturalists engaging in supplementary hunting, fishing and gathering, and some trading of minor forest products. While this is still very much the case for some Semai settlements in the interior, most today have become increasingly involved in the market economy. They grow cash crops such as fruit, collect minor forest products like rattan and bamboo for sale, and work for wages mostly as menial labourers.

In a study of a Semai village where I kept records of economic transactions for one year (1982 to 1983), I found the people to be greatly dependent on the market economy (Gomes 2004). They devoted about two thirds of their economic effort to production for the market to pay for their ever increasing dependence on the market for most of their food supply and other provisions. The subsistence economy has suffered as a result of people's focus on commodity production. I found that people did not cultivate swiddens as regularly as before, and, furthermore, whatever swiddens they planted were relatively smaller than the farms cultivated in the past. The impact of this market dependence on social practices is profound. Apart from a decline in subsistence-oriented economic pursuits, increasing involvement in the capitalist-oriented market has, among other things, led to incipient social differentiation in a community renowned for its egalitarianism, a change in the system and concept of land and property ownership from communal to private or individual, and a waning in sharing and other reciprocal practices. This social and economic transformation is by no means unique to the Semai village I studied or to the Semai group itself. In the mid-1960s, Robert Dentan (1965, 1979) observed the growing market economy involvement of the Semai, especially the people he referred to as "West Semai" living close to main towns along the western part of Peninsular Malaysia. Colin Nicholas (2000) has also reported similar changes in the lives of Semai living elsewhere, while numerous studies (Endicott 1979, 1984; Howell 1984; Gianno 1990; Karim 1995; Dentan et al. 1997; Nagata 1997; Benjamin 2002; Lye 2005; Gomes 2007; Dallos 2011; Riboli 2013; Tacey 2013) have documented the entanglement of Orang Asli communities with the market economy and its social, cultural, and economic ramifications.

Let us now turn to specific aspects of Semai ecological epistemologies. I shall focus on three cases drawn from my ethnographic work among the Semai in order to illustrate the nexus between indigenous onto-epistemologies (Williams et al. 2012) and ecological ethics, values, and principles.

WEAK KNEES, ERRANT "WIVES" AND DISAPPEARING ANIMALS

Bah Silang, a Semai man from the village I studied, emerged out of the forest looking weary. On his back was a rattan basket containing a machete, a bundle of tapioca leaves and a tobacco pouch. This was Bah Silang's third trip to his favourite hunting ground in the past week. The long hours trekking the forest in search of game yielded nothing but some edible greens gathered along the way. His fellow villagers have refrained from asking Bah Silang about his hunting. The machete in the basket and a blowpipe on the shoulder were sufficient indications that a person was out hunting. Enquiring where he is going or what he has obtained from his hunting or trapping is regarded as normatively improper and the potential cause of bad luck in such pursuits. If he had a successful hunting expedition, he would display his quarry but with explicit modesty. These are some of the rules and etiquette surrounding hunting which hunters and their friends or fellow villagers are expected to observe to ensure continual productive hunting and trapping and to avoid a hunting "drought". In the case of Bah Silang, it was not the contravention of one of these norms that had caused his spate of bad luck. Neither was it due to lack of skill, as I have observed him return with game on a more than regular basis. It was, as my Semai respondents diagnosed, the loss of his hunting soul, *kenah senlook*. Semai believe that a hunter's "luck" and skill are determined by this soul, which is referred to as "wife" (*kenah*) and said to be located in the knees. It is easily offended, especially if certain rules are not observed. For example, after an animal is shot or killed, the hunter is expected to apologize to the animal's spirit for taking its life. In the apology, the hunter would typically say that he had been driven to such cruelty by the necessity to feed himself and his family. Also a few rites are performed on the carcass before it is carried back to the village. If such entreaties are not performed, Semai believe that their *kenah senlook* would be angered and would leave the hunter's body. An errant *kenah senlook* spells ill fortune in hunting. To secure its return the hunter and his wife, with the assistance of a spiritual specialist, will carry out a special ritual in which an important part is the hunter's wife's consoling and cajoling her husband's *kenah senlook*. She would plead with the soul to return and not be jealous of her.

While this belief is an aspect of Semai religion, it is obvious that it is also linked to Semai interactions with nature. Among the Semai, as in many indigenous communities, ecological knowledge is not embodied in a distinct "discipline" as in western science, but is embedded in their cultural system. In other words, it does not exist as a separate field of knowledge. Anthropologists have for quite some time now recognized and documented this ethnographic fact. In a classic illustration of this, Roy Rappaport in his monograph entitled *Pigs for the Ancestors* found a close relationship between rituals and ecology among the Tsembaga Maring of New Guinea (Rappaport 1968). He revealed how ritual feasts among the Tsembaga Maring functioned as a regulatory mechanism in maintaining balance in the ecological system. During the time of his ethnographic research in the mid-1960s, the Tsembaga Maring, like the Semai living then, subsisted by cultivating swiddens, but, unlike the Semai, they herded pigs, numbering about 50 to 200 per clan of about 200 members, with pig numbers varying seasonally. The pigs were mainly slaughtered during rituals. Also, unlike the Semai, who are a peaceful people (Robarchek 1977; Dentan 1979), the Tsembaga-Maring engaged in regular warfare with its neighbouring tribes. During times of warfare, the Tsembaga-Maring hold a ritual pig sacrifice, referred to as *kaiko*, where large numbers of pigs are slaughtered to "repay" their debts to the supernatural and as an expression of gratitude to their neighbours who have aided them in their battles. Rappaport contends that this ritual ceremonial feast has ecological significance as a "ritually regulated ecosystem" (Rappaport 1967: 29). As Rappaport argues, the ritual slaughter restores the pig population to manageable levels both in terms of labour requirements and environmental carrying capacity, which in turn prevents land degradation that can result from herding too large a population of pigs.

Like the Tsembaga-Maring, Semai ecological knowledge and conceptions are embedded in their traditional religious systems, which can be described as "earthly" in the sense that they connect people with nature. In these societies, religion, ecology and society do not exist as separate fields of social experiences or cultural behaviour, but are enmeshed into a holistic realm. What is regarded as "sacred" is not confined to the Western notion of religion. To put it differently, the division between the sacred and the profane is indeterminate. Furthermore, it should be noted that what is sacred and profane is often an assumption of the observer rather than the observed.

To return to the discussion of *kenah senlook*, it would be plausible to state that the rather complex and intriguing set of Semai beliefs and practices related to hunting and trapping underlines the importance the people place on respect for nature. *Kenah senlook* can be considered as an idiom of this respect. This soul is part of the hunter and at the same time is intimately connected with the "laws" of nature: respect for fellow creatures, take only what you need, and the interconnectedness between humans, animals, spirits, and the environment. It would not be altogether implausible to say that *kenah senlook* serves as a guardian of both the hunter and the hunted.

Kenah senlook is not the only spirit or aspect of the spiritual world with ecological implications. As animists, Semai believe that the spiritual world consists of deities, spirits, elves and souls, and all these in some way or the other have ecological implications. Semai classify spirits into three types: *nyani, kitmoit* and *gunik. Nyani* are spirits found in natural features such as rocks, waterfalls, and certain trees. It is believed that every area has its own ground spirit which is referred to as *nyani kawul*. *Kitmoit* are spirits of the dead, while *gunik* are spirit familiars that shamans invoke during séances to assist in ritual curing. The main deity is *Ngku*, the thundergod, who is much feared and respected. It is believed that the breaking of certain taboos, such as teasing of or cruelty towards animals, actions that are called *terlaj*, will anger *Ngku* who would supposedly vent his wrath by causing severe thunderstorms.

Such religious beliefs are related to a wider conception of the forest held by the Semai and many other forest dependent peoples (Riboli 2011; Tacey 2013). Endicott (1979) has revealed that among the Batek, another Malaysian aboriginal people, forest-human relations are metaphorized in ritual and everyday discourse as an "adult-child caring" with the forest as a parent to be treated with affection and gratitude for its "gifts". This is in stark contrast to traditional Western or modern views in which, as Bird-David (1993: 121) argues:

> ... nature and humankind have been "seen" as detached and in opposition. Furthermore, they have been viewed within a "subject-object" frame: nature "seen" as a resource to be utilized, controlled, possessed, dominated, managed and (more recently) looked after by humankind.

It could be argued that the respect that the Semai and their fellow Orang Asli have for the forest has a utilitarian aspect to it. The forest is a provider of game obtained through hunting and trapping, and it is also where Semai cultivate their swidden farms. In swiddening, it is the "lord of the land" that is cajoled and appeased for the sake of a sustainable agriculture.

METAPHYSICS OF SWIDDEN HORTICULTURE

Swidden agriculture or "slash and burn farming" is widely practised among Orang Asli, but it is viewed with disdain by government and forestry officials who consider it an environmentally degrading form of agriculture. However, there is insurmountable evidence that suggests that this form of agriculture is well suited to tropical forested areas

(Spencer 1966; Kunstadter et al. 1978). As several researchers have indicated, what swidden farmers do is imitate the natural processes of forest disruption and re-generation in their cultivation and fallow cycle (Conklin 1957; Padoch et al. 2007; Cramb et al. 2009; Fox et al. 2009; Schmidt-Vogt et al. 2009). Even modern agroforestry and permaculture have adopted aspects of swidden farming techniques, but this is rarely acknowledged. Underlying the environmental sustainability and adaptability of traditional swidden agriculture as practised by the Semai and other such peoples in Southeast Asia is traditional and experientially grounded ecological knowledge. But what keeps swiddening ecologically sound is not simply a result of this knowledge; there is also a metaphysical element, and this relates to the animistic beliefs in the rice soul and the supernatural force that inhabits the land.

During my field research in the early 1980s, I observed that a Semai villager intending to cultivate a swidden will select a forested area, usually of secondary type, on the basis of several ecological features, such as the type of vegetation in the area and the appearance of soil texture. Upon deciding on a suitable location, the intending cultivator will clear a small area of about one square metre around the centre of the site and then standing at the clearing will announce aloud the intention to plant a swidden (*selai*) at the site. This announcement is meant as a request to the ground spirit (*nyani kawul*) believed to inhabit and control the area for permission to use the land. The response to the request, according to Semai belief, will be relayed through the dreams of the intending cultivator while he or she is asleep. According to Semai dream theory, the head soul (*ruway*) is believed to travel into the supernatural realm, and its experiences and encounters in this "world" form the content of the dreams. The dreams are then interpreted for omens which represent the response of the *nyani kuwul* to the request. Omens are classified into good and bad, and obviously good omens are taken to mean approval to cultivate a swidden on the land in question. Once "permission" is granted, the plot is cleared, allowed to dry and then burned, but with great care and respect for the land to avoid annoying the spiritual custodian. The area first cleared is turned into a shrine or altar where rituals are performed to placate the land spirit and to seek its good favour, especially in protecting the rice soul. Semai, like many other Southeast Asian peoples, believe that the rice plant possesses a soul that is timid, fragile and easily frightened. Any contravention of the "laws of nature", such as the degradation of the forest through over-utilization or excessive exploitation of the environment, is said to upset the *nyani kawul*, which is believed to vent its anger by casting a spell on the crops or the cultivators, causing crop failure or personal injury. As in the case of *kenah senlook*, the belief and practices associated with *nyani kawul* are not simply aspects of Semai metaphysics, but are intricately linked to Semai adherence to ecologically sustainable practices in their agricultural pursuits.

This belief in the existence of the land spirit and the sort of practices associated with seeking permission are not unique to the Semai. Many Southeast Asian cultures have similar beliefs. Kunstadter (1983) describes a similar case for the Lua of Thailand who believe in the existence of the Lord of the Land. He concludes:

> Swidden land is a community resource, "belonging" to the spirits as a result of their long and continued occupancy, but to which the Lua villagers also have some claim because of their long-term residence. Swidden land is periodically (though temporarily) accessible to villagers through payment to the spirits. (Kunstadter 1983: 143)

Kunstadter's conclusion applies to the Semai too. Members of a village may claim a demarcated area referred to as *negriik* as belonging to a land "owning" group (*mai pasak*), who have control over the area. But this claim is made relative to members of other villages. Hence, each Semai village will have exclusive control over a demarcated area. However, in their traditional conception of land ownership, land is "owned" by supernatural beings. Among the Igorot of the Philippines, Tauli-Corpuz (2001: 285), an Igorot researcher and activist, observed:

> We do not consider ourselves the owners of the ancestral territory and resources found therein. We are but the stewards, trustees, or custodians. The beings in the spirit-world and deities are the real owners of the land. Thus, it is imperative to consult these spirits and deities when land is used, converted, or transferred and when resources are harvested, planted, or hunted. The forms of consultation range from a simple petition, prayer, or chant to elaborate rituals in which every village member participates.

Interestingly, Tauli-Corpuz (2001: 287) goes on to say that "The beings in the spirit world are responsible for protecting the natural world from human greed."

Like the Igorot, what Semai have are usufruct rights to land that they obtain from the land owning ground spirit. They then are simply stewards of the land rather than owners. But they believe that they have to abide by the strict rules of nature in order to survive. An individual or family may use the swidden for one or two seasons. During this period the cultivators have exclusive rights to the plot and its harvest, but once they cease to use the land it reverts to communal property, controlled by the village but "owned" by the land spirit. However, the cultivators still retain "ownership" of whatever fruit trees they have planted on the plot. There are at least two ecologically sound principles associated with usufruct rights. First, people do not hold more land than what they can use. Second, given the ecological imperative of fallowing in a rotational form of agriculture, it would be in the interest of cultivators to take good care of the land for future use and for the use of future generations. They remove absolute rights to land from the individual and "places" these rights in some supernatural force which serves to sanction "proper" treatment of land and nature.

In recent years, this conception of land ownership seems to be declining in importance in Semai villages, which are experiencing radical changes in their economy as a result of their increased market involvement. In the early 1980s I observed a trend towards greater individualization of property ownership, and this seems to have spilled over into land ownership. Villagers who owned fruit trees began to extend their claim to the land on which their trees stood rather than as in the past when their ownership claims were restricted to just the fruit trees. Certain areas were regarded as belonging to either individuals or families. Also in some villages there was buying and selling of land among villagers. Since most Semai village land is legally considered either state land or aboriginal reserve, these commercialized land transactions are not legally sanctioned or recognized. But along with the increased commoditization of Semai property and land is a change in their attitude towards land and ultimately towards nature. It eventually leads to a change in their "history", as revealed in the following section.

SPACES, PLACES AND HISTORY

In his ethnographic research among the Penan of Borneo, Brosius (2001: 148) observes, "The landscape is more than simply a reservoir of detailed ecological knowledge.... It is also a repository for the memory of past events, and thus a vast mnemonic representation of social relationships and of society." Among the Illongot of the Philippines, Rosaldo (1980) discovered that people told stories about the past always in relation to the places significant to the tales rather than when they took place (the dates). To put it another way, Illongot's historical consciousness is spatialized rather than temporalized as in the narratives of Western or modern historiography:

> Stories usually are a series of relatively autonomous episodes that are united, like beads on a string, by winding thread of continuous movement through space, rather than by a rising plot line that points towards its own resolution in a climax. At their most elemental, Illongot stories may simply list a lifetime of place names where people have gardened or erected their houseposts. More elaborate stories, often about oratory, fishing, hunting, and headhunting, begin at home, move in gradual step-by-step fashion toward their destinations, and conclude with a quick return to the place of origin. (Rosaldo 1980: 15–6)

This is also the case for the Semai and apparently for many other indigenous minorities. Stories of the past were narrated in relation to where, rather than when, they happened. One could deduce from this that the "events" in people's history are not simply stored in their memories, but are also inscribed in the landscape. During my field research, trekking through the forest with the Semai was often also a "journey" into their past. We would stop at different sites or landmarks, and my companions would tell stories of past events that occurred at the site. On one occasion a Semai pointed out a large rock by the river and informed me that this was the rock Rawa Malay slave raiders used to sharpen their swords. Evidently the Malays frequently attacked Semai villages in the 1800s to capture Semai for the lucrative slave trade. I was told stories about the battles between Semai and Malays that the Semai refer to as *praak sangkil* almost always in relation to specific places. This spatialization of history gives more meaning to the environment. For Semai, then, nature is not just a bearer of "resources" but an archive of people's history. Space is historicized to become place coded with symbolic and social meanings. The intricate nexus between nature and history in Semai onto-epistemology would mean that the devaluing of one will lead to the devaluing of the other. And degrading or destruction of the natural environment or the "displacing" of Semai from their homelands is tantamount to the erasure of their histories and reciprocally, their identities.

CONCLUSION

In this chapter I have examined three different aspects of Semai indigenous knowledge and conceptions. Their hunting rituals and beliefs reveal their respectful attitude towards nature and animals. It is evident that Semai ecological wisdom is often embedded in their religious or spiritual beliefs and cultural practices. I have also shown that Semai connection to land and the environment is not simply spiritual but also historical. All this is now affected radically by Semai experience of modernity, especially capitalism in the form of commoditization, producing commodities for sale. What are the ecological implications of this commoditization? First of all, through commoditization a different form of valuing objects and resources is introduced. Instead of an item being considered as important for its use value, in commoditized economies things are regarded as valuable on the basis of how much they can obtain in exchange for other goods or money. Forests are considered important as a source of products to be extracted and sold. Everything has a price, and people are driven by market considerations and a desire to accumulate and create a surplus. This desire actually underlies the privatization of property and the individuation of production because people are becoming less and less willing to share production or harvests with others. These processes lead to the eventual breakdown of social institutions and the loss of indigenous knowledge that have very effectively operated thus far to protect the commons like the forest from over-exploitation and to prevent the careless and selfish use of resources by forest communities. Increasing market demand for certain products has impelled indigenous minorities to over-exploit their environments, in contradiction to indigenous systems and rules of resource management. But in the large number of ethnographic texts on the past lives of such communities and from a decreasing number of indigenous groups that have not been as entangled with modernity as the Semai and other Orang Asli and who still adhere to their traditional knowledge and epistemologies, one can find a rich array of beliefs, perceptions, conceptions and practices that could assist in formulating a normative or paradigmatic change that is ecologically sound and sustainable. We must reconnect our histories with nature and rekindle our spiritual connection with the land. In order to gain from the time-honoured and ecologically sound knowledge and conceptions of indigenous peoples like the Semai, we must make a conscious effort, as Henry Lewis poignantly remarked in relation to the Australian Aborigines, we have "to learn *from* Aborigines rather than merely to learn *about* Aborigines".

REFERENCES

Anderson, E.N.
    1996   Ecologies of the Heart: Emotion, Belief, and the Environment. New York and Oxford: Oxford University Press.

Berkes, F.
    2012   Sacred Ecology, Third Edition. New York and London: Routledge.

Benjamin, G.
    2002   On Being Tribal in the Malay World. *In* Tribal Communities in the Malay World: Historical, Social and Cultural Perspectives. G. Benjamin and C. Chou, eds. Pp. 7–76. Leiden: IIAS and Singapore: ISEAS.

Bird-David, N.
  1993 Tribal Metaphorization of Human-Nature Relatedness: A Comparative Analysis. *In* Environmentalism: The View From Anthropology. K. Milton, ed. Pp. 112–25. London and New York: Routledge.

Brosius, J.P.
  2001 Local Knowledges, Global Claims: On the Significance of Indigenous Ecologies in Sarawak, East Malaysia. *In* Indigenous Traditions and Ecology: The Interbeing of Cosmology and the Community. J. Grim, ed. Pp. 125–57. Cambridge, MA: Harvard University Press.

Conklin, H.
  1957 Hanunoo Agriculture: A Report on an Integral System of Shifting Cultivation in the Philippines. Rome: FAO.

Cramb, R.A., C.J. Pierce Colfer, W. Dressler, P. Laungaramsri, Q.T. Le, E. Mulyoutami, N.L. Peluso and R.L. Wadley
  2009 Swidden Transformations and Rural Livelihoods in Southeast Asia. Human Ecology 37(3): 323–46.

Dallos, C.
  2011 From Equality to Inequality: Social Change Among Newly Sedentary Lanoh Hunter-gatherer Traders of Peninsular Malaysia. Toronto: University of Toronto Press.

Dentan, R.K.
  1965 Some Senoi Semai Dietary Restrictions: A Study of Food Behavior in a Malayan Hill Tribe. PhD dissertation, Yale University. Ann Arbor, Michigan: University Microfilms Inc.
  1979 The Semai: A Nonviolent People of Malaya. Fieldwork Edition. New York: Holt, Rinehart & Winston.

Dentan, R.K., K. Endicott, A. Gomes and B. Hooker
  1997 Malaysia and the Original People: A Case Study of the Impact of Development on Indigenous Peoples. Needham Heights, MA, Allyn and Bacon.

Endicott, K.
  1979 Batek Negrito Religion: The World-view and Rituals of a Hunting and Gathering People of Peninsular Malaysia. Oxford: Clarendon Press.
  1984 The Economy of the Batek of Malaysia: Annual and Historical Perspectives. Research in Economic Anthropology 6: 29–52.

Fox J., Y. Fujita, D. Ngidang, N. Peluso, L. Potter, N. Sakuntaladewi, J. Sturgeon and D. Thomas
  2009   Policies, Political-Economy, and Swidden in Southeast Asia. Human Ecology 37(3): 305–22.

Gianno, R.
  1990   Semelai Culture and Resin Technology. New Haven, CT: The Connecticut Academy of Arts and Sciences.

Gomes, A.G.
  2004   Looking for Money: Capitalism and Modernity in an Orang Asli Village. Subang Jaya, Malaysia and Melbourne: Center for Orang Asli Concerns and Trans Pacific Press.
  2007   Modernity and Malaysia: Settling the Menraq Forest Nomads. London: Routledge.
  2012   Alter-Native "Development": Indigenous Forms of Social Ecology. Third World Quarterly 33(6): 1059–73.

Howell, S.
  1983   Chewong Women in Transition: The Effect of Monetisation on a Hunter-Gatherer Society of Malaysia. Occasional Paper 1 (Women and Development in Southeast Asia). Canterbury: University of Kent.
  1984   Society and Cosmos: Chewong of Peninsular Malaysia. Oxford: Oxford University Press.

Karim, W.J.
  1995   Transformations in Ma' Betisc' Economics and Ideology: Recurrent Themes of Nomadism. *In* Indigenous Minorities of Peninsular Malaysia: Selected Issues and Ethnographies. Razha Rashid, ed. Pp. 109–27. Kuala Lumpur: Intersocietal and Scientific Sdn. Bhd. (INAS).

Kunstadter P., E.C. Chapman, S. Sabhasri, eds.
  1978   Farmers in the Forest: Economic Development and Marginal Agriculture in Northern Thailand. Honolulu: East-West Center.
  1983   Highland Populations in Northern Thailand. *In* Highlanders of Thailand. J. McKinnon and W. Bhruksasri, eds. Pp. 15–45. Kuala Lumpur: Oxford University Press.

Lewis, Henry T.
  1989   Ecological and Technological Knowledge of Fire: Aborigines Versus Park Rangers in Northern Australia. American Anthropologist 91(4): 940–61.

Lopez-Gonzaga, V.
  1984   Peasants in the Hills: A Study of the Dynamics of Social Change
         Among the Buhid Swidden Cultivators in the Philippines. Diliman,
         Quezon City: University of the Philippines Press.

Lye, T.P.
  2004   Changing Pathways: Forest Degradation and the Batek of Pahang,
         Malaysia. Lanham, MD: Lexington Books.

Nagata, S.
  1997   Working for Money among the Orang Asli in Kedah, Malaysia.
         Contributions to Southeast Asian Ethnography 11: 13–31.

Nicholas, C.
  2000   The Orang Asli and the Contest for Resources: Indigenous Politics,
         Development and Identity in Peninsular Malaysia. Copenhagen and
         Subang Jaya, Malaysia: International Work Group for Indigenous
         Affairs and Center for Orang Asli Concerns.

Padoch, C., K. Coffey, O. Mertz, S. Leisz, J. Fox and R. Wadley
  2007   The Demise of Swidden in Southeast Asia? Local Realities and
         Regional Ambiguities. Danish Journal of Geography 107(1): 29–
         42.

Rappaport, R.
  1967   Ritual Regulation of Environmental Relations among a New
         Guinea People. Ethnology 6: 17–30.

Riboli, D.
  2011   "We Play in the Black Jungle and in the White Jungle": The Forest
         as a Representation of the Shamanic Cosmos in the Chants of the
         Semang-Negrito (Peninsular Malaysia) and the Chepang (Nepal).
         Shaman 19(1–2): 93–112.
  2013   Of Angry Thunders, Smelly Intruders and Human Tigers. Shamanic
         Representations of Violence and Conflict in Non-Violent Peoples:
         The Semang-Negrito (Malaysia). *In* Shamanism and Violence:
         Power, Repression and Suffering in Indigenous Religious Conflicts.
         D. Riboli and D. Torri, eds. Pp.135–48. Farnham, UK: Ashgate
         Publishers.

Robarchek, C.A.
  1977   Semai Nonviolence: A Systems Approach to Understanding.
         Unpublished PhD dissertation, Department of Anthropology,
         University of California, Riverside.

Rosaldo, R.
  1980   Ilongot Headhunting, 1883–1974: A Study in Society and History. Stanford, CA: Stanford University Press.

Schmidt-Vogt D., S.J. Leisz, O. Metz, A. Heinimann, T. Thiha, P. Messerli, M. Epprecht, Pham Van Cu, Vu Kim Chi, M. Hardiono and T.M. Dao
  2009   An Assessment of Trends in the Extent of Swidden in Southeast Asia. Human Ecology 37(3): 269–80.

Spencer, J.E.
  1966   Shifting Cultivation in Southeastern Asia. Berkeley: University of California Press.

Tacey, I.
  2013   Tropes of Fear: The Impact of Globalization on Batek Religious Landscapes. Religions 4: 240–66.

Tauli-Corpuz, V.
  2001   Interface between Traditional Religion and Ecology among the Igorots. *In* Indigenous Traditions and Ecology: The Interbeing of Cosmology and Community. J. Grim, ed. Cambridge, MA: Harvard Divinity School Center for the Study of World Religions.

White, L.T. Jr
  1967   The Historical Roots of Our Ecologic Crisis. Science 155(3767): 1203–7.

Williams, L., R. Roberts and A. McIntosh, eds.
  2012   Radical Human Ecology: Intercultural and Indigenous Approaches. Farnham, UK: Ashgate.

Part Six

CHALLENGES, CHANGES
AND RESISTANCE

13

Differential Responses to Development and Modernity among the Kintak Bong and the Ma' Betise'

Wazir Jahan Karim and Mohd Razha Rashid

DEVELOPMENT AND MARGINALIZATION

"Development" in the Malaysian context generally refers to programmes implemented under Five Year "Malaysia Plans", which are generally geared towards advancements in economic livelihoods through sustainable changes in work and lifestyles.[1] The current plan, the Tenth Malaysia Plan (2011–14), promotes sustainable development initiatives—explained as "structural transformation" in key sectors of agriculture, industry and science—with emphasis on successful adaptation to modern technologies in agriculture, advancements in bioscience and biomedicine and advanced specialization in tertiary education. For the Orang Asli, the focus continues to be on poverty alleviation, as they are among the 250,000 households on or below the poverty line (Tenth Malaysia Plan, Economic Planning Unit/EPU, Malaysia, 2011). In the Ninth Malaysia Plan (2006–10), RM361.8 million was allocated to the resettlement of the Orang

Asli, economic programmes and development of human capital (EPU 2006). The Malaysian government associates Orang Asli poverty with subsistence livelihoods dependent on the rainforest. Although resettlement programmes are geared to bring them closer to modern amenities, infrastructure and economic growth, Orang Asli generally resist departing from ancestral land and traditional life-styles (Karim 2001a; Khor 2004; Gomes 2007).² Gomes states that resettlement is better defined as "displacement" into new economic sectors unfamiliar to the Orang Asli. Activists like Colin Nicholas (2003) and Tijah Yok Chopil (2004) of the *Peninsular Malaysia Orang Asli Villages Network* (JKOASM) argue that rather than introducing resettlement programmes, it is more important to ensure that their land and cultural rights are not abused.³ Hence, in the context of Orang Asli "development" strategies, a dissonance exists between the theoretical expectation that they spur socio-economic mobility or the generation of new wealth and the observable social reality that they lead to further problems of economic and cultural poverty.

Both the Kintak Bong, who live in the rainforests in Kelian Intan, Ulu Perak in the north of Peninsular Malaysia (Map 13.1)⁴ and the Ma' Betise',⁵ who inhabit the areas on the margins of the mangrove rainforests on the west coast of Selangor and Carey Island (Map 13.2) have had a long history of avoidance of local authorities, having suffered denuded forests and hunting grounds, over half a century of "development" in Malaysia (Karim 1998a, 1998b, 2001b; Razha 2001).⁶

Malaysia's development initiatives intended to create new wealth for the working population, are incomprehensible to the beleaguered Kintak Bong at Bukit Asu, Kelian Intan, who are constantly looking for better hunting grounds deeper in the forests as their settlements are encroached upon by loggers (Razha 1995, 2001).⁷ For the Ma' Betise', exposure to development projects in the oil-palm sector is apparent as the plantations have expanded to the borders of their villages.⁸ However, they continue to be marginalized in national and local rural development programmes, which are geared towards greater professionalization and specialization in the agricultural sector. Poor education and low proficiency has denied them the competitive edge to take advantage of new job opportunities in industry.⁹ A few Ma' Betise'

Map 13.1 Kintak Bong settlements

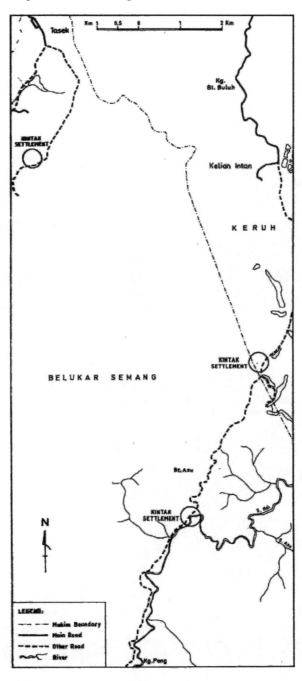

Map 13.2 Ma' Betise' settlements and land use

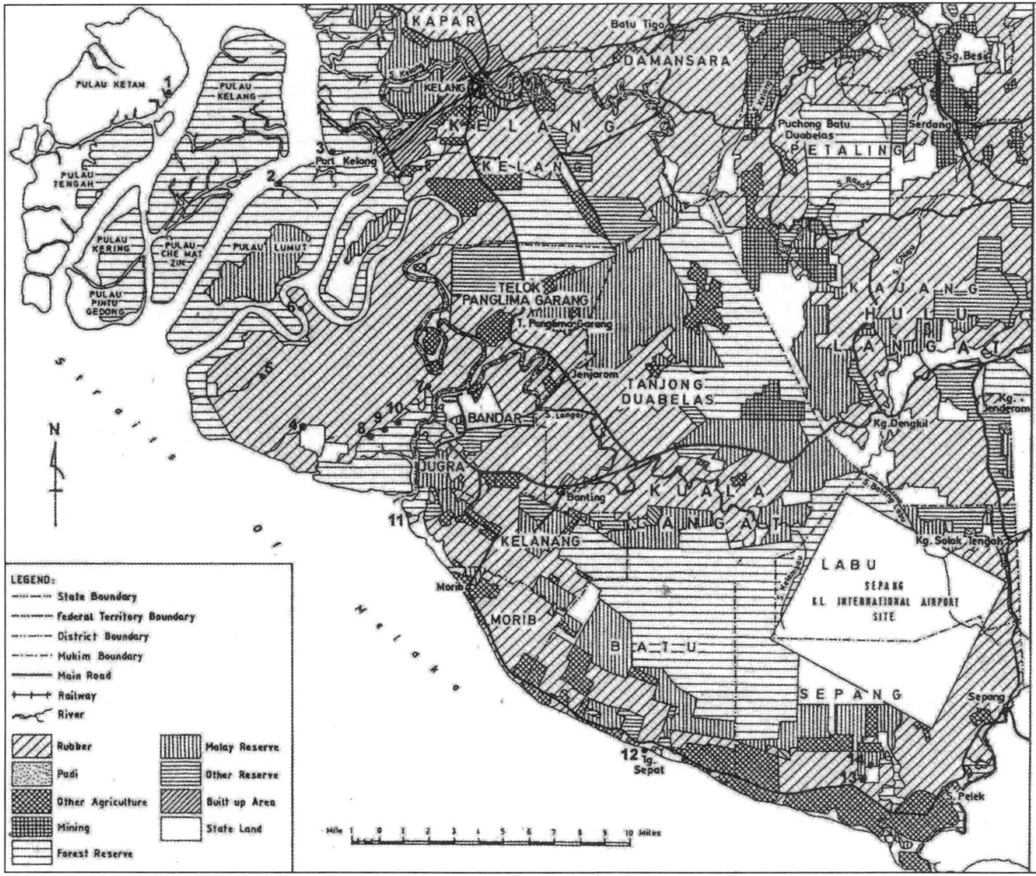

1 Pulau Ketam
2 Sg. Lumut
3 Tg. Gila/Kg. Halia
4 Sg. Judah
5 Sg. Rambai
6 Sg. Musang
7 Sg. Kurau
8 Sg. Bumbun
9 Sg. Mata
10 Sg. Sialang
11 Kg. Permatang Pauh
12 Koi (Tg. Sepat)
13 Bukit Bangkong
14 Ulu Tuchoh

Source: Director of National Map Office, Malaysia

graduates with diplomas have returned to the villages, stating that they cannot find work and that there is a general prejudice against the Orang Asli in the private and public sectors.[10] The level of education of the Kintak Bong is possibly the lowest in Peninsular Malaysia, with more than 80 per cent dropping out after primary schooling (Kamarulzaman Kamaruddin and Osman Jusoh 2008). School buses, uniforms, text books and school health and food are provided, but the majority of children are not motivated. They are unable to see the connection between formal schooling and socio-economic mobility or improved livelihoods.

MODERNITY AND ADAPTATION

"Modernity", from Charles Baudelaire's concept of "modernité" (1964), refers to the modern urban experience of street culture where the city entertains a "whirl wind romance" with consumerism and generates an insatiable consumer culture unattainable to most. Baudelaire and Baudrillard's (1973) poetic fears of growing social dissonance with urban experiences is remarkably similar to Kintak Bong and Ma' Betise' uneasiness with the city, in that they cannot belong in a world where they can only be part of the inferior "window-shopping crowd" who find consumer goods unattainable.

Berman's critique of modernity (1982) argues that it creates its own momentum of change and has been energized by the growing technocratization and commercialization of human society. As it increasingly alienates people and communities, it will inevitably give way to social levelling institutions. An outcome he could not have anticipated is the creation of intimate cyber communities within the Internet which defies the meta-narrative of modernity as oppressive and hegemonic. Unlike Berman, Osborne (1992) argues that modernity evokes subjective experiences which are not chronologically defined. For example the Kintak Bong live in "historical time" in a pre-modern habitat under conditions which resemble the Palaeolithic age (Skeat and Blagden 1906). Hunting, gathering and primary face-to-face social relations are crucial to their survival, but they are forced to reconcile with the surreal world of the faceless modern city. They resolve this dissonance by avoiding entry into the city. This suggests that the Kintak Bong have engaged in a subjective critique of modernity without a real or realistic encounter with modernity itself. The fear and mistrust of modernity removes the risk of a "quantum leap" urban experience in the city.

The Age of Information Technology in the 21st century has led to the creation of faceless cyber communities and networks which have diminished the significance of primary relationships and experiences. Writers like Baudrillard (1973) in introducing the media as "hyperreal" together with Lyotard's concept of the fluid knowledge society (1984) have positioned themselves to regard emerging societies in the Information Age as entities without a clear sense of social realities where the meta-narrative of interpretation of "truth" or "falsehood", "good" or "bad" must be seen from diverse perspectives. This phase of post-modernism has produced the reflexive or indigenous scholar in Orang Asli studies with a heavy slant towards advocacy research. The "people's point of view" is weighed against the writer's understanding of issues, without judgement or subjectivity (Razha Rashid 1995; Karim 1996, 1997; Nicholas 2003) or, alternatively, personal "native" experiences form the central database for advocacy (Williams-Hunt 1995; Tijah Yok Chopil 2004). The reflexive anthropologist functions as the "conscientized synthesizer"—the writer who investigates arti-culations of rights, needs and interests through different voices of a similar kind and who synthesizes these diverse representations through a common thematic experience (Karim 1993a, 1993b, 1997). The voices of different Orang Asli leaders and spokesmen converge on a common concern of underprivileged, marginalized minorities: the need to increase the influence of the native voice in print and social media.

The Kintak Bong preference for self-containment is a choice between a familiar natural environment and an unfamiliar urban ecology. Hunting and gathering societies in the pre-industrial age did not have these choices, since they were not juxtaposed, over different chronological time, against industrialization or modernity. Today the Kintak Bong live on the margins of the most urbanized communities in the Peninsula. The Kintak Bong indifference to national politics or development of a political voice beyond village issues is a "safety net" against public intrusions into their way of life. They are constantly being asked by government agencies to join main-stream society, but they reject this move for fear that the conditions of change may make them lose their autonomy. Adaptation to urbanism and state or national political culture brings them directly under the governance of the "modern urban Malaysian other".[11] They see towns merely as places to buy basic necessities, such as sundry goods and clothes. The reflexive anthropologist would regard this perspective as "rational", given that their semi-nomadic existence prevents them from accumulating goods in fixed abodes. Kinak Bong worry about whether they would be safe and comfortable in low-cost or affordable multi-ethnic housing schemes, despite built-up infrastructures and public conveniences. In the forest at least, they would not be "the monkey in the city"—equivalent to Baudrillard's (1973) city "gutter people".

The Ma' Betise', however, prefer a cautious approach, and modernity becomes a "window-shopping experience" with some misgivings and envy at not being able to indulge in the commercial experience of consumption. The Orang Asli in general and the Kintak Bong and Ma' Betise' in particular were marginal to trends of large-scale commercialization in farming and industrialization. The latter took off in Malaysia after the 1970s with the establishment of Free Trade Zones in major towns on the peninsula.[12] However, for the Ma' Betise', their shrinking habitats and exposure to modern technologies have thrown them into social disarray as they attempt to accommodate to the world of portable telephony, cybercafés, websites and on-line campaigns for land and cultural rights.[13] Those who have had success in tertiary education have taken advantage of these "socially levelling" institutions by creating their own discourses on marginalization and identity through social media.[14]

The Ma' Betise' accept the conveniences of modernity—physical and technological changes which improve their daily lives, such as fresh running water, electricity, access to new sources of cheap food, modern transportation, radio, television and social media. However they suffer the social costs of "wanting more", with unsustainable life-styles leading to bad debts. Usually their creditors are local Chinese businessmen or loggers. On Carey Island, Ma' Betise' men had to allow creditors to sleep with their wives as "interest" on unpaid loans, and this continues today in isolated examples of Ma' Betise' men who are gamblers or alcoholics and get into bad debts. They often find themselves working for slave wages as bonded labour and indebted to local creditors.

Dialogues of discontent reinforce the anthropologist's role as a sympathetic listener and "conscientized synthesizer" with a moral obligation to bring these messages to the right authorities. Social media reinforce the Orang Asli sense of marginality, that they have a weak political voice on the level of the state or nation. Ma' Betise' youth complain that even the Orang Asli radio station is dominated by the Semai, who have never used Betise' (or 'tise') language in their programmes. Their weaker political position among the Orang Asli makes them fully aware that they are "nobody" and discourages them from wanting to be "main-streamed"—like the Semai spokesmen on the radio station. Hence the village remains their source of solace. Lacking a national political voice, their cultural strengths become a resource for the future. The Ma' Betise' agree that cultural or conservation tourism is an important dimension of development and source of livelihood for the future. They prefer development initiatives such as entrepreneurial ventures in the village, which enable them to earn extra money to buy "modern goods". Hence they reject initiatives which require migration, resettlement and population intrusions into their neighbourhoods. Though both communities are emotionally bound to their places of origin, the Ma' Betise' are more open to some aspects of modernity, such as innovations in cultural tourism as a good alternative source of income.[15] This, however, does not mean that they want an alternative life in a multi-ethnic town or city.

Prominent American anthropologist Marshall Sahlins has argued (1998) that "development" does not lead to the "developed man", if the circumstances of change or modernity lead to the sacrifice of cultural identities. In 1998, Sahlins was introduced to the plight of the Orang Asli through several workshops on "Development Issues on the Orang Asli" at the Universiti Sains Malaysia, Penang.[16] He shared his thoughts with local social scientists on the real and potential failures of governments who main-stream cultural minorities by disregarding their cultures, imposing instead more widely and globally accepted practices of modern living. In other words, adaptation to urban life-styles, hybridity or assimilation with plural communities (which have become "universals" of modern living) may threaten the future survival of minorities. As minority communities with different cultures, languages and faiths, they could not successfully meet the challenges from outside or gain from hybridity.

A growing fear within both communities is the "loss of women" and eventual extinction, expressed as *diq* (finish; gone) by the Ma' Betise' and as *matik* (death) by the Kintak Bong. Both the Ma' Betise' and the Kintak Bong have lost some women to outside marriages with Malays, Chinese and Indians, and all these women, as minorities, have assimilated to their spouses' cultures, languages and faiths. In the villages of Sg Bumbun and Sg Sialang, two women have married Malay men and have not returned for several decades. At Ulu Perak, two women have married Malay men and have left the village. A Kensiu man who married a Malay woman in Memali, Kedah, has moved out of the village. Successful Orang Asli men who marry other ethnic groups generally are "lost" to the village. They move out and assimilate with Malays more easily. Most of them have not returned to their natal communities. The potential "loss of women" is a significant reason for rejection of outsiders (Karim 1994). To quote Sahlins (1998: 1):

> It seems to me that if the Malaysian government wishes to see the Orang Asli develop, as it surely does, it must take measures to safeguard the people's space and culture. For if anthropologists have learned anything about this problem in the last 30 years, it is that a living cultural tradition is the necessary means and measure of "indigenous people's" modernisation. The alternative is a condition of misery—which governments have found much more costly to deal with, since without the people's culture, there is no answer or end to it.

MODERNITY: FAMILIARITY VERSUS ALIENATION

The Orang Asli must "live like other Malaysians" is the vision of the Malaysian Government, but this policy ignores the reflexive position— voices of discontent in resettlement schemes, their differential phases on the road to development and modernity and issues which arise. The voices of anthropologists are also rebuked. Karim was once referred to as a "bleeding-hearted intellectual" by Dato' Seri Anwar

Plate 13.1 Wazir Jahan Karim (second from left) with her field family at
Carey Island

(Photo credit: Rashid Karim)

Ibrahim, then Deputy Prime Minister of Malaysia, when she brought
forward proposals of the kind suggested by Sahlins. The Ma' Betise'
point of view is "give us the conveniences without asking us to
move". "We will be the monkeys (*yen*) of the city", a Ma' Betise'
woman said, "and even monkeys can survive better than us." When
the same woman came to Penang to visit Karim in 2009, she noted
that her house had been overrun by macaques from the botanical
gardens, where surrounding forests had been cleared for housing.
She did not empathize with the macaques; they were once a familiar
source of food.[17] She exclaimed "So you have monkeys here—there
is abundant food for us! You never told us. We can live here."
She was not keen to move out of Carey Island, but said that if they
were squeezed out of Carey Island, Penang Island would be a good
alternative.

A few graduates from Ma' Betise' communities, like others from
the Semai and Temiar communities, have successfully lived in modern
multi-ethnic neighbourhoods. But they had assimilated to urban life

while studying in colleges and universities. However, there has been no incidence of an entrepreneurial Kintak Bong living in the city.

Orang Asli ideologies and ritual life adapted to the rainforests have evolved for thousands of years. Hence Orang Asli like the Ma' Betise' express familiarity with urban living when it evokes some iconic material association with the rainforests—for example, the botanical gardens or the epidemic of monkeys on Penang Island. This attachment to the rainforest, found in all Orang Asli groups, is not easily extinguished (Karim 1998a, 1998b).

For Ma' Betise' contentment removes feelings of *magnu* or "longing for family and the village". It also lessens states of *kempunan*, "deprivation", which open them to the dangers of the city. *Magnu* and *kempunan* both lead to serious feelings of deprivation and make them more vulnerable to illness.

Jamieson and Lovelace (1985: 31) explain that ecological dependency leads to "ideational phenomena" which "justify, give meaning to, or motivate behaviours that have already been demonstrated by experience to be necessary for continued existence in a particular environmental setting". Hence people, objects or words which evoke positive sentiments assist their capacity to adapt in the long term. Benjamin observed in his introduction to Schebesta's work (1973: v), that Schebesta viewed Semang cultural "primitivity", small population size and nomadism, as a "rational" adaptation to forest ecology, in the sense that the rainforests cannot accommodate large settlements without sacrificing the flora and fauna. Outside this context, Semang cultural "primitivity" would be misplaced. Anthony Williams-Hunt (1995) has said that Orang Asli have a deep-rooted spiritual connection to forests and land (see also Razha Rashid 1995). The city does not evoke a sense of belonging or comfort. Indeed, for the Ma' Betise', deforestation transformed forests into dangerous towns and cities, leading malevolent ancestral plant and animal spirits (*moyang*) to overrun their homes. This is a "bad" state since it upsets the balance between the "need to eat" plants and animals designated as food by their ancestors (*tulah moyang*) and the conservation of sacred plants and animals which have *kemali'* or mystical anthropomorphic attributes.

Deforestation, associated with the felling of trees and extraction of resources for commercial gain, leads to mystical retribution (*kemali'*) from *moyang*, a belief which is currently held by members of all generations (Karim 1981, 2004). The Ma' Betise' belief that humans have a right to eat plants and animals (*tulah*), but plants and animals can take retribution for their destruction (*kemali'*) expresses, in a more generic sense, the fragile ecological balance between Man and Nature. The rise of greed (*hagar kayak*) among Chinese and Malay loggers and developers has upset this balance, opening everyone to illness and death.[18]

Adaptation to socio-economic changes is a form of inventiveness, as communities adopt or let go of elements considered important or redundant for survival (Razha Rashid 2001). However, Schebesta argues there must be "all-round activity" and "all-round interest" to produce contentment. Only then can it be said that a life can develop "the whole man" (1973: 114). Sahlin's "developed man" must not feel he is the "monkey in the city", rather a useful and productive individual with something significant to contribute. Skeat and Blagden (1906, 1926) observed that at the height of British colonization in the last few decades of the 19th century, the Kintak Bong and other Semang groups had started to borrow Malay technology such as long knives (*parang*), cutting knives (*pisau*) and axes (*kapak*), which is reminiscent of Salisbury's "From Stone to Steel" study of technological change in New Guinea (1962). However, the Kintak Bong acceptance of new technology was to facilitate hunting and gathering; they were not striving to become the "modern Malay" or "Malaysian". Sure enough, by the end of the 20th century, instead of emerging from the forests as their hunting grounds decreased, they moved deeper into the forests.

Logging opened up Kintak Bong villages involuntarily to the outside world, and logging tracks came to be used to sustain lives which had become more dependent on processed food from grocery stores at the fringe of the forest. Roads were also used to bring out forest products which could be sold to buy food. Legumes, land turtles and birds were exchanged for rice, sugar and salt. Other than these exchanges, the Kintak Bong remained firmly entrenched in the forests.

The Ma' Betise' on Carey Island, however, adapted to estate life, and about 20 out of 300 families became dependent on the oil-palm estates for their economic livelihoods. They took up jobs as harvesters,

Plate 13.2 Tourists observing Ma' Betise' masked performers

(Photo credit: Wazir Jahan Karim)

but they were not very successful, turning up late for work, sometimes deciding to take the day off and generally being resentful of their low wages and loss of wages on rainy days. The majority pooled their resources and commercialized traditional crafts. They sold mats, bags, baskets and decorative head gear. A few women developed a craft weaving workshop where tourists could try their hand at weaving and thatching. The entrepreneur among them, Maznah, also organizes dance exhibitions at RM500 (US$167) per show, a good source of income for women. Some organized groups experiment with new choreography to render their dances (*jo-oh*) more dramatic, and others focus on designing new costumes of *nipah* palm leaves. Song composers have also added new tempos and beats to their *jo-oh* dances. Young woodcarvers have set up small workshops and stalls outside their houses to sell their wood carvings. This has been quite successful, as visitors prefer to visit workshops attached to houses against a natural mangrove setting, rather than the central design centre at Kampung Sg. Mata.

The Ma' Betise' have had a longer exposure to tourists and are able to engage in cultural tourism with greater confidence and innovation than the Kintak Bong, who need assistance in marketing their products to the same level as the Ma' Betise'. However, both communities prefer to engage in independent trading rather than being "main-streamed" in large-scale development projects.

MODERNITY WITHOUT WEALTH: INDIVIDUALISM AND SHARING AS PRINCIPLES OF SURVIVAL

While the Kintak Bong extract forest products for daily use, large-scale deforestation defies their imagined view of this kind of subsistence existence as "timeless". Reconciliation with deforestation implies a fully settled existence which they are not prepared to adopt. They will never be able to generate surplus from "family-scale" hunting and gathering and will never have enough to share with others.[19] They are unable to engage in generalized sharing like the Ma' Betise' and Semai. The semi-settled Kintak Bong now have their own plots of land where women plant tapioca, bananas and vegetables, but this does not lead to surplus. They complain that they are encroached upon by elephants and wild boar, and their crops are often destroyed. Deforestation increases the competition for food between hungry Kintak Bong and hungry animals.

In contrast, the Ma' Betise' are settled on larger plots of land behind the mangroves and have greater access to jobs in the townships of Teluk Panglima Garang and Klang. They buy food with wages, and this can produce a food surplus when the bulk of wages is spent on food. However, game surplus is a thing of the past, since most of the bigger animals they used to hunt, like wild boar and deer, are now extinct on the island. But they are not desperately searching the forests for food to satisfy daily requirements. Some have even quit their jobs in Chinese restaurants, citing poor working conditions and food. Significantly, they have developed modern values of "taste", "preference" and "quality" of food, unheard of among the Kintak Bong.

The Ma' Betise' uphold the principle of "generalized reciprocity", giving without calculating repayment, in food distribution, called *muntet-mulih* (a little for everyone) to ensure long-term survival of the community amidst unequal opportunities for families to procure food each day (Karim 2001b).[20] In other words, the community as a whole generates a daily food surplus, and food sharing enables everyone to survive over the long run.

Food sufficiency based on family subsistence and communal sharing does not generate a large-scale surplus which can produce wealth, defined by Malay words such as *kayak* ("rich") or *maju* ("developed"), which imply that wealth, above the procurement or satisfaction of daily needs, is a luxury, alien to Orang Asli and more closely associated with "the modern urban Malaysian other"—wage earners in towns and cities.[21] Hence, wealth is associated with urban living, where opportunities to be wealthy arise among other Malaysians. But to Orang Asli, *kayak* is also associated with greed. The Ma' Betise' use another Malay word, *tamak*, to indicate greed. *Tamak* refers to a person without morality and sensitivity to others, one who does not share profits for the general good.

Plate 13.3 Ma' Betise' feast for the ancestors

(Photo credit: Wazir Jahan Karim)

For these reasons, the Ma' Betise' continue to follow the principle of *muntet-mulih* to ensure the daily survival of the community. The family which willingly shares their food or game may have very little to eat on any given day, but they may go to one of those families they had shared their food with in the past and obtain a meal. During rice harvests or *Ari' Moyang* (Ancestral Day), all families cook a little rice, some game or fish and vegetable shoots and bring their pots to the ancestral hut (*hadu' moyang*), where everyone shares their food until all are satiated. Families take home their own leftovers for the evening meal.

Many Ma' Betise' elders express their fear that sharing by *muntet-mulih* may disappear if there is uneven wealth in the community, since those who are well off may refuse to share, to keep their surplus to themselves. According to the Ma' Betise', townsfolk are *kayak* because they refuse to share their surplus. Sure enough, Razha met Yusof, a Kensiu entrepreneur who married a Malay woman and lives comfortably outside the Kensiu settlement at Memali, Kedah. He refuses to be part of the community, and his explanation is that he will be rendered "poor" if he continues to engage in the communal sharing of food, even after satisfying the needs of his own family. He has a car, but said he will not offer free rides to the community since that would bankrupt him. When Razha mentioned this to the Kintak Bong, they said that they never have enough to share, but anthropologists who always have "surplus" food should share.

The process of adaptation to changes and exercise of choice among new opportunities—social, economic and political—synchronizes well with development and modernity. The Ma' Betise' have focused on cultural tourism in their adaptation to changes in their environment and the economic basis of their livelihoods. Their material culture has become their most saleable commodity (Karim 1996, 2001b). If sharing can be sustained, they welcome public conveniences and urban services as long as they are not separated from one another. For the Ma' Betise', to be rich is better than to be poor if one is generous and distributes resources widely, but, then again, if their culture deteriorates as a result of wealth, they would rather remain poor.

To conclude, both communities value their autonomy, but are not averse to development and modernity which advances their physical and economic livelihoods in their villages or settlements. However, changes based on new choices, opportunities and services are always qualified and measured against possible losses in culture and community solidarity. While the Ma' Betise' have ventured into Baudrillard's "window shopping" stage and have made economic advancements in tourism, the Kintak Bong refrain from full participation in the modern world, held back by the fear of alienation and loss of abode.

NOTES

1. The first plan was the First Malayan Plan, implemented in 1956–60.
2. Karim argues that resettlement leads to loss of cultural identities and resources, while Khor states that nutritional levels actually decline with resettlement. Gomes argues that resettlement does not necessarily lead to economic mobility.
3. Only 12 per cent of 27,800 hectares of Orang Asli land have been gazetted.
4. There are only about 100 Kintak Bong or 20 extended families living in Kelian, Ulu Perak.
5. The Ma' Betise' population is approximately 3,000. Wazir lived with the Ma' Betise' from 1974 to 1977 and again for several advanced projects on cultural conservation in 1985–87, 1996–97, 2000–01, 2010–12 and March–July 2013. She continues to do research on conservation anthropology and conduct many site visits to their settlements for evaluation of programmes on poverty eradication, including cultural property rights.
6. Razha Rashid has conducted research on the Kintak Bong since 1985 and frequently returns with biomedical teams and educationists to chart medical histories and design curriculums suited to the Semang.
7. The present Kintak Bong settlement has been deforested, and they now live in secondary forests.
8. The bunding and desalination of the mangroves from 2000 to 2013 for oil-palm cultivation have led to the collapse of the mangrove littoral belt, once rich with crustaceans and their major source of food and earnings.
9. For Orang Asli as a whole, despite an increase of more than 100 per cent attending secondary schooling, from 4,186 in 2000 to 9,684 in 2007, these numbers are significantly less than those who attended

primary school. In 2000, 19,033 attended primary school, but only 22 per cent went on to secondary school. By 2007, the primary school numbers increased to 26,124, but only 37 per cent went on to secondary school. Despite an improvement of 15 per cent over seven years, this is way below the national statistics for Malays, Chinese and Indians, among whom the dropout rate from primary to secondary schooling is less than 1 per cent.

10. This prejudice is however extended across the board to all Malaysian youth seeking entry into the private and public sector. Orang Asli youth—like some Malay, Indian and Chinese graduates—are unable to compete with graduates who can communicate fluently in English. Chinese graduates at least get entry into Mandarin-medium Chinese corporations.

11. "The modern Malaysian other" is a generic category of urban Malaysians who are waged or salaried and live in multi-ethnic neighbourhoods. They practise a cosmopolitan life-style which is generally alien to the Kintak Bong and the Ma' Betise'.

12. These Free Trade Zones were part of Malaysia's early drive towards manufacturing, when American and Japanese companies used Malaysian cheap labour, mostly rural Malay school-leavers. This drive did not penetrate into Orang Asli villages.

13. Since 1978, the Ma' Betise' on Carey Island and the coastal areas of Selangor have lost access to State forest reserves, all of which have been rezoned for oil-palm cultivation, infrastructural projects or housing.

14. For example, a visit to the facebook of Gerai Orang Asli, an online craft shop, will show the accomplishments of Diana Uju, a Ma' Betise' graduate in Administrative Sciences and Policy Studies from Universiti Teknologi MARA. It also features the 16th Public Lecture of the Centre for Malaysian Indigenous Studies (CMIS), University of Malaya by Shaq Koyok, a Temuan contemporary artist and graduate in Fine Arts from Universiti Teknologi MARA. shaqkoyok.blogspot.com

15. Karim's chapter on "Anthropology Without Tears ..." (1996) discusses new tensions and conflicts in cultural tourism in greater detail than can be provided in this chapter.

16. Marshall Sahlins, Emeritus Professor at the University of Chicago, was Visiting Professor at Universiti Sains Malaysia (USM) in 1998, at the invitation of Prof Wazir Jahan Karim (then Director of the Women's Development Research Centre, KANITA).

17. Monkey is a favourite meat of the Ma' Betise', but this source of protein has been almost wiped out by deforestation.

18. The phrase, *tulah moyang*, refers to the curse of ancestors on the spirits of certain plants and animals which assume human forms and trick humans into befriending them, only to kill them out of anger for destroying their habitat. The curse, "if a human be a human, if an animal be an animal, but do not be both" has now removed the ability of edible plants and animals to materialize into human forms, thus opening the way for humans to hunt and gather them for food.
19. Semai entrepreneurs stated that such generalized reciprocity is rapidly breaking down in Semai villages.
20. This principle will be explained in greater detail to explain other survival strategies with more long-term goals.
21. *Kayak* commonly refers to Chinese, Indian or Malay men who have cars, live in brick houses and often eat out in restaurants. It does not matter if they are seriously in debt or pay for their food through credit cards.

REFERENCES

Baudelaire, C.
    1964   The Painter of Modern Life and Other Essays. Edited and translated by Jonathan Mayne. London: Phaidon Press.

Baudrillard, J.
    1964   The Mirror of Production. St Louis: Telos Press.

Benjamin, G.
    1973   Introduction. *In* Among the Forest Dwarfs of Malaya, by P. Schebesta. Kuala Lumpur: Oxford University Press.

Berman, M.
    1982   All that is Solid Melts into the Air: The Experience of Modernity. New York: Verso Books.

Gomes, A.G.
    2007   Modernity and Malaysia: Settling the Menraq Forest Nomads. New York: Routledge.

Jamieson, N.L. and G.W. Lovelace
    1985   Cultural Values and Human Ecology: Some Initial Considerations. *In* Cultural Values and Human Ecology in Southeast Asia. K.L. Hutterer, A.T. Rambo and G. Lovelace, eds. Michigan Papers on South and Southeast Asia, No. 27. Ann Arbor, MI: Center for South and Southeast Asian Studies.

Kamarulzaman Kamaruddin and Osman Jusoh
  2008 Educational Policy and Oppression of Orang Asli: A Study on
         Indigenous People in Malaysia. The Journal of Human Resource
         and Adult Learning 4(1): 87–97.
Karim, W.J.
  1980 Ma' Betise' Concepts of Living Things. LSE Monograph No. 54.
         London: Athlone. Republished Oxford: Berg 2004.
  1981 Ma' Betisek Concepts of Humans, Plants and Animals. Bijdragen
         Tot de Taal, Land-en, Volkenkunde 137: 35–60.
  1993a With Moyang Melur in Carey Island. *In* Gendered Fields:
         Women, Men, Ethnography. D. Bell, P. Caplan and W.J. Karim,
         eds. Pp. 78–92. London: Routledge.
  1993b Epilogue: The "Nativised" Self and the Native. *In* Gendered
         Fields: Women, Men, Ethnography. D. Bell, P. Caplan and W.J.
         Karim, eds. Pp. 248–51. London: Routledge.
  1996 Anthropology without Tears: How a "local" sees the "local"
         and the "global". *In* The Future of Anthropological Knowledge.
         H. Moore, ed. Pp. 158–76. London: Routledge.
  1997 Jangan Lupakan Kami: Cendekiawan dalam Anthropologi
         Pribumi. Inaugural Professorial Lecture. Penang: Universiti Sains
         Malaysia.
  1998a Constructing Emotions and World of the Orang Asli. Public
         Lecture. Victoria, NZ: University of Wellington.
  1998b Shifting Cosmologies of Culture and Religion in Malaysia.
         Occasional Paper No. 13. Taipei: Academia Sinica.
  2001a Constructing Emotions and World of the Orang Asli. *In* Minority
         Cultures of Peninsular Malaysia: Survivals of Indigenous Heritage.
         Razha Rashid and W.J. Karim, eds. Pp. 13–26. Penang and Tokyo:
         Academy of Social Sciences and the Toyota Foundation.
  2001b Minorities of the Minority: Language Death and Patterns of
         Cultural Extinction. *In* Minority Cultures of Peninsular Malaysia:
         Survivals of Indigenous Heritage. Razha Rashid and W.J. Karim,
         eds. Pp. 69–74. Penang and Tokyo: Academy of Social Sciences
         and the Toyota Foundation.
Karim, W.J. and Razha Rashid
  2001 Material Culture as Technological Transformation. *In* Minority
         Cultures of Peninsular Malaysia: Survivals of Indigenous Heritage.
         Razha Rashid and W.J. Karim, eds. Pp. 33–58. Penang and Tokyo:
         Academy of Social Sciences and the Toyota Foundation.

Lin Khor Geok
    1994   Resettlement and Nutritional Implications: The Case of *Orang Asli*
            in Regroupment Schemes. *Pertanika* Journal of Social Sciences
            and Humanities 2(2): 123–32.

Lyotard, J-F.
    1984   The Postmodern Condition: A Report on Knowledge. Trans.
            Geoff Bennington and Brian Massumi. Manchester: Manchester
            University Press.

Nicholas, C.
    2003   The Orang Asli: First on the Land. Last in the Plan. Kajian
            Malaysia 21(1 & 2): 315–29.

Osborne, P.
    1992   Modernity is a Qualitative, Not a Chronological, Category: Notes on
            the Dialectics of Different Historical Time. *In* Postmodernism and
            the Re-Reading of Modernity. F. Barker, P. Hulme and M. Iversen,
            eds. Pp. 65–84. Manchester: University of Manchester Press.

Razha Rashid
    1995   As the Forests Become Thick with Ghosts: A Kintak Bong
            Narration of Time, Events and Space. *In* Indigenous Minorities
            of Peninsular Malaysia: Selected Issues and Ethnographies.
            Razha Rashid and Wazir Jahan Karim, eds. Pp. 74–85. Penang:
            Intersocietal and Scientific (INAS).

Sahlins, M.
    1998   The Indigenization of Modernity: New Cultural Formations of the
            Late 19th Century. Course in Advanced Anthropology. Pp.16–21.
            Penang: Universiti Sains Malaysia.

Salisbury, R.F.
    1962   From Stone to Steel: Economic Consequences of a Technological
            Change in New Guinea. Melbourne: Melbourne University Press.

Schebesta, P.
    1973   Among the Forest Dwarfs of Malaya. Kuala Lumpur: Oxford
            University Press [1928].

Skeat, W.W. and C.O. Blagden
    1906   Pagan Races of the Malay Peninsula. Vol. 1 and 2. London: Frank
            Cass.

Tijah Yok Chopil
    2004   Biodiversity and the Survival of Indigenous Identity. www.
            malaysiakini.com/browse/a/en/Tijah%20Yok%20Chopil, accessed
            24 Nov. 2013.

Economic Planning Unit (EPU)
  2006 Ninth Malaysia Plan. Kuala Lumpur: Percetakan Nasional
        Malaysia Bhd.
  2012 Tenth Malaysia Plan. Kuala Lumpur: Percetakan Nasional
        Malaysia Bhd.
Williams-Hunt, A.
  1995 Land Conflicts: Orang Asli Ancestral Lands and State Policies.
        In Indigenous Minorities of Peninsular Malaysia: Selected Issues
        and Ethnographies. Razha Rashid and Wazir Jahan Karim, eds.
        Pp. 36–47. Penang: Intersocietal and Scientific (INAS).

14

Livelihood, Locality and Marriage: Economic Flexibility and Its Consequences Among Hma' Btsisi'

Barbara S. Nowak

INTRODUCTION

This chapter examines how environmental destruction and subsequent changes in the subsistence activities have affected settlement patterns, post-marital residence and marriage among the 3,000 Southern Aslian speaking Btsisi' ("Mah Meri") of coastal Selangor, Peninsular Malaysia (see Wazir and Razha, this volume). Btsisi' have encountered severe land and forest losses along with other negative environmental changes over the past century. In response, Btsisi' livelihoods have also altered. This chapter suggests that these environmental and concomitant economic changes have affected Btsisi' marriage choices. Kinship and marriage data collected over 20 years suggests that controlling arable land has become Btsisi' households' priority when considering eligible marital partners.

This chapter falls into three sections. The first section describes environmental and economic changes over the past century. This is followed by a discussion of Btsisi' residential and marital choices as revealed by genealogical and census information, questioning members of the community and consulting ethnohistorical sources. The final section comprised of a summary and conclusions, viewing Btsisi' society as a "house society".

When possible each section describes three different time periods. The first period is the early 1900s, as revealed by ethnohistoric literature as well as stories from Btsisi' elders about their parents and grandparents. The next period is the 1970s–80s. The works of Dentan (1975), Ayampillay (1976) and Karim (1980a, 1980b, 1981) supplement data I collected during extended fieldwork between 1980 and 1982. The third period is from the mid-1990s to 2008 and rests on material I collected during brief visits.[1]

CHANGING ENVIRONMENT AND LIVELIHOODS

Before the recent destruction of the natural environment, a rich coastal environment allowed Btsisi' flexibility to shift livelihood activities depending upon people's wishes, opportunities and needs. Previously, I suggested that livelihood diversification can be a positive strategy used by a household to optimize abundance and take advantage of opportunities. I stated that diversity of subsistence resources underpins economic resilience (2003).

> [Resilience] … can be associated with success in achieving livelihood diversity and improved household living standards. Diversification may take place not only in poor households struggling to survive but also in wealthy households as a "… path to accumulation" (Murray 2001: 3). Livelihood diversity results in reduced pressure on natural resources, potentially eliminating future shocks and vulnerabilities that communities encounter rather than being a response to shocks and vulnerability. (Nowak 2008: 187)

Although diversification by poor households is more commonly accepted in the literature (e.g., Saith 1992), other *Orang Asli* also deliberately seek diversification as a hedge against the failure of a particular resource, for example by planting as many cultivars of as many crops as possible (Dentan 1971).

Loss of livelihood diversity can reflect a deteriorating natural resource base as was the case among Btsisi'. Not only has there been a serious reduction in the repertoire of economic activities Btsisi' are able to perform, but there has been a change in the types of livelihood options available.

Traditional livelihood activities included hunting and gathering in the lowland and mangrove forests, sea and littoral fishing, gathering littoral and mangrove fauna and cultivating swiddens. Livelihood strategies illustrate Btsisi' opportunism and flexibility, including shifting from one ecozone to another (cf. Endicott 1979). Mangrove activities included crabbing, using traps in high tides and *gnto'* (a prodding technique) at low tide; collecting snails; fishing with hook and line, gill nets, traps, poison and barricades; and collecting nipah and mangrove wood for house construction and fuel wood. Btsisi' seem to have preferred to live in the mangroves, moving outwards to the sea or inland to the forest to perform appropriate exploitative activities. On the sea, people used palisade traps, long lines and gill nets, and on the shore seine nets and barricade fishing. On the beach people crabbed, gathered snails and caught razor clams. Inland, they hunted, cleared and planted swiddens, and collected fruits and other forest products. The choice of which resource to exploit rested on factors including seasonality, monthly tidal cycle, distance to various locations, people's individual likes and inclinations, and the developmental cycle of the household (Nowak 1987).

At the beginning of the 20th century Btsisi' were residing from Batu Pahat, Johor, north to the Kuala Langat region of Selangor on the islands around Port Kelang including Pulau Carey, Pulau Ketam and Pulau Lumut. Before the plantation was established, only Btsisi' inhabited Pulau Carey and the neighbouring islands.[2]

Beginning in 1905 Edward Carey, an English planter, received a land grant from the Sultan of Selangor to establish a rubber plantation on Carey Island. Granted in stages, the plantation, then called Pataling Rubber Estate, today covers over 25,000 of the approximately 32,000 acres of the island, and is owned by the Sime Darby company.[3] This seizure of land and its bestowal on favoured parties was part of the expansion of the authority of the state over frontier peoples. The seizures, encouraged by the sultanate's British advisors, were under the

legal aegis of the infamous Torrens Doctrine, which declared that land
not secured by an official title was by default state-owned, *terra nullius,*
"no man's land", despite the fact that *Orang Asli* had inhabited it for
many years. Land gifts were a useful political tool in the expansion of
power (Juli 1976; Nicholas 2000; Doolittle 2005; Juli, Williams-Hunt
and Dentan 2009).

The Btsisi' began to feel the impact of colonialism through the
clearing of the lowland forest for cash crops: first rubber and coconut,
later coffee and, by the 1950s, oil palm. From the beginning, Btsisi'
were itinerant labourers for the plantation on Carey Island. The
company employed men to clear the land and help construct roads
and the bungalows for the future South Indian plantation workers, while
Btsisi' women worked in the plantation's nursery. The land cleared was
land Btsisi' previously used for their swiddens.

The Modern Economy and Shrinking Livelihood Choices

In the 1980s Btsisi' were aware of the fragility of the environment
and the impact the plantation was having on their traditional
livelihoods (Aziz et al. 2013). Loss of land and resources, coupled
with economic incursions by Chinese commercial interests, resulted
in Btsisi' becoming dependent on a cash economy (cf. Gomes 2004,
2007; Nobuta 2009). On Carey Island, by the 1960s, the plantation
had started planting oil palm not only on lowland forest areas, but
also in the mangroves, drying large tracts of the upper reaches of the
rivers through the construction of bunds or sea walls. The company
extended its ownership of the lands Btsisi' had traditionally used for
swiddening. By the 1980s, only a handful of older people, unable to
generate a cash income, continued to grow dry rice. In 2002 only one
household continued rice cultivation, but the land was nearing the end
of its fertility. With no access to arable land, in 2006, there were no
longer any households growing rice.

The plantation

On the 35,000 acre Carey Island, Btsisi' have access to approximately
1,100 acres of Aboriginal Reserve (Nowak 1985; Rahim 2007). Btsisi'

have become an almost landless proletariat (Nowak 1985, 2005). As Beckford (1972: 177) points out: "... inherent in a plantation system is a tendency toward monopolization of land by plantation owners as a device to deprive the majority of people access to an independent livelihood and therefore to ensure the plantation of labour supplies". In the 1980s, Btsisi' had to work as oil palm harvesters to generate necessary income. Typically either a married couple, a woman and her son or two teenaged brothers would partner for the work. The man or son of the partnership would cut down the oil palm fruit bunches and the palm fronds surrounding the fruit, then transport the fruit to the road. The woman and adolescents collected and bagged the nuts that dropped from the bunch, and stacked the cut fronds. Income from this work varied depending upon the season.[4] Btsisi' did not like plantation work. They called crabbing and fishing, like other unsupervised and unregulated activities, "fooling around". Plantation work was *krja,* "labour", from a Malay word. The term connoted labour's regimentation by others and its "alienation" in the Marxist sense that the workers did not get to consume the fruits of their labours or benefit directly from the sale thereof. Moreover, although the labour itself required a working couple, as just described, the plantation paid only the men who did the harvesting.

Few Btsisi' worked in the plantation by 2000. In the 1990s, the plantation began employing landless Malays and then Indonesian migrants. By doing this, the company was able to keep the wages at the same rates as in the 1980s. In addition, the managers assigned Btsisi' to oil palm tracts far from their villages, making access difficult and more time consuming. Btsisi' became less willing to engage in the heavy, alienating and underpaid labour. Chomsky (1996: 170) observed that banana plantations in Costa Rica divide workers' interests along racial, ethnic and nationality lines, which keeps workers from challenging or resisting company policy. This is similar to the situation Btsisi' oil palm harvesters faced. The introduction of Malay and then Indonesian workers kept wages depressed by dividing workers along lines of ethnicity and national identity. A few Btsisi' men continued to work for Chinese contractors, but by 2000 plantation work had ceased to be central to Btsisi' livelihood, except for the handful of men who worked as lorry drivers and a few women who worked applying pesticides and herbicides.[5]

Fishing: subsistence and commodity production

In 1980, the plantation had one oil palm processing mill on Carey Island; by the mid-1990s there were three. The mills discharge a boiling effluent heavy with fat residue and pesticides directly into the rivers. Btsisi' complained that the effluent was polluting the rivers that supported their fishing and crabbing activities. They observed that the fish and prawns were no longer spawning in the rivers, and catches were significantly reduced.

Although the estate is a signatory to the Roundtable on Sustainable Palm Oil, whose guidelines include maintaining a sustainable mangrove forest fringe along the rivers, on Carey Island, the fringe is too narrow to allow Btsisi' to pursue their traditional livelihood activities.[6] People from Sg. Bumbun complain that they can no longer even reach the headwaters of the Bumbun River, for which their village is named (Center for Orang Asli Concerns 2011).

In the 1980s, Btsisi' subsistence depended heavily on fishing and crabbing, often for sale to Chinese middlemen. Most households had a member who provisioned not only his own household, but also shared seafood and other mangrove products with kin. People consumed the less commercially valuable items and sold the rest to Chinese middlemen. However, by 2000, other factors diminished the importance of fishing, crabbing and gathering seafood in the Btsisi' economy. The high cost of buying and maintaining fishing vessels capable of competing with Chinese fishermen, the rising cost of diesel and the cost of fishing licenses all priced many households out of sea fishing. The poisoning of the rivers by mill effluent and the reduced mangrove have resulted in a compromised ecosystem with depleted resources (cf. Devi and Seabrook 2000), so that even rowing smaller boats long distances in the remaining mangroves did not produce a catch worth the effort. Some people tried to make do by buying outboard engines to go yet further towards the deltas or into the Straits, but rising petrol costs meant that many people could not keep running their boats. In desperation, some formerly independent producers turned to fishing for middlemen who would buy the petrol and let the Btsisi' use boats and engines the middlemen supplied. Btsisi' aver that the middlemen routinely bought the catch for under market value. Sometimes Btsisi' in this relationship would slip a portion of the catch to an independent buyer who then sold it at fair market prices. But in the long run many people discontinued the patron-client relationships, which left them feeling exploited besides having little to show for their labour.

Oil palm smallholdings

In the 1980s, the Malaysian Government provided seedlings to men interested in growing oil palm as smallholders.[7] Most of the seedlings did not survive, since, unlike the plantation managers, Btsisi' did not use herbicides and pesticides to ward off disease and destruction; nor did they allow cobras to proliferate to kill rats, nor plant strangler creepers from America to kill off plant competition. It took a second planting of seedlings independently bought to achieve success.

As men married, they requested land. I neglected to ask why women did not do so, since there are no restrictions on female land ownership. Traditionally, women controlled land they had cleared and planted with fruit trees or land they had inherited from their mothers. The only woman who I know requested land wished to marry a Malay, and it was her request that caused the elders to establish a policy restricting "outsiders". I suspect that government policies, which assumed patricentic households on the Malay Islamic model, may have affected Btsisi'. Perhaps because oil palm harvesting is men's work, and oil palm smallholding had become the focus of activity, women did not see the need to ask for land.

During the 1980s there was some wealth differentiation based on ownership of fruit trees and ownership of deep sea fishing boats (as opposed to the smaller outboard motor boats for fishing primarily in the rivers). But everyone had enough to eat; those less well-off worked for wages, sold *attap* ("palm thatch") or whatever marine produce they could get. By the mid-1990s, Btsisi' oil palm smallholdings were yielding fruit, and things began to change. I conducted a wealth ranking exercise (Pretty et al. 1995: 256–60; Thomas-Slayter et al. 1995: 87–90) in 2002, which highlighted that households villagers categorized as "wealthy" were oil palm smallholder households. The new income allowed some people to build permanent cinder block houses and to buy food and other commodities such as generators, televisions and even cars. "Poor" households were landless; they had not inherited land or members were too young to ask for their share of the communal land when it was available. Thus, oil palm has made some people's quality of life better. The depletion of natural resources leading to a reduction in commodity production activities (except for oil palm smallholding), reduced estate work, along with landlessness, intensified the wealth differences between households (Eversole, McNeish and Cimadamore 2005; cf. Dallos 2011).

Finding alternative income

Btsisi' have started to work in the wider Malaysian world. Teenaged girls are finding employment in the nearby seafood restaurants, a few men are working as security guards or lorry drivers for the plantation or at the multinational factories such as Toshiba and NEC; others are working at the port, while mainland women and men are employed as cleaners at Subang Airport. Sg. Bumbun villagers have developed a thriving tourist market selling their crafts. The loss of subsistence production and people's inability to establish new smallholdings results in a search for cash work off the reserve. What impact this will have on Btsisi' culture and Btsisi' future as a community remains unknown (cf. Karim and Razha, this volume).

LAND, RESIDENCE, KINSHIP AND MARRIAGE

People's changing relationship with the land has resulted in some major shifts in decision making as to who they will marry and where they will reside after marriage. In this section I will explore the changing preferences in choosing a marital partner.

Deme-*Opoh*: Residential Kindred Group

Traditionally, people preferred to build their houses strung out along the upper reaches of the rivers. Land had little value beyond its use as a swidden and a place to hunt and gather. It was not wealth which devolved generation to generation. With the plantations' expansion and the establishment of aboriginal reserves, people's options as to where they could reside decreased. While even as late as 1982 there were a few outlier households who built stilt houses in the tidal rivers, by the middle of the 20th century most people were living in "inland" settlements at the headwaters of rivers. A pioneering household or two would clear some land to establish their homestead and would then be followed by siblings. Settlements were typically a cognatic kin based cluster composed of a core sibling group and their in-marrying spouses. The traditional pattern of uxorilocality meant that most in-marrying spouses were husbands, but often the core sibling group included brothers as well as sisters.

Members of a deme-*opoh*, a cognatic local descent group of people descended from the founding ancestor through male and female links, held corporate rights to the land surrounding their settlement. While in-marrying spouses, shared corporate rights to local land and resources, they did so only so long as they resided in the hamlet. In-marrying spouses typically did not retain rights to land in their natal hamlets, but by virtue of retaining membership in their *opoh*, they could return to their natal hamlet and re-establish their claims (Karim 1980a).

A cluster of related households formed a hamlet, taking the name of the adjacent river. The result was kin-based hamlets, separated from other hamlets by hinterland forest. Over time, while the hamlets kept their distinct identities, including their hamlet names and their own ancestral house, they coalesced into a single village with a distinct name, on government-established Aboriginal Reserves. Each village had a Council of Elders whose job was to guide the community.

Post-Marital Residence

When discussing marriage in the mid-19th century, Logan says: "... Among the Besisi' a child of a few years old is not unfrequently betrothed to her intended husband who takes her to his house and brings her up" (1847a: 270). Logan thus implies that at least some marriages were patrilocal. However, when I spoke with elderly women about marriage they said that the groom would move to his bride's natal household. Later a couple might opt to shift to the husband's natal household if the husband or his parents desire, but they would ultimately settle near the bride's family. This pattern of village exogamy and ambilocality shifting to uxorilocality were the preferred post-marital residence pattern both traditionally as well as in the 1980s (cf. Dentan 1968: 73).

Upon dissolution of a marriage, the husband, especially if he was not well established in his wife's settlement, would return to his natal village. The increasing importance of permanent cash crops, however, made divorced men reluctant to leave their cash crops behind. Fruit trees created less of a problem than other cash crops, because a person not resident in a particular settlement could return to the settlement where he owned trees for the few weeks of fruit season or could ask his kinsmen to harvest the crop. But some crops require continuous care, for example, rubber (on the mainland), coffee and especially oil palm; the last need continual dosing with herbicides and pesticides and regular harvesting. A widowed or divorced man might balk at moving away from such crops which he had planted, and instead, if he could not find a wife within his adopted settlement, might choose to bring a new wife to live with him virilocally.

A similar kind of stress developed in the 1980s when young men began rejecting marriages that would take them away from wage work on the plantation, for example, when the potential wife's settlement was far away, such as on the mainland. Btsisi' males from Carey Island would fret over how they would earn an income if they married a mainland girl and lived uxorilocally.[8] Mainland women were equally concerned about moving to the groom's island village, where potable water was scarce, shops distant and alternatives to plantation work unavailable. Settlement exogamy would require men to sacrifice access to their livelihoods, something many were unwilling to do, resulting in what seems to be the beginnings of a shift in post-marital residence from settlement exogamy to endogamy, or at least residential propinquity in which both the bride and groom were from the island or the mainland.

In 2004 the tendency towards settlement endogamy was increasingly clear among young couples. Oil palm had replaced most other crops, including fruit trees, and, for reasons already discussed, men owned most of the oil palm smallholdings, building their houses in the midst of their smallholdings to facilitate access. Population growth within the settlements made it possible to find an appropriate spouse within the village.

Odo': The Household and the Couple

The household (*odo'*) is the principal socio-economic unit which provides the focus for daily interactions and activities. The married couple forms the focus of the household, with the husband and wife working together as a single unit for the benefit of the household (Nowak 1988, 2004). During a wedding for a never before married couple, the elders bestow on them a married name (*glaw odo'*) (Karim 1980b; Nowak 1987).[9] Thereafter, the community and the couple themselves use this name to address and refer to them both as a couple, as a household and also to them individually instead of by their birth names. The shared name is a reminder that they constitute a single socio-economic unit.

Btsisi' wedding ceremonies highlight the importance of the conjugal couple working in cooperation and sharing. One ritual in a wedding ceremony called *nyampak* (Malay, *nyapang*, "companion"), highlights the symbolic importance of unity among the conjugal pair (cf. Howell 1984; Skeat 1900; Skeat and Blagden 1906; Winstedt 1951). Under the watchful eyes of the community, the couple stands side by side, their arms around each other's shoulders. A woman feeds the couple some glutinous rice, then water followed by a betel quid. She tells the couple that they must share; when one eats the other eats, when one does not, neither does the other. She tells the couple, their arms still around each other's shoulders, to squat down and stand up seven times in unison, urging them to cooperate and coordinate their work. Otherwise, she says, the marriage will come apart, as the squatting and standing exercise would (Nowak 1987). Following the *nyampak*, the male elders, one after the other, lecture the couple on how spouses should treat each other (cf. Logan 1847b; Skeat and Blagden 1906; Williams-Hunt 1952).

Frank Ellis (1998: 5) notes that people's social institutions such as kinship relations and gender play a role in their livelihood choices. A couple must agree on the best activities they can perform to maximize their economic position, as well as allowing for individual needs and preferences. During different domestic stages, a household must strategize their livelihood activities, which frequently means altering their activities to accommodate their situation (Nowak 1987, 2003, 2008).

Filiative-*Opoh*: Parallel Filiative Kindred

In contrast to the deme-*opoh* described above, a filiative-*opoh* is a group of people who are cognatic kin of ego's same sexed parent. In this sense, a woman's *opoh* includes her mother's cognatic kin whereas a man's *opoh* comprised of his father's cognatic kin. Using this definition of *opoh*, a person's opposite sex parent and opposite sex siblings do not belong to ego's *opoh*. In a deme-*opoh* a brother and sister and both parents are in ego's *opoh* while in a filiative-*opoh* they are not.

While marriage creates a couple, it also unites kin groups. After one spouse dies, the survivor's kindred and the deceased's kindred join in a *craay kbuis*, "death divorce", formally terminating the couple's bond and the relationship between the respective kin groups. Many of the wedding rites, from arranging the marriage to the engagement ritual, and the wedding itself require the active participation of members of both kin groups. Before the formal engagement ritual and announcement to the community, the bride and groom each initiate a relationship with a *wali'* (guardian or representative), men in the bride and groom's respective filiative-*opoh*, who is the elder brother of the person's same-sex parent.[10] The *wali*'s role is to represent the interests of his ward and his sibling group in all community proceedings related to the marriage—both before and after the wedding ceremony.

Btsisi' assume that everyone will marry, and extensive genealogical information confirms this expectation. Serial monogamy is the norm, due to high mortality rates and the difficulties of maintaining the tight marital cooperation Btsisi' require for a successful livelihood outcome.[11]

Preferential Marriage Partners

In the 1980s, most first marriages were arranged by senior kin, either parents[12] or more probably grandparents. The prospective spouses rarely resisted, since weddings were so expensive that young people and their parents depended on financial help from their kinfolk. If the children insisted on making their own arrangements, that help will not be forthcoming. Previously married people usually did not face the same hurdles.

Cousin marriage

Btsisi' kinship terminology is "Hawaiian", meaning that the same terms are used for siblings and cousins (Murdock 1949: 160–1). Cousin terminology is by generation, with a peculiarly Aslian variant of distinction by relative age. Ego addresses elder siblings as *ye'*, "elder brother" (reference term *ke'ent*) or *ga'uk*, "elder sister" (reference term *ku'unt*). Younger siblings are *adi'*, from a Malay word, in reference and address. Cousin terminology rests not on the relative ages of ego and alter, but on the relative ages of the linking ancestors. Thus the son of ego's parent's elder brother is called the same as ego's elder brother, and so on.[13]

Elders in the 1980s stated unequivocally that traditionally cousin marriage was *somba'*, a term cognate with Malay words for "incest" and "arrogance". Ethnographers have glossed this term as "incest", which includes sexual misbehaviour among its denotations; but the general sense is of disorderly and disrespectful behaviour between particular categories of people. *Somba' banga* refers to cross-generational marriage and *somba' bois* to marriage within the same generation, typically between cousins, a taboo that extended to ego's second cousins. Third cousins were *lip ket,* distant enough that they were "others". The genealogies I collected in the 1980s indicated that older people, for the most part, had respected these restrictions.

In the marriage ceremony, people sing and dance the *main jo'oh,* around a *busut* (Malay, "mound"), a symbol of the centre of the world (Winstedt 1947: 27, 85), which re-enacts humanity's creation and celebrates the marital pair.[14] The *busut* symbolizes the mountain the original siblings, Pagar Buyuh and Busuh, elder sister and younger brother, circled around following the primordial flood that exterminated humankind. For seven days and seven nights, the siblings circled the mountain in opposite directions looking for marriageable mates, but found they were the only people left. God then permitted them to marry each other. In the *main jo'oh* song and dance cycle, by contrast, men and women circle the *busut* in the same direction, celebrating proper marriage according to the rules of *somba'* (Nowak 2000; Esa 2007).

Despite the traditional rules, some forms of cousin marriage were becoming popular by the 1980s. *Somba'* rules still applied to men who were *adi'* to their potential wives, so that cousin types E, F, G and H in Figure 14.1 were considered bad, but those in which the woman was *adi'* to the man, as in types A, B, C and D, had become acceptable. This change may reflect the increasing tendency for men to want to stay near their wage jobs or fixed assets like coffee and oil palm smallholdings after marriage. Since their cousins probably lived nearby, uxorilocal post-marital residence would not require them to move away.

Moreover, the preferred form of marriage for a man was with his younger patrilateral cross-cousin (Type A), so that both the "older" boy and "younger" girl would be marrying into their respective filiative-*opoh* described above. Following the principle of parallel filiation, a

Figure 14.1 Types of cousin marriage

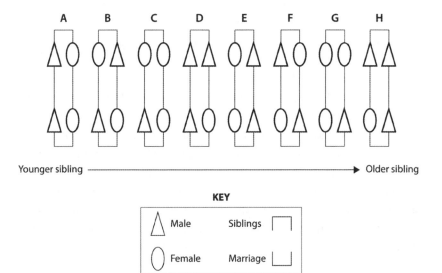

brother and sister belong to different *opoh*, a boy to his father's, a girl to her mother's. While parallel filiation cognitively separates brothers from sisters, and local exogamy keeps them spatially apart, patrilateral cross-cousin marriage reunites their children in marriage and their grandchildren as siblings; thus grandchildren replicate the grandparental brother-sister dyad, as illustrated in Figure 14.2, which I have called kinship involution, whereby the marriage and kinship system turns in on itself. This results in a bifurcate strategy, whereby the sibling pair is fractured only to be reconstituted in the following generation as a conjugal couple and then as a sibling set in the grandchildren's generation. Thus, Btsisi' have found a way to solve the dilemma of the original siblings while continuing to honour them regarding the laws that maintain humanity.

Figure 14.2 Kinship involution

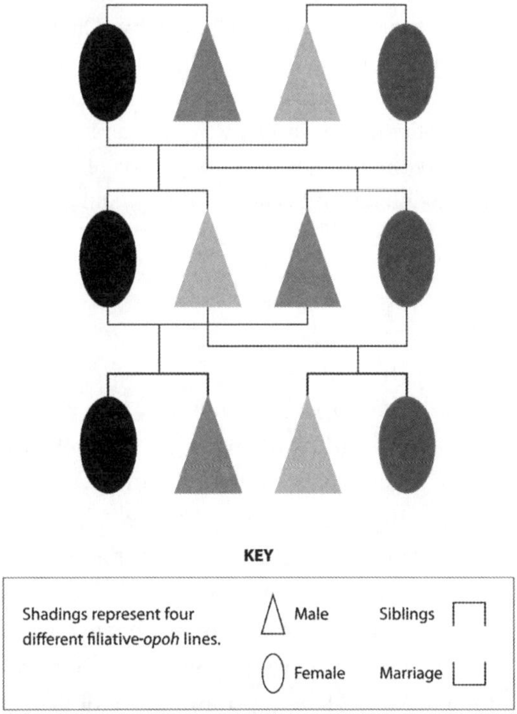

KEY

Shadings represent four different filiative-*opoh* lines.

△ Male △ Female

Siblings ⊓

Marriage ⊔

In the Btsisi' case this bifurcate strategy was implemented by tying inheritance to parallel filiation. Women inherited land and trees from their mothers and men from their fathers. The traditional pattern of settlement exogamy and marital uxorilocality separated men from their land and trees. The new patterns of preferential patrilateral cross-cousin marriage allowed a man to marry into his father's filiative-*opoh* and a woman into her mother's, along with parallel filiation providing a son to claim his father's property and a woman her mother's, results in parental property divided by opposite sexed siblings reunified through the siblings' children's marriage. The house arrangements turn the affinal link into a consanguineal one by turning the progeny of the married couple into siblings, thus reuniting the house. As Carsten and Hugh-Jones (1995: 39) say about house society:

> Married couples eventually produce new sibling sets in their children. These siblings are strongly associated with the unity of the house but are also differentiated by the order of their birth. This is often the basis of rank and hierarchy. On marriage these siblings divide and occupy different houses to begin the cycle anew. Marriage between houses is transformed once again into siblingship within the house. In this way we can see how the house represents not only siblingship but also marriage. In a continuous two-way process, siblingship becomes affinity, and affinity becomes siblingship.

HOUSE SOCIETY

Over the past century, the Btsisi' population has undergone dramatic changes. No longer self-sufficient with an expansive repertoire of livelihood activities, Btsisi' now must rely on generating an income either through commodity production or wage labour activities. Until around 2000, people were able to generate an income from traditional activities like fishing and crabbing, but with the expansion of the plantation, overfishing and pollution there has been a dramatic reduction in resources and a concomitant reduction in livelihood opportunities. No longer able to survive performing these activities, people must now support their households through smallholding oil palm. Establishing new smallholding is no longer feasible due to land scarcity, which means others must find wage work.

Previously, I argued that Btsisi' marriage patterns I observed in the 1980s were a contemporary development which looked very much like what Lévi-Strauss described as a "house" society (1982). Houses are corporate groups controlling material and nonmaterial wealth (titles, land, etc.). Houses use exogamous marriages to capture wealth and endogamy to consolidate wealth; with both strategies occurring simultaneously to achieve success.

The way Btsisi' adapted to the house pattern was to pass land down through parallel filiation; women inherited land from their mothers and men from their fathers. With the traditional marriage pattern of village exogamy and uxorilocality, men would not have remained near their land and trees. With parallel filiation and preferential patrilateral cross cousin marriage, a man married into his father's filiative-*opoh* and a woman into her mother's, thus allowing for the reunification of parental property. Land becomes part of the house's wealth. The house thus attempts to maintain the land as part of its endowment for future generations. It does so by turning the affinal link into a consanguineal one by turning the progeny of the married couple into siblings thus reuniting the house.

More recently this brilliant and subtle strategy seems to be drifting back to village endogamy, with land more likely coming under the control of men. Arranged marriage seems to be dying out, and with it, patrilateral cross cousin marriage. While these findings are tentative, they highlight the fact that Btsisi' continue to demonstrate enormous flexibility to adapt to new situations.

NOTES

1. Field research with Btsisi' of Carey Island and Sepang in 1980–81 was conducted with support from the State University of Buffalo Graduate Research Fund. Short visits in the 1980s were with assistance from Grinnell College, in the 1990s from Massey University and in 2006 from the Asia Research Institute, National University of Singapore. I wish to thank the JHEOA, *Jabatan Hal Ehwal Orang Asli*, now called JAKOA, *Jabatan Kemajuan Orang Asli*, the Malay-run government

agency which controls access to Orang Asli communities, for allowing me to work with Btsisi'. I would also like to thank Robert Dentan, Kirk Endicott and Peter Laird for reading earlier drafts of this chapter and providing helpful suggestions.

2. The Btsisi' traditional name for Pulau Carey is Pulau Gobok ("Mosquito Island").

3. The estate had a variety of owners under different names: from Pataling Rubber Estates to Jugra Land & Rubber Estates, then Harrison & Crosfield until it was sold to Golden Hope in 1982, which was later sold to Sime Darby.

4. Oil palm yields vary with the season. In the rainy season yields are higher and harvesters are paid more since their income is based on weight.

5. While supplied with boots and other protective gear, women said they did not wear them because it was too hot in the clothing.

6. In 2004, when I took a boat ride in the mangroves, I saw more wildlife, such as crab eating macaques, than I had ever seen. Btsisi' attributed this to the loss of the monkeys' habitat forcing them to become more visible along the mudflats.

7. The RSPO (2013) defines a smallholder as: "Farmers growing oil palm, sometimes along with subsistence production of other crops, where the family provides the majority of labour and the farm provides the principal source of income, and where the planted area of oil palm is usually below 50 hectares in size."

8. There was also a concern over mainland girls' morals.

9. According to Skeat and Blagden (1906, II: 655), the term for marriage, *kuyn-hodong*, was a composite word made up of the words husband (*kuyn*) and wife (*hodong*). It is interesting to note that in 1980 the term for household and marital couple was *odo'*, the term Skeat and Blagden defined as meaning "wife".

10. Sometimes a man may be *wali* to both bride and groom, notably in the case of patrilateral cross-cousin marriage.

11. Polygyny is acceptable although it rarely lasts except sororal polygyny, because two sisters cannot be angry with each other.

12. Fathers avoid a formal role in the decision-making process of who their daughters should marry for fear of being implicated in prostituting their daughters.

13. Karim (1980b: 140) states that only when a girl is the child of an older male sibling or a boy is the child of a younger male sibling was marriage avoided.

REFERENCES

Ayampillay, S.D.
  1976   Kampung Tanjung Sepat: A Besese (Mah Mei) Community of Coastal Selangor. Social Anthropology Section, Report No. 6. Pulau Pinang, Malaysia: Universiti Sains Malaysia.

Aziz, S.A., G. Clements, D.M. Rayan and P. Sankar
  2013   Why Conservationists Should Be Concerned About Natural Resource Legislation Affecting Indigenous Peoples' Rights: Lessons from Peninsular Malaysia. Biodiversity Conservation 12: 639–56.

Beckford, G.
  1972   Persistent Poverty: Underdevelopment in Plantation Economies of the Third World. London: Zed Press.

Carsten, J. and S. Hugh-Jones, eds.
  1995   About the House: Levi-Strauss and Beyond. New York: Cambridge University Press.

Center for Orang Asli Concerns
  2011   Mah Meri—The River Must Flow. http://www.youtube.com/watch?v=Y7QnpJPbXBc, accessed 12 June 2013.

Chomsky, A.
  1996   West Indian Workers and the United Fruit Company in Costa Rica 1870–1940. Baton Rouge: Louisiana State University Press.

Dallos, C.
  2011   From Equality to Inequality: Social Change among Newly Sedentary Lanoh Hunter-Gatherer Traders of Peninsular Malaysia. Toronto: University of Toronto Press.

Dentan, R.K.
  1968   The Semai: A Nonviolent People of Malaya. New York: Holt, Rinehart and Winston.
  1971   Some Senoi Semai Planting Techniques. Economic Botany 25: 136–59.
  1975   Fieldwork notes.

Devi, N. and J. Seabrook
  2000   Voices From the Ground: There are No Rich Fishermen Here… *In* Tanah Air Ku: Land Issues in Malaysia: Based on CAP's National Conference, Land: Emerging Issues and Challenges. Pp. 63–4. Penang: Consumer Association of Penang.

Doolittle, A.
    2005   Property and Politics in Sabah, Malaysia: Native Struggles Over
            Land Rights. Seattle: University of Washington Press.
Ellis, F.
    1998   Household Strategies and Rural Livelihood Diversification. The
            Journal of Development Studies 35(1): 1–38.
Endicott, K.
    1979   The Hunting Methods of the Batek Negritos of Malaysia: A
            Problem of Alternatives. Canberra Anthropology 2(2): 7–22.
Esa, Rashid.
    2007   Bunga Moyang: Seni Lipatan Daun Mah Meri. Siri Buku Seni
            Kraf Orang Asli. Kuala Lumpur: Kementerian Kebudayaan
            Kesenian dan Warisan Malaysia.
Eversole, R., J-A. McNeish and A. Cimadamore, eds.
    2005   Indigenous Peoples & Poverty: An International Perspective.
            London: Zed Books.
Gomes, A.
    2004   Looking for Money: Capitalism and Modernity in an Orang
            Asli Village. Subang Jaya, Malaysia: Center for Orang Asli
            Concerns.
    2007   Modernity and Malaysia: Settling the Menraq Forest Nomads.
            New York: Routledge.
Howell, S.
    1984   Society and Cosmos: Chewong of Peninsular Malaysia. Singapore:
            Oxford University Press.
Juli Edo
    2002   Traditional Alliances: Contact Between the Semais and the Malay
            State in Pre-Modern Perak. *In* Tribal Communities in the Malay
            World: Historical, Cultural and Social Perspectives. G. Benjamin
            and C. Chou, eds. Pp. 160–84. Singapore: Institute of Southeast
            Asian Studies.
Juli Edo, A. Williams-Hunt and R.K. Dentan
    2009   Surrender, Peacekeeping and Internal Colonialism: A Malaysian
            Instance. Bijdragen tot de Taal-, Land- en Volkenkunde 165(2/3):
            216–40.
Karim, W-J.
    1980a   The Nature of Kinship in Ma' Betisek Villages with an Introduction
            to the Ma' Betisek of Peninsular Malaysia. Federation Museums
            Journal 25 (new series): 119–35.

1980b The Affinal Bond: A Review of Ma' Betisek Marriages on Carey Island. Federation Museums Journal 25 (new series): 137–50.

1981 Ma' Betisek Concepts of Living Things. New Jersey: Humanities Press.

Lévi-Strauss, C.

1982 The Way of the Masks. Trans. S. Modelski. Vancouver: Douglas & McIntyre.

Logan, J.R.

1847a The Orang Binua of Johore. Journal of the Indian Archipelago and Eastern Asia 1(18): 242–93.

1847b The Ethnology of the Johore Archipelago. Journal of the Indian Archipelago and Eastern Asia 1(26): 336–40.

Murdock, G.P.

1949 Social Structure. New York: Macmillan Company.

Murray, C.

2001 Livelihood Research: Some Conceptual and Methodological Issues. Background Paper 5, Chronic Poverty Research Centre. http://papers.ssrn.com/sol3/papers.cfm?abstract_id=1754541, accessed Oct. 2003.

Nicholas, C.

2000 The Orang Asli and the Contest for Resources: Indigenous Politics, Development and Identity in Peninsular Malaysia. Copenhagen: IWGIA.

Nobuta Toshihiro

2009 Living on the Periphery: Development and Islamization among the Orang Asli in Malaysia. Subang Jaya, Malaysia: Center for Orang Asli Concerns.

Nowak, B.S.

1985 The Formation of Aboriginal Reserves: The Effects of Land Loss on the Btsisi' of Peninsular Malaysia. *In* Modernization and the Emergence of a Landless Peasantry: Essays on the Integration of Peripheries to Socioeconomic Center. G.N. Appell, ed. Studies in Third World Societies 33: 85–110.

1987 Marriage and Household: Btsisi' Response to a Changing World. Unpublished PhD dissertation, State University of New York at Buffalo.

1988 The Cooperative Nature of Women's and Men's Roles in Btsisi' Marine Activities. *In* Women in Fishing Economies. J. Nadel-Klein and D. Davis, eds. Pp. 51–72. Newfoundland: Institute of Social and Economic Research, Memorial University of Newfoundland.

2000   Dancing the Main Jo'oh: Hma' Btsisi' Celebrate their Humanity and Religious Identity in a Malaysian World. The Australian Journal of Anthropology 1(3): 333–44.

2003   Livelihood Diversification: Optimising Livelihood Strategies among Hma' Btsisi' Households of Peninsular Malaysia. *In* Proceedings of the 3rd Biannual Aotearoa/New Zealand International Dev-Net Conference. D. Storey, J. Overton and B.S. Nowak, eds. Pp. 294–308.

2004   Hma' Btsisi'. *In* Encyclopedia of Sex and Gender: Men and Women in the World Cultures. C. Ember and M. Ember, eds. Pp. 443–51. New York: Kluwer Academic/Plenum.

2005   A Comparative Examination of the Local Socio-Cultural and Environmental Impact of the Global Oil Palm Industry. *In* Proceedings of the 4th Bi-annual Aotearoa/New Zealand International Dev-Net Conference. K. Jackson, N. Lewis, S. Adams, and M. Morten, eds. Pp. 76–81.

2008   Environmental Degradation and its Gendered Impact on Coastal Livelihood Options among Btsisi' of Peninsular Malaysia. Development 51(3): 186–92.

Pretty, J., I. Gujit, I. Scoones and J. Thompson
1995   A Trainer's Guide for Participatory Learning and Action. IIED Participatory Methodology Series, Sustainable Agriculture Programme. London: International Institute for Environment and Development.

Rahim, R.
2007   Chita' Hae: Culture, Crafts and Customs of the Hma' Meri in Kampung Sungai Bumbon, Pulau Carey. Kuala Lumpur: Center for Orang Asli Concerns.

Roundtable on Sustainable Palm Oil, Smallholders: Definition. http://www.rspo.org/en/definition, accessed Oct. 2013.

Saith, A.
1992   The Rural Non-farm Economy: Processes and Policies. Geneva: International Labour Organization, World Employment Programme.

Skeat, W.W.
1900   Malay Magic: An Introduction to the Folklore and Popular Religion of the Malay Peninsula. New York: Benjamin Blom.

Skeat, W.W. and C.O. Blagden
1906 Pagan Races of the Malay Peninsula. Vol. 2. London: Frank Cass.

Thomas-Slayter, B., R. Polestico, A.L. Esser, O. Taylor and E. Mutua
1995 A Manual for Socio-Economic and Gender Analysis: Responding to the Development Challenge. USA: EcoGen.

Williams-Hunt, P.D.R.
1952 An Introduction to Malaysian Aborigines. Kuala Lumpur: Government Press.

Winstedt, R.O.
1947 The Malays: A Cultural History. London: Routledge and Kegan Paul.
1951 The Malay Magician: Being Shaman, Saiva and Sufi. London: Routledge and Kegan Paul.

chapter 15

Hazard, Risk and Fascination: Jahai Perceptions of Morality and Otherness in a Global World

Diana Riboli

INTRODUCTION

The aim of this chapter is to describe how the Jahai cope with their perceptions of hazard, risk and uncertainty coming from a world outside their ethnic group and the Orang Asli in general. The chapter argues that among peoples maintaining many of the characteristics of egalitarian social structure, hazard and risk, on the one hand, and fascination, on the other, create a sense of uncertainty. These sentiments are shaped by the differences and conflicts between different moralities and worldviews.

My long-term, multi-sited research takes place in the states of Pahang and Kelantan, with Batek and Jahai populations.[1] However, the case study presented in this chapter is entirely based on my research in Rual, Kelantan in northeastern Peninsular Malaysia, where formerly nomadic Orang Asli groups (mostly Jahai) living in the area were resettled in permanent villages by a government agency in the early 1970s. Despite the fact that the population can now be considered sedentary, they maintain many of the characteristics of typical hunter-gatherer social organization. Although rapid social change is taking place, they still lack centralized political power and hierarchy, and egalitarianism and gender equality are still strong. Social order is ensured by moral obligations, such as sharing, and by a long list of taboos (*lawac, telan*).

Despite the fact that the Orang Asli have probably never been totally isolated in their long history, especially during the last decade or so, their current degree of exposure to the outside world is unprecedented. In fact, they are called upon to respond/react to many major challenges and changes coming not only from other cultures and groups inhabiting Malaysia, but also from the globalized world (see also Tacey, this volume). New technologies, environmental pollution and politics, biomedicine, the lifestyle of the dominant culture, and western habits are perceived and experienced with a combination of fear and fascination. These tensions are particularly—but not exclusively—embodied in the younger generations.

Plate 15.1 Jahai women and kids at Kampung Rual, 2008

(Photo credit: Diana Riboli)

MORALITY, CULTURAL VALUES AND RISK

The well-being and psychophysical state of the Jahai, as well as of many indigenous groups the world over, are undoubtedly threatened by factors that have to do with "modernity" and the market economy. During recent decades, many anthropological works have focused on the common threats to native cultures. These include lack of land rights, environmental pollution, discrimination, racism, violence, inequality, poverty, human rights violations, epidemics and poor health. From these studies it becomes apparent that the conflictual and/or unbalanced relations with other national groups, as well as the inevitable encounter with the global world, contribute to the increase in what is defined as "social suffering" (Kleinman, Das and Lock 1997). Social suffering among indigenous peoples becomes dramatically tangible, first of all, in the increase of conditions like stress, depression and bad health, in an era when—on the contrary—technological and biomedical innovations should assure better living standards compared to the past.

In many parts of the world, racial, political and religious discrimination in accessing primary sources of livelihood, education and health facilities are the main causes of social suffering. Even in countries where some rights are granted and services provided, albeit in a "mediocre" fashion, the situation does not improve (see, for example, Dentan et al. 1997: 129 on the limitations of Orang Asli health care). In my opinion, the pivotal role of the moral world and cultural values, which shape the worldview of different groups, is still partly overlooked.

Jahai perceptions of the Otherness of members of the national or transnational outside world, are, first of all, not solely related to what is allowed or forbidden in a specific culture as expressed on an everyday, material level, such as what is suitable to eat or wear. In reality, all the "visible" or "tangible" aspects of Otherness stem from different moral and cultural values systems. In the words of Joel Robbins:

> I take cultural values to be cultural conceptions of the good or desirable. More than this, I also take them to be those cultural conceptions that arrange other cultural elements (such as cultural ideas about persons, kinds of actions, things, etc.) into hierarchies of better and worse or more and less desirable. (2012: 120)

Despite the fact that the terms morality and ethics are sometimes used as synonyms, I prefer to adopt Quetzil Castañeda's approach, according to which:

> [morality and ethics] ... can be placed in a hierarchical relation in which morals refer to a larger field of imperatives, norms, rights, duties, and criteria, whereas ethics refers to the application or embodiment of these principles in action or in the evaluation of action. Thus, in this usage, the term *morals* references social group and *ethics* the individual. (2006: 123)

The encounter with systems based on different or even opposing cultural values is experienced with a sense of uncertainty and fear. The perception is that this encounter is hazardous, potentially able to cause harm to the personal and/or social bodies. Hazard and therefore the fear of serious threat, opens the way to the risk dimension. In the words of Jakob Arnoldi:

> Risks are not *actual* but rather *potential* dangers ... risk is the opposite of pure chance, because it involves human agency. For the same reason it is also the opposite of random acts of nature. What we often refer to as natural causes is something that suspends human responsibility.... But when humans can be held responsible, risk emerges. (2009: 8–9)

Since the pioneering studies on risk (Douglas and Wildavsky 1982) and "risk societies" (Beck 1992 [1986]), this term is mostly used for capitalistic societies living in "high modernity" (Giddens 1991), while for non-industrial cultures the debate is more focused on danger. In this perspective, terrorism or nuclear power plants are risks, while a violent storm or the attack of a wild animal are dangers.

Actually, according to my studies, not only danger but also hazard and risk are—nowadays—important components of Jahai life. Danger was always a well-known dimension for them, while hazard and risk are connected to political, social, economic and cultural pressures, and to the conflicts resulting from the clash between different moral systems.

As mentioned above, Jahai cultural values and their general moral system are similar to those of other tropical forest dwelling foraging peoples of the world. Their life and culture are deeply intertwined with the rainforest and its non-human creatures. In recent decades, anthropological studies and debates have attempted to engage in a re-theorization of the famous nature-culture dichotomy and of the term animism, used to describe indigenous religions (Descola 1996, 2005; Bird-David 1999; Ingold 2000; Harvey 2005; Viveiros de Castro 2005). This term is particularly problematic when used within an evolutionary theory framework, as the precursor to "higher" forms of religion. What becomes clear from the study of indigenous cultures worldwide, including Jahai culture, is that "nature and culture are part of the same socio-cosmic field" (Viveiros de Castro 2005: 48) and that personhood in these systems "is open equally to human and non-human animal (and even non-animal kinds)" (Ingold 2000: 48). Respect for beings that are not human, a complex relational network and sense of brotherhood with such beings constitute the main difference between indigenous and non-indigenous perceptions not only of the natural, but also of the "moral" environment and world. The Jahai do not recognize a dichotomy or strict hierarchical relation between nature and culture or human and "other-than-human persons" (Hallowell 1960). In this sense their belief system can be considered animistic. Among the Jahai, great emphasis is put only on the difference—which often turns into a conflict—between the forest (*hep*) and the non-forest.

The forest is by no means perceived only as nature in the ecological sense of the word. The interpersonal, emotional and social relations with human and other-than-human persons with whom the Jahai feel they share the sense of belonging to the forest, constitute the fundaments of their worldview, morality, and the related concept of well-being. On the other hand, the non-forest is mainly understood as a foreign world that is ruled by very different—and therefore often incomprehensible—cultural values. I do not mean to imply that Jahai culture is static, a small and charming fossil trapped within modernity. All cultures are continually undergoing socio-cultural change, and the Orang Asli are not an exception. As brilliantly observed by Tim Ingold, if people were constrained to replicate a fixed pattern, "the effect would be similar to that of a needle becoming stuck in the groove of a record" (2000: 148). Music could not go on. But, despite the many more or less traumatic external and internal changes, it should not be forgotten that *"cultures have hearts"* (Sissons 2005: 33, italics in original), basically meaning that specific moral values continue to beat at the core of every culture. But "beatings" linked to different systems are often difficult to synchronize. In a not ethnocentric and hierarchical perspective the sound of these beatings is equally important to humanity, but possible problems and conflicts arise when a more powerful (socially, politically, economically and/or religiously) system intends to predominate over the other.

SHAMANISM, BIOMEDICINE AND BLACK MAGIC: INEQUALITY, RISK AND FEAR IN RUAL

Introduction

In this section I will present a clarifying case study highlighting the onset of inequality and risk perceptions among the Jahai of Rual, related to their acceptation and/or rejection of national and transnational cultures' different moral worldviews.

In 2006 I conducted my first fieldwork in Rual. This resettlement includes three villages (Kampung Rual, Kampung Manok and Kampung Kalok) and is inhabited mostly by Jahai, despite the fact that some members of other Orang Asli groups live in the community as a result of intermarriages. As pointed out by Alberto Gomes, a certain "ambiguity of ethnicity" (2007: 24) can be observed, as almost everybody claims to be a Jahai, even if one or both of his/her parents belong to a different group. For this reason, he prefers to use the more general term Menraq, a common Northern Aslian term for "human being", for the population of Rual.

Kelantan is the most conservative Muslim state in Peninsular Malaysia, and the Orang Asli resettlement is surrounded by Malay villages and small towns, where even the Chinese and Indian Malaysians form small minorities in the predominantly Malay population.

Most of the inhabitants of Rual have nominally converted to Islam. The Islamization policy of the government, which aims to assimilate Orang Asli groups into the Malay culture, started in the eighties, but it was kept almost secret until the nineties (Nobuta 2009: 38; see also Juli and Solahimi Fadzil, this volume). The reasons the Rual Jahai became Muslims are multiple: first of all, they felt fear and a sense of discomfort at residing in a Muslim neighbourhood, where the Orang Asli used to be (and, to an extent, still are) considered backward and primitive. Secondly, they hope for a better future generated by the governmental "positive discrimination" policy granting material, economical and educational benefits to Orang Asli who become Muslims (Dentan et al. 1997: 144–5). Recently, a new reason for being Muslim arose among the young generations, which stems from a combination of the above-mentioned two. Despite the still limited acceptance of Muslim rules, over the last three years or so I observed that young unmarried girls cover their hair and neck with the veil (*tudung*) not only at school, as in the past, but also during their free time, especially when walking around in the evening. The veil itself does not seem to refer to the religious faith, but more to the

Plate 15.2 Jahai women at Kampung Rual, 2008

(Photo credit: Diana Riboli)

idea of becoming a "visible" part of the dominant culture. Teenagers now consider the *tudung*—as well as the Malay female long dress (*baju kurung*)—important beauty accessories, which allow them to be more charming and modern. This—perhaps superficial—change was quite rapid, considering that, during my first visit, only one young man was strictly following the Islamic precepts, and, because of his observance of Muslim rules and customs, his friends were teasing him, calling him "*orang Perancis*", "the Frenchman", to underline his alien behaviour.

Equality and Inequality

In recent decades, the Jahai, like the Lanoh, another Semang group (Dallos 2011: 213), have experienced increasing social inequality, despite continuing to espouse an "egalitarian ethic". Of course, egalitarianism does not mean that there are no differentiations between, for example, the female and male worlds or between the younger and elder generations, but the fact is that globalization, the entrance into the market economy and the different levels of Jahai participation or assimilation into Malay culture are transforming differentiation into inequality.

In recent years, Jahai women, like women in some other Orang Asli groups (Gianno 2006: 106; Howell 2006: 88–9; Endicott and Endicott 2008: 145), have been losing their autonomy as they participate less in fundamental tasks, such as fishing and gathering, which fulfil the basic needs of the group (Gomes 2007: 137). In Rual, most of the profitable activities, such as the collection and trade of rattan and other valuable products of the forest, became male prerogatives. During my first visits in 2006, 2007 and 2008, women often gathered and fished in the forest. In fact, their expeditions outside the villages were particularly pleasant and sought out occasions not only for food gathering, but also for chatting about female topics and performing ceremonies mostly conducted by the traditional midwives (*bidan*). While in the forest, and especially during trips to waterfalls, which are particularly important places in Jahai culture, the women often told me that they felt happy and strong being in an environment that, unlike the villages, allowed them to be totally free and independent.

Plate 15.3 Jahai women fishing at Kampung Rual, 2006

(Photo credit: Diana Riboli)

Entering the forest, women basically re-adopt the important rules of their traditional moral code, which they are forced to modify or hide while in the villages. Probably one of the most important rules is to somehow become part of the forest, wearing fewer clothes and adorning body and hair with leaves and flowers. This action is fundamental in Jahai culture, to show respect and brotherhood for the forest and its non-human beings. Therefore, it strengthens the bonds with the world of the rainforest, while for Islam beautifying the body with ornaments is a sin. Even during my initial field trips the women removed the flowers and the leaves from their hair and waist before entering the village, as they were afraid of being accused of practising black magic by *gob* (foreigner, outsiders). The women's expeditions into the forest drastically declined since 2008, mainly because of the risk of sexual harassment. Women are afraid of encountering dangerous poachers, male seasonal workers—mostly Thais and Cambodians—who work in the plantations which surround Rual—as well as other *gob*.

During my most recent visit to Rual in 2012, with Ivan Tacey, women could no longer go to the waterfall in the proximity of their resettlements, since it is now surrounded by a new plantation belonging to a Chinese man. Most of the time, women are now "trapped" in their villages, taking care of the house and children and financially dependent upon their husbands. Currently, one of the main daily activities is watching Bollywood, Malay and other foreign movies. More often than not, these are rented from vendors who periodically visit Orang Asli villages in their vehicles, selling goods at quite high prices. While young girls are particularly fascinated by the rich Bollywood dancers' costumes and jewellery, boys are captivated by the powerful motorcycles, cars and weapons and by the violent actions in Asian and Western movies. In the last three years, the number of motorcycles and cars in the resettlement has multiplied. As a consequence, parents are now very concerned about the safety of their youngest children, who, until recently, were free to roam around alone, especially after a few—luckily not lethal—accidents. Boys try to impress girls by imitating the dangerous driving they see in the movies, and, when scolded by adults, they regard them as backward and not modern enough.

Through the years, I have also observed other events that denote an increase in inequalities and transcend the traditional social differentiation between younger and older generations. In 2006 and 2007, after obtaining a microphone, an amplifier and two powerful speakers from the JAKOA (*Jabatan Kemajuan Orang Asli* or Department of Orang Asli Development), people of all ages gathered in Rual almost every evening to play, sing and dance traditional Jahai or Orang Asli music and songs. These were very important occasions in terms of social cohesion; they were events during which people could share opinions, emotions and a sense of unity and belonging to the group. One year later, community elders no longer took part in the evening gatherings. Only teenagers used the electronic equipment to sing pop Malay songs and karaoke, while older people started to complain about the annoying noise. Due to the breakdown of the audio equipment, from 2009 onwards, people no longer held such gatherings. However, the distance between the young and elders remains.

Nowadays, among the younger generation, the tension between the sense of belonging to the group (deeply rooted on conscious and unconscious levels), their fascination with the habits of the dominant culture (superficially adopted and accepted, mostly on a bodily level), and, last but not least, the strong attraction towards foreign transnational habits promulgated in American and Asian (mostly B) movies (desired and envied, active on a imaginary level) increase a deep sense of uncertainty, which can lead to a problematic or even displaced identity construction process (Riboli 2013; Tacey 2013).

Health, Illness, Danger and Risk: New Concerns

Different moral perceptions, evaluations and worldviews—sometimes antagonistic, sometimes just opposite—are responsible for the rise of conflictual situations and not only in the young generation. This is evident when analyzing Jahai concepts of health and illness and related perceptions of uncertainty, danger, hazard and risk.

In Rual most families live below the poverty level, and the sanitary conditions are very precarious, first of all, because of environmental and water pollution. Child mortality rate is particularly high as are incidences of diseases, such as hepatitis A and B and tuberculosis. Most people are affected by dermatological and/or gastroenterological problems, which can be lethal, especially in young children. Many health problems are due to the consumption of polluted water, since the rivers in the proximity of the resettlements are dirty and probably contaminated with pesticides used in the nearby palm oil and rubber plantations.

Poor health conditions, malnutrition and diseases are not new threats to Jahai wellbeing (Gomes 2007: 157–62), but, throughout the years, I have observed a considerable increase in anxiety and depression —particularly evident in women—although widespread among the entire population.

In Jahai culture there are no specific references to evil spirits; nothing in the forest is considered evil. Of course, people are fully aware that, for example, animals and plants can be dangerous. The belief system, which permeates all aspects of their ontology and life, is not only animistic (not in the evolutionary sense of the term, as I have explained before), but also shamanic in nature. The people's cosmology and worldview features deep bonds and interrelations with the rainforest, natural phenomena, not-human and other-than-human beings and entities. Balance among all these spheres is the essential prerequisite for well-being, while unbalance corresponds to a state of suffering and illness, which can be healed only by shamans (see Gianno; Laird; Tacey, this volume).

The most powerful other-than-human person, known by different names among different groups (Endicott 1979: 163–8; Howell 1984: 79; Roseman 1991: 137; Lye 2005: 1, 28; Gomes 2007: 38–9; Dentan 2009: 68; Riboli 2013: 139–42; Tacey 2013: 244–9) is Karei: the master of thunder and thunderstorms, living in solitude somewhere in the sky or—according to other versions—on the peak of a jungle mountain. Karei is a distant figure, his only role being that of a punisher. He is irascible and manifests his anger and rage by sending devastating thunderstorms to humans. But even Karei, although deeply feared and respected by the Jahai, is not considered an evil being. The explanation is that, having great power, he is not able to control his feelings and—for this reason—his punishments are sometimes out of proportion, "a non-human example of the danger of uncontrolled anger" (van der Sluys 2006: 50). While his anger is sometimes undeserved, normally it explodes when human beings violate one of the numerous taboos that regulate the social life of the group and relations with the natural world. It is interesting to note that, recently, a relevant change in the perception of taboos has occurred. While many taboos are still related to the traditional lifestyle and moral code, which relates the human group to the forest and its creatures, for a few years now, great importance is attributed to the prohibition on mixing products of the forest with products coming from the world outside it, such as cooking processed and/or cultivated food with game, wild fruits and vegetables and honey (Riboli 2010, 2012; Tacey 2013). The consumption of non-forest food, which is inevitable nowadays, is perceived as a betrayal of the purity of the forest, a behaviour severely forbidden by the Jahai moral code, which can be very risky for the health.

The psychophysical conditions of the population are deteriorating, and combined with the everyday survival problems, people believe that everything is getting worse. For the last few years, there have been no *halak* (shamans) in the villages. There still are people who know magical spells (*jampi*) and traditional midwives (*bidan*), but they are skilled only in the treatment of minor problems. They certainly are not strong enough to deal with the increasing fear of black magic and ghost sickness. Only *halak*, in constant interrelation with the human and non-human spheres, had received very powerful therapeutic songs in dreams and—as in other shamanic cultures—they also played key roles as custodians of cultural values and guardians of the moral world. Thus shamans could face problems and states of imbalance threatening the sense of safety, morality and social justice.

Nowadays, illnesses are often believed to be caused by the aforementioned mixing of wild with cultivated and processed products and by attacks both on physical and magical levels. Illnesses are also connected to the concept of "evil" which—in turn—is most of the time related to the negative influence and actions of the *gob*.

The government is supposed to provide medical care and medicines for free to Orang Asli groups, and, in Rual, medical personnel visit the villages at least twice a month. But the Jahai were always suspicious of nurses and doctors because they are *gob*, Muslim Malays; so the Jahai are scared and hesitant to ask them for help. However, it should be noted that in the beginning the Jahai had high hopes for the promise of biomedicine. During the first years I visited the villages everybody was asking me for painkillers, mostly paracetamol, which

Plate 15.4 Jahai traditional midwives at Kampung Rual, 2006

(Photo credit: Diana Riboli)

they consider effective for all kinds of conditions (Riboli 2010). Over the years, however, trust in biomedicine declined, while quite new concerns related to black magic rose, causing a state of deep anxiety and suffering.

It should be noted that, in any case, the remedies of biomedicine were always perceived as treating only the symptoms, not the real cause(s), which are often not related solely to a physical condition. Only a *halak* could discover and deal with the true cause, whatever it might be, restoring the necessary balance between the bodily, personal, social, moral, human and non-human spheres.

In addition to recent changes in the perception of taboos, an important change has occurred in the perception of illnesses and sicknesses in general. Previously, according to the population of Rual, most diseases—such as malaria, dermatological problems, dengue fever and so on—were considered quite natural occurrences in human life. The forest provided remedies in the form of medicinal plants, and shamans and midwives knew healing spells and rituals. This is no longer the case.

Logging and pollution have had rapid and dramatic consequences for the natural environment and animal and plant species, rendering the search for medicinal plants more difficult and risky. While many plants are no longer readily available, or are not available at all, it must also be noted that other plant species, especially those with supposed aphrodisiac properties, are used in many Asian medical systems and are now traded mostly to Malays, Chinese and, recently, Pakistanis. This trade—a male activity—represents an important source of income for many families of Rual. But the money earned from such trade is mostly used for purchasing electronic devices such as mobile phones and televisions, rather than being used for the internal needs of the group.

Because of the deterioration of the environment and the increase in very serious diseases such as tuberculosis and hepatitis—for which, according to my informants, the forest does not have remedies to offer—the population of Rual gradually stopped attributing diseases to natural causes or the infraction of the traditional Jahai taboos or moral code. In fact, in recent years, the predominant perception is that *gob* black magic, dangerous ghosts and entities which belong to Malay or other outsiders' beliefs systems, are the causes hidden behind a wide range of diseases.

Fear is now tangible in Kampung Rual: fear of evil creatures and dark powers coming from outside, which are hostile to the world of the rainforest and its human and non-human inhabitants. The frequent illnesses are now interpreted in terms of magical attacks by dark shamans from other ethnic groups. The Jahai use the Malay term *bomoh* instead of *halak* when talking of shamans skilled in black magic. In Malaysia and Indonesia *bomoh* are shamans and healers who are often believed to be skilled in both white and black magic, linked to agricultural and urban environments. On the contrary, *halak*—to whom people of Rual do not attribute black magic skills—are deeply connected with the forest, wild animals and plants (Riboli 2009).

Because of the deterioration of health conditions in the last two or three years, the Jahai have started to believe that powerful *bomoh* insert black magic in the pills and tablets that doctors and nurses distribute in the villages. This new concern is due to the fact that—despite the efforts of governmental officers to convince them that biomedicine is "modernity" and is able to treat all kinds of sickness—in reality more and more people are getting sick or dying. Similarly, fear of being under violent magical attack is now making people suspicious of rice and other foods that they do not cultivate themselves. The new taboos regarding the prohibition of mixing products of the forest with products from outside are becoming stricter. Moreover, the health risks are no longer only in the "mixing" process, but also in the foods themselves, which are often consumed by everybody (and particularly by kids at school) on a daily basis.

Midwives and folk healers who recite spells can "feel" and recognize the black magic inside medicines or rice, but they are not strong enough to fight or destroy it. Only a *halak* could do that. In fact, the Jahai hold the *halak* to be more powerful than the Malay *bomoh*, since *halak* have the strongest power—that of the rainforest. From another point of view, the Malay neighbours, who are equally afraid of black magic, often consider the Jahai's deep links with the forest, consumption of wild products and—last but not least—the very dark colour of their hair and skin as possible signs of occult and harmful magical knowledge. Again, the clash between forest and non-forest manifests itself in the form of a conflict between two distinct worldviews and moral worlds, which direct similar weapons and accusations at each other.

Risk and fear not only refer to *bomoh*'s, and therefore human's, black magic, but also to dangerous ghosts and evil spirits. In Rual, people rarely approach the *surau* (Muslim prayer room) built by the government, especially at night, since many people report that they have seen a frightening ghost there, one similar to a very tall white female figure with long nails and teeth. The image resembles the *pontianak* of the Malay tradition, believed to be the dangerous ghost of a woman who died during delivery. Many illnesses and misfortunes are now believed to be caused by ghosts. In Rual, Jahai always use the Malay term *hantu* (ghost) to define these harmful beings. During my last visit, many witnesses told me that, just a few months before, a headless ghost attacked a young man in broad daylight, while he was walking with his companions on the main road that connects the three villages. The man fell to the ground, bleeding heavily from his mouth, nose and ears. He died within a few minutes. Bloodthirsty headless ghosts are central figures in many Malay and other Asian ghost stories and movies, but were not found among Jahai beliefs until recently.

CONCLUSION

Herein lies the paradox: Malaysia is rapidly moving toward "modernity", with the goal of becoming a self-sufficient industrialized nation by the year 2020 (*Wawasan* 2020). The country, where medical tourism is quickly expanding, provides cutting-edge medical technologies and facilities, which attract people worldwide. At the same time the health of people in Rual has deteriorated, and they see themselves as beset by evil beings, dangerous ghosts, black magic, dark shamans and images promoting inequality, thus causing a sense of uncertainty and anxiety.

The clash between the Jahai moral world, which connects their egalitarian social system to the local natural environment and its non-human beings, and the very different cultural, social and religious values of outsiders is the real cause of the dramatic social changes and collective psychological stress of the Rual Jahai. In recent years, taking a medicine or eating food that has been processed and/or cultivated outside the resettlement is not only perceived as a danger, but also as a risk, as it could be contaminated by unpredictable hazards like black magic. Risk is much more elusive than danger and, therefore, much more stressful. It is so stressful that it is now acquiring a tangible form as the terrifying apparitions of murderous monsters and ghosts. For thousands of years, dangers have been constant threats in Jahai's lives, while risk—for which a specific word in Jahai does not exist—is quite new and poorly understood. A snake bite or falling from a tree can be dangerous, but to eat rice or treat a sickness with antibiotic pills is risky. The difference lies in the fact that danger is well-known, and therefore can be calculated in advance. For the population of Rual, dangers rarely have any evil connotation, which is—on the contrary—intrinsic in risk.

The health and psychophysical problems are exacerbated by the sense of helplessness, as people believe that only a powerful *halak* could restore their well-being. The decreasing number of shamans, along with the destruction and pollution of the forest—which creates an open wound in the local environment and cultural values system—leave the Jahai feeling unprotected and unsafe. This seriously undermines their capacity for resilience in the presence of conflicts and adversities. Fascination and/or fear, acceptance and/or rejection of outsider values and practices are creating an unprecedented and quite unpredictable situation in Rual.

NOTE

1. I wish to express my gratitude to the following Malaysian agencies and institutions: the Economic Planning Unit (EPU), the Jabatan Kemajuan Orang Asli (JAKOA); the Department of Wildlife and National Parks (PERHILITAN); the State governments of Pahang and Kelantan; the University of Malaya and, in particular Professor Malini Ratnasingam, Professor Juli Edo and Mr. Kamal Solheimi (Department of Anthropology and Sociology, Kuala Lumpur, Malaysia). Special thanks to Professor Robert Dentan (University at Buffalo, New York, USA), Professor Kirk Endicott (Dartmouth College, Hanover, NH, USA) and Professor Alberto Gomes (La Trobe University, Melbourne, Australia) for their precious advice and support. Above all I must thank the people of Rual for their invaluable friendship, hospitality, patience and collaboration.

REFERENCES

Arnoldi, J.
 2009 Risk: An Introduction. Cambridge, UK: Polity Press.

Beck, U.
 1992 [1989] Risk Society: Toward a New Modernity. London: Sage Publication.

Bird-David, N.
 1999 "Animism" Revisited: Personhood, Environment, and Relational Epistemology. Current Anthropology 40: 67–91.

Castañeda, Q.E.
 2006 Ethnography in the Forest: An Analysis of Ethics in the Morals of Anthropology. Cultural Anthropology 21(1): 121–45.

Dallos, C.
 2011 From Equality to Inequality: Social Change among Newly Sedentary Lanoh Hunter-Gatherer Traders of Peninsular Malaysia. Toronto: University of Toronto Press.

Dentan, R.K., K. Endicott, A.G. Gomes and M.B. Hooker
 1997 Malaysia and the Original People: A Case Study of the Impact of Development on Indigenous Peoples. Boston: Allyn and Bacon.

Dentan, R.K.
 2009 Overwhelming Terror: Love, Fear, Peace, and Violence among Semai of Malaysia. Lanham, MD: Rowman and Littlefield.

Descola, P.
 1996 Constructing Natures: Symbolic Ecology and Social Practice. *In* Nature and Society: Anthropological Perspectives. P. Descola and G. Pálsson, eds. Pp. 82–102. London: Routledge.
 2005 Ecology as Cosmological Analysis. *In* The Land Within: Indigenous Territory and the Perception of the Environment. Alexandre Surrallés and Pedro García Hierro, eds. Pp. 22–35. Skive, Denmark: IWGIA.

Douglas, M. and A. Wildavsky
 1982 Risk and Culture: An Essay on the Selection of Environmental and Technological Dangers. Berkeley: University of California Press.

Endicott, K.
 1979 Batek Negrito Religion: The World-View and Rituals of a Hunting and Gathering People of Peninsular Malaysia. Oxford: Oxford University Press.

374   *Diana Riboli*

Endicott, K.M. and K.L. Endicott
   2008   The Headman was a Woman: The Gender Egalitarian Batek of
          Malaysia. Long Grove, IL: Waveland Press.
Gianno, R.
   2006   What Happened to the Female Midwives? *In* Orang Asli Women
          of Malaysia: Perceptions, Situations and Aspirations. A. Baer,
          ed. Pp. 91–106. Subang Jaya, Malaysia: Center for Orang Asli
          Concerns.
Giddens, A.
   1991   Modernity and Self-Identity: Self and Society in the Late Modern
          Age. Cambridge: Polity Press.
Gomes, A.G.
   2007   Modernity and Malaysia: Settling the Menraq Forest Nomads.
          London and New York: Routledge.
Hallowell, I.A.
   1960   Ojibwa Ontology, Behavior, and World View. *In* Culture in
          History: Essays in Honor of Paul Radin. Stanley Diamond, ed.
          Pp. 18–49. New York: Columbia University Press.
Harvey, G.
   2005   Animism: Respecting the Living World. Kent Town, Australia:
          Wakefield Press.
Howell, S.
   1984   Society and Cosmos: Chewong of Peninsular Malaysia. Oxford:
          Oxford University Press.
   2006   Chewong Women in Transition: The Effect of Monetization
          on a Hunter-Gatherer Society of Malaysia. *In* Orang Asli Women
          of Malaysia: Perceptions, Situations and Aspirations. A. Baer,
          ed. Pp. 61–90. Subang Jaya, Malaysia: Center for Orang Asli
          Concerns.
Ingold, T.
   2000   The Perception of the Environment: Essays in Livelihood,
          Dwelling and Skill. London and New York: Routledge.
Kleinman, A., Veena Das, and M. Lock.
   1997   Social Suffering. Berkeley: University of California Press.
Lye Tuck-Po
   2005   Changing Pathways: Forest Degradation and the Batek of Pahang,
          Malaysia. Lanham, MD: Lexington.

Nobuta Toshihiro
  2009 Living on the Periphery: Development and Islamization among the Orang Asli in Malaysia. Subang Jaya, Malaysia: Center for Orang Asli Concerns.
Riboli, D.
  2009 Shamans and Transformation. *In* Yogic Perception, Meditation and Altered States of Consciousness. D. Eigner and E. Franco, eds. Pp. 347–67. Vienna: Verlag der Φsterreichischen Akademie der Wissenschaften.
  2010 Ghosts and Paracetamol: Batek and Jahai Shamanism in a Changing World. Shaman 18: 99–108.
  2012 *"People Without Jungle are Dying People"*: Health and Illness in Semang-Negrito (Malaysia). *In* Anthropological and Socio-logical Approaches to Health. H. Oikonomou and M. Spyridakis, eds. Pp. 335–61. Athens: Sideris Publishers [in Greek].
  2013 Of Angry Thunders, Smelly Intruders and Human-Tigers: Shamanic Representation of Violence and Conflict in Non-Violent Peoples: the Semang-Negrito (Malaysia). *In* Shamanism and Violence: Power, Repression and Suffering in Indigenous Religious Conflicts. D. Riboli and D. Torri, eds. Pp. 135–48. Farnham, UK: Ashgate.
Robbins, J.
  2012 Cultural Values. *In* A Companion to Moral Anthropology. D. Fassin, ed. Pp. 117–32. Malden, MA: John Wiley & Sons.
Roseman, M.
  1991 Healing Sounds from the Malaysian Rainforest: Temiar Music and Medicine. Berkeley: University of California Press.
Sissons, J.
  2005 First Peoples: Indigenous Cultures and Their Futures. London: Reaktion Books.
Tacey, I.
  2013 Tropes of Fear: The Impact of Globalization on Batek Religious Landscapes. Religion 4: 240–66.
       http://www.mdpi.com/2077-1444/4/2/240, accessed 1 Nov. 2013.
van der Sluys, C.
  2006 Are the Jahai a Non-Violent People? *In* Orang Asli Women of Malaysia: Perceptions, Situations and Aspirations. A. Baer, ed. Pp. 43–50. Subang Jaya, Malaysia: Center for Orang Asli Concerns.

Viveiros de Castro, E.
2005 Perspectivism and Multinaturalism in Indigenous America. *In* The Land Within: Indigenous Territory and the Perception of the Environment. Alexandre Surrallés and Pedro García Hierro, eds. Pp. 36–74. Skive, Denmark: IWGIA.

16

Batek Transnational Shamanism: Countering Marginalization through Weaving Alliances with Cosmic Partners and Global Politicians

Ivan Tacey

This chapter focuses on how the Batek Tanum have realigned their religious and moral geographies in an increasingly globalized world. Under constant pressure from political, social and economic marginalization, stemming principally from being displaced from ancestral landscapes, they have demonstrated remarkable adaptability by incorporating new ideas, events and imagery into their religious practices and beliefs (Riboli 2013; Tacey 2013). This adaptability has allowed for change to occur while social and ontological continuity is maintained. The ability to transform the fabric of their religious landscape within the contemporary context of massive environmental degradation, territorial loss and social pressure constitutes an effective strategy of empowerment, a counter to the threats of marginalization. Examination of the ways these transformations take on a global dimension allows us to delineate the threads of Batek Tanum resistance to the devastating effects of transnational forces at work within their environment.

The Batek Tanum live to the west of the Batek Dè' and lay claim to a distinct traditional territory stretching across the states of Pahang and Kelantan in the Tanum, Yu, Relau, Galas and Tuang River Valleys. (Some Batek Tanum also live with Batek Dè' at the village of Marem which lies on the south-western border of the Taman Negara national park.) The Batek Tanum differentiate themselves from other Batek and Orang Asli and should be considered as a separate ethnic group, and this is not only due to their distinct territorial claims. Batek Tanum language differs considerably from Batek Dè' and other Orang Asli dialects, and the Tanum people also have a different history and cultural practices from other Batek groups. Lastly, the Batek Tanum only began to auto-identify as Batek following several massacres in the early 20th century (see below). Prior to this they called themselves Orang Maia (Maia People).

The Batek Tanum's experience with global actors is by no means restricted to the contemporary period. Present Batek perceptions of marginalization are framed by historical experience, as memories of past events and encounters feed into new experiences with Malays, Chinese, British, Japanese, and others. This inevitable temporal translation of the present through the past prefigures how Batek strategies to counteract marginalization can be constructed and imagined. The situation is complex, as the Batek Tanum's on-going modes and means of resistance to marginalization exist in a blurred domain where religious and political realms coexist, interlace and collide. In such a space, understanding of the present undergoes perpetual redefinition in response to spatially and temporally distant places and people.

The Batek Tanum actively seek to articulate alliances with international actors and groups they consider potential "powerful" partners to help them recover ancestral territories and resist social, economic and political marginalization. These alliances involve acting on an international stage at both earthly and cosmic levels. Worldly alliances are sought by sending letters and messages to human rights organizations, non-governmental organizations and foreign politicians via cultural intermediaries such as anthropologists, environmentalists and lawyers fighting for indigenous peoples' rights. Cosmic alliances are forged through dreams, shamanic journeys and relationships with human and "other-than-human persons" (Hallowell 1960). Batek leaders and shamans (*hala?*) are showing signs of acting at a transnational level, of becoming agents within a globalizing world. However, political and religious realities cannot be clearly differentiated as certain political acts take place at a cosmic level, and political allies are often encountered in dream states in the same way that other-than-human persons are. Everyday life and cosmic realms form an integrated reality for the Batek. The unbroken bonds that exist between the everyday world and the invisible world have profound implications for any understanding of Batek modes of empowerment.

TRANSNATIONAL SHAMANISM

A few days before I left the field in June 2013,[1] ʔey Wow, a headman from Becah Kelubi, one of three Batek Tanum villages situated in northwest Pahang, recounted the following account of Batek[2] shamanic response to the Japanese 2011 tsunami:

> Our shaman went to Japan today, he looked at the earth. The earth over there is broken. If the earth is fixed, there is no problem. In Japan, they have accepted the help of our Batek shaman. He went and looked at the earth below Japan today. There are many *Ey Dʒum* [other-than-human persons with extraordinary powers] over there, *Ey Dʒum* in the underworld and in the upper world. The Batek shaman made cosmic threads. Like the threads I told you about. [ʔey Wow illustrates by drawing a picture in my notebook]. This is Japan. Before, there was a huge tsunami over there. However, the Batek shaman took the threads, he took them here, and here, everywhere threads, like a spider's web [draws multiple threads like a web]. All the threads he took and weaved together. He saw the broken earth and he fixed the earth together. That is what the shaman did. Over there, in Japan.
>
> *Baji* [the underground rainbow snake] can't writhe anymore. I tell you *Baji* is now held firmly in place, the threads he made, all those threads, threads, threads … Threads here and threads there, everywhere he made threads. Now *Baji* is stuck in one place. She can't writhe anymore. The Japanese territory is now safe, it's good.

Keep a lookout this year, in the next few months, the shaman said it is safe now. The old man went to Japan. I heard he came back now. You check the newspapers. The Batek shaman helped. But if the Japanese can help the Batek, that will be good, they will be safe. But if they don't want to help us, maybe it is finished for them in the future.

How should we interpret this feat of transnational support for the Japanese people? Why would a Batek shaman go to the effort of aiding a people he has never met by fixing the damaged fabric of their underworld? ?ey Wow's words also contain a hint of menace that the Japanese may need to reciprocate help for the Batek to avoid future problems. Why would such a threat be suggested? The description's implications for understanding Batek positioning of self-identity on a global scale can be defined more clearly through the lens of Batek religion. The unpacking and interpretation of its meaning must also be situated within the Batek's contemporary experience of severe social, political and economic marginalization, environmental degradation and ever-increasing global flows.

Globalization theorists such as Roland Robertson have closely examined the effects of globalization on social relations and the way the world is increasingly experienced as a "single place" (Robertson 1992: 6). John Tomlinson describes this phenomenon as "unicity" or "complex connectivity" (Tomlinson 1999) while Anthony Giddens similarly addresses globalization's "stretching of social relations across distance" (Giddens 1990). The Batek shaman's dealings with the Japanese on a cosmic level present an intriguing modality of the complex connectivity of globalization. Tomlinson has remarked "[a]s connectivity reaches into localities, it transforms local lived experience but it also confronts people with a world in which their fates undeniably *are* bound together in a single global frame" (Tomlinson 1999: 12). Notably, the Batek choose to situate themselves as key agents on a cosmological level within this global frame. The shaman's act of weaving the cosmic threads which hold the world in place aptly figures the way the Batek bring together myriad images of faraway people, places and events within the very fabric of their own ontology and cosmology.

BATEK TANUM RELIGION

Batek Tanum shamans are specialists in weaving cosmic threads into gigantic webs which structure the architecture of the cosmos. One web holds the heavens in place to stop them crashing down to earth. Another supports the earth from collapsing into the underground sea below. And another holds the underground dragon or rainbow snake *Baji* in place. The Tanum people say that in the beginning there was just one thread which stretched through the centre of the cosmos connecting the upper-worlds, earth and lower worlds. Since then, their shamans have been continually weaving together more and more of these threads to create the underlying and invisible fabric of the cosmos. Threads are obtained from a class of beings called *Ey Dʒum* which shamans meet in altered states of consciousness, including trance and dream states. This concept of shamanic weaving of cosmic threads is unique to the Batek Tanum. Notably, Batek Dè' cosmology features descriptions of the thunder lord sending wind, rain, thunder and lightning down special cords or rope (*taliʔ*) (Endicott 1979: 69). Another Orang Asli people, the Semelai, believe that after a violent death a departing soul follows a red wind thread to the land of the dead. They also claim dangerous *pʔreʔ* spirits "attach threads between the victim and perpetrator of an impending accident" (see Gianno, this volume). However, these strands function in a more delimited way to the Batek Tanum's woven webs of cosmic cohesion that necessitate two-way movement between the realms of the real and invisible. Like shamans of other Orang Asli groups, Tanum shamans are said to be able to travel anywhere in the cosmos during their soul journeys and communicate with various other-than-human persons (Endicott 1979; Riboli 2008, 2009). Shamans slip through space instantaneously, travelling to far corners of the cosmos in a split-second, annihilating limits of space and time, thus embodying globalized interconnectivity. The Batek Tanum's cosmic threads were globalized long before the term "interconnectivity" was coined to describe the links, structures and networks inherent in globalization. Like the networks of international finance and the cybernetic webs which disseminate media imagery via satellites, cables and the Internet, the Batek Tanum's cosmic webs are invisible. However, rather than disseminating data, Batek webs hold the world together.

Cosmos

The Batek's tripartite conception of the cosmos divides into an upper-world, earth and lower world. Certain other-than-human beings such as the *Cenil,* the original creator beings, are said to dwell in both the upper and lower worlds, though they are most commonly associated with the lower world. The upper-world is the home of *Karei,* the thunder lord, and the place of the dead. In the underworld dwells *Baji,* the rainbow snake, and directly below her is the home of *Capoi,* an old woman closely associated with the rainbow snake. The Batek Tanum say *Capoi* is the mother of the sky-dwelling lord of thunder, *Karei,* while the Batek Aring call her *Ya'* or *'Aroc* and say she is his aunt (Endicott 1979: 168). Any transgression of ritual prohibitions (*talaiɲ*) infuriates the lord of thunder and the rainbow snake who respond by meting out devastating punishment. *Karei* sends thunderstorms and the rainbow snake writhes in anger, breaking free of the cosmic threads which hold her in place and releasing the waters of the underground sea, which surge through the earth's crust causing devastating floods.

Batek Tanum ritual prohibitions, like those of the nearby Batek Dè', vary from group to group and seem to change over time. Some of the most important concern avoidance of the following: eating or laughing at certain classes of animals; letting blood flow into streams, particularly menstrual blood, blood from childbirth or the blood of tabooed animals; mixing the odours of certain species of plants and animals through cooking them on the same hearth; mocking or imitating other-than-human persons or anything associated with them; and improper sexual or social behaviour, especially violence (Endicott 1979: 67–82). Olfaction is a key means of communicating with other-than-human persons, and it is the flow of odours which principally anger and placate the rainbow snake and thunder lord when taboos are broken and appeasement rituals are later performed (Endicott 1979; Lye 2004; Burenhult and Majid 2011; Riboli 2013; Tacey 2013).

Myths, stories and religious rules are frequently embedded within the landscape itself. As I have highlighted elsewhere, Batek "sacred sites are neither places of pilgrimage or ritual performance. In some

Plate 16.1 Batek Tanum elders with sacred site in background

(Photo credit: Ivan Tacey)

cases they mark the activities of culture-heroes' exploits in the past and in other cases the dwelling places of other-than-human beings which often become angered and dangerous if these sites are polluted or destroyed" (Tacey 2013: 254). Thus, displacement from their land and environmental degradation are closely connected with religious change.

The Tanum people, like other Batek communities, are increasingly claiming the thunder lord and the rainbow snake are angered not only by localized taboo-breaking but by contemporary destruction of the environment (Lye 2004) and transgression of ritual prohibitions by people in distant places (Riboli 2013; Tacey 2013). The Batek learn about world events from television, radio and newspapers, and they interpret these events in terms of their own religious practices and beliefs. For example, the Batek Dè' blamed the devastating Indian Ocean tsunami of 2004 on the rainbow snake and thunder lord's anger for Indonesian taboo breaking. In one explicatory account of the tsunami Indonesians were blamed for mocking animals (Tacey 2013). In another version, an Indonesian maid working in the Middle East, angry with her employers for abusing her, attempted to punish them through black magic and poured menstrual blood into a river or the sea, hence violating a major taboo and causing the wrath of the rainbow snake and thunder lord (Riboli 2013). Similarly, many Batek say Hurricane Sandy, which hit New York in winter 2012, was caused because the thunder lord and rainbow snake were angry at American violence in Iraq and Afghanistan. The 2011 Japanese tsunami was also said to be caused by the Japanese breaking taboos. Furthermore, these beings are increasingly angered at local landscape degradation, particularly by the destruction of forests which has taken on epic proportions in the Batek area and in the wider Southeast Asia region. By incorporating distant people and places into their cosmology the Batek are effectively expanding their concept of "moral community" (Endicott 1979; Lye 2004) to a global scale. Like ʔey Wow's story of the Tanum shaman fixing the underworld in Japan through weaving together cosmic threads, these interpretations of global catastrophes demonstrate the globalization of Batek religion and cosmology. Faced with the wholesale destruction of forests and their replacement with homogenous palm oil plantations—consequences of global demands for timber and palm oil—and with social, economic and political marginalization at a local level, the Batek now situate local problems alongside the seeming increased frequency of extreme weather and "natural" cataclysms that occur at a global level. As Batek Tanum shamans have been given the responsibility of weaving together the cosmic webs which hold the cosmos together and restrain the rainbow snake in the underworld they now identify themselves as key actors in this global struggle.

Plate 16.2 Mining has devastated Batek Tanum
landscapes

(Photo credit: Ivan Tacey)

Alliances with Other-than-human-persons

The Batek mediate social relations with other-than-human persons in
a number of ways. In dreams and trance states, the Batek say each
person's dreaming soul—*semangat* in the Batek Tanum and Mendriq
languages, *bayang* in Batek Dè'—leaves the body and visits various
places where they can encounter these persons. For non-shamans this
is normally the local environment of the forest. For shamans it also

includes the upper and lower worlds and anywhere else they choose to visit in the cosmos. Batek Tanum shamans enter trances through rhythmically rocking [*tiwŋiw*], and, once in a trance-state, other-than-human persons (*Ey Dʒum*) are said to enter the house (*hãyaʔ*) within the shaman's body. Then the shaman's soul leaves his/her body and can travel anywhere in the cosmos, even down to the depths of the underworld where powerful shamans can ride the rainbow snake. While shamans are the most adept at dreaming and trancing, encountering other-than-human persons in these states is not strictly restricted to shamans.

The Batek Tanum divide other-than-human persons into three main classes: *Cenil*—the original creator beings; *Ey Dʒum*—the personification of animals, rivers, mountains, waterfalls, fruit trees and other living things or landscape features whose help can be enlisted by shamans; and dangerous, often monstrous, disease-causing *Penyakit*, which hunt down human souls to devour.

Penyakit are divided into two further classes: *Penyakit batak* and *Penyakit djinn*. The terms *Penyakit* and *Djinn* are both loan words from Malay; the former can either mean disease or a disease-causing spirit, while the latter, originating from Arabic, literally means "hidden from sight". The word *Batak* is a collective ethonym used for several ethnic groups from the Lake Toba area in Sumatra who were infamous for practising cannibalism and for slave raiding other ethnic groups across the Malay-Indonesian world. The Batek often identify the Batak as murderous agents of the historical slave raids which targeted Orang Asli groups in the Peninsula until the 1930s. Thus the Batek's historical encounters with violent outsiders reverberates through the names given to the dangerous other-than-human beings associated with causing disease and death.

The *Cenil* appear in many Batek Tanum origin stories and are similar to the *Halaʔ Asal* of the Batek Dè' (Endicott 1979: 126). They heavily feature in Batek cosmogonical myths and are credited with creating the landscapes of the earth in the mythical past and teaching humans how to live. When the *Cenil* lived with humans in the past they were said to look like humans until they were tricked by the mouse deer and took on animal forms. Shortly after this the animals' souls became invisible and went to live in a beautiful place under the earth. Although most *Cenil* are associated with animals, the sun and the moon are also described in this category.

While *Cenil* are said to live in either the underworld or the upperworld, *Ey Dʒum* are said to live all around us. Shamans form long-lasting alliances with *Ey Dʒum* in order to battle *Penyakit* and as helpers in weaving the cosmic threads that hold the cosmos together. The most powerful *Ey Dʒum* is *Teʔ* (the earth being). Other important *Ai Dʒum* include the rainbow snake and the water being. The Batek can learn ritual knowledge from the *Ey Dʒum* and can communicate, marry and form long-lasting alliances with them. The Batek, like other Orang Asli groups, do not describe relations with other-than-human beings in figurative, metaphorical terms; instead these relationships are seen as having the same veracity as human-to-human relations (Endicott 1979; Dentan 2008; Howell 2011).

Plate 16.3 New technologies mean the Batek Tanum are connected to the wider world

(Photo credit: Ivan Tacey)

Plate 16.4 The Batek Tanum are becoming increasingly media savvy

(Photo credit: Ivan Tacey)

BATEK MARGINALIZATION AND ENVIRONMENTAL DEGRADATION

Kampung Becah Kelubi is the home to one of three Batek Tanum communities living between Kuala Lipis and Gua Musang. It is a typical Orang Asli resettlement village of about 60 people who live in 20 rundown government-built houses and a few traditional lean-tos scattered around the village. Houses in the village are sparse and often shared by more than one family. Possessions are limited to a few plates and dishes, some cooking pots, clothes and sarongs, a mattress or two, and a few tools. In many homes, NGO posters outlining Orang Asli rights are displayed, most of which have not been implemented. A small number of families own televisions, and in the evening friends and families often gather to watch shows, documentaries and films broadcasted via the Malaysian satellite television company Astro. The globalized-media imagery that flows into the community via satellite televisions, DVDs and newspapers has a powerful effect on how the Batek see the outside world. News coverage means the Batek are well aware of international catastrophes, wars, and extreme environmental and climatic phenomenon such as tsunamis, flooding, hurricanes and earthquakes. These types of events are consistently interpreted within the framework of Batek cosmology as punishments meted out by cosmic beings for the transgression of taboos. Entertainment programmes also bring direct evidence of other peoples' transgression of Batek taboos, such as mocking animals, committing violent acts and so on.

The authorities provided the Batek with no economic opportunities after settling them at Becah Kelubi, and life is extremely hard. The nearest area of primary rainforest is the Taman Negara national park which lies about 20 miles to the east, too far away for people to access on foot, and in any case the Batek are frequently told by the Department of Wildlife and National Parks (PERHILITAN) they can no longer forage in the park despite a major part of their ancestral territory falling within park boundaries. The village is encapsulated by Malay communities and a Federal Land Development Authority (FELDA) palm oil estate. A government body, which the Batek claim is associated with JAKOA (the Department of Orang Asli Development), gives each Batek household RM600 (US$188) per month as compensation for the use of this land, but the Batek consider this amount far too low for their needs. Northwest of the FELDA estate, the Batek can still access an island of logged-over secondary forest on foot where they fish, hunt and collect forest products. The area is said to be home to many benevolent other-than-human beings (*Ey Dʒum*). Other forest islands, situated to the east of the Kuala Lipis-to-Gua Musang railway line—within the fragmented landscape that has been carved up by FELDA palm oil plantations, rubber estates and open-cast mines—are regularly accessed by a few men from the village who go on scooters to collect rattan, hardwoods and other forest products. These men often camp out for weeks until they have collected all available rattan or other forest resources to sell to Chinese or Malay middle-men. Women, children and the elderly spend most of their time within the village except when making short trips to the forest near the village to fish, forage and collect flowers for bodily adornment.

Many Batek communities have now been obliged to settle in marginal forest-fringe villages like Becah Kelubi on the periphery of Taman Negara due to areas outside the national park being deforested and converted to oil-palm plantations and rubber estates. In resettlement villages, the Batek and other Orang Asli are under tremendous pressure to assimilate into mainstream Malaysian society, particularly via coercive attempts to Islamize the Orang Asli (Nicholas 2000; Gomes 2007; Endicott and Endicott 2008; Nobuta 2008). Like many other Batek resettlement villages, the Tanum people at Becah Kelubi converted to Islam en masse in the 1990s. Villagers claim conversion followed several visits from local Malays who aggressively coerced them to convert. After refusing conversion three times the villagers finally gave in when threatened with extreme violence. Batek in Kelantan also complain they were coerced into joining Islam, but not under the threat of violence (Endicott and Endicott 2008; Tacey 2013). Islam has had a more pervasive effect on the Batek of Kelantan than on communities in Pahang, where, for the moment at least, the only noticeable signs of Islam are Batek using Muslim Malay names when dealing with outsiders (Tacey 2013).

The key factor behind Batek marginalization, and that of the Orang Asli more generally, has been displacement and the loss of massive areas of their ancestral territories (see Subramaniam, this volume). No legal titles acknowledging the Batek people's ownership of their traditional territory have been recognized by the states of Pahang, Kelantan or the national Malaysian government. This places people in an extremely fragile legal position. Malaysian bio-political classifications of people and places, which allocates land rights and economic advantages to Malays while denying them to others, have resulted in many Orang Asli communities being relocated from their ancestral lands to resettlement villages like Becah Kelubi. Administrative landscape classifications, used to determine land use and rights of access, are another major factor behind Orang Asli marginalization, displacement and the intense environmental degradation of their landscapes. Administrative demarcations such as "National Parks", "Malay Reservations", "State Parks", "Forest Reserves", "Protection

Forests", "Water Catchment Areas", "Forested State Land", "Game Reserves", "Agricultural Areas" and "Mining Sites" have implications as to where the Orang Asli have a legal right to dwell, forage and collect forest resources. A pertinent example of this concerns the Batek and Taman Negara. While Batek communities living near the entrances to Taman Negara at Kuala Koh in Kelantan and Kuala Tahan in Pahang have been told by the Department of Wildlife and National Parks that they are allowed to forage for plants and animals within park boundaries, the Batek Tanum living near the Sungai Relau park entrance are forbidden to forage for any flora and fauna within the park. No Batek are allowed to collect forest products from the park to sell, which severely restricts economic choices and further pushes them into extreme poverty. A common complaint the Batek articulated during my fieldwork can be summarized in the following words of a headman:

> The Malays are getting rich, the Chinese are getting rich. Everyone is getting rich except us. This is our land, why aren't we getting rich?

Grievances like this are endemic among Orang Asli communities (Dentan et al. 1997) and will not abate until the Malaysian government recognizes the Orang Asli as the traditional owners of their ancestral lands. However, Batek complaints about environmental degradation and marginalization should not be mistakenly regarded as simply a desire to reap financial rewards via the economic development of landscapes. While some Batek do clearly pronounce their aspiration to collaborate as equal economic partners—with the British, Chinese, Japanese or Americans—the Batek are acutely aware of the dangers of uncontrolled development and environmental degradation. They frequently present these dangers within the framework of their cosmology and claim the repercussions of uncontrolled development will eventually result in the world's end, when the rainbow snake and thunder lord destroy the world in a final fit of anger at human actions on earth (Lye 2004). The Batek Tanum say they will be the only people saved as they enter the earth to join the *Cenil* (original creator beings) in the underground world.

GLOBAL POLITICAL ALLIANCES

It is within this context of territorial loss, severe marginalization and increased global flows that attempts to forge alliances with various powerful entities including foreign governments, politicians and companies must be understood. Immediately upon my arrival in the village of Kampung Becah Kelubi in November 2012, the Batek began articulating their grievances against the Malaysian government and their desire to create alliances of equality with national and international actors. They handed me piles of letters addressed to NGOs and human rights groups—including the Malaysian Human Rights Commission (SUHAKAM), the Malaysian Bar Council and also foreign governments and their leaders—in the hope that someone would be able to help them. The aims of the requests were far-reaching: autonomy from the Malaysian government, legal rights, recognition of their ancestral lands, and collaboration on equal terms with international partners to develop local resources. The over-arching struggle which the Batek Tanum articulate is that of regaining control over the ownership of their ancestral lands.

Batek attempts to form alliances continually blur the boundaries between literal political acts, religious experiences and the interpretation of transnational media flows. Literal political acts principally consist of writing letters to foreign governments and NGOs outlining grievances and asking for aid. Within the cosmic realm, alliances are sought through the religious experiences of shamanic soul journeys and individual revelations in dreams. Both the content of the letters and the imagery of the religious experiences are imbued with the Batek's interpretation of global media flows. Throughout my research, the Batek Tanum have articulated a fantastical desire for collaborative mining or timber projects with President Obama. Dream revelations are described where the Batek meet Obama, who communicates that he will soon be coming to Malaysia to help them. These dreams take a similar form to shamanic soul journeys where alliances are forged with other-than-human persons. However, the dreams in which President Obama is encountered and premonitions about American intervention in Malaysia are not just restricted to shamans, but are received by many Batek men and women. Dream revelations and premonitions also foretell Americans soon coming to the aid of the Batek, expelling the Malays, and assuming governance of Malaysia. The Batek support the validity of these dreams by referring to news events seen on television offering "proof" of Obama's imminent arrival. Naïve though they may seem at first encounter, the aspirational weaving together of desires, transnational media flows and potential international alliances within the Batek's everyday discourse and dreams should be seen as a mode of resistance, a counter to their contemporary social, economic and political marginalization. They represent a means of imagining resistance, a way of figuring out lines of positive force from the everyday encounters and features of their lives. But why have the Batek chosen the British, Americans, Chinese and Japanese as potential partners? Their choice can only be understood as an outcome of the Batek's perceptions of these peoples, which stem from historical experience with specific actors from these places—transformed and expanded into ethnic stereotypes—and of perceptions which have intensified in the contemporary period via the decoding of transnational media flows.

HISTORY AND GLOBALIZATION IN BATEK RESISTANCE

The Batek are well aware of Malaysian history in the pre-colonial, colonial and post-colonial eras and are able to express in eloquent terms how historical events and encounters with different peoples have led to their gradual marginalization. Batek Tanum encounters with Chinese, Malays, British and Japanese have radically affected their contemporary impressions of these peoples as potential allies. However, contemporary global media flows continue to inform Batek perspectives of these peoples and have radically transformed strategies for forming alliances.

The Batek Tanum claim that three entire Orang Asli communities in the Merapoh area—the Jelai People, the Bia? People and the Kiho? People—were slaughtered by Malays who moved into Batek lands in the early 20th century. They say if it wasn't for the British sending in the army at this time, all their ancestors would have been exterminated by the Malays. After these massacres the Tanum people split into three separate communities and adopted Batek ethnic identity as a strategy to avoid annihilation. Previously, the Batek in this area had been known as Orang Maia. Villagers told me the decision to switch from Maia to Batek ethnicity was to prevent Malays from targeting them as Orang Maia. Sadly, it is unlikely this strategy would have changed anything as Batek in Kelantan had also been targeted during slave raids in this period (Endicott 1997: 42) as had other Orang Asli communities across the Peninsula (Endicott 1983).

It is likely that, as is the case with other Batek communities, the Tanum people intermittently traded with Malays prior to the 20th century in times of peace and fled from them during the periods of slave raiding, which culminated in the massacres of the 1920s and 1930s (Endicott 1983, 1997). Batek Tanum encounters with most outsiders were probably of a fairly low frequency until the 1930s, following the construction of the Gemas-to-Tumpat railway line by the British colonial government. The railway's construction meant a rapid increase of Malays settling along the route and expansion of the towns of Gua Musang, Bertam, Manek Urai and Kuala Krai in previously Orang Asli dominant areas (Endicott 1997: 38). By the 1950s, large numbers of Malay farmers, mainly immigrants from Kelantan, were opening up agricultural land, encapsulating Batek communities and evicting the Batek from their ancestral landscapes. Malays are still greatly feared and mistrusted especially as violence continues through acts of coercive Islamization, territorial conflicts and institutionalized harassment. In contrast, the British are remembered as a powerful but benevolent people who stopped Malay aggression in the area. Repercussions of the past echo through statements such as the following from a Batek elder at Becah Kelubi:

> I want my country back; I want you to help me with your people, with your government. The *gob* [Malays] aren't from here. I'm frightened of the *gob*. I could blowpipe one or two but that wouldn't be enough. Come back with the British army. The *gob* should go back to Kalimantan, Sumatra and Thailand. I want them to go back to their countries.

The key point in the above quotation is that the Batek wish to regain the lands which have been forcibly taken from them. However, they know any form of armed resistance would be futile without the

Plate 16.5 ʔey Wow describes an attack on a Batek Tanum settlement near Kampung Pulai

(Photo credit: Ivan Tacey)

help of outsiders due to the massive imbalance of size between Batek and Malay populations. Representations of others that use the past are always history strategically rebuilt in the present. The Batek's choice of imagined future alliances speaks clearly of how they have chosen to pin their present hopes of security upon peaceable relations with powerful others from the past.

Due to fears of enslavement, the Batek Tanum kept their distance from most outsiders except the Chinese living at Kampung Pulai to the north, with whom they had close and peaceful relations ever since Chinese settlers moved into the Galas river valley looking for gold about 400 years ago. The Batek claim the Chinese were the first outsiders to settle in the area, and Batek-Chinese relations are always described as being peaceful. Chinese settlers ate the same forest foods as the Batek, are said to have learnt the Batek language and to have intermarried with the Batek. Oral accounts and archival research compiled by Tan Teng Phee (2012: 90–2) confirm what I was told by the Batek Tanum living at Becah Kelubi in 2012 and 2013 concerning Batek-Chinese ethnic relations in the Merapoh area. Like Batek-Malay relations, Chinese-Malay relations have been historically marred by violence. In 1825, following a quarrel over taxes, Malay forces slaughtered thousands of Pulai Chinese, after which "the river ran red with blood and the stench of decaying bodies polluted the air for miles" (Tan 2012: 91). Secondly, the Batek Tanum vividly remember a Malay attack on Kampung Pulai and a neighbouring Batek village in the post-colonial period. One Batek elder from Becah Kelubi described the attack as follows:

> At about 7pm in the evening mortar fire began raining down on the Batek. Boom, boom, boom! Fruit trees and crops were burning throughout the village. The people were terrified. Children were screaming and clutching onto their parents. The people decided to run. However, the shaman said "Stop! I can hold them off until the morning!" He conjured up a huge magical shield to protect the villagers. Bullets and mortar fire bounced off the shield all night long until fire ceased in the morning at around 8am. All the attacks were deflected by the shield. If we didn't have the Batek shaman we'd all be dead. Then, in the light of day, we all fled south through the forests towards Cegah Perah and set up camp there.

Despite confusion over the exact historical details of these events, the most important factor for the present discussion is the shaping of Batek perceptions of Chinese as "peaceful friends" versus Malays as "violent foes"; the perception is that to a certain degree the Chinese have been violently persecuted in the same way as the Orang Asli.

The Tanum people had only brief interactions with the Japanese during World War Two when the Japanese invaded Malaysia in 1941 and forced out the British colonial government until September 1945. However, the Japanese invasion meant the Batek became aware of Japan as a major global power capable of defeating the British, who in Batek eyes were already considered as immensely powerful.

Perceptions of Japanese, British, Chinese and Americans as potential allies are also greatly influenced by media flows. Although they have had no direct historical encounters with Americans, the Batek are well aware of American military power via media imagery of US wars ostensibly against Muslims in Iraq and Afghanistan. Imagery of

American military might has also been greatly exaggerated through Hollywood cinema and entertainment programmes. The Batek see Americans as anti-Muslim, therefore anti-Malay, and therefore highly desirable potential allies. Likewise, the British, Chinese and Japanese are seen as either non-Muslims or anti-Muslim and thus anti-Malay. It is within such a hotbed of distorted magnification of perceived similarities and stereotyped mutual oppositions that Batek ideas of potential international partnerships have been forged.

CONCLUSION

While British, Chinese, Americans and Japanese are seen as potential allies due to their perceived might, the Batek Tanum, like other Batek groups, frequently emphasize the weaknesses of these nations in the face of cataclysmic events caused by the transgression of taboos by people in these distant places. The Batek highlight the role they can play within the gap between the incredible military, political and socio-economic power of these nation states and the inability of these very same nations to prevent catastrophes such as flooding, hurricanes, earthquakes and tsunamis. The Batek believe they know the precise causes of these events (violence, environmental destruction, mocking of animals and so on), and the Batek Tanum claim they can repair the damage caused to the fabric of the cosmos and underworld by these disasters and can even prevent disasters from occurring through holding the rainbow snake in place with their cosmic threads.

Despite their marginalization and precarious legal position, the Batek have managed to remain as distinct ethnic groups, continued to live as foragers, and their religion has unequivocally retained its form, all while continually incorporating ideas from an ever-more-globalized environment. Rather than disappearing, Batek religion, like the Batek economy, incorporates change within its complex discursive fabric. How is this possible? Indigenous peoples are often considered as living a fragile existence in the shadow of the nation-state, under the constant threat of disappearance through assimilation. I argue that, far from being fragile, Batek descriptions of their society and religion should be considered as "antifragile" (Talib 2012). As Nassim Talib has highlighted, antifragility should not be confused with mere strength or resistance; it is "beyond resilience or robustness. The resilient resists shocks and stays the same; the antifragile gets better" (2012: 19). Via promethean-like adaption Batek religion has been able not only to recover from but also analyze and incorporate the external shocks it increasingly encounters. This is not to say the Batek's contemporary social position is not precarious because it certainly is. However, Batek religion has an in-built hydra-like antifragility which demonstrates a unique prowess for adaptation, a defiant ability to intelligently respond and reinvent itself under immense external pressure.

The basis for this antifragility results from the myriad plasticity of Batek social forms. Linguistic porosity of dialect groups, fluidity of group composition, complex shifting economies, open aggregation and shifting ethnicity have all been previously documented by anthropologists working with the Batek Dè' (Endicott 1979; Lye 2004) as well as anthropologists working with many other indigenous groups in Southeast Asia (Benjamin 2002; Scott 2009; Gibson and Sillander 2011). Notably, Batek religious beliefs and practices exhibit remarkable plasticity and fluidity. Far from being the only option left open to the weak, this prowess for adjustment and incorporation should be recognized as an effective countering manoeuvre against marginalization. It allows for change to occur while preventing the fragility associated with reification and standardization; things which become crystallized are easy to shatter. Clear recognition of the political strategies contained within such adaptability allow us to gain new insights into the modes of action that disenfranchised groups can utilize as means of maintaining social, cultural and ontological continuity. Batek political strategies are crystal clear in this respect. Faced with huge territorial loss, the Batek goal of creating political alliances aims to re-establish their claims to the ownership of their ancestral lands, areas which have been contested since Malays began moving into the area in the early 20th century.

Many of the metaphors commonly used to describe globalization are apposite to the Batek's contemporary experience of global encounters and resemble their own descriptions. Certainly the Batek Tanum's cosmic-threaded web of interconnectivity lends itself to such a reading. Yet such a seemingly close match must be approached with caution. Apparent metaphoric overlap between the descriptions may well just be that, "apparent". For within the self-descriptions of Batek religion and cosmology, extended "metaphors" are much more than elaborate rhetorical devices and are thoroughly embedded within underlying understandings of the world's structure. Indeed it could be argued that Batek figurations of their cosmology and religious experiences are not metaphoric at all in that they are literal descriptions of reality, albeit a reality which exists in an other-worldly sphere.

As locally-constructed meanings take new forms within a world of increasing global flows, it becomes necessary, as John Tomlinson highlights, to examine "how [globalization] affects people's sense of identity, the experience of place, and of the self in relation to place, how it impacts on the shared understandings, values, desires, myths, hopes and fears that have developed around locally situated life" (1999: 20). The Batek's exposure to current forces of globalization, informed by historical encounters with a variety of global actors, has radically affected their experience of place and the way their "desires, myths, hopes and fears" are imagined and articulated. In so many ways the dynamic of globalization exists just as forcibly as a mode of description as it does as a material process. Undoubtedly, Batek marginalization is the result of concrete global processes, yet it is also affected by the way these processes are represented in different discourses. Marginalization can reside as much within the discursive dimension of reality as within the literal. By carving out their own understanding of global pressures within the safe space of their cosmology, the Batek are able to imagine new ways to circumvent marginalization. Realigning their religious practice and belief in response to change has provided a means to explore the lines of force, both negative and positive, in their lives. With this in mind, there is much to learn from picking up the Batek Tanum's global threads and taking their critique of our fragile interconnected world seriously.

NOTES

1.   Research for this paper was carried out from July 2012 to June 2013 and was supported by a generous dissertation fieldwork grant from the Wenner-Gren foundation in New York. My research has been made possible by the Economic Planning Unit of the Prime Minister's Department, the governments of Pahang, Kelantan and Perak and JAKOA granting me

permission to carry out research. This permission would not have been possible without the help of Juli Edo from the University of Malaya who has acted as my local counterpart during my research periods. I must also thank Kamal Solhaimi from the University of Malaya for all the time and advice he has given me throughout my research. I would equally like to thank all the staff of the Department of Anthropology and Sociology at the University of Malaya for their help. Furthermore, I would especially like to thank all the academics working in the field of Orang Asli studies who have offered me invaluable assistance and advice throughout my studies. Particular thanks must go to Kirk Endicott who has been especially helpful and generous sharing his expertise and knowledge about all things Batek, offering me guidance throughout my research, reading drafts of my papers and of course editing this book. Special thanks must go to Diana Riboli from Panteion University in Athens; Robert Dentan from the University at Buffalo, New York; Geoffrey Benjamin from Nanyang Technological University, Singapore; Alberto Gomes from La Trobe University, Melbourne; Hood Salleh from the National University of Malaysia; Lye Tuck-Po from the Universiti Sains Malaysia and Colin Nicholas from the Center for Orang Asli Concerns in Kuala Lumpur. Finally I would like to thank my brother Richard Tacey who read through many previous drafts of this chapter and offered valuable criticisms, suggestions and feedback.

2. Henceforth, any reference to Batek will mean Batek Tanum unless specified otherwise.

REFERENCES

Benjamin, G.
2002 On Being Tribal in the Malay World. *In* Tribal Communities in the Malay World. G. Benjamin and C. Chou, eds. Pp. 7–76. Singapore: Institute of Southeast Asian Studies.

Burenhult, N. and A. Majid
2011 *Olfaction in Aslian. Ideology* and *Language.* Senses & Society 6(1): 19–29. doi: 10.2752/174589311X12893982233597, accessed 20 Nov. 2013.

Dentan, R.K.
2008 Overwhelming Terror: Love, Fear, Peace, and Violence among Semai of Malaysia. Lanham, MD: Rowman and Littlefield Publishers.

Dentan, R.K., K. Endicott, A.G. Gomes and M.B. Hooker
    1997   Malaysia and the Original People: A Case Study of the Impact of Development on Indigenous Peoples. Boston: Allyn and Bacon.

Endicott, K.M.
    1979   Batek Negrito Religion. Oxford: Oxford University Press.
    1983   The Effects of Slave Raiding on the Aborigines of the Malay Peninsula. *In* Slavery, Bondage and Dependency in Southeast Asia. A. Reid and J. Brewster, eds. Pp. 216–45. St Lucia, Queensland: University of Queensland Press.
    1997   Batek History, Interethnic Relations, and Subgroup Dynamics. *In* Indigenous Peoples and the State: Politics, Land, and Ethnicity in the Malayan Peninsula and Borneo. Monograph 46. R.L. Winzeler, ed. Pp. 30–50. New Haven, CT: Yale University Southeast Asia Studies.

Endicott, K.M. and K.L. Endicott
    2008   The Headman Was a Woman: The Gender Egalitarian Batek of Malaysia. Long Grove, IL: Waveland Press.

Gibson, T. and K. Sillander
    2011   Introduction. *In* Anarchic Solidarity: Autonomy, Equality, and Fellowship in Southeast Asia. T. Gibson and K. Sillander, eds. Pp. 1–16. New Haven: Yale University Press.

Giddens, A.
    1990   The Consequences of Modernity. Cambridge: Polity Press.

Gomes, A.G.
    2007   Modernity and Malaysia: Settling the Menraq Forest Nomads. New York: Routledge.

Hallowell, A.I.
    1960   Ojibwa Ontology, Behavior, and World-View. *In* Culture in History: Essays in Honor of Paul Radin. S. Diamond, ed. Pp. 19–52. New York: Colombia University Press.

Howell, S.
    2011   Sources of Sociality in a Cosmological Frame: Chewong, Peninsular Malaysia. *In* Anarchic Solidarity: Autonomy, Equality, and Fellowship in Southeast Asia. T. Gibson and K. Sillander, eds. Pp. 40–61. New Haven: Yale University Press.

Lye, T-P.
    2004   Changing Pathways: Forest Degradation and the Batek of Pahang, Malaysia. Lanham, MD: Lexington Books.

Nobuta Toshihiro
2008 Living on the Periphery: Development and Islamization among the Orang Asli in Malaysia. Kyoto: Kyoto University Press and Trans Pacific Press.

Nicholas, C.
2000 The Orang Asli and the Contest for Resources: Indigenous Politics, Development and Identity in Peninsular Malaysia. Copenhagen: IWGIA.

Riboli, D.
2008 Continuation of Shamanism among the Semang-Negrito of Peninsular Malayia. *In* Shamans Unbound. M. Hoppál and Z. Simonkay, eds. Pp. 53–9. Budapest: Akadémiai Kiadó.
2009 Shamans and Transformation. *In* Yogic Perception, Meditation and Altered States of Consciousness. D. Eigner and E. Franco, eds. Pp. 347–67. Vienna: Verlag der Φsterreichischen Akademie der Wissenschaften.
2013 Of Angry Thunders, Smelly Intruders and Human Tigers: Shamanic Representations of Violence and Conflict in Nonviolent Peoples: the Semang-Negrito (Malaysia). *In* Shamanism and Violence: Power, Repression and Suffering in Indigenous Religious Contexts. D. Riboli and D. Torri, eds. London: Ashgate Publishers.

Robertson, R.
1992 Globalization: Social theory and global culture. London: Sage.

Scott, J.C.
2009 The Art of Not Being Governed: An Anarchist History of Southeast Asia. New Haven and London: Yale University Press.

Tacey, I.
2013 Tropes of Fear: the Impact of Globalization on Batek Religious Landscapes. *In* Special Issue, "Religion and Globalization", *Religions* 4(2): 240–66. doi:10.3390/rel4020240, accessed 20 Sept. 2013.

Talib, N.N.
2012 Antifragility: Things That Gain From Disorder. New York: Random House.

Tan, T.P.
2012 Oral History and People's Memory of the Malayan Emergency (1948–1960): The Case of Pulai. Journal of Social Issues in Southeast Asia 27(1): 84–119. doi:10.1355/sj27-1c, accessed 5 Sept. 2013.

Tomlinson, J.
1999 Globalization and Culture. Cambridge: Polity Press.

chapter 17

Beyond Economic Gain: Strategic Use of Trade in Boundary Maintenance by Semang Collectors of Peninsular Malaysia

Csilla Dallos

INTRODUCTION: INTERETHNIC TRADE BETWEEN FORAGERS AND FARMERS—ITS HISTORY AND INTERPRETATIONS

This chapter deals with the meaning and implications of trade relations between foragers and farmers in Peninsular Malaysia, where, as in other parts of Southeast Asia, long history ties hunter-gatherers to agriculturists and to the state (Morrison and Junker 2002). Large scale trade in forest products which today compose the bulk of traded items is relatively recent. According to Metcalf, specialized collecting of rattan for instance only became common in the region in the 19th century under colonial rule (2010). Smaller scale trade in minor products such as "hunted meat, honey, rattan, resins and spices", however, likely extends back several millennia, significantly shaping regional politics as well as the development of maritime trading kingdoms and chiefdoms in Insular Southeast Asia (Junker 1996, 2002: 131).[1]

Trade relations between foragers and farmers in Southeast Asia have been subjected to considerable anthropological interest. In the late 1980s and early 1990s, as part of the ongoing debate about hunter-gatherers' cultural identity, several researchers studied the question of whether independent foraging was possible in tropical rainforest environments and concluded that, to make up for a deficiency in carbohydrates, hunter-gatherers must trade with farmers to survive (for example Headland 1987; Bailey et al. 1989; Headland and Bailey 1991). Though this conclusion has been subsequently contested by several scholars specializing in the indigenous groups of Peninsular Malaysia (for example Dentan 1991; Dallos 2011; Endicott and Bellwood 1991; for similar conclusions elsewhere, see Brosius 1991; Colinvaux and Bush 1991; Dwyer and Minnegal 1991), the narrowly economic framework in which revisionists interpreted foragers' trade with farmers has not been challenged.[2]

Yet, the economic framework contradicts foragers' own understanding of interethnic trade and their role as traders. This understanding is exemplified by Lanoh, a group of hunter-gatherer-collectors in Peninsular Malaysia, who, instead of perceiving trade as a desperate economic measure, less meaningful than hunting, take pride in their knowledge of forest products and in their identity as traders.[3] This is especially evident when they express a desire to protect the forest realm from intruders including, and especially, Malays. This interpretation suggests a so far largely unexplored political advantage to Semang of trade with local farmers. Apart from being a means to supplement their diet and tool kit, trade relations with Malays may have been instrumental in these foragers' ability to protect their autonomy and the autonomy of their domain over centuries of interacting with far more powerful Malays.[4]

INTERETHNIC TRADE AND ITS SIGNIFICANCE FOR LANOH

Lanoh (or *səmaʔ bloom*) are a central Aslian speaking indigenous group in Peninsular Malaysia. Though central Aslian languages are primarily spoken by horticulturists of the hills, Lanoh have nonetheless been classified as "Semang", because, in terms of lifestyle, they occupy a Semang niche. This means that, situated in the lowland between Malays of the coastal areas and Senoi horticulturists of the interiors, they have conducted the mobile, or semi-mobile, lifestyle of subsistence hunter-gatherers, while also participating in collecting forest products for trade. Since the 1980s, there has been increasing pressure by government agencies for Lanoh to resettle, primarily in one village, Air Bah, in northern Perak. In the past 30 years resettlement has impacted every aspect of Lanoh life, from hunting to social organization (Dallos 2011). Like other indigenous minority groups in Malaysia, they have been pressed to convert to Islam as well as to become agriculturists and engage in animal domestication. They have consistently resisted the latter two activities, as they also have resisted moving in or merging with other Orang Asli villages (Dallos 2011).

The organization and context of forest collecting and interethnic trade have also changed in recent decades. While trade in minor forest products—such as medicine, building materials, honey, camphor and aphrodisiacs—with Malay villagers has declined, large-scale specialized collecting of major forest products, primarily rattan and fragrant wood (*gaharu*), for Chinese middlemen has increased. Though dominating the life of resettled Lanoh today, this larger scale commercial collecting has been fraught with problems, not least because its organization is significantly different from, and even contradicts, the organization of individualistic collecting of minor products for Malay villagers in the past. The most important difference is that the middleman has a relationship with a whole group of collectors, as opposed to individuals. Albeit significant for economic reasons, this aspect makes trade with middlemen a frustrating experience for Lanoh, because their sociality is far better matched with ad hoc "village trade" conducted directly between individual collectors and the end users (Dallos 2011). In such trade, individual collectors maintain relationships with individuals and families in several Malay villages and drop in at these villages according to a seasonal schedule of demand and supply for forest products, which they subsequently collect and deliver. As a consequence, the relationship between village Malays and Orang Asli collectors is often quite close and stretches over generations. In spite of the current predominance of collecting major forest products, Lanoh in Air Bah eagerly participate in the small-scale intermittent exchange of minor products whenever possible, and, even today, Lanoh drop anything at a moment's notice to attend to Malay and Chinese villagers' request for frogs, medicine, or aphrodisiacs. The way village trade is presently conducted by Lanoh provides a glimpse into its impact in the lives of these hunter-gatherers.

Undoubtedly, trade has played a far more significant part in the life of forager-collectors than in the lives of village Malays. For Malay farmers, even in pre-development times when they relied on forest products to a greater extent than today, trade with foragers must have seemed incidental, a side activity, and their perception and treatment of foragers expresses this perceived insignificance.[5] For Lanoh collectors, on the contrary, their trade with villagers was a life-altering priority. In fact, it could be argued that the entire Lanoh lifestyle and social organization is geared toward such small-scale village trade. This is evident in their "outer orientation", which is similar to that of trade-oriented Malays (Benjamin 1985) with one important difference: while Malay social organization has a corporate quality, Semang social organization consists of individualistic social networks, which likely dominated the Semang lifestyle (Dallos 2011). For instance, while facilitating village trade, this individualistic and flexible character of Semang social relationships has most definitely hindered activities requiring cooperation in farming, big game hunting, and, as mentioned above, in more organized and specialized trade in major forest products (Dallos 2011). This life-altering significance of interethnic trade in hunter-gatherers' lives and farmers' mistreatment of the people who delivered these goods would seem to support the revisionist conclusion that hunter-gatherers depended on trade with Malay farmers and that they were politically subordinated to them. Lanoh's own interpretation of these relations, however, raises doubts about the validity of these conclusions and leads to an alternative explanation for this overwhelming significance of trade in the lives of forest collectors.

INTERETHNIC TRADE AND ITS ROLE IN LANOH CULTURAL IDENTITY

In terms of economic benefits and outcomes, without doubt, foragers have profited considerably from trade with outsiders. Today, like most Orang Asli, Lanoh are in an extremely disadvantaged political and economic position, increasingly relying on commercial activities for their livelihood. They consume a range of goods bought in the store or in the nearby logging town, rely on metal tools such as axes and bushknives (*parang*), and they even own a few shotguns, though not necessarily ammunition. In earlier times, too, they had exchanged forest products for items such as rice, tools and tobacco with farmers, which presumably made their lives more convenient in many respects. Yet, while acknowledging their increasing dependence on commercial products in recent years, people I consulted emphasized their economic self-sufficiency and self-reliance in the past:

> In the old days, the only difficult things to get were tools: a *parang* or an axe. They were very expensive, so one way to get these was to steal them. Whenever we were near Malay or Chinese farms, we would pick up tools left by these people. Everything else we could get from the forest. We could drink water from the river or roots. We could get paddy, tapioca, meat for food. We did not have cooking oil; we never used it. We could get honey for sugar. We got sour fruits as a substitute for salt, for instance, *mempelam* [mango, Mal.]. We boiled the *mempelam*. We mixed this with our meat whenever we were cooking, and chillies from the forest made food taste better than salt. We got lard from wild boar when we needed it. Even now, when we run out of salt and oil, we cook like that. We did not use pots and pans. We always cooked with bamboo. We put everything in the bamboo and cooked. For fire, we would use two stones on dry twigs and grass to spark a fire. Wild tobacco, we grew.[6]

In fact, in spite of the appearance of having the upper hand in their relations with foragers, Malays may have been more dependent on Orang Asli to supply forest products than Orang Asli collectors on products received from villagers.[7] Local Malay farmers not only obtained rare goods and luxury items from the forest, but also medicine, building material, aphrodisiacs, honey, camphor and scented wood.

Though their need for such products was limited both in quantity and frequency, these products were nonetheless welcome and, in the case of medicine, even essential.

This would indicate that, in spite of the relative significance of trade for collectors like Lanoh and in spite of the mistreatment they have suffered in the hands of Malays, instead of subordination, a power balance may have characterized the relationship of foragers and farmers—a power balance based on collectors' ability to turn an economic advantage (access to forest products—too dangerous and inconvenient for Malays to obtain) into a political one: an ability to maintain autonomy in spite of living in proximity to more numerous, organized and powerful Malays. This political significance, complementarity and power balance is evident in Lanoh cultural identity.

In anthropological discourse—often leaning toward essentialism—one of the major problems of recent years has been the difficulty in defining contemporary hunter-gatherers. In this discourse, extra-group relations of contemporary hunter-gatherers have often been relegated to the status of "secondary" significance, less relevant for understanding life in the world of pre-domestication hunter-gatherers. For hunter-gatherers like Lanoh, who see foraging and trade as parts of an integrated lifestyle neither of which is more or less important, this seems less of an issue. They think of themselves primarily as "forest people", and this designation includes both subsistence hunting-gathering and commercial collecting.[8] Nonetheless, when it comes to formulating and expressing their cultural identity, that is, who they are as people, trade and their relations with farmers appear to be the most significant.

This claim seems contradictory to the current importance of hunting and blowpipes (the tools associated with hunting) as symbols of indigenous identity. Yet, this recent emphasis likely reflects cultural and political pressures, especially the pressure to convert to Islam. In this confrontation, diet has assumed increased significance, and blowpipes and hunting have become symbols of their eating non-*halal* food and, thus, of non-Muslim indigeneity. Before these developments, though Malays may have considered Orang Asli an "uncivilized" race, they were presumably less concerned with what Orang Asli did or did not eat in the forest. It is probable that prior to recent politicization, blowpipes and hunting were more connected to masculine identity. Even today, attitudes toward blowpipes and hunting underline this point. Lanoh men spend many hours a day maintaining their blowpipes, which women are not allowed to touch. Beyond fulfilling subsistence needs, Lanoh also regard hunting as a sport performed by males (Dallos 2011). Men are proud of their skills and ability to hunt and cook meat (especially the squirrel's penis, a delicacy only consumed by men and boys) which are linked to masculinity and sexual prowess (Dallos 2011).

Unlike hunting, which is, therefore, a relatively recent cultural identity marker, trade and collecting forest products—the activities at the interface of the relationship between Malays and Semang—likely became important early in differentiating indigenous collectors of forest products from Malays—the recipients of these products. Even today, otherwise non-confrontational and overtly submissive Lanoh jealously guard their identity as forest collectors and, as the next quote indicates, express deep indignation when poorer Malays, themselves losing livelihood as small farmers or rubber tappers, "shamelessly" [*tak tahu malu*, Mal.] venture into the forest and engage in collecting forest products either for their own use or for commerce.

> They used to call us "jungle people" because of our work in the forest, but now [Malays] have become like us. The other day I met a Malay *haji* [person who has gone to Mecca] looking for frogs at Sumpitan. We were looking for frogs in the river. It was late and we decided to spend the night there. We were about to make a fire when we heard noises from the river. I went quietly to see what it was. Then I saw two people. One was a boy. He was carrying a sack. The man was in the river with a flashlight. I shouted, "Hey, who is that?" The man was shocked. He almost fell. Then I said, "We are Asli. We are looking for frogs. Who are you?" The man replied, "I'm looking for frogs too." The man came out of the water and approached me. Then I saw he was wearing the white cap of a *haji* on his head. I asked him, "Are you a *haji*?" He said "yes." Then I said, "How can you look for frogs? This is *haram* [forbidden food]." The *haji* replied, "Oh yes, this is not to eat. This is for sale. I'm not a rich Malay. I'm a poor Malay. Frogs are good money. This is all right. This is not wrong." Then I said, "Ah, now you are saying it's not wrong. Before, when we passed through the *kampung*, you, Malays, were always telling us, 'oh you are going

for frogs. How can you eat such things? They are so dirty.' If the
frogs are dirty, the money you get from selling them is also dirty."
The *haji* was very angry.[9]

This incident illustrates that Lanoh protect their role as collectors
and that their usual open-mindedness about territorial access does not
apply to intruding Malays. Especially today when space and resource
base are shrinking around resettlement villages and foragers' collecting
ranges increasingly overlap, competition with other Orang Asli occurs
almost daily (Dallos 2011). However, with other Orang Asli, there is a
pronounced ethic of permissiveness: "for Lanoh, everything is free for
everybody, for instance, Temiar can come here and look for food". Yet,
the same ethic loses its validity when it comes to Malays, who are not
at all welcome to look for resources in areas and in a manner Lanoh
consider their exclusive (Orang Asli) domain. Though Lanoh are fond
of saying that "people who make boundaries are people who are looking
for enemies, because boundaries attract enemies", this exclusivity
indicates the contrary, that physical and cultural boundaries with
Malays are, indeed, important, not the least because these boundaries
have played a role in defining who Lanoh are.

INTERETHNIC TRADE AND ITS ROLE IN
BOUNDARY DEFENCE

It has often been noted that hunter-gatherers' identity is strongly
linked to the forest (and forest skills) and is constructed in relation to
outsiders. For instance, Batek define the world of the forest in contrast
with the world of *gɔb*, or Malays, the primary reference group for
Batek (Lye 2005). Yount et al. similarly claim that in Madagascar
Mikea identity is constructed in contrast with agriculturists, fishermen
and pastoralists, and that existing contrasts between Mikea and their
neighbours "are usually magnified in the discourse of identity" (2001:
263). Furthermore, forager-collectors see themselves as the protectors
of the forest, and this guardianship also plays an important role in
hunter-gatherers' cultural identity. According to Lye, Batek believe that
one of their responsibilities entailed in being forest people is to look
after the forest (2002: 6). This attitude is consistent with a desire to

defend the forest world against invasion by outsiders (K. Endicott and K.L. Endicott 1986). However, small groups of hunter-gatherers are thought to have limited ability to engage in boundary (or frontier) defence.

Current theories of territoriality differentiate between two main mechanisms of boundary defence: "direct perimeter defence" (or "spatial boundary defence") and "social boundary defence", both of which are linked to the quality of resources in a group's environment (Cashdan 1983; Casimir 1992; Kelly 1995). While direct perimeter defence is said to correlate with relatively dense and predictable resources, social boundary defence, which operates via "more or less institutionalized reciprocal access" on the basis of reciprocal altruism, is likely to occur when resources are unpredictable and scarce (Casimir 1992: 12–3). Neither of these mechanisms is available to hunter-gatherers like the Lanoh. Direct perimeter defence requires military strength, that is, organization and numbers. Semang collectors are generally far too few in numbers and lack the organization necessary to engage in direct territorial defence.[10] On the contrary, Lanoh and other Semang, known for their nonviolent and non-confrontational ways, outwardly often appear submissive when in direct interaction with Malays. In fact as Kirk and Karen L. Endicott observe, the Batek Semang "[are not] territorial in any of the usual senses of the term" (1986: 140). Thus while some hunter-gatherer groups, for instance the !Kung of southern Africa, are known to engage in social boundary defence mechanisms, that is "reciprocal altruism through controlled access to the social group" (Cashdan 1983: 49), Batek do not observe any "kinship criterion for joining a camp", and "do not always know where other groups and individuals are" (1986: 144). Comments by Lanoh denying exclusive rights to resources, including fruit trees, echo these observations among Batek.

It follows that traditional thinking on territoriality would depict people like Lanoh as entirely defenceless. Yet, contrary to this prediction, the outcome of their long relationship with their farming neighbours indicates considerable success when it comes to boundary defence. After centuries of interaction, and until quite recently, they not only managed to keep their world, the forest world, and the world of farmers apart, but also to maintain their indigenous and independent lifestyle. This outcome suggests that our theory of territoriality and territoriality might be too limited, and that there could be alternative, so far little-explored, strategies available even to people whose numbers and social organization prevent other forms of territorial defence.

In the 1970s, Marshall Sahlins proposed what has become one of the most influential anthropological models of reciprocity and corresponding social relations (1972). In this model, social relations form a continuum in terms of social distance from the most familiar —domestic—arrangements, where "generalized reciprocity" takes precedence, to the greatest distance, where it is morally acceptable to cheat, even to harm the other (called "negative reciprocity") (1972). Yet, our current theories of territoriality and territorial defence fail to represent this continuum in its entirety. The above-discussed mechanisms of territorial defence correspond to one particular quality of social relations—each at the opposite ends of the social continuum. While social boundary maintenance mechanisms arguably operate among people towards the social end of the continuum,[11] direct perimeter defence occurs in situations where relationships approach the extreme asocial end.[12] Currently, however, there is no model of territorial defence representing the *middle range* of Sahlins' continuum, where social and economic relations are equally important. In terms of economic exchange, this middle range corresponds to "balanced reciprocity", a primary form of which is trade (or barter) (1972).

In the remainder of this section, I will explore the notion that, in certain situations, trade may operate as a special case of social boundary maintenance. However, instead of being based on kinship rules and regulations, it is based on social relations associated with balanced reciprocity. It may nonetheless effectively function in maintaining boundaries between populations and regulate access to land and resources. Equally important and relevant is the question whether people actively pursue trade as a strategy, making it a priority to achieve these desired ends. This is especially true considering that in anthropological debates about the meaning of hunter-gatherers' trade with outsiders, hunter-gatherer-traders are often portrayed as helpless victims of circumstance who are devoid of agency.

By engaging in trade in minor forest products with village Malays, Semang hunter-gatherer-collectors not only reduced the need and likelihood that Malays would enter the forest, but also managed to shift relations with their more powerful neighbours from the extreme asocial end to the middle, "friendlier", range of the above-discussed social continuum. With this shift, they successfully redefined the relationship, making it far less likely that Malays would engage in direct territorial intrusion, which, given the discrepancy in military strength between these two populations, could have resulted in the cultural and/or physical annihilation of the hunter-gatherers.

Although Sahlins emphasized that in balanced reciprocity social and economic relations mutually reinforce each other, his is still a predominantly economic model, in which it is easy to view social relations as vehicles in fostering and delivering continuous economic transactions. Yet, the current discussion emphasizing a political framework calls attention to the inverse relationship and directionality. In certain circumstances, for instance in the precarious geopolitical position occupied by Lanoh and other Semang groups in Peninsular Malaysia, continuous economic relations may, in fact, be employed to foster social relations. Indeed, Malay villagers frequently describe Orang Asli collectors, especially those with whom they and their families have had long-term relations, as their "friends". Thus, in spite of episodes of ill-treatment, having Malays thinking of their Semang neighbours in these terms arguably has gone a long way in discouraging these farmers from treating hunter-gatherers in their backyard as they would treat enemy strangers.

Nonetheless, territorial defence and boundary maintenance based on trade relations and balanced reciprocity differs from the other two forms of boundary defence in an important respect. While in both other mechanisms, there is a consensus that the arrangement, whether assigning rights of access or open warfare, is about territory and territorial access, there is no open admission, apparently not even recognition, that the trade relations have repercussions for territorial access. Evidently, there was a mutual satisfaction with the arrangement reinforcing the "symbiosis" interpretation of interethnic trade between foragers and farmers: Malays were pleased that they did not have to go to the jungle to get forest products, and Semang collectors were content to be left alone in the forest. Yet, a discrepancy in the perception of these social relations by the two parties indicates that hunter-gatherers may have approached this arrangement more deliberately than farmers.

While trade evidently and unequivocally shifts social relations from asocial and confrontational to "friendly" and neighbourly, it was not necessarily the case for both parties. While, as noted above, village Malays often refer to hunter-gatherers as their "friends", this warm feeling is rarely reciprocated by Lanoh, who never seem to completely relax their vigilance when dealing with Malays. Thus, this shift in terms of the quality of social relations has not occurred from a Lanoh standpoint. In spite of their continual engagement, they continue to relate to farmers as strangers, as if the relationship were still on the extreme asocial end of the continuum, where it is not morally wrong to cheat (Dallos 2011). They regard their relationship with Malays *instrumentally*.

This discrepancy and instrumentality on the part of Lanoh could indicate that forest collector Semang engage in trade relations with Malays as a more or less conscious strategy of appeasement. This assumes that they are active players, which goes against the (revisionist) tradition in anthropology of portraying hunter-gatherers as victims in their relations with outsiders. A similar tradition runs through Orang Asli studies as well, where the continuous fear caused by atrocities and mistreatment by majority populations and the implications of this for the behaviour of people in indigenous groups has long dominated scholarly treatment of these peoples. Researchers have emphasized that as a result of this power differential, Orang Asli have become fearful, nonviolent, with a tendency to flee danger (for example Robarchek 1977, 1979; Dentan 1992, 2008). This tendency has also been linked to hunter-gatherers' ability to preserve their cultural autonomy. Porath, for instance, considers that Menik in Southern Thailand have retained their autonomy because they were able to withdraw to the forest (2001: 135n3).

Without doubt, the atrocities such as slave raiding that Orang Asli have suffered at the hands of Malays were extremely menacing, and often when the hostility became untenable, hunter-gatherers, as well as other indigenous minorities of the peninsula, fled from this danger, retreating to the forest. [13] Yet, what is more extraordinary, that equally often, and even more consistently, they opted instead to remain near Malay villages at the boundary of the forest and agricultural landscapes. This *cultural response*, though seemingly counterintuitive, may have been far more effectual in the long term than the, perhaps natural, tendency to flee when facing persecution and mistreatment. In Peninsular Malaysia, geopolitical positioning has limited Semang's ability retreat to the forest, because, in many places, they are effectively sandwiched between two farming populations—Malays of the lowlands and Senoi of the interior hills. Although of these two groups, Malays have presented the greater threat, Senoi have also constituted an obstacle to their movements. Consequently, while in extreme cases, Semang would flee and engage in "silent barter", their more general strategy has been the opposite: in spite of the atrocities, and in spite of perceived danger, they *stayed* and continued to engage farmers.

CONCLUSIONS: INTERETHNIC TRADE AND HUNTER-GATHERER SOCIAL ORGANIZATION— QUESTIONS AND QUERIES

In this chapter, I have challenged the narrowly economic conception of foragers' trade with farmers and argued that the political significance of these trade relations may have outweighed their economic importance. In particular, I examined the potential role of interethnic trade in minor forest products with Malay villagers in the ability of Semang hunter-gatherers to retain their independence. I also suggested that the model outlined in this chapter represents an important change both from essentialism and victimization, which currently dominate the study of contemporary hunters and gatherers. I have emphasized that, even before their recent politicization within nation states, hunter-gatherers like Lanoh had been political players who successfully negotiated a complex set of ecological and social relations using strategies aligned with those attributed to one of their main cultural icons, the mouse deer (*kija?*).[14] Lanoh have several tales of *kija?*, and they love to tell them, especially because in these tales, *kija?*—the smallest, most vulnerable animal in the forest—outsmarts and outplays the most vicious, aggressive, and widely-feared animal, the tiger.

If we are to pursue this line of inquiry, if we are to understand better the role and potential of interethnic trade in boundary maintenance, it is crucial that we learn more about this mechanism as a (cultural) strategy and explore its dimensions on a cultural, cognitive and behavioural level. Given the significance of trade and continuing engagement with Malays for Malaysian hunter-gatherers, it is not surprising that trade has become a priority and cultural focus in Semang lifestyle and social relations, important enough to sacrifice internal coherence and structure. An interesting question, and one that has occupied anthropologists of hunter-gatherers since the 1980s, is whether and to what extent foragers' internal organization and relationships are shaped by their participation in interethnic trade with outsiders (Woodburn 1988). While James Woodburn considered the possibility that engagement in trade with neighbouring peoples may cause "fragmentation" in hunter-gatherers' social organization, there have been few suggestions as to the mechanisms of how this might occur. A study of the relationship between internal and external boundaries, and the effect of the emphasis on external boundary maintenance may shed a light on this question. It has been suggested that the lack of social boundary maintenance among Semang may be due to continuing persecution by Malays, and indeed often, it may have been the case (K. Endicott and K.L. Endicott 1986). Yet, alternatively this distinctive feature of Semang social life may reflect instead the need and urgency to focus on the even more consequential boundary these collectors strived to maintain with farmers. The fluidity and flexibility of Semang social organization and internal permissiveness when it comes to land and resource use by other Orang Asli has facilitated Semang in their participation in small-scale intermittent trade in minor forest products with Malays that thrives and depends on qualities that make internal boundary maintenance between Orang Asli unlikely and untenable.

Finally, a promising line of inquiry concerns the generalizability of this model. It is going to be interesting to see whether this potential of trade to maintain boundaries only applies to hunter-gatherers, or whether it can be extended to other minority populations in analogous circumstance, as, for instance, some of the essays on territorial strategies by peripatetics in Casimir and Rao seem to suggest (1992).

This direction could invigorate thinking on human territoriality and intergroup relations and call attention to opportunities historically available even to the manifestly weak and powerless in unequal interethnic encounters.

NOTES

1. It must be noted that interethnic trade between indigenous peoples and farmers in the region was far from uniform, but displayed a great variety from group to group and circumstance to circumstance (Endicott 1997; Gianno and Bayr 2009). It is also likely that these relations changed considerably due to "expanding maritime luxury good trade", which had an impact "on the economic choices, mobility and settlement strategies and social dynamics of tropical forest foraging populations in Southeast Asia" (Junker 2002: 135). As well, while interethnic trade between foragers and farmers has received considerable anthropological attention, foragers' trade relations have not been restricted to farmers. As evidenced by R.O.D. Noone's singularly interesting paper, trade between various Orang Asli groups has been similarly common and varied (1954–55, and Lye, personal communication).

2. For a critique of political economic approaches and the tendency in hunter-gatherer studies to focus on and overemphasize the economic aspects of forager-farmer interactions, see Griffin (1996).

3. This chapter is based on research conducted among newly resettled Lanoh in 1998–99 in northern Perak, Malaysia. This research was made possible by IDRC's Young Canadian Researchers' Award.

4. This point is consistent with the observation that, in North America and Siberia, hunter-gatherers engaged in trade during the colonial period were among those who managed to maintain their autonomy (Bodley 1999: 467).

5. The atrocities and mistreatment, including slave raiding, Orang Asli have suffered in the hands of Malays for centuries has been well-documented in the literature of the aboriginal groups of Peninsular Malaysia (for example, Dodge 1981; K.M. Endicott 1983; Dentan 2008; Dallos 2011).

6. A slightly modified version of this excerpt from my field notes appears in Dallos (2011: 72).

7. Claims about Lanoh relative lack of dependence on farmers' products does not necessarily have wider applicability. As Griffin notes, dependence by

hunter-gatherers on their farming neighbours varies from individual to individual and group to group (1996: 113).

8. As Griffin notes, hunter-gatherers are rarely interested in being "pure" hunter-gatherers; they are more interested in a good life (1996: 120).

9. The full version of this quote appeared in Dallos (2011: 90–1).

10. Semang constitute 3 per cent of the Orang Asli population, and they rarely number more than a few hundred per dialect group. At the time of my research the Lanoh numbered approximately 200, and Endicott estimates the total number of Batek around 700 (Dentan et al. 1997).

11. Even though social territorial defence mechanisms operate towards the social end of the continuum, they do not operate at the extreme social end. That would correspond to "generalized reciprocity", which, arguably, would be represented by unconditional permission granting to their land and resources among various Semang groups. (Though Lanoh would extend this unconditional permission granted to other non-Orang Asli as well, it is doubtful that this gesture is mutual. One could hypothesize that horticulturist Senoi operate on the basis of social territorial defence.)

12. Smith removes perimeter defence from the realm of social relations associated with reciprocity. Referring to the difference between social boundary defence and perimeter defence, he writes, "the first system is one of reciprocity, suitable for situations of fluctuating and unpredictable resources; the latter system is nonreciprocal, exclusionary, and adapted to cases in which the resource base is dependable...." (1983: 61, in Casimir 1992: 12). Yet, in examining Sahlins' continuum of social relations, negative reciprocity, the asocial extreme, can arguably be conceived of as the equivalent of exclusivity or lacking social relationships assumed in other forms of reciprocity.

13. There is evidence, however, that farmers recognized foragers' contribution to their economies and that this may also have mitigated the effects of slave raids. In a recent article, Peter Gardner argues that Hindus in South Asia had a vested interest in keeping hunter-gatherers from assimilating because they were valued as sources of forest trade goods and regarded as yet another occupational group (2013). Kirk Endicott made a related point when suggesting that slave raids by Indonesians were more violent than those by local Malay farmers, who valued hunter-gatherers' contribution as forest collectors (1983).

14. Griffin emphasizes the same point when remarking of Agta that they are political players who shape their fate and not helpless victims passively shaped by circumstance (1996: 116, 119).

REFERENCES

Bailey, R.C., Head, G., Jenike, M., Owen, B., Rechtman, R. and Zechenter, E.
    1989   Hunting and Gathering in the Tropical Rain Forest: Is It Possible? American Anthropologist 91: 59–82.

Benjamin, G.
    1985   In the Long Term: Three Themes in Malayan Cultural Ecology. *In* Cultural Values and Human Ecology in Southeast Asia. K.L. Hutterer, A.T. Rambo and G. Lovelace, eds. Pp. 219–78. Ann Arbor: Center for South and Southeast Asian Studies, University of Michigan.

Bodley, J.H.
    1999   Hunter-Gatherers and the Colonial Encounter. *In* The Cambridge Encyclopedia of Hunters and Gatherers. R.B. Lee and R. Daly, eds. Pp. 465–73. Cambridge: Cambridge University Press.

Brosius, P.J.
    1991   Foraging in Tropical Rain Forests: The Case of the Penan of Sarawak, East Malaysia (Borneo). Human Ecology 19: 123–50.

Cashdan, E.A.
    1983   Territoriality among Human Foragers: Ecological Models and an Application to Four Bushman Groups. Current Anthropology 24: 47–66.

Casimir, M.J.
    1992   The Dimensions of Territoriality: An Introduction. *In* Mobility and Territoriality: Social and Spatial Boundaries among Foragers, Fishers, Pastoralists and Peripatetics. M.J. Casimir and A. Rao, eds. Pp. 1–27. New York: Berg.

Casimir, M.J. and A. Rao, eds.
    1992   Mobility and Territoriality: Social and Spatial Boundaries among Foragers, Fishers, Pastoralists and Peripatetics. New York: Berg.

Colinvaux, P.A. and M.B. Bush
    1991   The Rain-Forest Ecosystem as a Resource for Hunting and Gathering. American Anthropologist 93: 153–60.

Dallos, C.
    2011   From Equality to Inequality: Social Change among Newly Sedentary Lanoh Hunter-Gatherer Traders of Peninsular Malaysia. Toronto: University of Toronto Press.

Dentan, R.K.
    1991   Potential Food Sources for Foragers in Malaysian Rainforests: Sago, Yams and Lots of Little Things. Bijdragen tot de Taal-, Land- en Volkenkunde 147: 420–44.

1992   The Rise, Maintenance, and Destruction of Peaceable Polity: A Preliminary Essay in Political Ecology. *In* Aggression and Peacefulness in Humans and Other Primates. J. Silverberg and J.P. Gray, eds. Pp. 214–69. Oxford: Oxford University Press.

2008   Overwhelming Terror: Love, Fear, Peace, and Violence among Semai of Malaysia. Lanham: Rowman & Littlefield.

Dentan, R.K., K. Endicott, A. Gomes and M.B. Hooker

1997   Malaysia and the "Original People": A Case Study of the Impact of Development on Indigenous Peoples. Boston: Allyn and Bacon.

Dodge, N.N.

1981   The Malay-Aborigine Nexus under Malay Rule. Bijdragen tot de Taal-, Land- en Volkenkunde 137: 1–16.

Dwyer, P.D. and M. Minnegal

1991   Hunting in Lowland, Tropical Rain Forest: Towards a Model of Non-Agricultural Subsistence. Human Ecology 19: 187–212.

Endicott, K.

1979   Batek Negrito Religion: The World-View and Rituals of a Hunting and Gathering People of Peninsular Malaysia. Oxford: Clarendon Press.

1983   The Effects of Slave Raiding on the Aborigines of the Malay Peninsula. *In* Slavery, Bondage and Dependency in Southeast Asia. A. Reid and J. Brewster, eds. Pp. 216–45. Brisbane: University of Queensland Press.

1997   Batek History, Interethnic Relations, and Subgroup Dynamics. *In* Indigenous Peoples and the State: Politics, Land, and Ethnicity in the Malayan Peninsula and Borneo. R.L. Winzeler, ed. Pp. 30–50. Yale Southeast Asia Studies 46. New Haven, CT: Yale University Press.

Endicott, K. and P. Bellwood

1991   The Possibility of Independent Foraging in the Rain Forest of Peninsular Malaysia. Human Ecology 19: 151–85.

Endicott, K. and K.L. Endicott

1986   The Question of Hunter-Gatherer Territoriality: The Case of the Batek of Malaysia. *In* The Past and Future of !Kung Ethnography: Critical Reflections and Symbolic Perspectives. M. Biesele, R. Gordon and R. Lee, eds. Pp. 137–62. Hamburg: Helmut Buske Verlag.

Gardner, P.M.
  2013 Understanding Anomalous Distribution of Hunter-Gatherers: The Indian Case. Current Anthropology 54: 510–3.

Gianno, R. and K.J. Bayr
  2009 Semelai Agricultural Patterns: Toward an Understanding of Variation among Indigenous Cultures in Southern Peninsular Malaysia. Journal of Southeast Asian Studies 40: 153–85.

Griffin, M.B.
  1996 The Cultural Identity of Foragers and the Agta of Palanan, Isabela, the Philippines. Anthropos 91: 111–23.

Headland, T.
  1987 The Wild Yam Question: How Well Could Independent Hunter-Gatherers Live in a Tropical Rain Forest Ecosystem. Human Ecology 15: 463–91.

Headland, T.N. and R.C. Bailey
  1991 Introduction: Have Hunter-Gatherers Ever Lived in Tropical Rain Forests Independently of Agriculture. Human Ecology 19: 115–22.

Junker, L.L.
  1996 Hunter-Gatherer Landscapes and Lowland Trade in the Prehispanic Philippines. World Archaeology 27: 389–410.
  2002 Introduction. *In* Forager-Traders in South and Southeast Asia. K.D. Morrison and L.L. Junker, eds. Pp. 131–67. Cambridge: Cambridge University Press.

Kelly, R.
  1995 The Foraging Spectrum. Clinton Corners, NY: Percheron Press.

Lye Tuck-Po
  2002 The Significance of Forest to the Emergence of Batek Knowledge in Pahang, Malaysia. Southeast Asian Studies 40: 3–22.
  2005 The Meanings of Trees: Forest and Identity for the Batek of Pahang, Malaysia. The Asia Pacific Journal of Anthropology 6: 249–61.

Metcalf, P.
  2010 The Life of the Longhouse: An Archaeology of Ethnicity. Cambridge: Cambridge University Press.

Morrison, K.D. and L.L. Junker, eds.
  2002 Forager-Traders in South and Southeast Asia. Cambridge: Cambridge University Press.

Noone, R.O.D.
  1954–55   Notes on the Trade in Blowpipes and Blowpipe Bamboo in
            North Malaya. Federation Museums Journal 1 and 2: 1–18.

Pellow, D.
  1996   Introduction. *In* Setting Boundaries: The Anthropology of
            Spatial and Social Organization. D. Pellow, ed. Pp. 1–9.
            Westport, Co.: Bergin and Garvey.

Porath, N.
  2001   Foraging Thai Culture: A Performing Tribe of South Thailand.
            In Parks, Property, and Power: Managing Hunting Practice
            and Identity within State Policy Regimes. D.G. Anderson
            and K. Ikey, eds. Pp. 117–38. Osaka: National Museum of
            Ethnology.

Robarchek, C.A.
  1977   Semai Nonviolence: A Systemic Approach to Understanding.
            Unpublished PhD thesis, University of California at Riverside.
  1979   Learning to Fear: A Case Study of Emotional Conditioning.
            American Ethnologist 63: 555–67.

Sahlins, M.
  1972   Stone Age Economics. Chicago: Aldine-Atherton.

Smith, E.A.
  1983   Comment on E. Cashdan, Territoriality among Human Foragers:
            Ecological Models and an Application to Four Bushman
            Groups. Current Anthropology 24: 61.

Woodburn, J.
  1988   African Hunter-Gatherer Social Organization: Is It Best
            Understood as a Product of Encapsulation? *In* Hunters and
            Gatherers 1: History, Evolution and Social Change. T. Ingold,
            D. Riches and J. Woodburn, eds. Pp. 31–65. Oxford: Berg.

Yount, J.W., Tsiazonera and B.T. Tucker
  2001   Constructing Mikea Identity: Past and Present Links to Forest
            and Foraging. Ethnohistory 48: 258–91.

chapter 18

Orang Asli, Land Rights and the Court Process: A "Native Title" Lawyer's Perspective

Yogeswaran Subramaniam[1]

INTRODUCTION

Orang Asli have suffered from decades of land loss legitimized by the national development agenda and state perceptions that Orang Asli lack security of tenure in and over their customary lands. However, the Malaysian courts' recognition and reaffirmation of Peninsular Malaysia Orang Asli customary land rights at common law have provided the Orang Asli community hope for a solution to their protracted land woes. Perhaps more importantly, the reinforcement of land rights by the judicial arm of the government provides a common source of inspiration for the untiring Orang Asli struggle to maintain the vitality of their cultures, identities and lives. The law, as it were, stokes optimism that the Orang Asli community may yet find their rightful place within Malaysian society as equal citizens with a difference.

With no executive or legislative recognition of Orang Asli customary land rights currently in sight, can the litigation process, the mode by which the judiciary has recognized Orang Asli customary land rights, be relied upon to provide land justice for Orang Asli? This chapter examines the effectiveness of this process.

After introducing customary land rights in an Orang Asli context, I examine the legal and extra legal challenges faced by Orang Asli communities who utilize the litigation route to claim customary land rights. The chapter concludes with a gaze into the future of such claims, and more generally, the Orang Asli customary land rights struggle.

ORANG ASLI CUSTOMARY LAND RIGHTS

The multi-dimensional relationship that Orang Asli have with their customary lands for their social, cultural, economic and spiritual nourishment, and general well-being cannot be overemphasized. Anthony Williams-Hunt (1995: 35–6), an Orang Asli activist and lawyer, has summarized the Orang Asli relationship with their land as follows:

> The Orang Asli share the same conception of land as other indigenous groups throughout the world.... Besides its material importance, land has special social and religious significance. It defines social relations and it is through common ownership of land that a group is bound into a society. Land is closely associated with definitions of territory, history and most important of all, culture and identity. It is thus a heritage, metaphorically embodied in the statement that "it is from the land that we come and it is to the land that we will eventually go". Land stands for the way of life of the Orang Asli, and symbolises the cultural vitality and continuity of the community....

However, the dismal record of the federal and state governments in protecting Orang Asli lands under the existing statutory Orang Asli land reservation system suggests the lack of a concerted will to protect and recognize this treasured element of Orang Asli well-being. As at 31 December 2010, only 14.21 per cent of officially acknowledged Orang Asli lands had been reserved (JAKOA 2011: 55). Compounding matters, officially acknowledged Orang Asli lands do not cover the full extent of lands, territories and resources traditionally occupied or otherwise used by Orang Asli. Degazettal of Orang Asli lands is also not an uncommon phenomenon. For instance, 76 per cent of reserved

Orang Asli lands were revoked in the state of Selangor between 1990 and 1999 (Nicholas 2000: 36–7).

From a legal perspective, the Department of Orang Asli Affairs ("JHOEA"; since 2011, the Department of Orang Asli Development, "JAKOA"), the government agency charged with the protection, well-being and advancement of Orang Asli, justifies these protracted land problems using two arguments.

First, the JAKOA attributes blame on the federal-state government power divide under the *Federal Constitution*. To the JAKOA, a federal government agency, Orang Asli land protection is out of its hands because land and forest matters come under the purview of the individual states (see *Federal Constitution*, Ninth sch List II – State List Item 2 and 3 respectively). While this justification may appear to be meritorious at first blush, it has equally been argued that the federal and state power divide is not a constitutional impediment to the legal recognition of Orang Asli customary lands, as there are adequate provisions to recognize these lands provided there is the political will to do so (Lim 1998: 183; Subramaniam 2012: 113–49). Article 83 of the *Federal Constitution* empowers the federal government to requisition land for federal purposes (including Orang Asli welfare, see *Federal Constitution*, Ninth sch List I – Federal List Item 16), while article 74 empowers the federal government to pass laws with respect to land tenure to ensure uniformity of land law and policy throughout Peninsular Malaysia. Further, the National Land Council, whose members consist of both federal and state government representatives and of which the federal government holds a majority of seats, can pass policies for the uniform recognition of Orang Asli customary land rights (see article 91).

Second, JAKOA also points towards the lack of statutory recognition of Orang Asli rights in and over Orang Asli lands unless the land concerned is reserved, or in local parlance, *diwartakan* ("gazetted") by the individual State Authority. Under the current statutory reservation system pursuant to either the *Aboriginal Peoples Act 1954* (hereafter "*APA*") or the *National Land Code 1965* (hereafter "*NLC*"), Orang Asli lands are declared as reservations at the discretion of the individual State Authority and are held in trust for a government-designated Orang Asli community. The statutory power for the creation, revocation and variation of such reservations lies in the hands of the individual State Authority [see the *APA,* sections 6(1), 6(3), 7(1) and 7(3) and *NLC*, sections 62 and 64]. Adequate compensation for the loss of reserved lands is not regarded by the executive as a right but is at the discretion of the State Authority (see *APA*, section 12). Mandatory compensation is limited to the loss of fruit and rubber trees belonging to Orang Asli but not to the loss of their lands (see *APA*, section 11).

Unreserved lands occupied by Orang Asli are accordingly regarded by the state executive as land available for possession, occupation, use and enjoyment by non-Orang Asli, subject only to the payment of discretionary and relatively paltry compensation. This extensive state executive fiat over Orang Asli land has enabled state governments to take Orang Asli land with relative ease. At the federal level, JAKOA has also not interceded by way of legal means to protect Orang Asli customary lands.

In holding that both the federal and state governments had breached their fiduciary duty to protect Orang Asli lands and not to act inconsistently with Orang Asli land rights, the Malaysian courts have held that the "lack of recognition" argument for taking Orang Asli lands is circular in logic and unacceptable. As put in rather emotive terms by Gopal Sri Ram JCA on behalf of the Court of Appeal in *Kerajaan Negeri Selangor v Sagong bin Tasi* [2005] 6 MLJ 289 ("*Sagong 2*") (2005: 314):

> These defendants [the federal and state governments] put it out of their contemplation that they were ones there to protect these vulnerable First Peoples of this country. Whom else could these plaintiffs [Orang Asli] turn to? In that state of affairs, by leaving the plaintiffs exposed to serious losses in terms of their rights in the land, the first [the state government] and/or fourth defendant [the federal government] committed a breach of fiduciary duty. While being in breach, it hardly now lies in their mouths to say that no compensation is payable because of non-gazettation which is their fault in the first place. I am yet to see a clearer case of a party taking advantage of its own wrong. [Clarification of parties involved in parentheses.]

Notwithstanding jurisprudential developments, Orang Asli land rights and land "grabbing" remain a live issue for Orang Asli. The federal government's attempted introduction of an Orang Asli land titles and development policy in December 2009 ("the land titles policy") for the granting of individual titles of between two and six acres to each Orang Asli head of household for cash crop cultivation, which would effectively eliminate communal land ownership and sharply reduce Orang Asli land holdings, was met with unprecedented resistance from Orang Asli. On 17 March 2010, more than 2,500 Orang Asli gathered at the nation's administrative capital, Putrajaya, to deliver a protest memorandum against the proposed land titles policy to the Prime Minister. Among the complaints against the land titles policy were the potential loss of customary land and communal arrangements, lack of free, prior consent and engagement, and selective consultation (*POASM* and *Gabungan NGO-NGO Orang Asli Semenanjung Malaysia* [Peninsular Malaysia *Orang Asli* NGO Network] 2010: 5). During the recently completed National Inquiry on Indigenous Land Rights undertaken by the National Human Rights Institution ("SUHAKAM"), Orang Asli lodged 289 complaints in connection with their customary lands (Agam 2012). Unfortunately for Orang Asli, the land titles policy and similar variants continue to loom over Orang Asli with Government policies still geared towards the ultimate grant of individual titles. These policies pay little heed to communal customary land arrangements and tenure of the Orang Asli.

RECOGNITION OF ORANG ASLI CUSTOMARY LAND RIGHTS

The Malaysian courts have recognized the rights of Peninsular Malaysia Orang Asli in and over their customary territories since 1996 (*Adong bin Kuwau v Kerajaan Negeri Johor* [1997] 1 MLJ 418 ("*Adong 1*")). *Adong 1* involved a claim by 52 Jakun for adequate compensation in respect of 53,273 acres of their *ungazetted* ancestral lands that were alienated by the Johor State Government to the Singapore government for the construction of a dam. The *Adong 1* decision was upheld on appeal by both the Court of Appeal and Federal Court (*Kerajaan Negeri Johor v Adong bin Kuwau* [1998] 2 MLJ 158 ("*Adong 2*"); *Sagong 2* 2005: 302). The Federal Court, the apex court of Malaysia, unanimously reaffirmed the recognition of Orang Asli customary land rights *as a matter of law*, stating that such recognition "reflects the common law position with regard to native titles throughout the Commonwealth" including Malaysia (*Superintendent of Land and Surveys Miri Division v Madeli bin Salleh* [2008] 2 MLJ 697 ("*Madeli*") 2007: 692). The common law of England and Wales as applied and developed by the Malaysian courts in accordance with local circumstances forms part of the law in Malaysia. Article 160 (2) of the *Federal Constitution* defines "law" to include case law or more specifically, the common law as received by the courts and customs or usages having the force of law. Following the legal principle of *stare decisis*, legal pronouncements made by Malaysian superior courts, particularly those of the Federal Court, are binding upon lower courts (*Kerajaan Negeri Malaysia v Tay Chai Huat* [2012] 3 MLJ 149).

How Do Orang Asli Customary Land Rights Arise?

Orang Asli customary rights arise from pre-existing laws and customs observed by Orang Asli over their customary lands and continue to exist unless these rights are taken away by clear and obvious words in a statute (*Madeli* 2007: 691–2; 696–7). Contrary to the previous legal misconception that state land is held by the State Authority on behalf of the individual state sultan ("monarch") as beneficial owner, the Malaysian courts have since held that the radical title held by the state can be legally burdened by pre-existing title or interests of natives of Sarawak and Sabah and Orang Asli (*Madeli* 2007: 692; *Sagong 2* 2005: 301, 315). The Malaysian courts have also conclusively established that Orang Asli rights to their customary lands have not been extinguished or taken away by the *APA*, *NLC* and the statute providing for the application of the common law in Malaysia, namely the *Civil Law Act 1956* (*Adong 2* 1998: 164; *Sagong 2* 2005: 307–8; *Madeli* 2007: 689, 698). In other words, pre-existing Orang Asli customary land rights continue to remain in force in Peninsular Malaysia notwithstanding the existence of statutes regulating Orang Asli land and tenure.

Orang Asli customary land rights therefore do not require explicit recognition by any statute or executive act (*Kerajaan Negeri Selangor v Sagong bin Tasi* [2002] 2 MLJ 591 ("*Sagong 1*") 2002: 612). As such, legal recognition of these rights is not defined by whether or not these lands are reserved Orang Asli lands under any applicable statute. Rather, these pre-existing rights are already recognized and enforceable through the courts.

However, these rights: (1) are limited to Orang Asli (in respect of Peninsular Malaysia); and (2) arise from their early and continuous occupation of the land claimed and the maintenance of a traditional connection with such land through the observance of particular Orang Asli sub-group laws and customs (*Sagong 1* 2002: 610).

What Do These Rights Mean?

Orang Asli have the right to occupy, use and enjoy their customary lands or territories in accordance with their specific laws and customs without any impediment. Based on the common law doctrine and the fundamental rights to equality (article 8) and property (article 13) under the *Federal Constitution*, Orang Asli also have the right to be adequately compensated if they are deprived of these lands (see *Adong 2* 1998: 164; *Sagong 2* 2005: 309–10). Adequate compensation here includes compensation for the deprivation of livelihood of current and future generations, solatium ("injured feelings"), erected structures, and the market value of the land. By virtue of the fiduciary duty owed by the federal and state governments to Peninsular Malaysia Orang Asli, both governments should also not act inconsistently with Orang Asli customary land rights unless the full consent of the affected Orang Asli is obtained (see *Sagong 2* 2005: 313–4).

Unlike in Australia where the Australian government passed the *Native Title Act 1993* (Cth) to recognize and regulate Aboriginal native title at common law after the recognition of native title in the landmark decision of *Mabo v Queensland [No 2]* (1992) 175 CLR 1, Malaysia's federal and state legislatures and executives have not taken any formal step towards recognizing Orang Asli customary land rights at common law. Malaysia's repeated support for the 2007 *United Nations Declaration on the Rights of Indigenous Peoples*, where Malaysia has undertaken a moral obligation to take appropriate measures to recognize a comprehensive set of contemporary indigenous rights, including rights to customary lands, territories and resources has also not prompted any

reforms to the existing law. Much to the contrary, the federal and most
state governments continue to contest Orang Asli customary land rights
claims or claims for breach of fiduciary duty with renewed vigour,
constantly attempting to reopen settled issues on common law Orang
Asli customary land rights, perhaps with the objective of reversing this
line of jurisprudence.

In the meantime, JAKOA and the state governments, particularly
those controlled by the *Barisan Nasional* political coalition, have in
2012 commenced to reserve some Orang Asli lands with the ultimate
aim of eventually moving Orang Asli towards the acceptance of
individual titles. Complaints of the lack of consultation and under-
gazettal, where land reserved is less than the total customary land area,
during this exercise have fallen upon deaf ears.

Consequently, the only legal recourse available for Orang Asli
seeking to enforce their land rights lies in the courts. The following
sections examine the interplay between Orang Asli claimants, lawyers
and the court process with a view to unearthing the main challenges
faced by Orang Asli in pursuing a customary land rights litigation.

A DISTINCTIVE SOLICITOR-CLIENT RELATIONSHIP

Assertion of land rights and indeed fundamental liberties among Orang
Asli through the use of the civil courts is a relatively new phenomenon,
gaining momentum over the past 15 years. The unique context of the
Orang Asli poses a particular challenge for lawyers seeking to build
and maintain a solicitor-client relationship with potential Orang Asli
claimants.

The Orang Asli Association of Malaysia ("*POASM*")[2] has been
demanding the recognition of Orang Asli land rights by legislation and
the gazetting and granting of titles in respect of these lands for the past
two decades (Dentan et al. 1997: 156; POASM 2005). In negotiating land
rights, Orang Asli had previously taken a subordinate position due to a
lack of bargaining power and the lack of legal protection for their lands
(Juli 1998: 321–5). The defensive strategy employed is understandable
as Orang Asli have in the past experienced negative repercussions
from engaging in more open opposition towards the state (Idrus 2008:

76–7). Dentan has attributed the difficulty Orang Asli face in rights activism to, amongst other factors, Orang Asli culture (2000: 226). As an example, he argues that the cultural response of *Semai* to being badly treated is to *krad'dii* ("to withdraw or sulk for a while") rather than to confront the problem at hand. Historical subordination by dominant cultures adds to Orang Asli hesitation in the active assertion of rights.

However, the continued failure of the government to protect Orang Asli customary lands has prompted some disgruntled Orang Asli to overcome their traditional conservatism and assert their rights through the courts. As observed in the previous section, Orang Asli have done so with reasonable success. Recent public displays of discontent by Orang Asli also show them moving beyond past non-confrontational responses to the violation of their fundamental rights.[3]

Nonetheless, "old-school" conservatism and reticence in asserting Orang Asli rights through the courts still pervade some quarters of the Asli community. State practice does not help nurture this new-found Orang Asli empowerment and can be said to arrest its development. As far as other government agencies are concerned, JAKOA is still the first, and at times the only point of contact for matters affecting Orang Asli lands. Despite possessing the right to claim customary land rights at common law and to sue the federal and state governments for breach of their fiduciary duty, Orang Asli who raise their land issues with JAKOA and other government agencies are frequently advised that they have no land rights beyond those formally granted by the state. Indeed, it would be remarkable for JAKOA and the relevant land authority to advise otherwise given that they are usually at the receiving end of Orang Asli customary claims. In short, the government does not support Orang Asli customary land rights claims.

Further, the continued dependency of Orang Asli on JAKOA for assistance with education, healthcare and other aspects of their daily life reinforces the reluctance of some Orang Asli to "bite the hand that feeds them". Concern that assistance from JAKOA may not be forthcoming if a community were to commence legal action involving the federal and state governments, whether unfounded or not, adds to Orang Asli reluctance to litigate customary land claims. Government-fuelled pessimism about the repercussions of legal action complements

the pre-existing reticence among some Orang Asli to confront the
government in a head-to-head legal tussle.

Professional Challenges

This section examines how the distinctive situation of Orang Asli
clients in a customary land rights claim plays out in the course of
building and maintaining a solicitor-client relationship. As observed in
the previous section, neither the federal nor state governments support
Orang Asli customary land rights claims. Many Orang Asli communities
also lack the financial means to pursue customary land claims. Both
factors limit the number of lawyers willing to handle Orang Asli
customary land rights claims. Beyond financial considerations, having
conduct of matters that usually involve suing the federal and state
governments, government agencies or large corporations may not be
an appealing prospect for some lawyers. Possible concerns about suing
the government and conflict of interests that may arise due to previous
work done for these potential defendants further shrink the pool of
available lawyers.

Plate 18.1 Lawyer-client conference with the Jah Hut of Kampung Mai,
Jerantut, Pahang, 2010

(Photo credit: Y. Subramaniam)

Although there is a small band of lawyers who are willing act for Orang Asli pro bono in customary land rights claims (currently numbering not more than 20), the issue of legal costs is far from settled. Losing a customary land rights claim may well involve Orang Asli claimants having to pay the costs of the successful party. Realistically, the prospect of being saddled with the costs of protracted litigation is not relished by anyone, let alone an underprivileged Orang Asli community.

Framing an Orang Asli customary land claim is also a time consuming process as every claimant group has a distinctive set of oral histories, laws and customs and history of official land use. The acute shortage of Orang Asli researchers necessitates lawyers having to conduct archival and historical research to corroborate Orang Asli evidence. Many lawyers are ill-equipped or simply do not have the time or resources to conduct such inquiries. Logistical matters compound problems. Orang Asli claimants located at remote areas are not easily accessible and have limited access to the Internet and telecommunication coverage. Repeated trips to these remote areas for instructions can be taxing on lawyers. It is equally costly for Orang Asli to make regular trips to meet and instruct their lawyers.

Consistent with Orang Asli customary land arrangements, customary land claims are typically communal claims that are filed in court via representative or class actions. These actions require representation and a general consensus from the community. Due to extensive government intervention into traditional Orang Asli decision-making institutions, an Orang Asli village may be represented by a *batin* ("headman"), JKKK ("Village Development and Security Committee") and a traditional institution (for example, a *lembaga adat* in the case of *Temuan*) who may all be different people. Despite the delays involved, it would therefore be prudent to seek the free, prior and informed agreement of a majority of adult community members for the appointment of community representatives and lawyers.

Community representatives in an Orang Asli communal land claim would ideally consist of the *batin*, chosen elders, a younger adult and a woman, all of whom should be knowledgeable in their particular laws and customs. The appointment of representatives can therefore be slow, exacerbated by the reticence discussed in the previous section. Such delays can be potentially detrimental to a claim particularly where Orang Asli are faced with land problems that require urgent action, for instance, logging activities that encroach on customary lands.

The recent efforts of Jaringan Kampung Orang Asli Semenanjung Malaysia (JKOASM) and other Orang Asli rights non-governmental organizations (NGOs) in helping Orang Asli villages establish village action committees in respect of land issues and in initiating village community mapping exercises have sped up the process. After the completion of a community map and the selection of village representatives, lawyers usually offer legal advice on the viability of the claim in the light of the strength of evidence supporting the claim and other land interests that overlap with the claimed land. Consensus and tactical compromises regarding the extent of a particular customary land claim requires deliberation and at times can only be settled after a number of meetings.

Once the community representatives have been selected, lawyers also usually explain to them the possible legal effects of any past and potential compromise arrangements between Orang Asli and the government or the encroaching party. In this regard, the seemingly admirable Orang Asli strategy of flexibility and keeping options for surviving in their changing world (Endicott 2000: 114–8) may not be entirely appropriate, and in certain circumstances can be prejudicial to a land claim. In the failed judicial review application by the *Chewong* and *Temuan* people against the construction of the Kelau dam, the fact that some members of the affected community had accepted a resettlement and compensation offer was a factor considered by the Court in arriving at its decision.

Despite all these challenges, Orang Asli have been extremely resilient in adapting to this relatively alien mode of enforcing their rights. There are currently 11 customary land claims pending before the courts, an exponential increase from the time of the landmark cases of *Sagong bin Tasi* and *Adong bin Kuwau* when Orang Asli land claims were considered to be isolated occurrences. More encouraging from a rights advocacy perspective is the fact that there are around another ten villages that are in the process of preparing customary land claims.

THE COURTS AND PROOF

In *Sagong 1* (2002: 603–10), the Court held that the lands in dispute were *Temuan* customary lands by reason of the following findings of fact:

(1) the plaintiffs were an Aboriginal society within the meaning of the *APA*;
(2) their continuous occupation of the land for "generations";
(3) they were descendants of *Temuan* who had resided on the land since "early times";
(4) the traditional connection with the land had been maintained from "generation to generation"; and
(5) the customs in relation to the land were distinctive to *Temuan* culture.

As the superior courts are yet to elaborate the requirements for proof of Orang Asli customary title, the above factors are considered to be the threshold for the proof of such title. The standard of proof required for Orang Asli to establish this civil claim is on a balance of probabilities rather than the higher criminal standard of proof "beyond reasonable doubt". It is also important to note that if changes in the location and customs of the Orang Asli claimants are such that the court considers the claimants as no longer: (1) "Orang Asli"; or (2) having a connection with the land claimed, a claim of this nature may potentially fail.

Definition of an Orang Asli and an Organized Society

In order to fall within the definition of an Orang Asli within section 3 (1) of the *APA*, Orang Asli claimants must establish that they are a distinct tribal division of Orang Asli as characterized by culture, language or social organization, speak an Orang Asli language and habitually follow an Orang Asli way of life and Orang Asli customs and beliefs.

The first point of objection to this requirement, usually spearheaded by the federal government and JAKOA, is that the claimants are not Orang Asli. Considering the extensive records maintained by the JAKOA on Orang Asli, it is disappointing that the federal government has to resort to such objections particularly in the case of officially-acknowledged Orang Asli claimants or villages. Despite these persistent objections, there has yet to be a decided case where an Orang Asli customary land rights claim has been denied on the ground that the claimants are not Orang Asli.

A more meritorious argument could be that the claimants, while being Orang Asli, may not be an organized society that collectively follows an Orang Asli way of life and Orang Asli customs and belief pursuant to section 3(1) of the *APA*. However, this ground would be tenuous in the case of a group of claimants who are members of an officially-classified Orang Asli village. That said, additional evidence of an organized society may be necessary where Orang Asli claim areas within their broader customary territory which are no longer officially regarded as part of their village.

In *Sagong 1* (2002: 606–7), the Court held that the plaintiffs continued to exist as a society notwithstanding that:

(1) they no longer depended on foraging for their livelihood in accordance with their tradition;

(2) they cultivate the lands with non-traditional crops such as palm oil;

(3) they also speak other languages in addition to *Temuan*;

(4) some members of the family embrace other religions, and/or marry outsiders;

(5) some family members work elsewhere either before or after the acquisition of the land; and

(6) a Village Security Committee was set up by the JHEOA to manage their affairs.

However, the *Sagong 1* decision is a decision of first instance and not a decision of the superior courts. Another judge can depart from the liberal findings in *Sagong 1* on the impact of changes foisted upon Orang Asli by the government on their "aboriginality". For example, the Court in *Pedik bin Busu v Yang Dipertua Majlis Daerah Gua Musang* [2010] 5 MLJ 849 (2010: 855) held that *RPS* (a state scheme to regroup Orang Asli communities) lands resided on by the *Temiar* plaintiffs were not customary lands.

Part of demonstrating that particular claimants are an organized Orang Asli society includes the continued observance of laws and customs distinctive to a particular Orang Asli sub-ethnic group. The observance and acknowledgment of Orang Asli laws and customs, much like mainstream laws, have undergone change and adaptation to cater for the mutable environment in which they exist. These changes should not necessarily deprive Orang Asli laws and customs of their distinctive character. Unfortunately, there is a dearth of recent ethnographic research to support the adopted or changed observance of Orang Asli laws and customs. While changes in practices have proven detrimental to native claims in Australia, they have not as yet functioned to defeat Orang Asli customary land claims.

In Peninsular Malaysia, establishing a genealogical connection with Orang Asli who resided on the lands claimed from "early times" has not been very strict so far and is usually proven by primary oral evidence from Orang Asli claimants that is supported by any available official documents. The courts have not established how far Orang Asli have to go back in time to prove a genealogical connection with lands claimed. In the successful *Sagong bin Tasi* and *Mohamad bin Nohing* claims, both *Temuan* and *Semelai* claimants managed to prove, through oral histories and other supporting official records, a genealogical continuity of seven and six generations respectively. The challenge lies in sourcing secondary evidence to support the genealogical link. Save in cases where Orang Asli communities have been the subject of early anthropological and sociological fieldwork, specific genealogical records of particular Orang Asli claimants before the colonial assumption of stewardship over Orang Asli in the early 1950s are by no means comprehensive and in many cases, scant.

Early and Continuous Occupation

The Federal Court in *Madeli* (2007: 694–5) has ruled that there can be legal "occupation" without physical presence on the land provided "there exist (*sic*) sufficient measure of control to prevent strangers from interfering". This ruling potentially allows Orang Asli to prove occupation of areas beyond their settlement areas but within their customary lands or territories.

In addition to the problem of providing corroborative evidence of "early" and "continuous" occupation of the lands claimed, these criteria pose two practical challenges to potential Orang Asli claimants. The "early" occupation criteria may function to exclude Orang Asli communities which have been relocated, regrouped or resettled beyond their traditional customary lands. While "continuous" occupation for the purposes of aboriginal or native title at common law in other comparable common law jurisdictions does not require uninterrupted occupation but only the maintenance of a traditional connection of the land,[4] the Malaysian courts have not authoritatively determined the issue of whether, for instance, Orang Asli communities which were relocated temporarily during the Emergency fulfil the requirement of "continuous occupation". A conservative interpretation of "continuous occupation" of the land claimed or, as will be observed in the next section, "the maintenance of a traditional connection" with the land claimed may work against Orang Asli claimants.

Maintenance of a Traditional Connection with the Land

Following *Sagong 1*, the maintenance of a traditional connection with the land from generation to generation in accordance with customs distinctive to the claimant group is relevant in establishing Orang Asli customary title at common law. The main issue for establishing a "traditional connection" would be the extent to which customs can change before they are no longer considered "traditional" for the purposes of an Orang Asli customary title claim. For example, would a connection to customary lands used for the extraction and sale (as opposed to barter) of rattan be considered a custom distinctive to Endau *Jakun* culture?

As observed earlier, the Court in *Sagong 1* held that the *Temuan* claimants had maintained a traditional connection with their lands notwithstanding their cultivation of non-traditional crops like palm oil. In determining that the claimants had maintained a traditional connection with the lands claimed, the Court considered the continued observance of laws and customs including those relating to lands as relevant rather than engaging in an inquiry on whether each and every activity on the land was "traditional". The extent of "continuity" required and the level of change, adaptation and interruption of Aboriginal laws and customs allowable has worked to defeat native title claims in Australia (Young 2008; McRae et al. 2009: 348–51; Strelein 2009: 74–81). In this respect, there is a dire need for ethnographic research that focuses on the adaptability of Orang Asli laws and customs and their observance to suit the changing environment.

Evidentiary Challenges

According to Alice M. Nah (2008: 231–2), the lack of familiarity with the court system and language difficulties make attending court and giving evidence an extraordinarily difficult experience for Orang Asli litigants. The social and political realities of the relationship between Orang Asli and their "protectors" would understandably cause some trepidation to Orang Asli witnesses when giving evidence against the government. The adversarial nature of civil proceedings where answers and explanations required from litigants are limited by the law potentially conflicts with the participatory and informal manner in which many intra-communal Orang Asli disputes are resolved (see Hickson and Jennings, this volume). If these problems are not appreciated and appropriately managed, the outcomes can be potentially disastrous for Orang Asli litigants.

Oral testimony of prior occupation and laws and customs from Orang Asli knowledgeable in these matters, while admissible under sections 32 (d) and (e) of the *Evidence Act 1950*, may not be given due weight by the court if not supported by secondary materials. Expert evidence is relevant here. There is a scarcity of experts on Orang Asli matters who are willing to give evidence on behalf of Orang Asli claimants. Such shortage may be attributable to the fact that most potential Orang Asli expert witnesses are employed by the government. These potential witnesses may be reluctant to give evidence against the government particularly in matters requiring the witness to be critical of government policies. In fact, the *Statutory Bodies (Discipline and Surcharge) Act 2000* and regulations provide for disciplinary action to be taken against any employee of a public education institution critical of government policies. A court-appointed expert may produce similar results for Orang Asli claimants particularly where the expert appointed works with the government. On the other hand, engaging foreign Orang Asli experts to give evidence on behalf of Orang Asli claimants may prove too costly. The shortage of available expertise on Orang Asli land matters has contributed to the backlog in the commencement of proceedings mentioned earlier.

Managing Settlement

Any order of court or alternatively amicable settlement between the parties must ensure that the claimant community enjoys the fruits of its litigation in an equitable manner. Settlements or orders may include a variety of matters including the restitution and registration

Plate 18.2 The arduous road to justice: the Jakun of Kampung Peta and pro bono lawyers outside the Court of Appeal, Putrajaya after successfully obtaining leave to review a state decision to evict these Jakun from their customary lands, 2012

(Photo credit: Machang, Kampung Peta)

of communal property in the name of a legal entity established by the community, joint management of communal property with the state and the direct payment of monetary compensation. Each settlement arrangement poses its own challenges, but these matters are beyond the scope of this chapter. Once again, consensus and the representivity of the community should be participatory, transparent and clear.

However, taking such steps does not necessarily translate to sustainable or in some cases, responsible management of these funds. For instance, one of the lawyers in the *Adong bin Kuwau* case, who subsequently became the joint-trustee of the multi-million *ringgit* compensation payout, is currently facing a claim for breach of trust for, among other things, allegedly appropriating RM11 million of the compensation fund.

While a trust or corporation model which empowers the successful Orang Asli community to manage their funds or property may be desirable, it nonetheless poses potential problems in terms of community membership, power structures, leadership, representation and accountability. The lack of expertise in financial matters may further work to the disadvantage of the community. Unfortunately, there are no fool proof measures. Independent checks and balances and effective community participation in transactions beyond a certain threshold may reduce the risk of property being squandered or embezzled. Having the court supervise a settlement payout by way of a court order, as done in the *Sagong bin Tasi* case, may also be helpful, but there is only so much the court can do to monitor the day-to-day management of Orang Asli communal property. The assistance of NGOs who work regularly with the community concerned may also provide helpful perspectives, but, in the end, sound legal advice still requires painstaking attention to the particular community.

CONCLUSION

There is little doubt that the recognition of Orang Asli customary land rights at common law has provided Orang Asli inspiration for the resolution of their land problems and, more broadly, has supported their identity and rights as citizens, Orang Asli and indigenous peoples. However, both Orang Asli and their lawyers face formidable legal and extra legal challenges in utilizing the civil litigation process to deliver true land justice to Orang Asli. In spite of the courts' relative liberalism in adjudicating Orang Asli cases so far, the scales of justice may well tip against the Orang Asli in the future.

Erica-Irene A. Daes (2001: paragraph 93), in her capacity of UN Special Rapporteur preparing a working paper on indigenous people and their relationship to land, aptly observed, "it is safe to say that the use of judicial mechanisms may be risky because of the problem of different interpretive tools, the subjective and highly political nature of these state-chartered forums, and continuing cultural biases demonstrated by Governments".

Without legislative and executive intervention supporting the recognition of Orang Asli customary land rights, there can be no assurance of security of tenure for Orang Asli lands. Further, to expect the courts to achieve what the legislature and executive can do in a comprehensive and inclusive programme of customary land reform is to place an inordinate burden on the judiciary and risks the judiciary encroaching on the powers of the other two branches of government.

That said, the recognition of Orang Asli customary land rights at common law provides added hardware for Orang Asli in their war of attrition to force land reforms in favour of the recognition of Orang Asli customary land rights. As suggested in this chapter, anthropological and sociological research that focuses on the contemporary observance of Orang Asli laws and customs, particularly those in relation to lands, territories and resources, are a vital component of this struggle. In addition to being corroborative evidence in a customary land rights claim and a valuable aid to Orang Asli land reform initiatives, the documentation of these laws and customs potentially serves a more holistic yet practical purpose. These laws and customs may be seen as a source of pride and identity for Orang Asli, including the younger educated generation, rather than a set of malleable norms that can be arbitrarily discarded to facilitate the intended "integration" of Orang Asli into mainstream Malaysian society.

NOTES

1. This chapter is current as at May 2013.
2. *POASM* was established in 1976. Originally it consisted mostly of *JHOEA* employees. As at 2011, *POASM* membership had swelled to around 30,000 (Khoo 2011).
3. See Heikkila and Williams-Hunt, this volume. For instances of peaceful assemblies and civil disobedience by Orang Asli in relation to their land rights, see for example, the Center for Orang Asli Concerns ("COAC") website at http://www.coac.org.my and the *Facebook* pages of COAC and Jaringan Kampung Orang Asli Semenanjung Malaysia ("*JKOASM*") at http://www.facebook.com.
4. See *Delgamuukw v British Columbia* [1997] 3 SCR 1010, [153] (Supreme Court, Canada).

REFERENCES

Agam, H.
   2012   Opening Address. Speech delivered at the Public Hearings of the National Inquiry on Indigenous Land Rights, Kuala Lumpur, 27 March.

Daes, Erica-Irene A.
   2001   Indigenous Peoples and their Relationship to Land: Final Working Paper Presented by the Special Rapporteur. UN Document E/CN.4/Sub. 2/2001/21 (2001).

Dentan, R.K.
   2000   The Semai of Malaysia. *In* Endangered Peoples of Southeast and East Asia: Struggles to Survive and Thrive. Leslie E Sponsel, ed. Pp. 208–32. Westport, CT: Greenwood Press.

Dentan, R.K., K. Endicott, A.G. Gomes and M.B. Hooker
   1997   Malaysia and the "Original People": A Case Study of the Impact of Development on Indigenous Peoples. Boston: Allyn and Bacon.

Endicott, K.
   2000   The Batek of Malaysia. *In* Endangered Peoples of Southeast and East Asia: Struggles to Survive and Thrive. L.E. Sponsel, ed. Pp. 101–22. Westport, CT: Greenwood Press.

Government of Malaysia
  n.d.   Federal Constitution (Malaysia).
  1954   Aboriginal Peoples Act 1954 (Act 134).
  1965   National Land Code (Act 56 of 1965).
  2000   Statutory Bodies (Discipline and Surcharge) Act (Act 605).

Idrus, Rusaslina
  2008   The Politics of Inclusion: Law, History and Indigenous Rights in
          Malaysia. Unpublished PhD dissertation, Harvard University.

Jabatan Hal Ehwal Orang Asli [Department of Orang Asli Affairs]
  2008   Data Maklumat Asas [Basic Information Data]. Kuala Lumpur:
          Planning and Research Section, Department of Orang Asli Affairs,
          Malaysia.

Jabatan Kemajuan Orang Asli [Department of Orang Asli Development]
  2011   Pelan Strategik Jabatan Kemajuan Orang Asli 2011–2015
          [Department of Orang Asli Development Strategic Plan 2011–
          2015]. Kuala Lumpur: Planning and Research Section, Department
          of Orang Asli Development, Malaysia.

Juli Edo
  1998   Claiming Our Ancestors' Land: An Ethnohistorical Study of
          Sengoi Land Rights in Perak. Unpublished PhD dissertation,
          Australian National University, Canberra.

Khoo, S.
  2011   Emergency Fund for Orang Asli. The Star (Malaysia), 5 September.

Lim, Heng Seng
  1998   The Land Rights of the Orang Asli. *In* Tanah Air Ku [My
          Motherland]: Land Issues in Malaysia. Consumers' Association of
          Penang, ed. Pp. 170–95. Penang, Malaysia: Consumers' Association
          of Penang.

McRae, H., G. Nettheim, T. Anthony, L. Beacroft, S. Brennan, M. Davis and
T. Janke
  2009   Indigenous Legal Issues: Commentary and Materials, 4th edition.
          Sydney: Thomson Reuters.

Nah, A.M.
  2008   Recognising Indigenous Identity in Postcolonial Malaysian Law:
          Rights and Realities for the Orang Asli (Aborigines) of Peninsular
          Malaysia. Bijdragen Tot de Taal-, Land und Volkenkunde 164:
          212–37.

Nicholas, C.
2000   The Orang Asli and the Contest for Resources: Indigenous Politics, Development and Identity in Peninsular Malaysia. Subang Jaya, Malaysia: IWGIA, Center for Orang Asli Concerns.

POASM [Orang Asli Organisation of Peninsular Malaysia]
2005   Memorandum kepada YB Dato Seri Abdul Aziz bin Shamsuddin, Menteri Pembangunan Luarbandar dan Wilayah, Malaysia [Memorandum to the Right Honourable Dato Seri Abdul Aziz bin Shamsuddin, Minister for Rural and Regional Development, Malaysia].

POASM and Gabungan NGO-NGO Orang Asli Semenanjung Malaysia [Peninsular Malaysia Orang Asli NGO Network]
2010   Memorandum Bantahan Dasar Pemberimilikan Tanah Orang Asli yang diluluskan oleh Majlis Tanah Negara yang Dipengerusikan oleh YAB Timbalan Perdana Menteri Malaysia pada 4hb Disember 2009 [Protest Memorandum Against Orang Asli Land Title Grant Policy Approved by National Land Council in a Meeting Chaired by the Right Honourable Deputy Prime Minister of Malaysia on 4 December 2009].

Strelein, L.
2009   Compromised Jurisprudence: Native Title Cases since Mabo, 2nd edition. Canberra: Aboriginal Studies Press.

Subramaniam, Yogeswaran
2012   Orang Asli Land Rights by UNDRIP Standards in Peninsular Malaysia: An Evaluation and Possible Reform. Unpublished PhD dissertation, University of New South Wales, Sydney.

Williams-Hunt, A.
1995   Land Conflicts: Orang Asli Ancestral Laws and State Policies. *In* Indigenous Minorities of Peninsular Malaysia: Selected Issues and Ethnographies. Razha Rashid, ed. Pp. 35–47. Kuala Lumpur: INAS.

Young, S.
2008   The Trouble with Tradition: Native Title and Cultural Change. Sydney: Federation Press.

Part Seven

THE FUTURE

chapter **19**

Orang Asli Women Negotiating Education and Identity: Creating a Vision of the Self with Socially Available Possibilities

Shanthi Thambiah, Zanisah Man and Rusaslina Idrus

INTRODUCTION

Malaysians' general view of Orang Asli in education is that they are academically weak, lack confidence, are incapable of making decisions on their own, depend on others to do everything for them and are lazy (Chupil and Joseph 2003). This prejudiced view has hindered the delivery of quality education to the Orang Asli. This has led to poor educational results, which have limited social and economic mobility, thus causing the Orang Asli to remain the poorest segment of the Malaysian population (Nadchatram 2007; Nicholas 2010).

The Orang Asli face many educational disadvantages. The teaching method, which follows the rigid curriculum of the national school system, does not take account of their cultural differences from other populations (Nicholas 2010). Because most Orang Asli live in rural areas, they often live far from the nearest schools, which causes low rates of enrolment and attendance, thus impeding their academic performance (Johari and Nazri 2007). Moreover, in multi-ethnic schools, Orang Asli students are subject to bullying and harassment by non-Orang Asli students (Lim Hock Chye 1984).

Government officials tend to blame Orang Asli parents for not emphasizing the importance of education and the children for not being interested in studying and not being able to cope with being scolded by teachers (*The Star* 14 April 2006, cited in Nicholas 2006: 1; cited in Rusaslina 2013: 275). But Majid Suhut, the president of POASM (*Persatuan Orang Asli Semenanjung Malaysia*, Association of Orang Asli of Peninsular Malaysia) stressed in a speech on 30 April 2006 delivered at the Annual General meeting of POASM that it is "a false assumption that the problems are caused by the children being lazy and their parents unsupportive towards schooling". Majid argued that the problem lies instead in the disparity in the quality of education available to Orang Asli children and the fact that the educational environment does not take Orang Asli culture into account (Rusaslina 2013: 275).

These problems have led to high dropout rates among Orang Asli students (Nicholas 2006: 5). According to Hasan Mat Nor (1997) the most numerous dropouts occur during the transition from primary to secondary school, which is often the transition from local schools to distant boarding schools. According to the Orang Asli Strategic Development Plan (JAKOA 2010), the percentage of Orang Asli students who passed the public examinations in primary and secondary schools is low, and only 880 Orang Asli students completed their tertiary education between 1971 and 2010.

Looking at the question of Orang Asli identity and education, Endicott and Dentan (2008) showed how the JHEOA (*Jabatan Hal Ehwal Orang Asli,* Department of Orang Asli Affairs) until 1995 used education as a key mechanism to assimilate the Orang Asli into the Malay ethnic group, improve their standard of living and give them new occupational opportunities (Mohd Tap 1990: 257–8). Some government officials have advocated assimilating Orang Asli into the Malay community so that they cease to exist as a separate ethnic category (Jimin et al. 1983: 55–6; Mohd Tap 1990: 112–9; also cited in Dentan and Juli 2008 and Endicott and Dentan 2008).

This chapter will discuss some of the issues mentioned above and will describe how Orang Asli women engage with the educational process in the voices of the Orang Asli themselves. In studying Orang Asli women and education we need to recognize negotiations as a key factor in their understanding of identity. In this chapter we deal with identity in its active form as a performance and therefore regard identity as a process rather than a static state. Ivanič recognizes that "this process of identifying with socially available possibilities for self-hood links individual social action to larger processes for social change" (1998: 11). Similarly, Davies and Harré (2000) speak about "positioning", how one discursively positions oneself as one self-identifies, as being the key to understanding personhood. This has also been perceptively explained by Tania Li for tribal or indigenous people: "a group's self-identification as tribal or indigenous is not natural or inevitable, but neither is it simply invented, adopted, or imposed. It is, rather, a positioning which draws upon historically sedimented practices, landscapes and repertoires of meaning, and emerges through particular patterns of engagement and struggle" (2000: 151). In this chapter we consider self-identity as a narrative about one's location and positioning.

METHODOLOGY

To understand how Orang Asli women conceptualize their identity and experience in education, we examine a rich range of experiences in the form of narratives from in-depth interviews with six Orang Asli women who have completed tertiary level educational programmes. Two of the interviews were conducted in Semelai, one in Malay, one in English and another two in both Malay and English. The language used was upon the request of the informants. As the Orang Asli women in this study recounted their educational experiences, they recreated for us a discursive geography of their lives in their villages, in primary and secondary schools, and in the colleges they attended for their higher education. In the analysis of the narratives for this research, mapping this geography was important to understanding each woman's discursive relationship to her educational process.

The six Orang Asli women interviewed, who were predominantly in their 30s, varied in their marital status and socio-economic position and also in their level of comfort at discussing their experiences. The interviews were conducted from July to September 2013 at locations of their choice. Data used in this chapter include transcripts from one-on-one interviews. The women were all interviewed individually. These interviews produced narratives (Connelly and Clandinin 2000) that show how meaning is situated in the multiple contexts of these women's lives, culture and experiences. We looked for the way these women defined issues and themes as they talked about themselves and how they position themselves in the educational process (Davies 2000).

The Orang Asli Women interviewed were as follows:

MM, from Bukit Rok, Pahang, married, 32 years old, Semelai; occupation teacher, and her husband is a teacher too. Parents' occupation rubber tappers. Comes from a large family of 8 siblings (4 male and 4 female). Highest level of education—Bachelor's Degree in Education.

SM, from Bukit Rok, Pahang, single, 39 years old, Semelai; occupation rubber tapper. Comes from a large family of 11 siblings (3 male and 8 females). Highest level of education—Master's Degree.

RY, Pekan, Pahang, married, 36 years old, Jakun; occupation x-ray technician. Parents' occupation village work (*kerja kampung*). Highest level of education—Diploma.

LA, Petaling Jaya, Selangor, single, 30 years old, Semai; occupation uncertain because not employed yet. Parents' occupations: father lecturer and mother housewife. Highest level of education—Diploma in Management in Office Technology/Office management.

ZM, Bukit Rok, Pahang, single, 33 years old, Semelai; occupation lecturer. Highest level of education—Master of Science. Currently PhD candidate in social anthropology.

JE, Kampung Parit Gong, Jelebu, N. Sembilan, single, 31 years old, Temuan; occupation coordinator assistant. Parents' occupation rubber tappers. Highest level of education—Diploma in Early Childhood Education.

VILLAGE, CHILDHOOD AND EARLY EDUCATION

Each woman spent her youth and adolescence closely connected to her Orang Asli community. When they were asked to talk about their home and the community they grew up in, most of them had happy memories of their childhoods, but they also experienced a variety of challenges. JE said:

> I was born in the village of Parit Gong and I grew up there, in the village. Mmm I think my childhood was a little different from children born in the 80s ... the rubber plantation was my playground.... So everything was in the village. There were animals that were venomous, not poisonous; you know the grass that causes itch was like my toy.... I did not go to a kindergarten. During my time there was no kindergarten in the village. So I started my education at the age of eight years due to my sickness, in my childhood.... So all my brothers and sisters are my friends.... All my cousins came home and played with me. Most of the time I tried to sneak off ... to play a little far away, but when I got home I was scolded.... So that was my routine until I was six to seven years old. (JE, Temuan)

ZM said:

> When I was growing up I love to play a game we called *kentui*. *Kentui* is a game where you climb a tree and move from tree to tree and one of your friends becomes the *kentui*. So you will jump from tree to tree as they try to touch you. When he succeeds in touching you, you will have to replace him and your position now is on the ground and his will be on the tree. That's really interesting. We always play that game, me and my sister ... and there's another person, my cousin, a boy from my father's second brother ... we also played combat.... Yes. Combat ... we form a team ... because I am the same age as my cousin ... we are always in one team and then they form the other team and then we play communist and soldier.... Communist has to hide. I hate soldier because you have to seek but I love being communist because ... I like to hide.

And then the other game that I really love is umm it's a traditional game. You just build huts. As far as I remember I built three huts with my sister. It's a real house and sometimes we sleep inside and sometimes we would collect materials from the surrounding forest and sometimes the hut will be used by my father because it's like a tradition in the family.... It was really interesting because your family, and then your extended family will come and say "Oh this is really nice, your floor is neat, the way you tied it is really neat, and your roof and everything is good". That's the most interesting part. And then you cook and they will supply you food, rice and everything. (ZM, Semelai)

The early education of the informants in this study was informed by their immediate surroundings and through play. Everything that they knew was about the community and their surroundings, and their early learning was developed in this context. The village and the community were central to their early learning, and this also informed their identity. Family, brothers, sisters, cousins and friends were very important in their early childhood.

EDUCATIONAL EXPERIENCES

Mothers' and their Children's Education

Although all family members were keen and supportive of children's education, most informants emphasized the special importance of mothers. They said that mothers' encouragement and efforts helped improve their academic performance. According to them, the mothers spent a lot of time sending their children to school and visiting children living in dormitories compared to the fathers. SM said:

If back then, if children were going to school ... they did not care much. Now they do care. The children are sent to school. They make an effort to send their children to school. All (parents) want their children to go to school. During PTA meetings, some of the parents are not present. But mostly the women are more aware of the importance of education for their children. Men do not bother much. If you notice carefully, mostly it is like that. (SM, Semelai)

Teachers and Learning

Due to the lack of exposure to the outside world and the lack of money to buy reference books and additional work books, students rely heavily on the creativity and enthusiasm of their teachers to provide educational input. Parents cannot help the students at home because the syllabus has changed compared to their time or they do not know how to read. RY said that reading and revision is usually only done when the students are in the school, hostel, or their teacher's house and seldom when they are with their friends and family. The Semelai informants also said that if teachers were not very efficient, the school clerk also played the role of educator to the students in the Orang Asli School. RY said of teachers:

> ... they want us to be successful.... They conducted extra classes ... sometimes we are taken to their homes that are close to the school like the one near Tasik Chini ... they take us to their house and teach us there too. (RY, Jakun)

SM said:

> Sometimes we are taught by the school clerk in our primary school ... his name is Manaf ... when we were sitting for our Standard Five assessment exams he taught us ... he became our teacher.... (SM, Semelai)

Informants also emphasized that the quality of education is dependent on the commitment of the teacher, the relationship with the teacher and the motivation given by them to the students. The teaching method and syllabus also contribute to student performance. RY questioned the present performance of teachers and talked about the importance of motivation:

> Primary school performance down ... weird! The teachers have low morale. They are happy their pay is high ... so lazy. The teachers nowadays.... It is the teacher's fault for not being nurturing. We can succeed if the teachers are good....Teachers have to motivate. Motivation is important. You'll have to learn ... to help your family move out of difficulty.... Every day if they talk like this the student will keep it in her head.... Ha! (RY, Jakun)

Coping with Limited English Language Proficiency

English language proficiency was mentioned as a challenge, which becomes more serious as Orang Asli students enter secondary school. LA, who lives in a city, said that she has a better command of the language because she was in an urban school. Informants who went to school in the rural areas, such as SM, saw the poor English language training there as a major handicap. Most of the Orang Asli women interviewed said that they make it a point to try to learn the language in order to succeed in their education. For example, LA said:

> ... people ask me to speak in English only ... my English language is kind of ok. I do not want to say I am excellent, but I'm ok. It is better than average. The reason is that since childhood, we lived in Gombak and later PJ [Petaling Jaya], and we have not lived in Orang Asli village. Orang Asli use more Malay....
> (LA, Semai)

In addition, punishment imposed by the teachers makes it even more critical to improve in English, and at the same time it also instilled fear amongst the students. For example, SM said:

> Ah English also la. We are not good at English. If you do not pass, the headmistress will hit us. Midah teacher (headmistress)....
> So we are constantly in fear. (SM, Semelai)

SM also mentioned that Orang Asli are weak in English because the teachers are also weak in the English language:

> Oock I am not good in English la. The reason is because the teachers are also not good at it.... (SM, Semelai)

Bullying and Discrimination

A major problem facing Orang Asli students in multi-ethnic schools is being bullied. One strategy employed by Orang Asli students in dealing with bullying that was mentioned by the informants was to ignore abusive words and discrimination levelled at them by the students of other ethnic groups. RY said:

When you're mixing and being friends for a long time ok je. However, there are others who like to insult us. Normal la. Orang Asli are always insulted but we do not bother with them.... We just ignore them. Continue to learn.... When they see that we have passion to learn, so they learn from us la.... When we can endure the insults and discrimination we are encouraged to retaliate but by studying and to get better grades ... sometime we feel that we do not want to continue with schooling. We have to develop the courage to face it by just ignoring them. I don't care, I just want to study, and I want to succeed in my studies ha.... Sure we can move up.... (RY, Jakun)

Sometimes Orang Asli students also face discrimination by teachers. JE told us how she was asked to do some of her teacher's household chores, like throwing away her rubbish:

So there was an incident that happened when I was in primary school ... every morning, the teacher will ask us to throw away her household garbage, every morning we were called by the teacher, her name was Roziah.... So that was the worst part of my education.... My father will send us to school very early in the morning so when we reached early this teacher would ask us to help her.... She would ask us to remove all her garbage and throw it away at the dump behind the school. Then we were rewarded with ice cream.... When we were the only ones to be asked to sweep the rubbish that means something is wrong ... that is the thing that made me angry later on. When I started to understand what was happening here.... (JE, Temuan)

Financial Challenges

When Orang Asli students pursue tertiary education, most of them face severe financial problems. In addition to increased educational costs, students have to deal with the rising cost of living in terms of food, accommodation and clothing expenses. The challenge when students begin to learn to manage their own finances is to balance their spending among competing needs. The informants mentioned that they are expected to participate in sports and non-sports activities and also to fit in with other students in terms of fashion and lifestyle. Such non-educational expenses also contribute to the financial stress they experience during their journey through tertiary education. ZM mentioned that she had to manage her money so carefully that sometimes she even compromised on the quality of food she ate:

> You have to really manage your money and then I cooked and I ate a lot of burger because it was ... the cheapest so sometimes I only eat burger so during dinner or during lunch it was Maggi. So it was really bad. I was so skinny and I never ate banana because we can get it in the village but it was really expensive at the place where I was studying. But when I entered second year I couldn't take it anymore. I bought it. (ZM, Semelai)

In the early stages of university admission, the Department of Orang Asli Development (JAKOA) paid the tuition fees for most informants, but the payments were usually not made until the middle or end of the semester. Therefore, before the first semester began, the informants needed to get financial support from their families. Once at university, they had to manage their own finances. They emphasized the need for experience and maturity in handling money.

NEGOTIATING EDUCATION AND IDENTITY

Overcoming the Lack of Confidence and Self-esteem

Reaching a higher level of education causes an increase in distance between the Orang Asli students and their family and friends and from their village. Thus the informants mentioned that they increasingly feel isolated and alone in their learning environment, facing challenges alone. This isolation made them become more sensitive to differences between themselves and the non-Orang Asli people around them, and they feel inferior. MM said that she has to be among the best in order for her not to feel inferior:

> I work in KL [Kuala Lumpur]; of course I'm an Orang Asli. I was working in Selangor and at my work place I was the only Orang Asli. I tried to not act like Orang Asli because they will look

down upon me. So I wanted to be the same as others or higher than the others in my achievements. So that is the reason why I wanted to pursue higher education. So that's why I always want to learn. Ok first, why I wanted to pursue it? I know my career in education will always be changing. The reason for why I constantly want to improve myself. I do not want to lag behind. So I always wanted to put myself among the best. The reason for this is that I worry that if I am left behind in knowledge I will feel inferior. (MM, Semelai)

Distancing or Displacing Oneself

There were many emotional challenges expressed by informants when they entered secondary school. Competition and continuous interaction with non-Orang Asli students in academic and non-academic matters creates some issues and challenges. To maintain high levels of achievement in education, the main challenge, as voiced by the informants, was to maintain the excellent performance they achieved during primary school and secondary school.

Most of the Orang Asli women interviewed mentioned that achieving success in higher education meant isolation from their fellow Orang Asli. This isolation includes being in a different class (for example, Science Stream) or studying in a non-Orang Asli school. Despite feeling alone, displacing oneself from one's community is a calculated decision at a critical stage in their educational progression where they eventually build endurance, both mentally and emotionally, to forge ahead to achieve better results. MM said:

> At that time I was the best student so the teacher sent me to the Science Stream. But in fact I could not accept it … it was hard for me to follow. I just understood when the teacher explained it to me. But when I went back to the hostel.... Because at that time I was the only Orang Asli in Science Stream so when I wanted to study with the students from my class none of them stayed in the hostel.... Most of the students in my class were not staying in the hostel—Malays and Chinese students.... If I wanted to consult with my friends, Malay or Chinese it has to be in the morning only. There was always no time so I felt stressed up.... (MM, Semelai)

Ambitious Orang Asli students felt that they had to avoid mixing or being influenced by weak and troubled students; socializing with peers was mentioned by the informants as very important for success in their education. The desire to succeed is so powerful that some of the informants took the drastic decision of changing schools and displacing themselves from their community because they did not want to mix with fellow Orang Asli students who were considered weak. They wanted to be in an ethnically more mixed school because the quality of education in those schools was considered to be better than in Orang Asli schools. For example, SM said:

> I did not want to go to school in Mengkarak and mix only with Orang Asli students. Orang Asli children are playful. They are not serious in their learning. I do not want to keep playing only. That is the reason why I went to study alone for I do not want to mix with Orang Asli students only. I want to study seriously.... I want to be successful. (SM, Semelai)

LA said:

> I guess my family ... my dad did not want me to go to a school that has a lot of Orang Asli students because he feared that I will be influenced by them. He does not want us to be like that ... but this is not because we are arrogant but he was concern that we will take it easy with our school work ... because many have dropped out of school at an early stage of their schooling ... many students quit early, right? So my father did not want us to be like that, he did not want us to be influenced, so I went to Anglo Chinese School for two years. (LA, Semai)

Aligning with Non-Orang Asli Ideas and Practices

The women interviewed also discussed their experiences vis-à-vis the non-Orang Asli "other". The "other" includes Malay or Chinese teachers and fellow students. The non-Orang Asli "other" is at times used as a benchmark to compare themselves to. JE aligned herself with non-Orang Asli practices like watching and learning from Sesame Street:

> So I got my early education ... by watching television. And I saw my brother brought back school books, wear school uniform,

school shoes. It was very interesting for me. But I could not follow him because he went to school in a truck. But I got to know school from the television so I used charcoal and went down the house, to write to follow ... you know Sesame Street? ... That was my Kindergarten.... Because I prepared myself with Sesame Street so I was a bit special I think and the teachers who taught me were happy. "JE best of all, you already know ABCD". I already knew how to spell when I was 6, 7 years old, I already can spell in English. When I entered primary one, though I was eight years old I could understand and spell....
(JE, Temuan)

The urge to upgrade oneself can be seen in the informants' willingness to compete with non-Orang Asli students. Although there are informants who think state primary schools in Orang Asli areas are of poor quality and do not encourage competition, some students want to succeed despite being in rural areas. This might be influenced by the students' access to electronic media and television. Competition was mentioned as important to encourage Orang Asli students to improve in their studies. RY had this to say:

Who would want to stay in hostels, ha...? So, the thing is, depending on the student je. Orang Asli student from my village was the best student in our town's school. This means it depends on the student whether she wants to be clever. Whether she wanted to compete ... the student can become clever because she wants to compete with the other students. She was the best student in the school and an Orang Asli student got 8As. (RY, Jakun)

MM also said that it is important to embrace the competitive spirit:

I think the challenge is when we are not able to focus. We think we are inferior when placed in the lowest class. Then, we start to compare ourselves with others ... Chinese female student are aggressive. Indeed they are aggressive in school.... I'm scared. This is an uncomfortable situation when learning la. Then, when I was in form 3, ok, I was happy that I was sent to a better class ... I did try because I wanted to jump class. Then, when I was in Form 3, I was able to go to the first class. That's when I started to focus and to compete and be focused on learning.
(MM, Semelai)

Informants also said that they wanted to keep up with their non-Orang Asli friends or to even be better than them:

> When I look at my friends move up, I want to be like them ... can I achieve that kind of success. Do not want to maintain status quo. Or be paralyzed by fear, or do not dare to speak when dealing with educated people. Therefore, I was determined to improve myself parallel to the other people in education and career. (MM, Semelai)

All the Orang Asli women in this study viewed the ability of the Orang Asli to be successful as their ability to be comparable to non-Orang Asli. As RY said:

> ... If we feel we are too low, we will end up with very low self-esteem, how are we to succeed? The way we speak.... Our appearance.... Not wanting to show off too much but be very adaptable to the circumstances so that we can be comparable with other people ... when we go out what are the languages that we should use. Our language Bahasa Asli ... English language? Bahasa Malaysia? We have to change our ways. Look at our situation ... even the way we dress has to be the same. In the village we wear whatever je ... we do not care. If we are educated, we have to follow ... with modesty ... as long as we do not overdo it ... appropriate to us as a student so that we can have friends, we can learn easily, what is comfortable. The lecturers will also feel comfortable with us. We have to be careful in the way we present ourselves ... we cannot not bother about it until people become uncomfortable with us.... It becomes difficult for us to compete ... to learn ... to seek knowledge ... it is akak's [elder sister's] opinion. This is important ... we have to adjust to the situation. (RY, Jakun)

Pressures to Assimilate/Convert

Much has been written about how education was a mechanism to assimilate the Orang Asli into the Malay ethnic group by converting them to Islam (Dentan and Juli 2008; Endicott and Dentan 2008). Two of the informants in this study experienced this, and the strategy they used was to avoid the religious teachers (Malay *ustaz* [male], *ustazah* [female]) or to refuse their assistance. SM said:

Ustazah was also the same. If it was our break time, she adamantly told me to meet her. I only went to see her once. After that I did not go to see her. Do not expect la! (SM, Semelai)

RY said:

There were many Ustaz. There were also many Ustazah. So when they know that we are not Muslims ...They will try to become close to us ... they educate us on Islam.... What is not Islamic ... much of their syllabus emphasizes on Islamic civilization ... all—all right. But we did not refuse. We acted normally.... But without doubt we were worried, a little worried ... concerned ... but we thought, Alahai why call us to talk about Islam.... We do not want to think in that direction ... to say it was a challenge—it was not so and to say that it is a problem I don't know lah. But this did happen. (RY, Jakun)

The teachers who wanted to talk religion made them uncomfortable, and they tried to get away from such influences. Most informants mentioned that some religious teachers made efforts towards converting them to Islam through support and assistance, and most of the time they refused such assistance.

Going Back to their Land: Not Forgetting their Roots

The women in this study said that Orang Asli identity and roots are linked to their land. Most of them continue to connect with their ancestral land by visiting their family and attending weddings and funerals in their villages. Besides that most of the informants have a house they can call their home in the village. These women also said that indigenous women's rights have to be integrated into land issues. The empowerment of women in land matters is also an effective way of combating land dispossession, since women—who carry a great deal of responsibility for the well-being and future of the family—tend to be stronger guardians of lands than men. Most of the informants said that they had land in their village, but only one is working on her land (SM), although she has a master's degree. She decided to return to working in the village after giving up her urban employment:

If they (women) who have an education do not know how to use her knowledge/education they will undergo hardship too. While those without education think that their farm is big but they are not able to go too far (financially) because they are not knowledgeable.... If you have an education you can use it (the land) in the right way. (SM, Semelai)

Most of them also said that the way their parents distributed their land was usually very fair:

The Jakun people ... majority of them treat their children equally.... They are not bothered whether the child is the eldest or the youngest ... majority of them if they have four children and if they have four acres of land ... one acre la for each child! (RY, Jakun)

... my mum is willing to pass it (land) on to me ... land that I already have is a fruit orchard ... Rubber from my mother and the fruit orchard from my father. I'm happy because my father is fair and each of us got a piece of rubber plantation and a fruit orchard. (JE, Temuan)

Share equally ... because the land is my father's so far it is under his name. So far I don't know how he is going to share it out ... maybe he will divide it equally amongst us but I don't know lah. So far he has not mentioned anything about it. He only said that if he is no longer there he wants us to keep the land productive, to work the land ... because it is the family's land. (LA, Semai)

One informant said that having land alone is not sufficient to succeed in life. She said that Orang Asli should have both education and land. With education, they will be able to work on the land with better outcomes:

If we have 20 acres of land or 30 acres but if we do not know how to read I think it will be difficult la.... We can farm no problems. Dig, dig, dig and plant palm trees, rubber trees. It will grow and we can tap it.... When we have no knowledge we actually cannot manage things well.... If the woman has a lot of land and do not have an education ... I think she will not know how to manage

her land. At best she will get some income ... she can tap the
rubber trees ... we can get results but not the best possible la!
(RY, Jakun)

Most of the women in this study mentioned that education
is important, but they have to own land. They also linked it to the
Orang Asli struggle to maintain their rights over their land and their
identity. LA, who is the youngest informant and the most urbanized
of all, said:

> We are here (in the city) and the land is in the kampung. Education
> is like a bonus but land we must have la ... it is because our people
> have been fighting for it (their land rights).... Because when we
> do not have land ... we really don't know where we are heading.
> Because we want our rights, right? For example if I stopped work
> suddenly and I want something to do (go somewhere) it is important
> that I have something that I can say is mine and not something that
> belongs to others.... Something that I want as my own ... that's
> our right la. (LA, Semai)

CONCLUSION

Inequality acquired a central place in these women's efforts to
understand the struggle for an education. This discursive space as
a location of possibility has the power to inspire a realization that
they have agency to deal with the discriminatory experiences that
often characterize Orang Asli education. They also dealt with the
crushing bullying and discrimination in school by ignoring it and
building the courage to face it. The six women varied in their level
of comfort and the amount of support received in the mainstream
academic environment. Some narratives showed efforts to distance
themselves from their own people as a kind of strategic displacing
of themselves in their educational journey, creating associations or
benchmarks by comparing their performance with that of non-Orang
Asli people.

In the analysis of the narratives for this research, it was important
to understand each woman's discursive relationship to her educational
process. In these discursive spaces, we observed that they acknowledged

their histories and cultures, and they valued knowledge from both the Orang Asli and non-Orang Asli worlds. Another important observation was that the Orang Asli women in this study negotiated their identity by aligning themselves with non-Orang Asli ideas and practices to improve their academic performance as a strategy to survive in a rather harsh educational environment. These experiences such as learning to be competitive, which is very subdued in Orang Asli cultures, were transformational for the women in this research, infusing them with a sense of confidence when they talked about the ways in which they identified with their education. It is interesting to note that the narratives from the interviews showed the influence their educational journey had on their identity, and the narratives also affirm Tania Li's (2000: 151) view that self-identification is not natural or inevitable, but that it is a positioning which draws upon particular patterns of engagement and struggle.

REFERENCES

Chupil, T. and J. Joseph
    2003 Creating Knowledge for Change: A Case Study of Sinui Pai Nanek Sengik's Educational Work with Orang Asli Communities in Malaysia. Malaysia Indigenous Education Program Case Study. Mumbai: Asia South Pacific Bureau of Adult Education.

Connelly, E.M. and D.J. Clandinin
    2000 Narrative Inquiry: Experience and Story in Qualitative Research. San Francisco: Jossey-Bass.

Davies, B. and R. Harré
    2000 Positioning: The Discursive Production of Selves. *In* A Body of Writing 1990–1999. B. Davies, ed. Pp. 87–106. Walnut Creek, CA: Altamira.

Dentan, R.K. and Juli Edo
    2008 Schooling vs. Education, Hidden vs. Overt Curricula: Way of Thinking about Schools, Economic Development, and Putting the Children of the Poor to Work—A West Malaysian Example. Moussons 1(2): 3–34.

Endicott, K. and R.K. Dentan
    2008   Into the Mainstream or into the Backwater? *In* Civilizing the Margins: Southeast Asian Government Policies for the Development of Minorities. C.R. Duncan, ed. Pp. 24–55. Singapore: NUS Press.

Hasan Mat Noor
    1997   Kajian Keciciran di Kalangan Pelajar Orang Asli Peringkat Sekolah Rendah. Bangi: Penerbit Universiti Kebangsaan Malaysia.

Ivanič, R.
    1998   Writing and Identity: The Discoursal Construction of Identity in Academic Writing. Philadelphia, PA: John Benjamins.

Jimin Idris et al.
    1983   Planning and Administration of Development Programmes for Tribal People (The Malaysian Setting). Kuala Lumpur: Jabatan Hal Ehwal Orang Asli.

Johari, T. and M. Nazri
    2007   Bagaimana Kanak-kanak Orang Asli Gagal di Sekolah. Jurnal Pengajian Umum Asia Tenggara 8: 51–76.

Jabatan Kemajuan Orang Asli Malaysia (JAKOA)
    2010   Laporan Bahagian Pembangunan Minda dan Pendidikan. Annual Report. Kuala Lumpur: JAKOA.

Lim, H.C.
    1984   On the Way to a Better Future. Problems in their Education. Malay Mail, 28 July 1984.

Mohd Tap Salleh
    1990   An Examination of Development Planning among the Rural Orang Asli of West Malaysia. Unpublished PhD thesis, University of Bath.

Nadchatram, I.
    2007   Folklore Inspiration to Improve Malaysian Orang Asli Children's Literacy. UNICEF Malaysia (Online). http://www.unicef.org/malaysia/media_7099.html, accessed 5 Aug. 2011.

Nicholas, C.
    2006   The State of Orang Asli Education and its Root Problems. *In* Orang Asli: Rights, Problems, Solutions. Suhakam, ed. Subang Jaya, Malaysia: Center for Orang Asli Concerns. http://www.coac.org.my/codenavia/portals/coacv2/images/articles/OA%20Education.pdf

2010   Orang Asli: Rights, Problems, Solutions. Kuala Lumpur: Suruhanjaya Hak Asasi Manusia.

Li, T.
2000   Articulating Indigenous Identity in Indonesia: Resource Politics and the Tribal Slot. Comparative Studies in Society and History 42(1): 149–79.

Rusaslina Idrus
2013   Left Behind: Orang Asli under the New Economic Policy. *In* The New Economic Policy in Malaysia: Affirmative Action, Ethnic Inequality and Social Justice. T. Gomez and J. Saravanamuttu, eds. Pp. 265–91. Petaling Jaya and Singapore: SIRD, NUS Press and ISEAS.

chapter **20**

Spaces of Self-Determination: Divining Contemporary Expressions of Indigeneity from Orang Asli Blogs

Karen Heikkilä and Anthony Williams-Hunt

INTRODUCTION

Indigenousness, in various political and socio-economic contexts the world over, carries the unfair connotations of resistance to development and modernization, apathy to global concerns, non-participation in greater society, and illiteracy (Stea and Wisner 1984; Shaw et al. 2006; Johnson et al. 2007; Denzin et al. 2008). Such stereotypes have, to a greater or lesser degree, characterized the indigenous peoples of Peninsular Malaysia, collectively known as the Orang Asli. These groups have been portrayed throughout Malaysian history as jungle-dwellers, primitive, indigent and in need of state assistance to "develop". Such notions are systemic, having taken root in the imperial project of Malaya, and something that Sibley (1995) might describe as being representative of an identity politics that is manifested in the binary of superior Self/inferior Other. In contemporary, post-colonial Malaysia, the idea of "Orang Asli as savage" has become firmly lodged in the national mindset via its formalization in the state apparatuses of legislation, social welfare, media, religion and education. Malaysian census data, for instance, in reporting consistently for years on Orang Asli underachievement in literacy and educational attainment (see Khor and Shariff 2008) indicate a lack of upward social mobility for this particular population; together with media portrayals of Orang Asli poverty and vulnerability to poor health, natural hazards and landlessness, such data have reproduced and thus affirmed the inferior and marginal status of aboriginals in Malaysian society.

The binary of superior Self/inferior Other is also expressed in the purification/defilement of space (Sibley 1995). As "Others" in Malaysian society, Orang Asli belonging and exclusion seem dependent on the "imagery of defilement, which locates [them] on the margins or in residual spaces and social categories" (Sibley 1995: 69). The Orang Asli are "invisible" in mainstream spaces, an instance being urban-dwelling Orang Asli, who Malaysians consider "no longer aboriginal" based on the presumption that a traditional indigenous forest lifestyle has been renounced by these people for a "modern" life in towns and cities (personal observation). A simultaneous fascination and revulsion exists in the Malaysian image of the Orang Asli: on the one hand, they are "noble savages", belonging in a jungle idyll; on the other, they are heathens and socially backward, to be rescued and helped.

This chapter offers a glimpse into the compelling, but overlooked, phenomenon of Orang Asli-generated weblogs (henceforth, "blogs"). The presence of these blogs indicates a thriving community of literate and politically aware Orang Asli. Many of the bloggers are youth and write blogs as a way of recording their impressions of village life and government decisions affecting the Orang Asli as well as recounting aspects of indigenous culture, language and oral history. The blogs are primarily intended for an Orang Asli audience and written in Malay, the language used by the different Orang Asli groups to communicate with one another. Anyone who possesses basic reading and writing skills and who has access to a computer and Internet can open and maintain a blog. Internet cafes, common throughout Peninsular Malaysia, offer the convenience of connecting online and are where younger rural-based

Plate 20.1 Waq Lady typing her interview notes on a laptop at her house in Ceñhòòy, a Semai Orang Asli hamlet on the outskirts of Tapah, Perak. Electronic gadgets, including mobile telephones and the laptop, got re-charged every evening when the hamlet's diesel-fuelled generator was turned on for two hours. Generally, it is still a challenge to connect to the Worldwide Web in rural Peninsular Malaysia; nonetheless, smartphone usage is on the rise among Orang Asli. Thus, while not necessarily computer literate, many Orang Asli are digitally literate.

(Photo credit: Karen Heikkilä)

Orang Asli, for instance, go to surf the Internet for information and to network (see Ajani 2012). Explored in this chapter is the significance of the Internet as a space where literate Orang Asli can keep informed of and participate in discourse relating to issues critical from an Orang Asli standpoint. Particularly significant is the role of the Internet as a form of political organization and indigenous solidarity; blogs and social networking sites not only connect Orang Asli from diverse linguistic groups but put them in contact with other indigenous peoples, such as those from Sabah and Sarawak. As spaces of self-determination, blogs and social networking sites map the geographies of indigenous exclusion and resistance in 21st-century Malaysia from an Orang Asli standpoint.

ORANG ASLI IN THE NEWS

Mainstream and Alternative News Sources

The first news stories on the Orang Asli were produced during the colonial era, in the local Malayan presses (Nicholas et al. 1989). In that period, reportage on the Orang Asli peaked during the communist insurgency, commonly referred to in Malaysian history annals as the Malayan Emergency (1948–60) (see Leary 1989; Nicholas et al. 1989).[1] Of late, particularly in the last five years, the emergence and popularity of Internet social networking communications have enhanced public access to news on the Orang Asli. Major Malaysian English and Malay language newspapers, such as *The Star*, *New Straits Times*, *Malay Mail*, *Utusan Malaysia* and *Berita Harian*, post newsfeeds online and report regularly on the Orang Asli.[2] These media reflect the Malaysian government's point of view.

Besides newspapers, there exist several online alternative news sources that also carry reports on the Orang Asli, for example *Aliran*, *Malaysia Today*, *Malaysia Kini*, the *Nut Graph*, the *Center for Orang Asli Concerns*, *Malaysian Bar Council*, *Selangor Kini* and *Perak Speak* websites. These sites feature news digests from the major Malaysian dailies and weeklies, but notably differ from the online newsfeeds of the conventional presses in that they engage in commentary and analyses of current affairs. Reader and columnist opinions and editorials frame the presentation of news items, engendering a *vox populi* interpretation of current events. Assuming a citizen or human rights advocacy role, these sites provide reportage from an altogether different journalistic slant compared to that of the mainstream presses. For instance, the statement by Deputy Prime Minister Tan Sri Muhuyiddin Yassin announcing the government's plan to award land titles to the Orang Asli and covered as a general news item in the major presses (for instance, *The Star*, 4 Dec. 2009) was followed up by *Nut Graph* (29 March 2010) in an opinion piece. Appearing under the "Holding Court" column, the story used as its lead the March 2010 Orang Asli protest against the proposed land titles at Putrajaya, Malaysia's administrative capital. Yassin's words to the press, "The land is given in perpetuity and is part of efforts to take the [Orang Asli] community out of poverty" (*The Star*, 4 Dec. 2009) were in particular scrutinized. In a column headlined "Giving Orang Asli Land" (*Nut Graph*, 29 March 2010), the essential facts of the government's proposition were thus laid bare:

> ..."beware Greeks bearing gifts". Or in this case, it may be wise for the Orang Asli to be wary of overtures from a government with a proven track record of *taking* land away from them, rather than awarding it. What's the catch? Orang Asli say if they accept the land under the new policy, it would deprive them of a further 200,000 acres of customary land which they currently occupy. In addition to that ... the land cannot be rented out, leased or pawned without the permission of the state. Ownership of the land cannot be transferred until the first owner has held it for at least 15 years. Orang Asli who accept the land grant cannot claim ... any other land in that area or any other Orang Asli area. They also cannot make any claims for ... "roaming area[s]". The land would be developed with crops such as oil palm and rubber and these plantations would be managed by developers. Orang Asli would have to pay ... surveying costs, premiums, registration and "other payments advanced by developers" out of the proceeds from the land. Existing land gazetted as Orang Asli reserves can be re-gazetted and parcelled out under this new policy ... the government could evade recognising and paying compensation for potentially 200,000 acres belonging to Orang Asli....

The rise of independent online presses is consistent with the Malaysian public's growing lack of confidence in the accuracy and fairness of reporting by the mainstream presses (see *Aliran*, 2 March 2008). The fact that major political parties or their investment arms own stakes in mainstream newspapers (see Kim 2001) diminishes faith in the reliability of news coverage and reporting. That being so, mainstream news is of questionable repute in the public mind; a niche now exists for alternative news sources as a means to subscribe to multiple readings of a news story, to engage in the democratic activity of criticizing and comparing accounts, and to enter into civic discourse representative of a broad socio-economic and political spectrum. Presumably, with Malaysians increasingly reading online alternative news accounts, their exposure to marginalized groups, such as the Orang Asli, and the issues impacting them, also increases.

Orang Asli Representation in the News and the Paradox of Preservation

However, does being informed of accounts that highlight the marginalized status of the Orang Asli in Malaysia lessen the group's stigmatization, or do they conversely affirm societal prejudices and fixed views of aboriginals? Generally, news on the Orang Asli is negative, evidenced by the recurring news pegs of their abject poverty, illiteracy, gullibility and helplessness; charitable acts bestowed upon the Orang Asli in the form of donations of food and clothing; their low educational attainment; Orang Asli families or communities that have been displaced from their homes and lands due to a natural calamity or to appropriation of their ancestral territories by the state or large corporations; outbreaks of disease or pestilence in the Orang Asli villages; and the impending loss of culture and identity as the Orang Asli establish themselves in cities and take on an urban lifestyle. It would seem that other than extensive coverage given to Orang Asli success in litigating the state over infringement of aboriginal title and rights as in the *Sagong Tasi* and *Adong Kurau* cases (Subramaniam 2012), there is negligible coverage of the community's achievements, for example university graduations, successful business ventures, and the publication of novels, music and artwork.[3] Hence, a skewed understanding exists among Malaysians of the distinctiveness of the Orang Asli in contemporary times. This may be attributed to both mainstream and alternative news reporting being nuanced by notions of aboriginal primitivity, savagery and rurality. As a consequence, a specious, unidimensional status of quaint, childlike, jungle peoples on the verge of becoming extinct is accorded to the Orang Asli, accompanied by the logic of preserving them, or at least remnants of their culture.

"Preservation" of the Orang Asli is, however, paradoxical and problematic, delineated along the lines of people versus the culture they practise: the Malaysian government's policy of safeguarding the Orang Asli communities assumes a severance of links with the aboriginal way of life, but a safekeeping of aboriginal relics as mementoes of a bygone society. The first sense of "preservation" of the Orang Asli may be understood as the strategy of integrating the community with the country's Malay or Muslim majority, and of settling and reorganizing the community into a proletariat (Nowak n.d.). The second sense of "preservation" of the Orang Asli is observed in state actions to "conserve for good" the Orang Asli, via the visible, material aspects of their culture in museums and officially approved *sewangs* (healing rituals) and blowpipe hunting performances for tourism purposes (see Nowak 2000). It is such connotations of Orang Asli preservation that are sanctioned and commemorated by the state, and through them, the motifs of primitivity, tribal savagery and rurality recur, are made valid and gain currency in the Malaysian imagination.

ORANG ASLI-GENERATED NEWS AND VIEWS ONLINE

The advent of the Internet has meant countless possibilities for ordinary citizens to broadcast their views on issues that interest them. With the aid of easy-to-use desktop and online publishing tools, websites and blogs can be instantly constructed, with as much creative flair as one chooses. Indigenous groups have used websites and blogs to publish information about their histories, languages, treaties and other agreements they have entered into with governments as well as government abuses of their autochthonous rights (see Maybury-Lewis 1997; Dyson 2010). A special function of indigenous online narratives and reflections is their correction of mainstream views that relegate indigenous groups to categories of social and economic backwardness and ideological obscurity. The Bukit Lanjan Temuan Orang Asli, for instance, published an article on its community website regarding the sale of ancestral territory to property developer, MK Holdings. The sale, brokered in 2002 by the Department of Orang Asli Affairs, saw the relocation of the entire community from their traditional lands at Bukit Lanjan to the newly established housing estate of Desa Temuan. Besides being given houses to live in and a community centre, the Temuan were also compensated in the form of shares, an educational fund and state-allocated funds for further development of their new

settlement (see *The Star*, 18 April 2009). General opinion holds that
the Temuan won a significant cash windfall from the sale along with
the added bonus of free housing; thus it was a shock to many when
reports began to circulate after a few years that the resettled Temuan
were socially isolated and largely unemployed in Desa Temuan and
were choosing to return to the forest. Written in English (presumably
to reach a wider audience), "Back to the Forest that We Love" (Ajani
2009b) is the online article in which the Temuan community shared
its reality of living in Desa Temuan:

> At first the Temuan living [in Desa Temuan] cherish[e]d their
> new home[s] … a bungalow house … [was a] symbol that [the]
> Orang Asli [had] entered the mainstream…. After a few years [of]
> inhabiting [their] concrete home[s] the Temuan began to feel
> [insecure] with all the tax[es] and utility bills they had to pay [to
> rent] their bungalow[s] to outsider[s]. [Some] Temuan rent their
> homes to kindergarten owners (there are about four kindergartens
> in Desa Temuan) and some to a security company for [the
> company] employees to stay. [Others rent their homes to companies
> specializing in old age care.]

> Where [do] the Temuan of Desa Temuan … go after renting [out]
> their homes? Well, the answer is simple. We went back to the forest
> that we love … The Temuan of Desa Temuan … [have migrated to
> other Temuan villages] such as Bukit Lagong, Air Kuning, Sungai
> Buloh, Sungai Kelubi, Serendah and Kuang, [where it is still possible
> to make a living from the forest].

> [Many] Temuan at Desa Temuan can't afford to pay [their]
> electricity bills, so some … home[s] are [in total darkness at
> night]. If you [are] visiting Desa Temuan at night, don't think
> that the Temuan switch off their light[s] [as part of] the Save the
> Earth campaign…. [They just can't afford to pay their electric
> bills!]

> Outsiders [think] that the Temuan of Desa Temuan are …
> millionaire[s]. They [are] wrong. The Temuan here are not rich and
> the average working Temuan … earn[s] only RM 500 [per] month
> from [renting their low cost houses].

[Many of us] are not ... educated. Maybe some ... have succeed[ed] in going to university and college but the majority of ... Temuan ... are primary school [dropouts]. [They] work ... as [labourers] in the nearby citi[es] of Bandar Utama and Bandar Sri Damansara. Some ... work at factor[ies] located at [the] Sunway Damansara Technology Park.

[Many] Temuan elder[s] [feel that the] Desa Temuan environment [is too] hot ... [They] ... miss [the original Temuan village that was here before] ... the peaceful, [cool] environment full of ... trees that protected them from the sun.... The high cost of living in the city and the minimum [amount] of money that Temuan earn [here] are the main factor[s] for them to migrate to [other] Temuan villages that are [near] the forest. Maybe it's Temuan nature that [they] cannot be separated from the forest [where] everything is free and [where] they won't need to spend a nickel because all their need[s] are provided by Mother Nature. Maybe it's time to go back to the forest that we love.

Online self-expression by the Orang Asli has been through blogs more than community websites. Routine web searches for news and information on the Orang Asli carried out in English reveal blogs and websites written primarily by non-aboriginal Malaysians. However, when searches were conducted in Malay, several blogs written by the Orang Asli themselves emerged. This was evident from the fact that most blogs carry a blogger profile: even when pseudonyms are used, bloggers tend to reveal their gender, age and the Orang Asli group to which they belong. Moreover, the blogs contain links to other blogs, many of which are written by Orang Asli; these linkups have served as a useful sampling technique to identify and examine Orang Asli blogs.

Blogs are pervasive in cyberspace, symbolizing a multiplicity of experiences and perspectives. Herring et al. (2005) claim that as an online activity, blogging has increased exponentially since 1999 as a direct result of the creation of blogging software such as Pitas, Blogger and Groksoup; in particular, they trace the grassroots power of blogs and their potential as alternative news sources to two recent historical events: 9 November 2001 and the 2003 American-led war on Iraq. Hookway (2008), Eastham (2011) and others view blogs as a resurgence, and even a revolution, of the traditional diary, and conceive the blog as a type of human document relating personal life and serving as a conduit for the mundane and profound in an individual's record of his/her life. However, blogs are utilized for reasons other than as a personal journal. Both filter and notebook blogs cull news and events, but differ in the amount of blogger opinion featured. The former offers little or no opinion, while the latter features lengthier, purposive commentary on feature stories (Herring et al. 2005: 145). Journals, filters and notebooks seem to be the typical forms assumed by Orang Asli blogs. Some blogs serve the purpose of recording life events and personal reflections, while others appear angst-driven, containing strong reactions to current events and government policy. Certain blogs act as forums, containing commentary and long discussion threads on specific issues. Other blogs function as information repositories, where the blogger collects news and information from several sources and posts these items on his/her blog. The blogs introduced below were selected for inclusion in this chapter because of their aboriginal self-defining content.[4] Firstly, the blogs generally host articles about the Orang Asli from the local presses, which is noteworthy as it exhibits a keenness to keep abreast of and publicize the issues affecting the Orang Asli communities. Secondly, the blogs contain opinion on government policies, current events and international human rights legislation. These views are unique because they are provided from an Orang Asli perspective and often include cross-references to the bloggers' own life situations or that of their communities. Thirdly, some blogs feature a glossary of terms and sayings in the aboriginal language of the blogger, as well as the mythico-historical significance of places on aboriginal ancestral lands. These may be interpreted as Orang Asli attempts to make known in writing, languages and narratives that have been hitherto transmitted only orally and are in danger of becoming obsolete as the Orang Asli communities adapt to rigorous, fast-paced changes. In sum, the Orang Asli seem to utilize a tool of self-expression, the blog, to exercise the right to define themselves: to voice issues impacting their communities, to write their own histories and languages, and to educate their own people about basic human rights issues.

Blog 1

Distrust of the mainstream media has ostensibly motivated the writing of Blog 1. The blogger complains about the taken-for-granted nature of news reporting in Malaysia, which he thinks falsely promulgates an image of normalcy where Malaysian public life is concerned. In an entry on racial discrimination in Malaysia, the blogger discusses the Satu Malaysia (1Malaysia)[5] concept. He disagrees that the concept will bring about equal opportunities for all Malaysians, irrespective of race, religion and class, and views the concept as state propaganda. The blogger also alleges that the Satu Malaysia concept is focused on the needs of the country's three major ethnic groups—Malays, Chinese and Indians—to the exclusion of minorities such as the Orang Asli. He stresses that the state has not adequately championed the idea of Satu Malaysia in indigenous communities, and he questions the role of the press in ensuring that the concept reaches every Malaysian. Here, an important point is raised regarding Orang Asli access to news and information—the blogger mockingly states that government messages would only reach Orang Asli households if they had satellite or cable television. The reality that most Orang Asli still live in remote areas, without the basic amenities of electricity and running water, and isolated from civic rights and participation in national debates and events, is registered in the blogger's remark.

Blog 2

The blogger maintains his blog for the primary purpose of furnishing news, opinions and publications relevant to his own village. In an entry on Satu Malaysia, the blogger satirizes the "citizens first" spirit of the concept, citing the tokenism and doublespeak that seem to inhere in political addresses to the Orang Asli communities. Using as an example the visit of a Member of Parliament to his village, the blogger recounts the seemingly commiserative speech that was delivered by the MP, in which he acknowledged the existence of the village from time immemorial and the various injustices perpetrated on the villagers that have led to a loss of traditional lands and forced relocations.

However, as the blogger argues, underlying this rhetoric are the actual daily struggles of an Orang Asli village, which seem to be kept in abeyance by politicians: the unrelenting process of petitioning state authorities for basic services (piped water, electricity, schools, etc.) and for the protection of ancestral lands against being logged or developed in other ways. The irony of appealing to the government to continue living on their own ancestral lands (to which Orang Asli have at least customary rights) is not lost here. As the blogger witnesses, the state evidently places more importance on gazetting the community's ancestral territory as a wildlife sanctuary than on fulfilling its fiduciary responsibility to an aboriginal group. To emphasize this point, the blogger recounts other instances in the history of his village where the government has extinguished the community's rights to land, simultaneously negating the people's status as indigenous inhabitants of the land and relegating them to the position of tenants at will. The blogger ends this entry by renouncing the Satu Malaysia concept as unadulterated bombast, something that cannot provide real solutions to the problems faced by the Orang Asli.

Blog 3

Blog 3 captures the daily life events of an Orang Asli village. The blogger critically narrates the goings-on of the village from an aboriginal rights perspective. The blog starts with a reflection on the various derogatory terms used against the Orang Asli, the blogger's intent being to situate readers in the problematics of Orang Asli segregation and marginalization. In an entry focusing on land use in his village, the blogger observes that the village is impoverished compared to Malay villages located nearby because his community has chosen to continue an aboriginal subsistence way of life. The Orang Asli villagers hunt, fish, gather and cultivate swiddens, and are relatively self-sufficient, except in cases of seasonal resource scarcity. There is no road access to the village, other than a dirt track through an oil-palm estate. Because of the non-intrusive nature of indigenous subsistence land use, village lands still include virgin jungle. The village's remoteness, coupled with its thick forests and absence of permanent agricultural plots, makes it seem uninhabited and "available" to outsiders. Thus, it was only a matter of time before agriculture department officers came to the village and cleared hectares of land to grow rubber and to establish a freshwater prawn farm. The Orang Asli villagers were not consulted prior to these developments nor were they compensated for land appropriated by state authorities. The blogger claims that the villagers were instead offered the opportunity of caring for the rubber trees for a duration of three years, which in his opinion is a shoddy attempt by the authorities at bringing training and progress to an Orang Asli village. Of note in this entry are the topics of aboriginal land entitlement and the continuance of indigeneity, which seem to be correlated issues to the blogger. He concludes the entry by stating that should their traditional lands continue to be encroached upon and developed, the Orang Asli would have no land available to them in the future and thus, no real opportunity to lead a forest-dependent lifestyle. In other words, without a land base, the only choice that may be left to the Orang Asli is to urbanize and immerse themselves in mainstream culture and wage employment.

Blog 4

Similar to other Orang Asli blogs, news digests and commentaries pertaining to the various aboriginal communities are available on this blog. An interesting feature of the blog, nonetheless, is its devotion to Orang Asli language and cultural matters. An example is the blog entry on the place name, Temerloh, whose etymology and lore provide fascinating insight into the history of Orang Asli–Malay relations.

Temerloh, nowadays the name of a town in the state of Pahang, once designated an entire territory under the rule of the Semelai Orang Asli headman, Batin Serindun. The territory was the valley lying between the mountains, Gunung Senyum and Bukit Gebuk. According to the story, Batin Serindun's territory would eventually fall into the hands of the Minangkabau prince, Sujudbilang. When Sujudbilang and his brothers left Sumatra, they sailed up to Daik and onwards to Pahang. Upon landing, they paid their respects to the Bendahara Pahang, and continued their journey inland, travelling upstream on a bamboo raft. When they tried to land at Sentang Mukim Kertau, they were driven away by hostile local Malays. Moving further upstream, Sujudbilang spotted Orang Asli encampments on both the east and west banks of the Pahang River. The party mollified the aboriginals with gifts of salt and tobacco and was soon accepted and welcomed each time it disembarked at an encampment. Sujudbilang was impressed by the vast jungle hinterland and intimated to his brothers that he would take an Orang Asli wife to lay claim to the bountiful country before his eyes.

Eventually, Sujudbilang reached Batin Serindun's territory. There was instant rapport between the two men, with Sujudbilang accompanying Batin Serindun on daily hunting trips. From dawn to dusk, the men looked for food in the forest and even slept by the same hearth each night. The custom of separate sleeping spaces for men and women was obviously enigmatic to the visitors, for they gave the place where they slept each night the name temerloh (from the Semelai word mereloh, meaning "sleepy", "needing to sleep"). The stream closest to the place was given the name Sungai Temerloh.

The friendship between Sujudbilang and Batin Serindun was further strengthened when the headman's daughter's hand was given in marriage to the prince. The marriage created a situation whereby the entire house of Batin Serindun as well as his kinfolk from along the Pahang River became Sujudbilang's subjects. This occurred when the prince converted the Orang Asli to Islam. It is believed that this incident caused the spread of Islam in central Pahang.

Accounts such as this may be needed to complete Malaysian history, which is heavily reliant on Malay oral history as transcribed and codified in the *Sejarah Melayu*, *Hikayat Hang Tuah* and *Hikayat Merong Mahawangsa* and on English accounts of Malaya as a colony. Orang Asli oral narratives re-told in writing can broaden perspectives on the Orang Asli past; at present it is limited to biogeographical and archaeological reconstructions. Unquestionably, these evidence-based accounts should be balanced by aboriginal accounts of history (cf. Cruikshank 1998), in order to fully appreciate the contemporariness of the Orang Asli and not merely their adaptive/genetic links to early humans.

Blog 5

This blog features pan-indigenous content and is interesting for its inclusion of slideshows and photographs depicting traditional ceremonies, arts and crafts, and species of medicinal value. News and information digests are featured as well, and extend beyond the Orang Asli communities of Peninsular Malaysia to coverage of issues impacting the indigenous communities of Sabah and Sarawak. Of interest also, is the blogger's enthusiasm for communicating in his own aboriginal language: two blog entries are dedicated to teaching readers basic vocabulary and sayings.

An especially intriguing entry is one that provides a plain language explanation of the United Nations Declaration on the Rights of Indigenous Peoples (UNDRIP 2007). The blogger's intention here is to provide the gist of the declaration to readers, so that its implications are understood alongside legislation such as the Aboriginal Peoples' Act (1954, revised 1974) and the Wildlife Act (1972), which affect Orang Asli land and resource rights. Starting with an explanation of the genesis of the UNDRIP, the blogger proceeds by discussing the intent of the declaration. He points out that the declaration is akin to an international law that protects the rights of indigenous peoples, including their traditions, territories and ways of life. Other than the Aboriginal Peoples' Act, the blogger emphasizes that the UNDRIP should be honoured by the state as a means to ensuring that aboriginal rights are given the same legal recognition as that given to the rights of other Malaysians. The concept of indigeneity is also explored at this juncture, where the aboriginal way of life is shown to be distinct from that of other societies, in terms of oneness with and reliance on the natural environment as a basis for identity, sustenance and spirituality, and Fourth World solidarity as peoples discriminated against on the basis of their indigenousness. Practising aboriginal beliefs and ways of life are stressed here as a basic human right, with the reminder to readers that the Orang Asli do not need to convert to other religions because they already possess their own belief systems which also promote peace and goodness.

All nine divisions of the UNDRIP are summarized in this blog entry, with special attention given to the "Development and Consultation" and "Lands and Resources" divisions. This is likely due to the rampant abuses of power in Peninsular Malaysia surrounding the appropriation of aboriginal customary lands (see Nicholas et al. 2010). The notion of free and prior informed consent (FPIC) is discussed at length here, where the state and industry, as initiators of land development schemes, bear the onus of meaningful consultation in seeking the consent of aboriginal communities prior to the commencement of development projects. The blogger emphasizes that the process of consultation must be conducted early (months ahead of the proposed project), freely (without coercion or inducement) and unequivocally (any and all information pertaining to the proposed project must be presented in lay terms, including foreseeable risks and benefits to the aboriginal community involved). The spirit of FPIC fosters the recognition of the *sui generis* ties between aboriginal peoples and their territories, including aboriginal title to and use of those lands. Within this context, the blogger draws attention to the issue of adequate compensation in the event of development projects being initiated on aboriginal lands without prior consultation; he makes the point that in such cases, the state as protector of the Orang Asli (per the Aboriginal Peoples' Act) has the ultimate responsibility of compensating aboriginal communities for the loss of lands and resources.

The entry ends with the blogger's opinion that since Malaysia was party to the ratification of the UNDRIP, the state is obliged to honour the declaration in all its dealings with the Orang Asli. This is a significant point and one that will conceivably emerge in future court rulings over interpretations of extant legislation governing aboriginal title and subsistence rights. In fact, a recent proposal to amend the Aboriginal Peoples' Act was met with opposition from the Malaysian Bar Association, whose vice-president cited the UNDRIP as grounds for the state to meaningfully consult with the Orang Asli on all matters pertaining to their welfare: "Even though Malaysia voted in favour of the UNDRIP, the key concept of free, prior and informed consent appears to be honoured more in its breach than in its observance" (*The Star*, 13 May 2011).

DISCUSSION AND CONCLUSION

In focusing on Orang Asli use of blogs as a particular form of aboriginal self-definition, this chapter highlights "cyberspace as a new frontier for social research" (Hookway 2008: 92). Even indigenous authored books are gaining a virtual life of their own through online promotions and advertising. The implications of this are wide-ranging, particularly when considered in the context of e-research: the multi-sitedness of online inquiry allows instant access to geographically and socially distant groups of people. Also, due to the open access nature of online content, researchers are able to engage in uncensored observation of the minutiae of daily life and forms of popular culture, which generally do include a measure of sensitive and private information. It has been argued that the primary benefits of relying on blogs as data sources are: their cost-effectiveness and easy availability; their textual form obviates the laborious tasks of listening, note-taking and transcribing that are the drawbacks of the interview technique; greater success with gathering sensitive information compared to the traditional survey or interview; and the possibility of better capturing the phenomenological present. The latter refers to the enduring nature of blogging—because bloggers tend to consistently record daily life events, the problem of memory attrition (faced in interview- and focus group-orientated research) is hardly ever encountered (see Tremayne 2007; Hookway 2008; Eastham 2011). Despite these benefits, a degree of ethical uncertainty overshadows the use of blogs, in particular, as data; the analogy of peeping into someone's diary may well apply here, although it may be conversely argued that if one did not wish to make one's private life public, posting information about oneself online should simply be avoided.

Nonetheless, it remains that the demarcation between public and private is not necessarily straightforward in cyberspace. As Eastham (2011: 353) states: "Blogs are simultaneously private and yet quite public.... The private nature is reflected in the 'intimate, often ferocious expression of the blogger's passions', whereas the public nature is inherent in the very fact that anyone with Internet availability can access and read those intimate expressions." Hence, researchers are obliged to carefully assess the ethical implications of their use of online content as data and to follow the relevant institutional review precautions of guaranteeing anonymity and confidentiality to their research subjects (Eastham 2011). Care was employed in this paper to conceal the identity of bloggers, so as to guard against possible repercussions (libel, imprisonment, etc.).[6]

Ironically, protecting the identity of bloggers, which necessitates secreting URLs and blogger profiles as well as avoiding the use of direct quotes, raises suspicion about the credibility of one's data sources. More fundamentally perhaps is the concern regarding potential identity ruses and deception. How does one assess the veracity of claims made by an online personality to Orang Asli membership, for instance? One is bound to encounter such a challenge when dealing with the seemingly unconfined yet simulated world of blogs, websites and social networking sites. However, a way of circumventing the problem is to supplement blog content as research data with interview data (see Hookway 2008). Interviews not only enable researcher and blogger to become personally acquainted, but offer the chance to verify (and correct if necessary) the researcher's interpretations and understandings of blog messages.

This chapter is intended as an initial contribution to examining Orang Asli online expression. It confirms the presence of a burgeoning sphere of writing that is fully representative of the Orang Asli. In doing so, the chapter introduces the potential of Orang Asli blogs as sources of Orang Asli perspectives on a variety of issues. Unlike the blogs and websites on Orang Asli issues maintained by non-aboriginal organizations and individuals (see for example the *Jabatan Kemajuan Orang Asli* and *Center for Orang Asli Concerns* websites, and the *Portal Permata Orang Asli* and *Anthropological Notebook* blogs), the blogs discussed in this chapter are written by Orang Asli individuals and may be viewed as situated and grounded accounts, reflecting their moral worlds and realities. Further research is needed on the evolving nature of Internet use among the Orang Asli; while Orang Asli blogs can still be tracked in cyberspace, they are not being updated or used as frequently as they were five years ago. This is likely due to the popularity of social networking sites such as Facebook, MySpace and Twitter among the Orang Asli of late (Ajani 2012: 69–70). Through

Facebook, for instance, closed group platforms can be created to post and comment on information privately (that is, to permitted members of the group only); an example is the recent release of the Human Rights Commission of Malaysia's Report of the National Inquiry into the Land Rights of Indigenous Peoples (SUHAKAM 2013) and Department of Orang Asli Development's refutation of it, which were vigorously discussed, debated and strategized by Orang Asli leaders and community members via Facebook closed groups.

To conclude, the use of Malay by the Orang Asli in blogs may at first seem alarming, due to widespread reports about the waning viability of aboriginal languages (see Smith 2003); however, Malay usage in these instances should be viewed more optimistically, as a sign of Orang Asli inter-group solidarity as well as a counter-hegemonic strategy. Malay remains the *lingua franca* that enables communication between the linguistically and culturally distinct groups of Orang Asli; it is also the language of unity and cooperation for the Orang Asli groups, the workings of which are conspicuous in Orang Asli protest marches and rallies and in the *Persatuan Orang Asli Semenanjung Malaysia* (Orang Asli Association of Peninsular Malaysia) annual general meetings. The imperialism of Malay is thus subverted, the language serving as a means "[to challenge] labels which signal rejection ... [and resurrect] the hope that, through political action, the humanity of the rejected will be recognized and the images of defilement discarded" (Sibley 1995: 69).

NOTES

1. A valuable undertaking to gauge the newsworthiness of Orang Asli issues is to survey the frequency of news reports between the Emergency and milestones in aboriginal rights recognition, such as the *Adong Kurau* (1998) and *Sagong Tasi* (2005) court cases. It is assumed that the Malaysian press reported more frequently on Orang Asli issues during and following these cases, and that there was a lull in reports of the same in the interval preceding the cases.

2. For instance, a search on Press Display, searchable for 60 days of back issues from date of search, produced 331 hits for the search term "Orang Asli", appearing in both headlines and the body of articles.

The newspapers scanned were the English language *The Star* and *Borneo Post*, and the Malay language *Migguan Malaysia* and *Utusan Malaysia*.

3. Orang Asli writers, for instance, often employ online media to advertise their publications. Akiya Mahat China, a Semai Orang Asli author, maintains a blog where he showcases his works and reviews of them, which have appeared in the Malay presses. His novel, *Perang Sangkil* (2007), reveals the buried history of Rawa enslavement of the Orang Asli that occurred in the late 1800s. Another author, Mor Ajani, from the Temuan community of Bukit Lanjan, advertises his writing online on the *Temuan Orang Asli Website*. His books, *Semangat Muyang* (2009a) and *Temuan: Histuri, Adat, Kepercayaan* (2008), are written in the Temuan language and address the community's ancestral knowledge and customs.

4. To protect the identity of bloggers, actual blogger names or pseudonyms, age, gender, community of origin, blog names and direct quotes from the blogs, are not revealed in this chapter. He/his/him are used to refer to all bloggers regardless of gender. See final section for a discussion of the ethical implications of undertaking e-research.

5. The concept of a united, "one" Malaysia was introduced by the Prime Minister, Datuk Seri Najib Razak, in 2009 to quell sentiments of racial discontent among the non-Malay/Muslim public. Waves of racial unrest arise periodically as a result of disgruntlement with affirmative action policies that specially favour *bumiputra* Malaysians.

6. The year 2008 saw a number of government crackdowns on Malaysian bloggers (see Aliran, 20 Feb. 2008). The bloggers were threatened with charges of subversion under the Internal Security Act, the Sedition Act and Section 121b of the Penal Code, if they continued to blog "against" the government.

REFERENCES

Ajani, M.
   2008   Temuan: Histuri, Adat, Kepercayaan [The Temuan: History, Customs, Beliefs]. Kuala Lumpur: Blue Crystal Enterprises.
   2009a Semangat Muyang: Ca'ak Hidup Kami [The Spirit of the Ancestors: Our Way of Life]. Kuala Lumpur: Blue Crystal Enterprises.

2009b Back to the Forest that We Love. Temuan Orang Asli Website. http://
       www.oocities.org/etemuan/earticle.html, accessed 26 Sept. 2013.
2012   Uwang Asli Moden/Orang Asli Moden [Modern Orang Asli].
       In New Malaysian Essays. S.H. Yin, ed. Pp. 59–78. Petaling
       Jaya: Matahari Books http://www.mataharibooks.com/NME3.pdf,
       accessed 26 Sept. 2013.

Aliran
2008   A Year of Bull, Broken Promises. Aliran, 20 Feb. http://aliran.
       com/aliran-monthly/2007/200711/a-year-of-bull-broken-promises-
       blog-heads-bigots-and-bravehearts/, accessed 6 March 2014.
2008   Cyber Activism, the New Frontier. Aliran, 2 March. http://aliran.
       com/aliran-monthly/2007/200711/a-year-of-bull-broken-promises-
       blog-heads-bigots-and-brav Aliran.

Anthropological Notebook
n.d.   Fieldwork Photos, blog entry by Lye Tuck-Po. http://fieldsketches.
       blogspot.fi/p/on-fieldwork.html, accessed 6 March 2014.

Center for Orang Asli Concerns [COAC]
n.d.   About COAC. http://www.coac.org.my/beta/index.php, accessed
       6 March 2014.

Denzin, N., Y. Lincoln and L. Smith, eds.
2008   Handbook of Critical and Indigenous Methodologies. Thousand
       Oaks, CA: Sage.

Ding, J-A.
2010   Giving Orang Asli Land. Nut Graph. http://www.thenutgraph.com/
       giving-orang-asli-land/, accessed 5 July 2011.

Dyson, L.
2010   Indigenous Peoples on the Internet. *In* The Handbook of Internet
       Studies. R. Burnett, M. Cosalvo and C. Ess, eds. Pp. 251–69.
       Chichester: Blackwell Publishing Ltd.

Eastham, L.
2011   Research Using Blogs for Data: Public Documents or Private
       Musings? Research in Nursing and Health 34: 353–61.

Herring, S., L.A. Scheidt, E. Wright and S. Bonus
2005   Weblogs as a Bridging Genre. Information Technology and People
       18: 142–71.

Hookway, N.
2008   Entering the Blogosphere: Some Strategies for Using Blogs in
       Social Research. Qualitative Research 8: 91–113.

Jabatan Kemajuan Orang Asli [JAKOA]
   n.d.   Portal Rasmi JAKOA. http://www.jakoa.gov.my/web/guest/home,
           accessed 26 Sept. 2013.

Johnson, J., G. Cant, R. Howitt and E. Peters, eds.
   2007   Creating Anti-Colonial Geographies: Embracing Indigenous
           Peoples' Knowledges and Rights. Geographical Research 45:
           117–20.

Khor, G.L. and Zalilah Mohd Shariff
   2008   The Ecology of Health and Nutrition of "Orang Asli" (Indigenous
           People) Women and Children in Peninsular Malaysia. Tribes and
           Tribals 2: 67–77 (special volume).

Kim, W.L.
   2001   Media and Democracy in Malaysia. The Public 8: 67–88.

Koshy, S.
   2011   Delay Act Amendment. The Star, 13 May. http://www.thestar.com.
           my/Story.aspx?file=%2F2011%2F5%2F13%2Fnation%2F8672079&
           sec=nation, accessed 5 July 2011.

Leary, J.
   1989   The Importance of the Orang Asli in the Malayan Emergency
           1948–1960. Clayton, VIC: Centre for Southeast Asian Studies,
           Monash University Working Paper No. 56.

Mahat China (Akiya)
   2007   Perang Sangkil. Kuala Lumpur: PTS Fortuna.

Mazwin Nik Anis
   2009   Orang Asli to Get Land to Boost Quality of Life. The Star, 4 Dec.
           http://www.thestar.com.my/story.aspx/?file=%2f2009%2f12%
           2f4%2fnation%2f20091204193625&&sec=nation, accessed 5 July
           2011.

Maybury-Lewis, D.
   1997   The Internet and Indigenous Groups. Cultural Survival Quarterly.
           http://www.culturalsurvival.org/publications/cultural-survival-
           quarterly/none/internet-and-indigenous-groups, accessed 6 March
           2014.

Nicholas, C., A. Williams-Hunt and Sabak Tiah
   1989   Orang Asli in the News: The Emergency Years, 1950–1958.
           Petaling Jaya: Center for Orang Asli Concerns.

Nicholas, C., Jenita Engi and Yen Ping Teh
  2010   The Orang Asli and the UNDRIP: From Rhetoric to Recognition. Subang Jaya: Centre for Orang Asli Concerns and Jaringan Orang Asal SeMalaysia.

Nowak, B.
  2000   Dancing the Main Jo'oh: Hma' Btsisi' Celebrate their Humanity and Religious Identity in a Malaysian World. The Australian Journal of Anthropology 11: 333–44.
  n.d.   A Comparative Examination of the Local Socio-Cultural and Environmental Impact of the Global Oil Palm Industry. Proceedings of the 4th DevNet Conference: Development on the Edge.

Portal Permata Orang Asli
  2009   Pengenalan, blog entry by Group Pengkaji Tamadun Asli Universiti Malaysia Pahang (UMP). http://permataorangasli.blogspot.fi/, accessed 6 March 2014.

Subramaniam, Y.
  2012   Orang Asli Land Rights by UNDRIP Standards in Peninsular Malaysia: An Evaluation and Possible Reform. Unpublished PhD dissertation, University of New South Wales, Sydney.

Shaw, W., R.D.K. Herman and R. Dobbs.
  2006   Encountering Indigeneity: Re-Imaging and Decolonizing Geography. Geografiska Annaler 88B: 267–76.

Sibley, D.
  1995   Geographies of Exclusion: Society and Difference in the West. London: Routledge.

Smith, K.
  2003   Minority Language Education in Malaysia: Four Ethnic Communities' Experiences. International Journal of Bilingual Education and Bilingualism 6: 53–65.

Stea, D. and B. Wisner.
  1984   Introduction. Antipode 16: 3–10.

SUHAKAM (Human Rights Commission of Malaysia).
  2013   Report of the National Inquiry into the Land Rights of Indigenous Peoples. http://www.suhakam.org.my/documents/10124/1326477/SUHAKAM+BI+FINAL.CD.pdf, accessed 28 August 2013.

Tremayne, M.
    2007   Harnessing the Active Audience: Synthesizing Blog Research and Lessons for the Future of Media. *In* Blogging, Citizenship, and the Future of Media. M. Tremayne, ed. Pp. 261–72. New York: Routledge.

Yip, Yoke Teng
    2009   Desa Temuan Orang Asli Settlement in Limbo. *The Star*, 18 April. http://www.thestar.com.my/story.aspx?file= %2f2009% 2f4%2f18%2fcentral%2f3695416, accessed 26 Sept. 2013.

List of Contributors

A.S. Baer is an adjunct faculty member of the Departments of History and of Integrative Biology at Oregon State University. Previously she was on the faculty of the University of Malaya, San Diego State University and the University of California, Berkeley. She has done fieldwork during two Fulbright fellowships to Malaysia and is the author of *Health, Disease, and Survival* (1999), on Orang Asli problems, and *Vital Signs*, a survey of health in Sarawak. She and her co-authors published *Orang Asli Women of Malaysia: Perceptions, Situations, and Aspirations* (2006). Previously, she edited *Heredity and Society: Readings in Social Genetics* (1973) and authored *The Genetic Perspective* (1977).

David Bulbeck is a specialist in the archaeology and palaeoanthropology of Peninsular Malaysia and Sulawesi. His MA from the Australian National University (ANU) involved the description and analysis of human burial remains from Gua Cha (Malaysia) and Leang Buidane (Talaud Islands, North Sulawesi province). His PhD, also from the ANU, included a survey of 13th to 17th century CE sites associated with the rise of Makassar as a trading emporium in southwest Sulawesi between the 16th and 17th centuries. His postdoctoral research projects include a comparative analysis of human skeletal remains from South Asia and Southeast Asia. Since 2009 he has been a Visiting Fellow and research associate at the ANU's Department of Archaeology and Natural History, devoting most of his activities to a project, headed by Sue O'Connor, on the prehistory of the lowlands near Lake Towuti in southeastern Sulawesi.

Niclas Burenhult is Associate Professor of General Linguistics at Lund University and Research Associate at the Max Planck Institute for Psycholinguistics, Nijmegen. His research interests include the relationship between language, cognition and culture, with a particular focus on the representation of space and perception, as well as ecological knowledge. He is a leading expert on the Austroasiatic languages of the Malay Peninsula and has conducted extensive field-based language description and documentation among speakers of Jahai, Lanoh, Menriq and Semnam since 1998. He is the author of a grammar of Jahai (2005) and curator of the *Tongues of the Semang* documentation corpus in the DOBES digital archive. He is co-director of the *Repository and Workspace for Austroasiatic Intangible Heritage* (RWAAI), a digital multimedia resource dedicated to the maintenance of research materials documenting endangered Austroasiatic communities in Southeast Asia and India.

Csilla Dallos, PhD (McGill), is a sociocultural anthropologist specializing in the study of hunter-gatherers. Her most important academic influences included Borneo specialist Jérôme Rousseau, legendary archaeologist Bruce Trigger, hunter-gatherer specialist Richard B. Lee and beloved mentor Shuichi Nagata, who introduced her to the Orang Asli and Southeast Asian hunters and gatherers. Her thesis and subsequent book, *From Equality to Inequality: Social Change among Newly Sedentary Lanoh Hunter-Gatherer Traders of Peninsular Malaysia* (2010), based on an ethnographic study of Lanoh foragers, analyze the consequences of recent regroupment and resettlement in terms of general theories of egalitarianism and emerging social complexity. Her research interests include social change, gender and complexity theory, as well as the link between hunter-gatherer traders' social organization and their relationship with neighbouring peoples, especially in Southeast Asia. She is an Associate Professor and Chair of the Department of Anthropology at St Thomas University in New Brunswick, Canada.

Kirk Endicott, PhD (Harvard) and DPhil (Oxford) is Professor Emeritus in the Department of Anthropology at Dartmouth College. He is a sociocultural anthropologist with special interest in Orang Asli cultures; hunter-gatherer economies, social organization and gender relations; indigenous religions; human rights of indigenous peoples; human violence and cooperation; and the relevance of hunter-gatherer studies for understanding human evolution and human nature. He has carried out fieldwork with the Batek and other Orang Asli groups intermittently since 1971. His publications on Orang Asli include *Batek Negrito Religion* (author) (1979), *Malaysia and the "Original People"* (co-author with R.K. Dentan, A. Gomes and M.B Hooker) (1997) and *The Headman Was a Woman* (co-author with Karen Endicott) (2008). He was also editor of the *Orang Asli Studies Newsletter* from 1982 to 1995.

Juli Edo, PhD (Australian National University), is an Associate Professor in the Department of Anthropology and Sociology at the University of Malaya. A member of the Semai Orang Asli group, he has studied aspects of Semai culture and history and has worked for Orang Asli rights since his undergraduate days at the Universiti Kebangsaan Malaysia. His doctoral thesis is entitled "Claiming Our Ancestors' Land: An Ethnohistorical Study of *Seng-oi* Land Rights in Perak, Malaysia" (1998).

Alan G. Fix is Professor Emeritus in the Department of Anthropology, University of California, Riverside. He is a biological anthropologist interested in the role of sociocultural factors affecting the population genetics and demography of small-scale human populations. His PhD project (Michigan, 1971, "Semai Senoi Population Structure and Genetic Microdifferentiation") and much subsequent work was based on extensive fieldwork with Semai Senoi (1968–69; 1987) supplemented by computer simulation experiments. The general topic of human colonization, of which the present chapter is an example, was presented in *Migration and Colonization in Human Microevolution* (1999), and the specific model relating to the Orang Asli was developed for the symposium, Dynamics of Human Diversity in Mainland Southeast Asia (2011).

Rosemary Gianno is a Professor in the Department of Sociology, Anthropology and Criminology, Keene State College, USA, where she has been since 1990. She studied anthropology at Queens College, CUNY, where she graduated *summa cum laude* in 1976. She subsequently earned her PhD in anthropology from Yale University in 1985. Prior to Keene State, she held research fellowships at the Conservation Analytical Laboratory, Smithsonian Institution. Her research, primarily based on several extended ethnographic fieldtrips, mostly with Semelais, has come to focus most specifically on different aspects of Semelai culture within a comparative, cultural, ecological and ethnohistorical framework. She has published on a variety of topics relative to Semelai culture, including resin technology and trade, midwifery, ethnicity, and agricultural patterns. In 2000, she received a grant from the Wenner-Gren Foundation for Anthropological Research to establish the Orang Asli Archive at Keene State, which she continues to support.

Alberto G. Gomes is an Emeritus Professor at La Trobe University, Melbourne and the Global Director of the Dialogue, Empathic Engagement and Peacebuilding (DEEP) Network. An anthropologist by training, much of his scholarly work is on the impact of capitalism, development and state policies on the Orang Asli, especially the Semai and the Menraq (Semang). He has also published work on cultural identities, inter-ethnic and inter-religious relations, civility and interculturalism in Malaysia and Goa in India. His books include *Modernity and Identity: Asian Illustrations* (editor) (1994), *Malaysia and the "Original People"* (co-author with R.K. Dentan, K. Endicott and M.B. Hooker) (1997), *Looking for Money* (author) (2004), *Modernity and Malaysia: Settling the Menraq Forest Nomads* (author) (2007) and *Multiethnic Malaysia* (co-editor with Lim Teck Ghee and Azly Rahman) (2009).

Karen Heikkilä completed her undergraduate work, including a teaching degree, at the University of British Columbia, Canada. Her Master's degree, focusing on Dakelh (Northern Athapaskan) toponymy, was completed at the University of Northern British Columbia in collaboration with the Tl'azt'en Nation. Karen is currently completing a doctorate in geography at the University of Helsinki. She works on the toponymy and oral narratives of the Semai Orang

Asli communities whose customary territories form the Bukit Tapah Forest Reserve in lower Perak, Malaysia. Karen's research explores the links between place-naming, ethnogeography and place attachment and the wider socio-cultural significance of the forest environment to indigenous memory and being. Her long-standing interests centre around indigenous education, geographical conceptions and language documentation.

Andy Hickson, PhD, has lived with the Temiar Orang Asli on a number of occasions. His MA thesis concerned the Temiar concept of *selantap*. Andy is a theatre and film director and Director of Actionwork Worldwide (www.actionwork.com). He has been a consultant to the governments of the UK, France and Gibraltar and has developed theories and practice of social theatre leading to empowerment and cross cultural understanding. Andy currently spends time between the UK and Asia delivering specialist creative training and producing international events.

Duncan Holaday received a BA with honours in anthropology from Wesleyan University, an MA from Cornell, and a PhD from the Annenberg School of Communication at the University of Pennsylvania. He was Fulbright Professor at the University of Indonesia and Universiti Sains Malaysia. He did original research with the Jah Hut people of Pahang in 1969–70 and published *Bes Hyang Dney and Other Jah Hut Stories* (1985 and 2003). His film, *Metos Jah Hut*, is in the Human Studies Film Archive at the Smithsonian Institution. From 1995–99, he was Head of the Division of Research and Director of Graduate Studies at the School of Communication Studies, Nanyang Technological University in Singapore. Since then he has been a distiller in Vermont. He lives with his wife, poet Chin Woon Ping, in Barnet, Vermont.

Signe Howell is Professor at the Department of Social Anthropology at the University of Oslo. Her DPhil from the University of Oxford (1981) was based on fieldwork in 1977–79 with Chewong—a small hunting, gathering and shifting cultivating Orang Asli group who then lived deep inside the Kerau Game Reserve in Pahang. She has made many subsequent visits, the last one in 2010. Since 1984 she has also undertaken fieldwork with the Lio people on Flores in Indonesia. Her main research interests fall within the anthropology of religion in a broad sense, including classification, modes of thought, concepts of personhood and ritual practices. She has also written on gender and kinship. Her extensive publications include *Society and Cosmos* (1984 and 1989), *The Ethnography of Morality* (1994), *For the Sake of our Future: Sacrificing in Eastern Indonesia* (1996) and "Metamorphosis and identity: Chewong animistic ontology" (2013).

Sue Jennings, PhD (SOAS), Dip Soc Anthrop (LSE), LRAM, LGSM is an anthropologist, author, storyteller and specialist in Neuro-Dramatic-Play. Her early career in professional theatre as dancer and actor led into social theatre and theatre in education. She pioneered theory and practice of dramatherapy in UK and many countries and published extensively on this work, culminating in her ground breaking book *Healthy Attachments and Neuro-Dramatic-Play* (2011), which brings together neuroscience, play and early child development. Leeds Metropolitan University held a festschrift to honour her work in 2012. She conducted doctoral fieldwork with Senoi Temiar in Malaysia beginning in 1974, which led to her book *Theatre, Ritual and Transformation: The Senoi Temiar* (1995). Sue has held academic appointments at the universities of Exeter, Leeds and Coleraine and is currently Visiting Professor at HELP University in Malaysia. She is planning further research with the Temiars on storytelling and play.

Kamal Solhaimi Fadzil, MA (SOAS) is a Lecturer in the Department of Anthropology and Sociology at the University of Malaya. His research interests centre on the impact of development on Orang Asli, education and the problems of disadvantaged children in Malaysia. One of his recent projects is "Understanding the Impact of the State on Orang Asli in the Belum Temengor" (2012–13).

Wazir Jahan Karim is Distinguished Fellow and Founder of the Academy of Socio-Economic Research and Analysis (ASERA), a global think-tank and research collective focusing on economic justice, and is a Life Member of Clare Hall, University of Cambridge. She is also a co-founder of Gender Studies in Malaysia, Founding Director of the Women's Development Research Centre (KANITA) at Universiti Sains Malaysia and the founder and Founding President of the Southeast Asian Association for Gender Studies. She has authored, co-authored and co-edited over 100 scholarly publications, including *Ma' Betise' Concepts of Living Things* (1981 and 2004), *Emotions of Culture: A Malay Perspective* (1990), *Women and Culture: Between Malay Adat and Islam* (1992), "Male" and "Female" *in Developing Southeast Asia* (1995), *Gendered Fields: Women, Men, Ethnography* (1994), *Cultural Minorities of Peninsular Malaysia: Survivals of Indigenous Heritage* (2002) and *Straits Muslims: Diasporas of the Northern Passage of the Straits of Malacca* (2009), *Feasts of Penang: Muslim Culinary Heritage* (2013).

Nicole Kruspe is a Research Fellow at Lund University and leading specialist in the Austroasiatic (Aslian) languages of the Malay Peninsula. She obtained her PhD from the University of Melbourne in 2000 for "A Grammar of Semelai", which was published in 2004. Since then she has undertaken field-based language description and documentation projects in Mah Meri, Ceq Wong, Semaq Beri and Batek communities. Her research interests include grammatical description, structural and semantic typology, the history of the Aslian languages, and the relationship between language and culture. Her current research investigates perceptual modalities across languages and cultures in the Malay Peninsula. She has compiled a dictionary of Mah Meri (2010) and is curator of the Ceq Wong and Mah Meri corpus in the ELAR (SOAS) digital archive and the Semaq Beri and Batek corpus in the DOBES digital archive. She is co-director and curator of the Repository and Workspace for Austroasiatic Intangible Heritage (RWAAI), a digital multimedia resource dedicated to the maintenance of research materials documenting endangered Austroasiatic communities in Southeast Asia and India.

Peter Laird, PhD (Monash), is an ethnographer and acoustic ecologist who began fieldwork with the Temoq in 1973. However, almost all of his field research on Temoq shamanism is post-doctoral, initially funded by the University of Malaya while employed as a Lecturer. He has also taught anthropology and religious studies in Australia and the United States. Currently he is an Honorary Research Fellow in the Faculty of Arts and Education, Federation University, Australia. His interests lie in ethnography, ethnopoetics, ritual studies, religion, visual anthropology, indigenous knowledge systems, translation theory and practice, indigenous rights, and Southeast Asian Studies. He is writing "Temoq Shamanism: Songs of Life and Healing in a Malaysian Rain Forest Society", and "Teng Kijai: Temoq Shaman Paq Loong's Journey to Putri Bungsu's Cloud-Mountain Healing Pool", the latter being a complete shamanic performance of six "songs" with accompanying audio recordings.

Sandra Khor Manickam is a historian specializing in colonial British Malaya, the history of Orang Asli and anthropology and the history of ideas of race. She obtained her PhD in history at the Australian National University (2010), was Visiting Fellow at the History Department, National University of Singapore (2011) and Junior Professor of Southeast Asian Studies at the Goethe University of Frankfurt, Germany (Feb. 2012–Sept. 2014). Since November 2014, she holds the position of Assistant Professor of Southeast Asian history at Nanyang Technological University, Singapore. Her first monograph, *Taming the Wild: Aborigines and Racial Knowledge in Colonial Malaya*, is part of the Asian Studies Association of Australia (ASAA) Southeast Asia Series and has recently been published by NIAS and NUS Press.

Barbara S. Nowak is a development consultant and independent scholar. She earned her PhD in anthropology from SUNY Buffalo where she was a student of Robert Dentan. Barbara's initial research with Hma' Btsisi' focused on gender relations, which later extended to the impact of development on Btsisi' livelihood and gender relations and a general interest in the environmental degradation caused by plantation economies. She taught at Massey University where she became the Head of the Institute of Development Studies. While there, she participated in a New Zealand delegation to Aceh following the 2004 earthquake and tsunami. This led her to take up a Senior Research Fellowship in the Asia Research Institute at the National University of Singapore (with support from World Vision) where she explored the impact of rehabilitation, reconstruction and redevelopment and the re-establishment of livelihoods for inhabitants of the regions affected by the tsunami.

Mohd Razha Rashid, PhD (Toronto), is Associate Professor at the School of Distance Learning, Universiti Sains Malaysia where he teaches social anthropology, philosophy and ethics of social research. He is also Executive Director of the Academy of Socio-Economic Research and Analysis, a non-profit organization committed to economic justice, and Vice-President of the Penang Heritage Trust. His studies of the Orang Asli span 40 years, from his undergraduate years in USM under Professor Anthony Walker and his graduate studies under Professor Suichi Nagata, at the University of Toronto. He has conducted extensive research on the Kintaq Bong in Ulu Perak and has also participated in collaborative research with the Kensiu in Kedah and the Akha, Lisu and Karen of Northern Thailand. Razha has co-edited two volumes on the Orang Asli: *Indigenous Minorities of Peninsular Malaysia: Selected Issues and Ethnographies* (1995) and *Minority Cultures of Peninsular Malaysia: Survivals of Indigenous Heritage* (2002).

Diana Riboli, PhD, is Assistant Professor of Social Anthropology at the Department of Social Anthropology, Panteion University of Social and Political Sciences, Athens, Greece. Since 2011 she has been Vice-President of the International Society for Academic Research on Shamanism. She has carried out ethnographic research among the Chepang of Nepal (1991–2000) and, since 2006, has directed a research project on the resilience of Batek and Jahai religions and ethnomedical systems in Peninsular Malaysia. Her published works include *Tunsuriban: Shamanism in the Chepang of Southern and Central Nepal* (2000), *Shamanism and Violence: Power, Repression and Suffering in Indigenous Religious Conflicts* (co-edited with Davide Torri) (2013), and *Consciousness and Indigenous Healing Systems: Between Indigenous Perceptions and Neuroscience* (2014). She is the author and co-author of numerous articles and essays on shamanism, indigenous concepts of health and illnesses, altered states of consciousness and strategies for survival of indigenous cultures.

Rusaslina Idrus is a Senior Lecturer in the Gender Studies Programme, University of Malaya. She received her BSc from Cornell University, Masters in Environmental Sciences from Yale University, and PhD from Harvard University. She is a social anthropologist with research interests in gender, political ecology, indigenous peoples, Orang Asli and women in history. She has published on Orang Asli land issues and rights.

Yogeswaran Subramaniam earned a doctoral degree in law from the University of New South Wales for his research on Orang Asli land rights. He is currently co-legal counsel in a number of pro bono Orang Asli land rights cases, including notably the 2014 decision of the Court of Appeal in *Yebet binti Saman v Fong Kwai Loong* that reaffirmed Orang Asli customary land rights at common law. He served on a task force established by the Malaysian federal government to study the 2013 Human Rights Commission of Malaysia (SUHAKAM) Report on the National Inquiry into the Land Rights of Indigenous Peoples. He also serves as the Chairperson of the Committee for Orang Asli Rights of the Malaysian Bar Council and is an associate member of the Centre for Malaysian Indigenous Studies and the Centre for Legal Pluralism and Indigenous Law at the University of Malaya, Kuala Lumpur, Malaysia.

Ivan Tacey is a PhD candidate in sociocultural anthropology at the University of Lyon in France. He has taught a variety of subjects at French universities for over 13 years. His doctoral research with the Batek, a foraging people of Peninsular Malaysia, explores how processes of globalization and marginalization have led to realignments of environmental relations, moral geographies, and claims to places. He is particularly interested in transformations to the interactions between humans, animals and other non-human beings as landscapes are reshaped by severe environmental degradation, land loss and increased global and national flows. His publications (individual and in collaboration) explore the impact of globalization on Batek lives, environmental change, violence and shamanism. During his research he has worked closely with several wildlife and human rights NGOs in Malaysia as well as with geographers, sociocultural and evolutionary anthropologists, and biologists from Europe, the US and Malaysia.

Shanthi Thambiah is Associate Professor and formerly coordinator of the Gender Studies Programme, University of Malaya. She is currently the Deputy Dean of Post Graduate Studies at the Faculty of Arts and Social Sciences. She studied social anthropology at the University of Malaya, University of Cambridge (MPhil, 1989) and the University of Hull (PhD, 1995). She has conducted research and published widely on cultural change and changing gender relations in indigenous communities in Sarawak and amongst the Orang Asli in Peninsula Malaysia. She has been dealing with mobilities in her work with modern day hunter-gatherers in Malaysia and has extended that interest into migration studies. Her most recent publication entitled "Mobile and Changing Livelihoods Constituting Gender among the Hunter-Gather Bhuket of Sarawak" was published by NIAS in 2015.

Anthony Williams-Hunt is an advocate and solicitor of the High Court of Malaya. He currently practises at Williams-Hunt & Associates in Ipoh, Perak, Malaysia. He has been involved with Orang Asli rights advocacy since the 1990s and was President of the Peninsular Malaysia Orang Asli Association (POASM) from 1987 to 1991. He is currently a member of the Committee for Orang Asli Rights under the Malaysian Bar Council.

Zanisah Man is a PhD candidate at the Department of Anthropology and Sociology, University of Malaya. She is also a Lecturer at the Universiti Kebangsaan Malaysia in the Institute of Development and Environmental Studies. Her PhD research is on the subject of Semelai connection and relationship to their land.

Index